The military dimension of the Chinese revolution

The military dimension of the Chinese revolution

The New Army and its role in the Revolution of 1911

EDMUND S.K. FUNG

UNIVERSITY OF BRITISH COLUMBIA PRESS
VANCOUVER AND LONDON

Published 1980 by University of British Columbia Press
For sale only in North America, U.K., Europe, and Africa
ISBN: 0 7748 0129 8

Canadian Cataloguing in Publication Data

Fung, Edmund S. K., 1944-
   The military dimension of the Chinese Revolution

   Bibliography: p.
   ISBN 0-7748-0129-8

   1. China. Lu chün. 2. China — History —
Revolution, 1911-1912. 3. China — History,
Military. I. Title.
UA837.F86 951'.03 C80-091219-5

Printed in Hong Kong by Colorcraft Ltd

To Lucia and Eugene

Preface

ALTHOUGH THIS book is not based on my PhD thesis, I began to develop an interest in the late Qing army when I was doing post-graduate work at the Australian National University on the revolutionary movement in Hubei Province during the period of the 1911 Revolution. Hubei provided an interesting case study of the role of the New Army in the revolution, but I later found that in order to understand better and more fully the role of the New Army in the ultimate fall of the Qing dynasty it was necessary to take a wider view and look beyond the confines of Hubei and the activities of the revolutionaries. After publishing a few articles out of my thesis, I started to undertake further research on a fuller range of military development during the period 1903 to 1913.

Most of the research which resulted in this book was conducted at Griffith University with the aid of inter-library loans from the Australian National University and the National Library of Australia in Canberra. I also spent some time in Canberra in the summer of 1976-7 (the southern hemisphere), in the Mitchell Library (Sydney) in July 1977 and in the Public Record Office (London) in the winter of 1977-8 (the northern hemisphere). When I was a PhD candidate, I also had the opportunity of visiting the Guomindang Archives in Taiwan and the Tōyō Bunko in Tokyo.

In this book Chinese names and terms are romanised according to the *pinyin* system. There are, however, some exceptions for the sake of convenience. Treaty ports and other cities where foreign missions were established are romanised in their conventional postal spellings: thus Tsinan not Ji'nan, Tientsin not Tianjin, Canton not Guangzhou. Peking is used instead of Beijing, Taipei (in the citation of sources) instead of Taibei, Mongolia instead of Menggu, and Tibet instead of Xizang. Names of famous personalities commonly known in English-language writings by non-Mandarin names are also rendered in the usual, conventional way. Hence, Sun Yat-sen not Sun Yixian.

This book owes much to the encouragement, guidance and support of a number of people to whom I wish to express my deepest gratitude. Professor Wang Gungwu, my mentor at the Australian National University, deserves the first place. He encouraged me at every stage of my research. He read the last drafts and offered helpful comments and suggestions. I should also mention Emeritus Professor C.P. FitzGerald, Professor Jerome Ch'en and Professor Ernest P. Young, whose criticisms of my PhD thesis showed me the way to a more careful and wider study of the New Army. At Griffith University two fine colleagues, Professor C.P. Mackerras·and Dr D.H. McMillen, read the manuscript, criticised it, and helped improve the style of my prose. The errors and shortcomings that remain are, of course, my sole responsibility.

Chapter 9 of this book was originally published in *Papers on Far Eastern History*, 19 (March 1979). I am grateful to the Department of Far Eastern History, Australian National University, for its permission to reproduce it in this book.

All the photographs in the book are taken from *Revolution in China*, a contemporary photographic collection published in Germany. They were made available by courtesy of Griffith University Library.

I am also indebted to Griffith University for its financial support, without which my field work in Canberra, Sydney and London would not have been possible. My thanks are due to Mrs Jennifer Parkes and Ms Em Pelecanos for typing the manuscript with great care. I also wish to express my appreciation to the staff of the Australian National University Press for editorial and other advice.

Finally, I must acknowledge the moral support of my wife, Lucia, without whose understanding and encouragement this book would not have been written.

Brisbane   E.S.K.F.
November 1978

CONTENTS

TABLES

MAPS

PLATES

Introduction

OF ALL traditional Chinese institutions, probably none was regarded by the West with such contempt as the military organisation. 'An utterly negligible quantity' was the verdict that had often been pronounced on the Chinese army by foreigners acquainted with China. The results of a series of conflicts between the Middle Kingdom and the foreign nations in the nineteenth century appeared to bear this out. It was only natural that when the imperial government announced its plan to reorganise the Chinese army on modern lines in 1903, foreign observers should express serious doubts about the ability of the Chinese ultimately to put their military house in order.

Yet, in spite of a traditional aversion to militarism, China had always had the raw material of a good army. The Chinese were, generally speaking, fatalists by nature, obedient and with few needs. Under the most trying circumstances they were capable of displaying the endurance and faithfulness which were the finest attributes of the fighting man. The Chinese soldier could subsist on little and undertake long marches, and did not resent having to sleep on the ground if necessary. He could put up with insanitary conditions and seemed to be immune to some common diseases which had destroyed many Western armies. Although he lacked the fighting instincts of the Japanese soldier and was more fitted for passive defence, he could be made formidably aggressive if good leadership and competent officers were provided.

The newly organised *Lujun* (the Land Forces), consisting of many divisions to be distributed throughout China, was intended to be a national army as distinct from the provincial troops. The first six northern divisions, generally known as the Beiyang Army, were the most efficient and the best equipped. In the south the term *Lujun* did not appear to be in common use and the new divisions there were often called *xinjun* (new army). To avoid confusion, the term New Army is used in this book to denote all the troops which constituted the *Lujun*, wherever they were maintained.

The objectives of the New Army scheme were both national and dynastic, to defend China against encroachments and aggrandisements from outside and revolutionary challenge and internecine conflicts from within. It was an integral part of the imperial reform

movement designed to strengthen the imperial position in dealing
with foreign aggressors and domestic rebels. Like the reforms instituted in the civil administration, the New Army displayed both
merits and defects. There was a steady growth of military spirit and
a steady uplifting of the military profession. There was improvement
in the morale of the army — a better *esprit de corps*. On the other
hand, the officers were far from efficient. There was a lack of uniformity in drill and armament. Military transport and communications were deplorably inadequate. Corruption was still rampant. All
in all, the New Army was far from modern by Western or Japanese
standards, despite the substantial progress it had made since its
inception. Nevertheless, it was seeking to modernise; thus it could
be regarded as a modernising army, in which remarkable changes
were taking place for the first time in Chinese military history.

Military reform had a significant impact on the Chinese attitude
towards soldiering. The educated Chinese had traditionally looked
down upon the fighting man, and it was questionable whether they
did not still do so in the late 1900s. Nevertheless they at least appeared to show less contempt for the soldier, and many actually
chose a military career. Furthermore, the new generation of Chinese
scholars and students realised that, in order to survive, China needed
a strong, modern army and the Chinese people required a psychological reorientation towards military values. The cause of Chinese
militarism was espoused by the intellectuals and the imperial government as a means of building a powerful, respected China.

The Qing dynasty came to grief in 1911 when it failed to control
and exercise the New Army effectively against the revolutionary
assault. The army, as the government well realised, was disaffected.
As an institution, it was not insulated or self-encapsulated; rather it
was permeable to outside influences, ranging from the soldiers'
social backgrounds to exciting political currents. In other words the
soldiers were not immune to the forces that spawned revolution,
and the state of affairs in the country had alienated them as much as
it had the civil elite, the rural masses and the urban poor. Indeed, the
army had been subverted by foreign ideas, domestic influences,
traditional grievances and revolutionary propaganda before the
revolution. No sooner had the revolution broken out than large
sections of it in the southern provinces declared for the republican
cause. The Beiyang Army, although politically favourable to a constitutional monarchy, was also partially disaffected, thus contributing
to the undoing of the imperial government.

This book is concerned with the New Army and its role in the
ultimate fall of the Qing dynasty. Part I deals with army reform and

the social order, Part II with the process of military subversion and mutinies, and Part III with the revolution and its aftermath. The new military movement in the early twentieth century can, of course, be traced back to the conclusion of the Sino-Japanese War in 1895, but for the sake of brevity, military developments before 1903 will not be treated in detail. Also, relatively little attention will be paid to the old-style provincial troops which were in a process of demobilisation. The book concentrates on the period 1903-13 for the reason that the New Army owed its inception to the Commission for Army Reorganisation, which was formed in December 1903, and that the Chinese Republic, though established in 1912, was not firmly under the new president's control until 1913. However, there will be little coverage of the so-called 'second revolution' except in so far as the attitude of the army is concerned. Nor will there be a detailed account of army reorganisation in the early Republic, in order not to render the book intolerably bulky.

In dealing with the military dimension of the 1911 revolution, it is necessary, first of all, to examine the whole range of changes instituted, successfully or otherwise, in the Chinese military profession and organisation. This is done in chapters 1-3. We should then develop our thoughts on the relationship of the New Army with the social order in terms of support, fiscal, moral and intellectual, in terms of use in keeping domestic order and suppressing disturbances, and in terms of reinforcing or diminishing the social power of different groups. Not all these issues are adequately dealt with in this book; but an attempt is made to discuss some of them, mainly in chapter 4 and somewhat loosely elsewhere.

Parts II and III of the book are not intended to be a study of the revolutionary movement, on which there is already an extensive literature. The emphasis is on a hitherto neglected area, the disaffection of the army and its contribution to the Revolution of 1911. Earlier studies of the revolution had tended to focus on the Tongmenghui (Revolutionary League) movement, the role of Sun Yatsen, Huang Xing and other revolutionary leaders.[1] Recent scholarship, however, has shown much interest in the role of the non-revolutionaries, notably the reformist elite,[2] the constitutionalists, the provincial assemblymen, gentry merchants, and so on. Much interest has now been shown in the reforms made in the late Qing administration and various aspects of Chinese society. Considerable attention has also been given to the social change occurring in the post-Boxer decade which led to the emergence of new social groups who made new demands on the government, demands which Peking was both unwilling and unable to meet. Consequently, the theme that reform led to revolution has been well developed in a few recent works which invariably conclude that the ultimate fall of the dynasty was attributable to the alienation, by 1910 and 1911, of the reformist elite, rather than to the revolutionary movement which was weak and divided. The imperial government would have survived the political upheaval of the 1900s had it complied with the demand of the reformist elite for the early opening of parliament and had it been willing and able to lead the way to constitutionalism more promptly and decidedly than it did.[3]

The new interest shown in the role of the reformists, notably the constitutionalists, elucidates the weaknesses and inadequacies of the late Qing government to which the fall of the dynasty could be attributed. It also corrects narratives which have focused on the cult of Sun Yat-sen and the leading personalities in the Tongmenghui. However, in stressing the contributions of the reformists, constitutionalists and provincial assemblymen, recent scholarship seems to have resulted in the other extreme — denial of the contributions of the revolutionaries who belonged to a variety of occupational and regional groupings. For all its factionalism and organisational weaknesses, the revolutionary movement, whether or not it was led by the Tongmenghui, was important in laying the groundwork for the overthrow of the dynasty.

This book contends that, as far as the New Army was concerned, the revolutionary movement in Hubei was fairly well organised, with features which distinguished it from the revolutionary movement in other parts of China. The revolutionary strength in Wuchang was unusual, an achievement which could not simply be discounted as being fortuitous.[4] The Wuchang uprising was premature, but it was no accident that it succeeded where all earlier uprisings had failed, that is in becoming a beacon for the other provinces to revolt.

Indeed, despite earlier studies of the revolutionary movement in Hubei, there is still room for a more thorough inquiry into the structural evolution of the subversive societies there. Such an inquiry (chapter 5) will show not only a marked continuity in their development but also the ways in which they were similar to and, more significantly, different from revolutionary bodies elsewhere in terms of organisation and strategy. It will show, too, that the Wuchang uprising was not a spontaneous movement but that it was a military coup, planned and premeditated, even though its actual outbreak was accidental in the sense that it was forced to take place under the most adverse circumstances after it had been postponed indefinitely. A plot was conceived after the Canton uprising of April 1911 and particularly in the following September to initiate revolutionary action. Although they were a divergent group, the revolutionary soldiers agreed to sink their differences, at least temporarily, in an attempt to launch an uprising. To recognise this plot does not mean that conspiracy theories are adequate in explaining revolutions. Of course they are not, and one must examine the social, political and economic forces which spawn revolutions. Nevertheless, it would be as unrealistic to dismiss the role of conspiracy altogether as to exaggerate its importance. The truth is that revolutions are most likely to occur when conspiracies and plotting take place at the most appropriate 'psychological moment', or alternatively in the most 'revolutionary situation' brought about by a variety of forces.

Consideration of the case of Hubei, however, should not deny the fact that the revolutionary movement which existed in many parts of China was generally fragmented and largely ineffectual. Local revolutionary groupings operated with little co-ordination, which partly accounted for the weaknesses of the Tongmenghui movement. There were Tongmenghui revolutionaries operating in many provinces, but they had failed to achieve organisational unity, with the result that their activities were largely confined to individual efforts.

To compare and contrast the Hubei army with armies elsewhere, a few other provinces will be examined. These provinces include Hunan, Anhui, Jiangxi, Zhejiang, Jiangsu, Guangdong, Yunnan, Manchuria and the metropolitan area where the Beiyang Army was stationed. Here again, for the sake of brevity, many other provinces will be omitted in this investigation. But it will suffice to show that disaffection existed in the New Army to varying degrees, and that the loyalty of the troops, with the exception of the 1st Manchu Division and the Imperial Guard Corps, was highly suspect. There were revolutionaries at work in most of the regular units, although army disaffection was due to a variety of factors, of which revolutionary influence was only one.

There was indeed a process of military subversion. The term military subversion is used here in different senses. It denotes, first, a revolutionary process whereby the army was subverted by revolutionaries and radical nationalists operating within or outside the military organisation. It refers, second, to the alienation of the soldiers for a variety of reasons which made them defy the military authorities from time to time. These soldiers were not necessarily associated with any revolutionary party. Third, it means the erosion of the loyalty of the troops by the forces of environment, that is the impact of a general socio-political situation on the entire population, of which the army was a part. The soldiery, in spite of their arms and uniforms, were not politically different from the discontented civil population, from whom they were not isolated. In the first case military subversion was planned and organised, involving infiltration of the army and intensive revolutionary propaganda. For discussion purposes, it may be referred to as revolutionary subversion. In the second and third cases the behaviour of the troops was influenced by traditional grievances, personal ambitions, nationalistic sentiments and spontaneous feelings towards the social unrest which spawned revolution. All these cases were interrelated situations which were often present at the same time in varying proportions. The end result was to undermine the allegiance of the armed forces on which the perpetuation of the Qing authority depended.

There were many factors which contributed to military subversion. The main ones are outlined (not in order of importance) as follows:

a. *The social composition of the New Army:* The emergence of a new, scholar-officer class, the entry into the ranks of educated youths, and the enlistment of thousands of bankrupt peasants and the urban poor, all combined to change the social composition of the Chinese army and gave it an awareness of the social, economic and political conditions in the country. The modern-educated officers became increasingly concerned with the national problems of the time. Young nationalists and radical students who had joined the army exerted their influence among the common soldiers.[5] The rank and file were restive in times of social and economic distress, as they had their own interests at stake. Furthermore, being mostly natives of the province where they were garrisoned and being largely of peasant origin, they were sympathetic to the local peasantry with whom they retained close ties through their families and other social organisations. Hence, they often found family ties, provincial affinities and personal sentiments affecting their behaviour.[6] The soldiers could not be used as a repressive agent of the state indefinitely, for their sentiments were often those of the poor people and their fellow-provincials.

b. *Revolutionaries at work:* In some places subversion of the army was part of a broader political movement to overthrow the government. Young revolutionaries operating within or outside the military organisation propagated subversive ideas and formed various kinds of cultural societies as legal fronts behind which to carry out revolutionary activities.

c. *Nationalism and anti-Manchuism in the army:* A form of modern nationalism developing in some significant sections of the New Army proved to be subversive of the military order. Many young officers became radical nationalists and developed anti-Manchu feelings as the dynasty proved unable either to meet the foreign challenge or to deal with its internal problems.

d. *Traditional grievances of the soldiers:* Corruption in such forms as embezzlement of funds and peculation of the soldiers' pay was still rife among some senior officers. The army life was not meant to be easy. There was incessant hard work both on the parade ground and in the classroom. The intensive gymnastic training was often dangerous and unnecessarily tough. In some places, food and sanitation were poor and the living conditions appalling. Discipline was strict, and corporal punishment was still in force in some divisions. The officers often treated the men badly, and were socially remote from them. Moreover, as conscription in a modified form was enforced, many young men appeared to have enlisted against their will.

e. *Natural disasters:* Floods, famines, droughts, plagues and the like caused a great deal of misery to the people in the last years of the dynasty. Scarcity of food and high prices of rice led to civil disorders which reacted on the local soldiery.

f. *Military cut-backs:* The impoverished state of the economy throughout the country led to serious cut-backs in military expenditure in 1910 and 1911, after a period of army expansion. Very few new divisions were created; the incomplete ones remained far below strength. Morale of the officers slipped as career prospects diminished. The privates became agitated because their pay was often in jeopardy.

g. *The increasing literacy of the common soldiers:* This rendered the troops more susceptible to revolutionary propaganda as well as to the influence of the local press in local and national affairs. Newspapers were more widely read than ever before, and revolutionary literature found ready acceptance among the disaffected soldiery.

All these factors will be elaborated in Part II of this book in the context of each individual army. They were not either singly indispensable or collectively necessary for the growth of army disaffection. However, they did contribute to it and a combination of them, or of some of them, would suffice to undermine the established military authority.

For the revolutionaries who had no army that belonged to their own organisations, the New Army was one of the two principal sources of military power to which they sought to gain access. Initially, Tongmenghui revolutionaries led by Sun Yat-sen set great store by the secret societies, which provided the basis for a series of abortive uprisings during the years 1900 to 1908. These societies were 'primitive rebels', to borrow E.J. Hobsbawm's words, or alternatively 'amateur soldiers' as Lyon Sharman called them, forming the bulk of the so-called 'people's army' *(minjun)* whose function was to challenge the local authority.[7] Even though they had proved unreliable and limited in their military capabilities, Sun was reluctant to consider suggestions that he should review his strategy and start subverting the New Army. For he was convinced that the secret societies, less powerful as they were than the government troops, were the only force which dared to initiate bold actions. To Sun, every uprising, though abortive, was 'a seed of success', which had a considerable impact on society.[8] Until 1910, he persisted in this attitude, confident that the army would in the end respond spontaneously to his cause.

Other revolutionary leaders were more realistic, and saw a need to tap the potential of the New Army. This shift of focus led to a new emphasis on the role of the city in the revolutionary movement. Before 1910, most of the *putsches* were launched in the countryside, rural towns and border areas, where the imperial authority was at its weakest. The revolutionaries had to deal with the old-style provincial troops, but were careful to avoid taking on the better trained and better equipped regular troops stationed in the capital cities. Sun's optimism had led him to believe that once the rural towns had been seized, the administrative centres in the provinces would quickly fall into line through spontaneous revolts. But the failure of the *putsches* only showed that the further they were from the administrative centres, the less was the impact on the urban population and the bureaucracy. The support of the urban population would not have been decisive, if Sun and company had tried a peasant revolution in the communist sense. But the Tongmenghui had never contemplated a peasant revolution, and had evidently failed to. mobilise and organise the peasantry, in spite of its choosing the countryside in which to mount the uprisings. Revolutionary infiltration of government troops would result in an urban-based revolution, thus further divorcing the rural masses from the revolutionary mainstream. It was now necessary to seize the capital cities, which would not only yield control of the state apparatus and economic and communication nodes, but also provide the symbols of political legitimacy. This was a movement aimed at 'the struggle for the troops', led by young revolutionaries of a new generation who had been educated either locally or abroad, or both. The importance of the city could not be overemphasised. For those who wanted to use the New Army more than the secret societies, the immediate targets were the garrisons, the yamens (Chinese civil or military courts) and the symbols of government.

There were various ways of infiltrating and subverting the New Army. One of these was to use the military cadets in Japan who were scheduled to return to China for service. A substantial proportion of them joined the Tongmenghui at the time of its founding. In 1906

Huang Xing, a revolutionary leader from Hunan who maintained good relations with them, selected a few of the most reliable and truly committed ones to form a military society known as the Iron and Blood Man Corps *(Tiexue zhangfutuan)*. There was an initial membership of twenty-eight, prominent among whom were Li Liejun from Jiangxi, Yan Xishan from Shanxi, Luo Peijin from Yunnan, Kong Geng from Hubei, and Huang Fu from Zhejiang. Later the membership increased a little, but never became very large. The members were in the main from good socio-economic backgrounds. Some of them were wealthy enough to buy their way in to official-dom, on their return to China, avowedly to further the revolutionary cause from within the bureaucracy.[9]

Others who did not join the Iron and Blood Man Corps were also expected to play a similar role back home. Many of them in fact did so in their capacity as commissioned officers and military instructors. But they did not follow a clearly defined policy laid down by the Tongmenghui, for there was no such policy.[10] The formation of the Iron and Blood Man Corps was more the result of Huang Xing's personal initiative than of Tongmenghui planning. Consequently, while Sun Yat-sen and his Cantonese lieutenants concentrated their efforts on south China, others went into operation elsewhere with little co-ordination.

A second way in which the revolutionaries sought to win over the army was to use the friendly ties which some of them had cultivated with individual commanders. It was dependent upon personal rela-tions, involving no organised activity and thus having little chance of success. Discharged revolutionary officers (usually junior ones) also maintained clandestine contacts with the common soldiers and enjoyed a good rapport with them. Old ties were renewed and strengthened, in order to establish communication between the dis-affected troops and civilian leaders of the Tongmenghui. These tactics were used by revolutionaries in Canton (see chapter 7).

There was yet another mode of 'struggling for the troops'. It was an approximation of 'going to the common soldiers', involving as it did a great deal of hard work over a relatively long period. It required that the revolutionaries should identify themselves with the rank and file whose support they attempted to recruit. This meant that radical elements and revolutionary nationalists had to join the army in the first place, either as officers or as privates. It then necessitated organised activity under the cover of legal cultural societies and study groups. Sympathetic soldiers were approached, won over and organised clandestinely. The hallmark of this movement was the fact that both leaders and followers were part of the soldiery and that the revolutionary societies existed and operated within the local army, independent of the civilian organisations which revolved around the Tongmenghui. They were aware of the mood of the troops, knowing at first hand the conditions in the military circle as well as the extent to which the troops were prepared to go one way or another. This was the case with Hubei (see chapter 5).

The emphasis on the New Army did not require dispensing with the secret societies altogether. In fact, these societies still played an auxiliary role, contributing much to the infiltration of the army. There was nothing new about secret society members joining the army. The old-style troops had always contained a large number of them. Conversely, many secret society elements were ex-soldiers. Demobilisation of the old-style troops had resulted in many being drafted into the regular forces. Others were attracted by the terms of service in the New Army. Still others were asked to infiltrate it by revolutionaries who took advantage of their anti-Manchu tradition, and used them as an intermediary between the ordinary, apolitical soldiers and the radical activists behind the scenes.

These revolutionary tactics were used in different circumstances with varying degrees of success, which depended as much on the organisation of the revolutionaries as on the extent of disaffection already among the soldiers.

The importance attached to the New Army should not suggest that the revolution was made by revolutionary soldiers or the conspirators who deliberated in secret meeting-rooms or in army barracks where they resided and enlisted support.[11] It is the contention of this book that the opening phase of the revolution in 1911 was determined by the disaffected New Army. It was only after the New Army had shown the way to revolution in six provinces before the end of October 1911 that the alienated constitutionalists and provincial assemblymen threw in their lot with the revolutionaries, realising that they now had a better chance of succeeding than at any previous time. The army officers welcomed the defection of the provincial assemblymen and collaborated with them, a strategy which contributed to the rapid collapse of Manchu power.

This collaboration began with the establishment of the Hubei military government, and it soon became a pattern of revolution in many provinces which declared their independence. The army officers represented a section of the new Chinese elite by virtue of their family backgrounds, modern education, professional training, nationalistic aspirations and their modernising outlook, all of which distinguished them from traditional officers. It is true that they came from lower social levels than the intellectual elite, as men of real standing and influence in the army were still rare. However, many of them expressed much concern about China's political future, and were therefore in tune with the civil elite. This common concern, coupled with a common desire for private self-interests which were not necessarily incompatible with national interests, helped bring about the co-operation of the civil and military elites. Like the civil elite, the army commanders in 1911 believed that a quick restoration of law and order following the outbreak of civil war would be in China's best interests. The Beiyang Army supported Yuan Shikai not because of its personal loyalty to him but because of the popular feeling that Yuan was the only man capable of establishing a new order that would avert the danger of foreign intervention.

The events of 1911 were more than a military movement, and the dynasty was not lost on the battlefield. The final act that overthrew the dynasty was one played out by a diversity of participants, including the locally based revolutionaries, the military, Tongmenghui leaders, the constitutionalists, the provincial assemblymen, the rich merchants and industrialists. The emphasis on the contributions of the New Army is not intended to denigrate or deny the role played by other social groups. There were many other factors contributing to the fall of the dynasty, the study of which is beyond the scope of this book.

ONE

Formation of the New Army

DESPITE SOME attempts at military reform following the Opium War, no serious endeavour was made by the Chinese government to overhaul its army until after the disastrous war with Japan in 1894-5. The so-called self-strengthening movement that preceded the war represented an early, half-hearted effort to build up China's maritime defences in the wake of Western intrusion. It was based on the *ti-yong* dichotomy (Chinese learning for essential value, Western learning for practical use) and the assumption that the acquisition of modern weaponry would suffice to enable China to keep the foreigner at bay. Much attention was given to the building of steamships and the manufacturing of modern arms. But there were no plans to create a new, national army, or to introduce institutional change in the civil and military establishments.[1]

Neither the Hunan army nor the Huai army of the Taiping period was intended to be a defensive force against foreign invasion. Their training, despite the use of some Western arms, was short and still largely traditional. Once the Taipings had been suppressed, they were ordered to disband by Peking which was disturbed by the growing power of the provincial leaders.

On the other hand, there was an extensive and costly effort to build a modern navy, despite the fact that the Manchu rulers had always ignored the sea and had held an anti-maritime attitude which reflected the traditional Chinese view that the Inner Asian frontiers were the most important strategic area. It was the presence of foreign gunboats in Chinese waters that altered this military thinking. The recognition of naval power as a chief index of great power status led to the establishment of a modern Chinese navy in 1882.[2] The army then tended to be neglected until the Beiyang Fleet was ignominiously annihilated by the Japanese in the Yellow Sea in 1894.

The new military movement since 1894
The focus on the army in the post-1894 era reflected a shift back to

the primacy of land defence. The navy had been a disappointment to its patrons and well-wishers. For many years thereafter, previous efforts to develop naval power were not followed up, and the army continued to play an important part in Chinese military development. One salient feature of the new military movement was the initiative displayed by the central government. Previous military reforms had been largely spasmodic and isolated efforts made by a few provincial leaders, which had made it possible for Peking to co-ordinate the navy during the war with Japan. Peking now saw the need to effect some central planning and control of the armed forces, a Herculean task which would require fundamental changes in the relationship between central and provincial authorities, among other things. It was also realised that power could not simply be equated with armament. Institutional change was necessary.

The first modern-drilled army, the Pacification Army *(Dingwujun)* was raised during the war by an official named Hu Yufen at Xiaozhan, a garrison about thirty-five kilometres south-west of Tientsin. At the suggestion of von Hanneken, a German military expert in the Chinese employ, it was created by the newly formed Bureau for the Supervision of Military Affairs *(Duban junwuchu)* headed by Prince Gong and Prince Qing. A total of ten battalions numbering 5000 men had been formed by November 1895 when Hu was appointed director-general of the Tientsin-Peking railway. Yuan Shikai was then commissioned to take over the training and command of the brigade which was renamed the Newly Created Army *(Xinjian lujun)* and brought up to a strength of 7000 men, consisting of infantry, cavalry, artillery, engineers and some auxiliary sections.[3] It remained under the control of the Bureau, although Yuan was rapidly establishing his personal influence among the troops. The fact that its expenses were defrayed by the Board of Revenue[4] seems to have enabled the central government to exercise much control over it.

In the meantime, Zhang Zhidong, then Acting Viceroy of Liangjiang, was organising a new brigade called the Self-Strengthening Army *(Ziqiangjun)* at Nanking. Based on the German model, it comprised the three basic forces and an engineer corps, all of which were trained and drilled by thirty-five German officers. When he later returned to Wuchang to resume duty as Viceroy of Huguang, he initiated a new plan for the training of modern troops there. In 1896 a bodyguard, 1000 strong, consisting of two battalions and an engineer corps was established. It was financed by the provincial treasury and directly under the viceroy's control.[5] A small group of the German officers had been transferred to Wuchang, but only three of them were used to train troops. Later they were relieved of this duty and were employed only as advisers and instructors in the military school.[6]

In December 1898, the Military Defence Army *(Wuweijun)* was formed in Zhili, with Ronglu, a Grand Secretary and Superintendant of the Northern Sea, as commander-in-chief. It comprised five divisions: the front, the left, the right, the rear and the central. Yuan's Newly Created Army was transformed into the Right Division *(Wuwei youjun)*, which he took to Tsinan when he was appointed Governor of Shandong in 1899. Three of the remaining divisions were dispersed after the Boxer uprising, while the fourth, namely the Left Division *(Wuwei zuojun)*, continued to exist in a debilitated state. In 1901 Yuan was appointed Viceroy of Zhili and brought his division to Tientsin.[7]

In early 1900 when the Germans took advantage of the Boxer uprising to further their own ends in Shandong, Yuan found it necessary to expand his Right Division. Shandong, with its long coastline, could not be defended without a large modern force. Yuan's division had only 7000 men, and the old-style provincial troops were too decrepit to be of any real value. With Peking's sanction, Yuan transformed twenty battalions of the provincial troops into the Vanguard of the Right Division *(Wuwei youjun xianfengdui)*, which later evolved into the 5th Division of the New Army. At the end of June, when the allied forces were at war with China, he recruited a further four infantry battalions and transformed some provincial troops into a left-wing, a right-wing, and a coastal defence corps.[8]

One of the most important consequences of the Boxer catastrophe was the change wrought in the military organisation. The Empress Dowager Cixi, now converted to an advocate of far-reaching reforms, gave effect to most of the radical reforms which had been advocated unavailingly in the 1890s. An edict of 29 August 1901 abolished the traditional military examinations to clear the way for modern military education. Another decree of 1 September recognised the value of trained officers by directing all provinces to establish military schools as soon as possible. A third decree of 2 September ordered the division of army units into standing armies *(changbeijun)*, first class reserves *(xubeijun)* and gendarmeries *(xunjingjun)*.[9]

At this juncture it may be suggested that the reorganisation of the Chinese army after 1900 can be analysed on two interrelated levels as far as the motivations of the imperial government and the ardent reformers were concerned. The first is that of national security. The sense of national humiliation brought about by the political events culminating in the allied invasion of Peking in 1900 convinced the scholar-officials that unless a viable defence system were developed,

China would sooner or later be partitioned by the powers. Military reorganisation was a first essential step towards securing China's territories and sovereign rights.[10]

Yuan Shikai, for one, was concerned about the impingements of the foreign powers. While his troops were educated in the traditional values of loyalty and righteousness, he exhorted them 'to remember the national humiliations'. One of his ten 'military commandments' ran:

> It is your duty to defend the country against invasion. You ought to be ashamed and indignant at the sight of the plundering enemy bullying us, encroaching upon our land and territory, and killing our people. The shackled pig and the long snake are advancing step by step. When they are near, they will become wicked and peevish to the danger of yourself and your family. There will occur all sorts of devastation [which I] dare not imagine. Cherish the feeling of revenge and wipe out the [national] disgrace . . . Bear this in mind unremittingly.[11]

The 'plundering enemy' and 'the shackled pig and the long snake' referred to the Japanese with whom Yuan had many unpleasant experiences as Chinese Resident in Korea from 1882 to 1894.

Similarly, Zhang Zhidong was extremely critical of the old-style troops which, although they could still be relied upon to deal with local revolts, were utterly incapable of offering resistance to a Western or Japanese force. On many occasions he expressed his apprehensions of the foreign threat to justify his efforts to build a large, strong army in Hubei.[12]

The Japanese threat to China was growing. If it could not be eradicated at once, at least it should be contained. As the United States military attaché said early in 1904:

> Possibly moved somewhat by the spectre of Japan's military power looming up on her horizon, China, realizing that if she were ever to be allowed to exert again real sovereign rights over Manchuria, [she] must necessarily be in condition to assure the Powers of her ability to preserve order and secure property in that province, institute efforts towards putting her military house in order. To that end a commission with H.I.H. Prince Ch'ing at its head was organized to frame regulations for the government of the forces.[13]

The impending Russo-Japanese war provided another impetus to military expansion. It was to be fought in Manchuria, threatening to get China involved despite her neutral stand. In April and May 1904, Peking was obliged to take precautionary measures to secure its north-east frontiers. Sections of the Beiyang Army were moved outside the Great Wall. The 1st Division of Yuan's standing army was dispatched to Yongpingfu, near Shanhaiguan, while orders were given for the immediate formation of two more divisions of similar strength and composition. The war furnished a good reason for demanding funds from the nation for military purposes, and an imperial edict was issued to that effect. Later in the year another division began to be formed, Yuan's intention being to raise his standing army to 40,000 men.[14]

Japan's victory over Russia in 1905 could not fail to make a deep impression on China: never before had it demonstrated so clearly that the East was not essentially inferior to the West, and that an Asian army, if well trained and well organised, could be a match for any Western army. It would be possible for China, as for Japan, to ward off the aggressive powers if she adopted Western military institutions and methods. The mood was summed up by a correspondent of the *Far Eastern Review:* 'What Japan could do, China could do, for are we not the superior race, reasoned the latter.'[15]

The emergence of Japan as a fully fledged imperialist power added to Peking's sense of insecurity and accelerated the nascent Chinese nationalist movement. Much resentment was expressed against the fact that two foreign nations, while at peace with China, had selected a battle ground in absolute disregard of China's neutrality and sovereign rights.[16] The war did not spell the end of Russo-Japanese rivalries in the Far East. On the contrary, their conflict continued to grow unabated, which made China all the more anxious to assert her sovereignty over Manchuria and other border regions. The build-up of Chinese forces in the frontier provinces in the following years was evidence of a new forward policy in that direction.

Apart from Manchuria, Xinjiang and Mongolia were also threatened by the Russians. In 1909 the Chinese were reported to have stationed a large force, 40,000 strong, equipped with modern rifles and drilled by Japanese instructors, at Ürumqi. The strength of this force had been grossly exaggerated. The fact was that the military governor of Yili was ordered to proceed with the training of at least one division of modern troops in his district, where Russian aggression was most to be feared. In Mongolia, which originally was not included in the New Army scheme, another large Chinese force was being organised, while plans were being made to install wireless telegraphy in Mongolia and Xinjiang for communication with Gansu. One foreign traveller who explored the whole length of the Great Wall in the spring of 1910 observed widespread military propaganda throughout the country; new troops were being drilled almost everywhere, even in the remotest villages, and it appeared 'all part of a general plan to prepare secretly an enormous Army'.[17]

A similar policy of asserting Chinese sovereignty was carried out in Tibet. In 1906 the reassertion of Qing authority was acknowledged in an Anglo-Chinese agreement. In 1907 the Chinese and the Russians agreed that both would refrain from interference in Tibet. In 1910 Peking initiated a broad reform scheme, suppressed uprisings in east Tibet and sent a punitive expedition to Lasa (Lhasa), forcing the Dalai Lama to flee to India. It was also Peking's intention to secure the support and co-operation of the Tibetans in the development of a military force.[18]

Another area where Chinese sovereignty was at stake was Yunnan. The French construction of a metre-guage railway from Hanoi up the River to Kunming (Yunnanfu) in the 1900s, coupled with highly exaggerated reports that the French had sent some 20,000 Annamites to Yunnan to carry out imperialist activities, alarmed Peking. The Chinese felt that the Yunnan army, with only one infantry brigade and two artillery battalions in 1909, should be increased to two divisions immediately. To meet this contingency, 2,000,000 taels were appropriated from the central government.[19] When the British acting consul-general at Kunming asked the local authorities why it was considered necessary for a poor province like Yunnan to have two divisions, the answer was that it was 'to guard Yunnan against French aggression'. If necessary, the three divisions in Sichuan could serve as reinforcements when they were completed.[20]

In 1910, Edwin J. Dingle, an English journalist who had travelled extensively in China, spoke of the enormous improvements in the development of the Yunnan army:

> China is determined to work out the destiny of Yün-nan herself, and she is working hard — the West has no conception how hard — so as to be able to be in the position of safeguarding — vigorously if necessary — her own borders.[21]

Again, in early 1911, Dingle reported:

> She [China] is making preparations to be in a position to be able successfully to defend Yün-nan in time of emergency. Go any day you wish over the roads leading to the capital and you will find string after string of pack-horses laden with foreign ammunition and rifles. In my tramp from Chung-king, the uppermost port of the Yangtze to Yün-nan fu, a distance of nearly nine hundred miles, I was never out of sight of this new military equipment. *And it is all for the purpose of keeping the French out of Yün-nan.*[22] [Emphasis added]

Only a few years before, the Yunnan army had been held up to ridicule by every passing traveller. But by 1911, in the course of three years, it had achieved a standard higher than most of the richer and more populous provinces of China. It was backed by the Sichuan army, and together they represented a considerable force in China's western frontiers, a development which the British authorities in Burma were watching with much interest.[23]

China had been humiliated too often and for too long, and this condition, she realised, should not be allowed to continue indefinitely. China was awakening, and every time she suffered a fresh humiliation she renewed her effort to achieve military efficiency. Truly, as a contemporary writer who saw 'the haughty Manchu princes . . . smarting under repeated humiliations' described it, the New Army was forged as 'an instrument of revenge'.[24]

The new military movement can also be seen as a response to internal challenge. While Chinese nationalism was a natural response to the impact of modern forces and to the challenge of modernity, anti-imperialism was not the only reason for the importance attached to the New Army. As Paul Cohen has ably demonstrated, the conceptual framework of 'Western impact' and 'Chinese response' is not a satisfactory approach to late Qing history.[25] Any study of late Qing developments must involve analysing China's response to the internal situation which was affected by the Western impact.

As Samuel Huntington has asserted, the traditional monarchies of the twentieth century have generally recognised the need for reform or modernisation for domestic reasons, because the stability of a traditional society was threatened not so much by foreign armies as by foreign ideas and influences. Nineteenth-century monarchs, he maintains, modernised to thwart imperialism, while twentieth-century monarchs have done so to thwart revolution. Since the consolidation of power was the prerequisite for reform, it was necessary for a traditional monarchy to create an efficient loyal, rationalised, and centralised army.[26]

China's new military scheme must therefore be understood, in part, as a response to an internal situation where the revolutionary upsurge coincided with the imperial reform movement. It was directed as much to the internal challenge as to external threats. Yuan Shikai understood from the very beginning that the functions of his troops were 'to defend the honour of the country and to suppress violence on behalf of the people'. For Yuan, the term country *(guo)* meant as much the dynasty as the Chinese nation, and he repeatedly stressed 'the graciousness of the Throne and the corresponding debt of gratitude owed by the people'.[27] Zhang Zhidong, likewise, was well known for his loyalty, and had no qualms about using his new troops to assist in the suppression of local revolts. Naturally, then, the dynasty found the New Army a useful instrument of political control until the soldiery themselves became disaffected.

These two levels, national security and internal challenge, are not mutually exclusive. By the beginning of the twentieth century, the security of the nation had become intertwined with that of the dynasty, the latter being dependent upon the former. It was the government's weak and unsuccessful foreign policies towards the powers rather than the alien rule itself that caused the growth of Chinese nationalism and anti-Manchu sentiment. That was why in their last years the Manchu rulers were anxious to pursue a nationalistic foreign policy and address themselves to the problems facing the nation as well as the dynasty. For if the nation collapsed, the dynasty would go down with it. On the other hand, if the nation was secure from external threats, the dynasty would find itself in a stronger position to deal with the internal problems.

Given this analysis, it becomes more meaningful to describe the actual formation of the new troops after 1900. With the blessing of the Old Buddha in Peking, military reform progressed fairly quickly. In 1902 the modern-drilled army in north China had a strength of approximately 50,200 men, which was not a bad start. Yuan Shikai's Right Division, 7850 strong under the command of Liu Yongqing, Duan Qirui and Wang Shizhen, was the most outstanding of all. About 5500 of them were quartered in Peking and the Summer Palace, while a large proportion of the Left Division commanded by Ma Yukun and the Valiant Army *(Wuyijun)* by Jiang Guiti, were within fifty kilometres of the capital. Other troops including the Self-Strengthening Army (now transferred to Baoding) and a few battalions of inferior quality were stationed in various places. It was obvious that although the Manchu Banner force still existed in a semi-moribund condition, the dynasty as well as the country depended entirely on Chinese troops for survival.[28]

In Hubei, meanwhile, there were about 9500 modern-drilled troops, of whom 7060 furnished the nucleus of the Wuchang body-guard which consisted of two infantry regiments and one battalion each of cavalry, artillery, and engineers.[29] The military preparatory school *(wubei xuetang)* had 120 students, taught by three ex-officers of the German army and twelve Chinese military graduates from Canton and Tientsin. The school for non-commissioned officers *(jiangbian xuetang)* had one hundred students selected from literate junior officers from each battalion. It was under the direction of a Japanese lieutenant-colonel, who was assisted by three captains, two sergeant-majors and two translators.[30] The graduates were appointed non-commissioned officers, and had the prospects of promotion to commissioned officers after serving for a period of time in the ranks.[31]

Similar developments took place in other parts of the Yangzi region, but their progress was much slower than that of Zhili and Hubei.[32] It is noteworthy that previously modern-drilled troops had been confined to large garrisons along the river, but now Chinese instructors graduating from military schools were drilling them in the inland towns as well. There was a general improvement of the worst troops, while the efficiency of the best troops was only moderate.[33]

Impressed with the progress made in Zhili and Hubei, the imperial government directed the other provinces in 1902 to emulate their successes and to reorganise the troops under their control. Selected officers from Henan, Shandong, and Shanxi were to be sent to Zhili for training, while those from Jiangsu, Anhui, Jiangxi and Hunan were to go to Hubei. They were afterwards to return to their original provinces for service.[34]

By 1903 a beginning in the formation of standing armies was being made in various provinces: they were either freshly raised or formed through conversion of large sections of the existing forces. Their size and strength was determined by considerations of strategic factors and financial resources, as a result of which there was no uniform standard of training and efficiency. To remedy this, the Commission for Army Reorganisation *(Lianbingchu)* was established in Peking on 4 December 1903, with Prince Qing and Yuan Shikai at its head and Tieliang as assistant director. In the following year it formulated a general policy dealing with a wide range of issues, including tables of organisation, the functions of officers, recruitment, medical and supply services, standardisation of equipment, classes of troops, pensions, and so on. Plans for the creation of a system of military education were also made.[35]

The completion of the six northern divisions by the autumn of 1905 marked the beginning of the Chinese New Army.[36] Since then the standing armies in the provinces had been transformed into new divisions or brigades. In April 1906 Peking ordered the creation within ten years of thirty-six divisions to be distributed among the provinces (see Appendix 1). In the following year the date of their completion was advanced to 1912, but this proved to be impracticable owing to financial constraints.[37] On the eve of the revolution only fourteen divisions (excluding the Imperial Guard Corps) of more or less full strength had been completed, to which must be added eighteen mixed brigades and two brigades of varying strength (Appendix 2). The actual total fighting strength was about 190,000.[38]

The strategic distribution of these troops came under four groups. The Peking metropolitan group consisted of the Imperial Guards,

1st, 2nd, 4th, 5th and 6th Divisions and the Taiyuan and Kaifeng Mixed Brigades. A second group was concentrated in Manchuria, where the 3rd, 20th, 23rd Divisions and the Mukden (present Shenyang) and Tsitsihar (Qiqihaer) Mixed Brigades were stationed. There was also the central China group along or near the Yangzi comprising the 7th, 8th, 9th Divisions and seven mixed brigades quartered in Wuchang, Suzhou, Changsha, Nanchang, Kiukiang, Anqing and Hangchow. These three groups were linked by rail and inland water communications. The Tientsin-Pukou railway had brought the 5th Division into the Peking group in 1910 and was expected to facilitate better communication on its completion in 1912. The remaining units constituted yet another group, the isolated divisions and brigades maintained in other parts of the Empire, including Foochow, Chengtu, Tibet, Yunnan, Xi'an, Lanzhou, Ürumqi, Yili, Canton, Guilin, Guiyang and Rehe (Jehol).[39]

The organisation of a division

The organisation of the New Army was copied to a great extent from the Japanese. A division *(zhen)* consisted of two infantry brigades *(xie)*, one regiment *(biao)* each of cavalry and artillery, one engineer battalion *(ying)*, one transport corps battalion, and a band. An infantry brigade consisted of two regiments, each of which (infantry or artillery) was made up of three battalions (or squadrons if cavalry). The strength of a division was 12,512 as shown in Table 1.

Table 1   The strength of a division

Unit	Officers	Men	Coolies	Total	Guns (artillery)
Divisional staff	12	50	5	97	—
2 Brigade staff	16	36	4	56	—
6 Regiment staff	68	84	12	164	—
12 Infantry battalions	384	6 924	600	7 908	—
3 Cavalry squadrons	78	813	198	1 089	—
2 Artillery Field battalions	60	882	194	1 136	36
1 Artillery Mountain battalion	30	453	109	592	18
1 Engineer battalion	32	577	58	667	—
1 Transport Corps battalion	36	573	143	752	—
Band	2	44	5	51	—
Total	748	10 436	1 328	12 512	54

Source: *Qingchao xuwenxian tongkao, juan* 219, *bing* 18, pp. 9662-4; FO 371/637, Annual report on China, 1908, p. 34; FO 371/866, Annual report on China, 1909, p. 37; MP 312/119, Notes on the organisation of a Chinese division, by Lieutenant-Colonel Pereira, 2 September 1980; Leonard, pp. 78-87.

Sometimes the artillery regiment consisted of two mountain battalions and one field battalion, or even three mountain battalions. In speaking of the strength of a battalion, the Chinese usually gave figures only of the men in the ranks, exclusive of officers, carpenters, shoe-makers, and so on. An infantry battalion (504 men) was divided into four companies *(dui)*. A company consisted of three sections *(pai)*, each forty-two strong. A section was divided into three squads *(peng)*, each of fourteen men. Each squad had one sergeant *(zhengmu)*, one corporal *(fumu)*, four first-class soldiers *(zhengbing)* and eight second-class soldiers *(fubing)*. A squadron of cavalry had four troops *(dui)*, each fifty-six strong. A troop had two sections, each of two squads (same strength as for infantry).

A battalion of artillery had three batteries *(dui)* each of 126 men with six guns, and was sub-divided the same as for the infantry, namely, into three sections, each of three squads. A mixed brigade *(hunchengxie)* was a brigade composed of infantry, cavalry and artillery with a few engineers and transport corps, varying in size between 2000 and 7000 men according to local circumstances.

In times of war the infantry would be doubled from the first reserve (assuming, of course, that the reserve was forthcoming), but cavalry and engineers were always maintained on a war footing. According to United States intelligence sources, the full strength of a Chinese division, inclusive of a hospital company, a balloon section, and a machine-gun section, was 12,768. When fully completed, the Chinese army with thirty-six divisions would have a strength on a peace footing of 450,000 officers and men and on a war footing of 1,085,976.[40] As the Chinese government published few reliable figures, the above estimates were only approximate, and it must also be pointed out that nearly every division was more or less under strength.

Officers and men
The efficiency of a modern army depends in large measure on the quality of its officers. Herein lay the greatest weakness of the Chinese army. Not only was there no military tradition, but the mere acquisition of the scientific knowledge essential to modern tactics and strategy was alien to Chinese custom and sentiment. The social contempt for the soldier had discouraged any men of education from serving in the army. The root of it, as Mary Wright observed, was the absence of a social class that could produce competent officers.[41] The traditional officer was uncultured and had no real knowledge of military science. Like the rank and file, he was drawn from the lower class. Even those who by education and position would seem

fit for commissions were almost invariably unsuitable owing to a total lack of military qualities, which received little social appreciation. There could be no way of achieving a competent officer corps until the traditional attitude towards soldiering was radically changed.

Serious endeavours were now made by the government to attract educated men to the military profession and particularly to improve the quality of officers through a new system of military education (see chapter 3). In future all officers were to be graduates of a military school, local or overseas. But before a sufficient supply of such graduates was assured, the old officers were not to be dismissed altogether. Those who had demonstrated exceptional abilities, diligence, skill, and a willingness to learn, were to receive continuing appointment, but they would also have to be educated properly.[42]

As with officers, the common soldiers needed to develop a character and spirit befitting a modern army. A first step towards achieving this was to remove the centuries-old concept that the army was only for the worthless, the ruffians, ex-criminals, opium smokers, and all those who could not otherwise eke out a living. Significant change was to be effected in the social composition of the soldiery, coupled with a serious effort to render the profession of arms both popular and lucrative. The new recruitment regulations[43] included an age limit (between 20 and 25) and certain physical requirements, both of which seemed to allow a certain degree of flexibility in practice. What the regulations emphasised was the social origins and characters of the recruits. It was a must that a recruit be indigenous and with family connections. He was required to make a statement of the members of his family for three generations and his place of residence as identification. Opium smokers, vagabonds, discharged soldiers, irresponsible people, and those with criminal records were not to be considered. The village headmen, elders and local constables were required to submit a list of worthy young men and were not to omit anyone who satisfied these requirements.

In order to attract promising lads, the government was prepared to grant some privileges to the recruits. Under the rule a soldier, after three months' probation, was to be remitted a land tax of thirty *mou* (about five acres). If he had no land tax to be remitted, he would enjoy the exemptions ordinarily granted to a student of the Imperial Academy. As well, his family was to be accorded careful protection against oppression by local officials, bullies or rowdies. In the case of any members of his family being implicated in a law-suit, they were to be represented in court. All these privileges were to be withdrawn upon his retirement or when he was dismissed.

The government's determination to raise the status of the soldier to a level almost comparable with that of the student of the Imperial Academy who formed part of the privileged gentry class marked a significant departure from the great tradition. It seems to have been Yuan Shikai's idea, since he was the central figure in the Commission for Army Reorganisation. It may nevertheless be added that Zhang Zhidong had been training new troops in much the same way for some years. The men of Zhang's choice were preferably 'settled elements' owning some property or having a trade of some sort who could live without relying heavily on the military stipend and were willing to retire after completing their service. Not only were they to have no criminal record, but the recommendations of the local gentry and village elders plus the endorsement of local officials were required. The age limit was between eighteen and twenty-four. Enlistment was for three years, at the end of which the men retired and went into reserve in their original place of registry.[44] Already in 1902 Zhang had proposed to the imperial government that retired soldiers be granted certain privileges as an inducement to enlistment. Under his proposed scheme, retired soldiers were to receive a certificate of three different grades. Those in the first and second classes were to be appointed non-commissioned officers or instructors, while third-class soldiers passed into the reserve. These 'certified' soldiers were to be exempted from the *corvée*, and were not to be arrested or insulted by officials for allegedly committing an offence until concrete evidence was produced. When implicated in a law-suit, they were allowed to plead their cases without torture before their title was removed.[45] Although this proposal was not approved, it may have had a bearing on the recruitment policy of the Commission for Army Reorganisation.

Under the new system, the rates of pay were liberal. A regimental commander with allowances got 500 taels a month, and battalion commander 400 taels. A subaltern received 50 taels, while a first-class private got 4.50 taels and a second-class private 4.20 taels.[46] A portion of the soldier's pay was given to his family, after deductions were made for rations, usually between 1.20 and 1.80 taels subject to local prices.[47] He was provided with winter and summer uniforms, and was reasonably well fed and quartered.

The idea of forging a new, respectable image of soldiering seems to have taken hold among progressive provincial leaders. Of course, it would be some years before this idea gained wide popular acceptance. But it was important that at least some sections of the troops should be literate. The commission's expectation was modest: that when a new battalion was formed the first one-fifth of the recruits had to be literate men serving as first-class privates who would normally be promoted to corporals after five months' probation and to sergeants after another three months' drill.[48] Zhang Zhidong was more ambitious, demanding that at least half of his troops be able to read and write. To that end, he required all those who wished to enlist to take a written examination, the content of which was based on local affairs and Confucian ethics.[49] Consequently, a large proportion of the Hubei soldiers were literate to varying degrees (see chapter 5).

It is impossible to ascertain the number of literate soldiers in the Chinese army, and certainly it varied from province to province. On the whole, however, the Chinese educated class seems to have reacted favourably to army reorganisation and a good many of them enlisted for a variety of reasons (see chapter 4). This is not to deny that the bulk of the recruits were still principally from the peasant class and few from the merchant class, but is meant to show that some significant change was taking place in the social composition of the Chinese army.

Territorial enlistment

The geographical origin of the soldier was another area of interest to the military reformer. The rule was that every division was to be composed of natives of the province where it was maintained. This raised problems when not enough natives were willing to enlist, problems which could be solved by the introduction of conscription. In the traditional army voluntary enlistment was the rule, though conscription was common in times of war. The Qing government, in principle, continued the policy of voluntary enlistment, but actually conscription in a modified form was in force, that is local authorities were called on to find the quota of recruits required, and where volunteers were not forthcoming compulsion was resorted to.[50] Such integration of conscription and territorial enlistment had several advantages. There would be little difficulty in getting recruits and bringing up the divisions to full strength whenever funds were available, and all the non-natives who had joined earlier could be replaced in time. It ensured to some extent that the recruits were from decent families as their origins could be checked; and finally, it served to promote mutual help among the troops based on local affinity, thereby discouraging desertion.

With a very few exceptions, territorial enlistment was in force in the provinces. Most of the conscripts, known as *zhengbing*, were *bona fide* natives, while the volunteers *(mubing)* were largely from outside provinces, hirelings, in fact, as the Chinese term implied. (Not to be confused with the *zhengbing* and *fubing* which meant first and second class soldiers and their degree of proficiency.) There were large numbers of volunteers recruited before the new policy was announced, and it would take a few years to replace all of them. For instance, in 1902 the Hubei troops consisted of many non-natives, but in 1905 of the 12,317 men there, 9915 were natives, with only 1916 coming from Zhili, Henan, Shandong, Anhui, and Hunan, and 486 Manchu Bannermen garrisoned at Jingzhou.[51]

In late 1906, 90 per cent of the 1st Manchu Division at Baoding were Peking Manchus, the remainder being Manchus from other colonies. About 75 per cent of the 3rd Division stationed nearby were conscripts mostly from Zhili, with a good number from Hunan, some from Anhui and a very few from Shandong. Those of the 2nd Division were all natives of Zhili. About 90 per cent of the 7th Infantry Brigade and the 4th Artillery Regiment of the 4th Division stationed at Machang on the Grand Canal were Zhili men. The majority of the troops of the 5th Division in Shandong were conscripts, 90 per cent of them being locally recruited. The 6th Division was a little different in that while 75 per cent of the men were conscripts, most of them came from Hunan or the Zhili border near Henan, and some from Shandong and Anhui.[52] The trend to replace the non-natives was set. By the end of 1908, in the Beiyang Army, very few soldiers were left who came from outside provinces.[53]

However, some provinces encountered more difficulties than others in getting good local recruits. In 1906 the troops in Canton were principally Anhui and Sichuan natives; there were no Cantonese because, in the opinion of Acting Viceroy Cen Chunxuan, they were too quick-tempered and untrustworthy. Of the 1800 soldiers of the Guangxi army, 1500 were Hunanese, the others being from Jiangxi, Anhui, and only a few from the home province. In Zhejiang three-fifths of the infantry regiment stationed at Hangchow were natives, and the authorities were anxious to recruit only local men in future.[54]

The recruiting process at Boading illustrates the way in which recruits were obtained in north China. There was a recruiting office *(zhaobingchu)* in every prefecture, with branches in various places. The recruiting office was in the same place as the depot for the reserves, both of which were managed by reserve officers. When a unit was to be formed, the general commanding officer determined which prefecture to draw on. An officer was then sent to the recruiting office, where the reserve officer, in conjunction with the local magistrate, issued a proclamation stating the quota of recruits required. The magistrate then apportioned the numbers to the villages and held the local elders responsible for filling them. If there were not enough recruits in one prefecture, they would be found in another one. Volunteers were expected; if they were not forthcoming, as was often the case, the majority of the men would enlist under compulsion.[55] It is not clear, however, what types of compulsion were used.

In every other province, similar recruiting offices were established. Wherever possible, only natives of the province were to be recruited, except in special provinces like Zhili, which had to furnish several divisions. Such provinces might recruit outside their own boundaries, provided they did so from localities in the neighbourhood of, or travelled by, the railways.[56]

In Hubei the soldiers were obtained chiefly by conscription, the rule being that each prefecture was responsible for furnishing one regiment. The cavalry regiment was drawn from Wuchang prefecture, the artillery from Xiangyang prefecture, and so on. The rationale was that certain districts were well known for producing people most suitable for each of the three forces. In 1907, the system was not working properly, as suitable recruits in fact had come from different places; so it was adhered to in theory only.[57] Elsewhere, the Hubei pattern was never followed, and recruits were drawn from any prefectures where suitable young men were available.

Territorial enlistment resulted in rendering the Chinese army, for all its national aspirations, a semi-territorial one. Troops raised in this way would be more difficult to control in the event of local uprisings because of local feeling and affinity. On the other hand, they were easier to recruit, mobilise, drill and discipline in the beginning than a mixed army.[58]

Drill, armament, transport, communications and medical service
The drill of the New Army was a combination of German and Japanese elements. The Beiyang divisions were excellent in the ordinary ground drill, in the handling of arms and in close order. The American military attaché who inspected them in 1908 found the movements in the 3rd Division particularly impressive. They were 'executed with snap, regularity, and precision, the set-up, military appearance, soldierly bearing and attentiveness of the men leaving little to be desired'.[59] Likewise, the British military attaché found them 'exceedingly smart, and the training of the troops seemed to be everywhere carried out on a uniform system'.[60] In the Yangzi region the 8th Division was equally splendid. There was a strong German element in the drill, although the Japanese were gradually exerting a great influence. The infantry was distinctly good, while the cavalry, as in other divisions, was the weakest force.[61]

The armament was of a mixed kind. The 1888-model Mauser rifle manufactured at the Hanyang arsenal was widely in use. The cavalry was armed with the same model carbine. As from 1908, the infantry also used the 6 mm Japanese rifle, model 1903, and had Japanese accoutrements, while the cavalry and artillery had 6 mm Japanese carbines and 75 mm Japanese Arisaka field guns, respectively. German arms were used too, such as the 75 mm Krupp mountain guns, the Vickers-Maxim and the Schneider-Canet (Creusot) of the same calibre.[62] In 1910 an order was placed with Krupp for fifty-four 75 mm Q.F. (field) guns for the Imperial Guard Corps.[63]

The Chinese had always been anxious to manufacture their own weapons and munitions of war. The new military scheme provided for one large arsenal in the north, one in central China and one in the south, all of which were equipped with modern machinery and expected to turn out uniform weapons for use throughout the Empire. There were other small ones in various provinces, but many of them were abolished or converted to repair shops. As late as 1908 the new arsenals were as yet unable to achieve a high level of efficiency owing to technical and administrative problems, lack of managerial skill, shortage of funds and corruption. Their products were not modern enough and rather poor in workmanship. Worse still, production was by no means uniform.[64] By the end of the decade, there was some obvious improvement. Foreign observers seemed to agree that the Hanyang arsenal was the most efficient, Canton second, and Jiangnan (Shanghai) third. Two other important ones were in Kaifeng and Tsinan. Among the products turned out in large quantities were Q.F. mountain guns and ammunition, magazine rifles, carbines and machine guns, samples of which were on display in the Nanking Exhibition in the summer of 1910. The new arsenal at Chengtu (opened in May 1910) had a branch for making a German-pattern water-jacketed machine gun of Maxim type. In addition to these, there were factories which manufactured smokeless powder. It appeared that China was 'becoming increasingly independent of foreign countries in the supply of iron and steel for the manufacture of her munitions of war'.[65]

Unfortunately, the Chinese army lacked uniformity in the use of arms, which seriously affected its efficiency. As an example of the resulting confusion, one can point to the 1st Division, which was armed with three different patterns of guns — three batteries each of Arisaka field guns, Gruessen field guns, and Krupp mountain guns. So, too, with the rifles, either imported or locally made.[66]

The organisation of the transport corps usually conformed to local conditions, with companies of boats, pack, cart, or wheelbarrow. For communication, flag and lamp signalling were practised generally. The Morse system was adopted. Field telegraphs and telephones were used where there was a complete engineer battalion. A wireless telegraph station was started in Shanghai in 1910. Some divisions and brigades had a few bicycles, but they were not in common use.[67]

The medical service was the most backward part of the Chinese army because of an inadequate supply of modern-trained doctors. But generally sanitation was given careful attention, dispensaries were kept clean and tidy. The native doctors who had the confidence of the troops were useful, while the rank and file of the medical service *(yibing)* functioned as dressers and hospital orderlies. There was a lack of veterinary surgeons, but the horses were well looked after and kept in good condition.[68]

Reserves and mobilisation

The army was divided into three classes: the regulars, the first and second reserves. After serving for three years, the regulars were given a certificate and sent back to their native villages, where they passed into the first reserve for three years on reduced pay and periodic drill. They were to follow their ordinary occupations and would be activated in times of war. After three years, the reserves became second reserves on half pay, and were required for drill only in the second and fourth years, at the end of which they retired as private citizens. It would then still be possible for those with exceptional abilities to be examined and appointed as sergeants, corporals, even officers commanding the first and second reserves in various districts.[69]

In theory there would be a large pool of reserves after a few divisions had been completed for three years. In fact, however, such was not the case because the reserve regulations, except in the 2nd, 4th and 9th Divisions, those in Zhili, Shandong and Jiangsu, had remained a dead letter. In 1908 there ought to have been a first reserve of 70,000 men since the Beiyang Army and the 8th Division had been established for over three years. But actually there were only about 13,400. The number rose to 18,200 in 1909 and to 20,000 in 1910, all of them being trained as infantry only. No attempt was made to form a reserve for the cavalry and artillery.[70] Up to 1911 the second reserve still did not exist.

Several factors accounted for the slow formation of reserves. First, contrary to earlier expectations that the regulars were *bona fide* natives who would retire to form a sort of territorial reserve, by 1910 only a few of the completed divisions had all their troops recruited locally, and this resulted in the reserves being lost to those divisions which were filled with men coming mainly from outside provinces. At the expiration of their service, they returned to their native provinces, thus losing connection with their old organisations.[71] The 3rd Division, which had been transferred from Baoding to Manchuria, was a case in point. When it was formed in 1904 the troops mainly came from Shandong, Hunan, Anhui and south Zhili, and none from Manchuria. In 1907 General Fengshan, Inspector-General of the New Army, seeing the difficulty in forming reserves, recommended to the Throne that those who had completed their service be allowed to re-enlist in the Division or elsewhere, or join the provincial troops and police in Manchuria.[72]

Second, the Peking government seems to have had no objection to re-enlistment. Up to the end of 1907, 3000 men in the 2nd Division had completed their service, but 1000 of them subsequently joined the 4th Division, thus leaving only 2000 for the reserve.[73] In the Manchu divisions (the 1st Division and the Imperial Guard Corps) discharged soldiers were allowed to re-enlist.[74]

Third, in some provinces retired soldiers were absorbed in the police and old-style army units. This was particularly true of Hubei, where many discharged soldiers from the 8th Division had gone into the railway guards and the provincial troops, thereby improving the quality of the latter organisations but defeating the purpose of wartime mobilisation. Finally, large numbers of them were originally taken on from the old armies, that is they were recruited under the old regulations and could not be compelled to join the reserve if they did not wish.[75]

There was no army corps forming part of the peace organisation of the New Army, but the mobilisation regulations provided for its formation in times of war. Each army corps was to consist of a regular division increased by 5170 men, a reserve division (eight battalions of infantry with 3720 men) and three depot battalions (900 men from the second reserves). It required a total of 17,230 reserves to expand a division to a war strength army corps. The total reserves available in 1910 would suffice to form a little more than one.[76]

The provincial troops

A corollary to the formation of the New Army was the demobilisation over a period of time of the old-style troops which consisted of the Manchu Bannermen *(qibing)*, the Green Standard *(lüying)*, the old 'braves' *(yongying)*, the trained militia *(lianjun)* and the local militia *(tuanlian)*. In 1905 the reorganisation of all the provincial troops was ordered. The best of the existing troops were to be drafted into the New Army, the second best to form the Patrol and Defence Force *(Xunfangdui)*, and the remainder to be demobilised.[77] The Patrol and Defence Force was also to be drilled on modern lines, well armed and well equipped, and officered to some extent by the regulars and graduates of the modern military schools. There remained a great many undrilled units, the worst of which were the bodyguards of viceroys and governors *(qinbing)*, whose only skill was in the use of the halberd and the trident.

The Patrol and Defence Force furnished a constabulary force assisting in the suppression of brigandage, local revolts and frontier disturbances. Although these troops were not supposed to be used outside the confines of the province where they were maintained, in practice provincial authorities often called upon each other for aid in the event of local uprisings. A second function of this force was to act as a reserve to the New Army until such time as the regular reserves had been completed. In other words, they were designated as the second lines of defence within their own provinces in times of war, to perform garrison and line-of-communication duties, collect supplies and guard depots, so as to release the regular troops for active operations. Some of them, notably those in Guangxi who had the experience of fighting the French, were considered to be valuable as 'guerrilla or partisan troops against an invading force'.[78]

Unlike the New Army which was concentrated in the capital cities, the Patrol and Defence Force was scattered throughout each province. Its organisation was not uniform in spite of temporary regulations drawn up in June 1907 to bring them into one system. It was normally designated by districts *(lu)* usually called 'centre', 'left', 'right', 'front', and 'rear', each consisting of a varying number of battalions *(ying)* infantry and cavalry. A battalion contained three or five companies *(shao)*, each of three or five sections *(dui)*. The smallest unit was the squad *(peng)*, a number of which formed a section. The provincial general *(tidu)*, who was assisted by a few lieutenant-generals *(zhentai)* in various districts, was in command of the troops.[79]

There were infantry and cavalry, but no artillery. Their quality varied tremendously between provinces. For instance, in Shandong, Anhui and Manchuria, they were of little value. On the other hand, those in Jiangxi were of a higher standard than the 7th Division quartered in Jiangbei.[80] Generally, they were well trained in Tientsin, Nanking, Wuchang and the other important provincial capitals. The best of them were quite efficient. In the opinion of Lieutenant-Colonel Pereira, the British military attaché, they would make better soldiers than those of the New Army, if the same care was given to their organisation and training.[81] Not surprisingly, the reorganisation of the Patrol and Defence Force in some provinces showed substantial progress from a military point of view. In 1909 a number of well educated officers and non-commissioned officers were introduced to it, thus improving the quality of its training.[82]

Probably all the men, or at any rate most of them, were soldiers by choice, as the provincial troops were not bound by strict regulations. Generally, they were from lower class backgrounds and received less favourable treatment than the New Army. Their normal pay was 4.20 taels a month. In some provinces like Guangxi, it was only three taels.[83] Deductions were made for rations as in the regular troops. Their uniforms and equipment, quarters and, above all, status were inferior to those of the New Army. There was neither transport nor medical service.

Yet, interestingly enough, they were loyal to the government. Not only was there an absence of mutinies, but they were often used by the government to suppress with pitiless energy riots and revolts, as well as mutinies attempted by the less reliable troops of the New Army. They evinced a pronounced animosity towards the new troops who showed much contempt for them. Moreover, territorial enlistment was not the rule, and hence lack of local sentiment made them particularly effective in dealing with local revolts and disturbances. For this reason the government was interested in maintaining them along with the New Army for as long as necessary, so that when one turned against it, the other might come to its aid.[84]

As regards their total strength, Lieutenant-Colonel Willoughby, the new British military attaché in Peking, estimated it at 246,730 in December 1909, exclusive of the local militia and other undrilled organisations.[85] At the end of 1910 his American counterpart put the number at 157,087, taking into account the usual discrepancy between the full strength on paper and the actual strength.[86] Meanwhile, the general movement for the abolition of the Green Standard troops and the drafting of the best of them into more modern organisations had made substantial progress. In November 1910 Zhejiang became the first province to have completely demobilised the Green Standard troops.[87]

The Manchu troops

A study of the Qing army will not be complete without mention of the Manchu troops. The Bannermen had been first-rate warriors before they were debilitated by long peace, prosperity and corruption in the eighteenth century. They constituted a hereditary, privileged class, receiving grants of land, livestock, rice, cloth, and a small pension, as well as favourable treatment before the law.[88] But their social status, which had been higher than any Chinese soldiers' since they belonged to the ruling race in China, had also been declining because of the same factors which contributed to the rapid deterioration of their physical prowess. Thus it had become necessary to reorganise them as well.

Their reorganisation proceeded in three directions: first, the formation of one or two modern divisions composed entirely or predominantly of Manchus: second, to give some modern training to those who could be made to perform some of the functions of the Patrol and Defence Force; and third, to disband the Manchu garrisons and force the Bannermen to adopt commerce, agriculture or industry.

The 1st Manchu Division of the New Army was well established by 1906. It was commanded by General Fengshan, under whom were two Chinese brigadier-generals, Cao Kun and He Zonglian, who had control of the 1st and 2nd Brigades, respectively. The chief of staff was also a Chinese, Wang Dingzhen by name, who had been educated in Japan. There were twelve infantry battalions which were smart on parade and well drilled. Of cavalry and artillery there were three battalions each.[89] Judging from its performance in 1908, it compared unfavourably with the 4th, 5th, 2nd and 6th Divisions, but was superior to the 3rd Division.[90]

The other Manchu division was the Imperial Guard Corps *(Jinweijun)*, the formation of which was decreed on 3 December 1908.[91] Designed as a special force for the protection of the Imperial Palace, it was under the direct control of the Prince Regent and the General Staff. The soldiers were raised entirely from the best candidates among the Bannermen, both as regards physique and training; others were picked from the 1st Division. The officers were graduates from the Nobles' College *(Guizhou xuetang)* who had served for six months in other divisions. By 1909, only one regiment of infantry and one squadron of cavalry had been formed. It was the aim of the Prince Regent to make the Imperial Guard Corps the model organisation of China's military system. The troops were equipped with the best armament, diligently drilled, well attended to, and were much better paid (privates receiving eight taels per month) than the average soldier in the ordinary divisions. When completed with 30,000 men, the new troops would help perform police duties in the capital, and the Peking gendarmerie would be abolished.[92]

In November 1910 the High Commissioner for the training of the Imperial Guards proposed a new system of enlistment whereby Chinese were to be recruited as well.[93] This appeared to be a sop to Chinese feeling rather than an indication of the Manchu rulers' confidence in the loyalty of the Chinese population towards the alien dynasty. In any case the effect of the new system was by no means great, as the Bannermen still formed the vast majority. Moreover, as has been pointed out, the Manchus were normally permitted to re-enlist after completing their service.

There were Manchus in other New Army divisions, especially in those raised in Fengtian, Jilin, and Heilongjiang. Elsewhere their numbers were extremely small. Other Manchu troops could be found in the Patrol and Defence Force. The most outstanding of them was the Awe-Inspiring New Army *(Zhenwei xinjun)* at Jingzhou, in Hubei. Lieutenant-Colonel Pereira, who visited it in May 1907, found them young looking, aged between eighteen and twenty-six, and more or less equal to the New Army in training and drill. As regards physique, they were the smartest men he had ever seen in China, some being as tall as six feet and in better physical condition than was usual with Chinese troops. In other Manchu colonies, such as those at Canton, Nanking, Hangchow, and Rehe, Manchu troops were also trained on modern lines.[94]

On 27 September 1907 a decree was issued ordering the Manchu garrisons to be disbanded and absorbed among the Chinese population.[95] Excluding Peking, there was a large number of Manchu garrisons throughout the country. In various places they lived as a caste apart, under their own officials' government, and were not amenable to the Chinese jurisdiction. But this did not prevent them from becoming impoverished in time, as they were forbidden to engage in trade or agriculture. Their existence was indeed an outstanding example of the decay of the ruling race in China. The government therefore proposed that the provincial authorities, in conjunction with the Tartar-generals, take a census of the Bannermen and then assign them land for cultivation while their stipend was reduced in proportion. After they had adopted agricultural pursuits, they were to be treated equally as ordinary people regarding land tax and lawsuits. Initially they were to be provided with a means of livelihood which would render a continuation of the government doles unnecessary.

However, even up to the end of 1909 not very many Bannermen throughout the country had become ordinary citizens like the Chinese. A decree of 26 December reaffirmed the government's policy to help all Bannermen earn a living, but added that it had no immediate intention of abolishing their pensions.[96] This indicated that the edict of September 1907 had not been carried out very effectively and that there must have been some resistance from the Manchus themselves.

It is nevertheless of interest to see how far the Manchus had participated in the development of a modern Chinese army. A French source reported that by March 1910 out of 5,000,000 Manchus and 'naturalised' Manchus (like Mongol Bannermen), about 227,000 had been compelled to undergo military training; 33 per cent were trained;

38,395 men belonged to the New Army or were affiliated to it; 29,292 were either indifferently trained in the Patrol and Defence Force or assimilated into it. Military education for members of the imperial clan was provided by the Nobles' College in Peking.[97] Evidently, a substantial proportion of the Manchu troops constituted part of the modernising army of late Qing China.

To sum up, China was serious in attempting to reorganise her army along modern lines in the post-Boxer period. The new military movement was not confined to a small number of provinces or regions. Rather, it was nationwide, with guidelines and regulations laid down by the imperial government, which took the initiative from the provincial leaders who had been the moving spirit in the early reform movement of the nineteenth century, and thereby assured the nation and the people that it was determined to improve the national defence system and the military profession. For the first time in Chinese history, a modern, professional army was in the process of formation. To facilitate this process, it was necessary to secure the co-operation of the provincial authorities, the social elite and the population at large. There were many obstacles to military development. The nature of these obstacles and the ways in which the imperial government sought to overcome them will be treated in the following chapters.

TWO

Administrative reforms and military finances

MODERN ARMIES are cohesively organised and highly structured institutional forces which specialise in the rational use of violence through the application of modern techniques and technology. They are, as Lucian Pye puts it, 'essentially industrial-type entities'.[1] Like the civil administration, they have specialised functions, with particular structures and institutions for their accomplishment. China in the post-Boxer decade was seeking to build up a Western-style army, and this meant that some kind of structural differentiation in the military organisation was required. Military administration was in need of specialisation by reforming the old institutions or establishing new ones. Officers were required to achieve a certain degree of professionalism through education in a modern military academy.

'Centralized power is a pattern of organization familiar to the military.'[2] In implementing the military reforms, the Peking government pursued a policy of political centralisation, which could be justified in terms of military efficiency, as the emerging New Army of China was to be a national army. However, this met with considerable resistance from the provinces owing to the financial control which accompanied it.

The question of finance was indeed an important one. Not only did it show how expensive the New Army was, but it had a significant bearing on the relationships between the central government and the provinces. The success of the imperial reforms depended to a great extent on the conditions of the imperial exchequer and the provincial treasuries. This chapter seeks to show the administrative reforms made in the military organisation and the ways in which these reforms were hampered by political and financial problems.

The Commission for Army Reorganisation
Military administration in imperial China had always been distinct from the command of the armies on the battlefield, being a privilege of the civil elite and part of the general administration, whereas military command was the function of largely uneducated officers.

The Board of War was fundamentally a civil institution. Although it was supposed to administer the armed forces of the Empire and to formulate military policies, its functions had been almost completely administrative and logistical. It had no authority over the Manchu Bannermen or the old-style Imperial Guards *(shiwei)*, and no jurisdiction over the provincial forces. The training of modern troops necessitated a modern institution administered by progressive officials who appreciated the value of modern training, modern strategy and logistics. The Commission for Army Reorganisation set up in December 1903 was intended to be an interim body to institute a specific military program. Its principal objective was to place the organisation, training, and armament of the emerging New Army under one system.[3]

The commission consisted of three departments: military administration *(junzhengsi)*, military command *(junlingsi)* and military education *(junxuesi)*. Military administration had six sections *(ke)*, charged with organisational matters, personnel, pay and quartermaster, medical, legal, and armament responsibilities, whereas military command had four sections dealing with strategic planning, cartography, communications and staff officers training. Military education was also divided into four sections, charged with training, education, compilation and translation, and naval affairs.[4] While Prince Qing and Tieliang were the director and assistant director, respectively, Yuan Shikai, the associate director, actually dominated the commission. Liu Yongqing, Duan Qirui, and Wang Shizhen were appointed chiefs of military administration, military command and military education, respectively.[5] They owed their appointments to the influence of Yuan, with whom they were closely associated. But it is only fair to add that they were able men most suitable for the jobs.

Duan Qirui came from a family with a long tradition of military service. He himself graduated from the Beiyang Military Academy *(Beiyang wubei xuetang)* in 1887, and had subsequently studied military science in Germany and received practical training in artillery engineering at the Krupp armament works. In 1895 he was appointed commander of the artillery battalion of the Newly Created Army and director of an artillery training school. In 1901 he became one of Yuan's chief military aides as well as head of the staff section of a provincial department of military administration.[6]

Wang Shizhen was a graduate of the Tientsin Military School and had fought in the Sino-Japanese War. In 1896 he served as chief assistant to Yuan and commander of the engineering corps in the Newly Created Army. In 1901 he was appointed commander of the 1st Infantry Brigade and also placed in charge of military training in

Tientsin.[7] Liu Yongqing had not been academy-trained. He had served as a commercial attaché in Korea during Yuan's Residency. In 1895 he was placed in charge of military provisions and battalion administrative affairs in Tientsin. In 1901 he was an inspector and staff officer in Yuan's Right Division, and a year later became head of instruction and training in the provincial department of military administration.[8]

In addition to them, Xu Shichang, a former chief of staff in the Newly Created Army and Yuan's sworn brother, was appointed senior administrative officer, with the rank of lieutenant-general.[9] Early in 1904 Yuan also recruited about sixty young Japanese-trained military graduates from Hubei and other southern provinces, where they had served for a period of time.[10] It was evident that the commission had a staff of modern-educated military graduates, with Yuan himself coming from a remarkable background that was both civil and military.

The commission was empowered to formulate plans and regulations for army reorganisation and military education, and had a special function to raise funds to meet the expenses of the Beiyang Army. As well, it dealt with the manufacture, purchase and distribution of arms and munitions of war. It was not a policy-making body, but its recommendations were normally accepted by the Throne, thus becoming imperial orders. Although it was supposed to co-operate with the Board of War, in fact it had little consultation with the latter, even in matters of promotion and transfer of military officers. Its juxtaposition with the Board tended to create friction between them, owing to their respective powers and jurisdiction not being clearly defined, as well as to some overlap between their responsibilities. This led to rivalry and competition for power and influence. The government realised that it would be difficult for them to exist side by side for too long, and there seemed to be plans for the commission to be abolished at a later time or to be assimilated eventually to the Board when the latter was reformed.[11]

Yuan's dual position as Viceroy of Zhili and associate director of the commission made him a very powerful man. Tientsin, the traditional seat of the Zhili viceroy, now became a most important centre for military training in China. There was a local war board called *dulianchu*, which shared a compound with the viceroy's office.[12] Like the commission, it was divided into three departments: administration *(bingbeichu)*, general staff *(canmouchu)*, and education and training *(jiaolianchu)*. The administrative department was responsible for the troops' conformity to military regulations and obedience to orders. It was also in charge of rewards and punishments, judicial proceedings, current supplies, and the preparation of supplies for the commissariat, artillery and medical services. The general staff department examined the quartermaster organisation and arranged for its proper administration. Furthermore, it collected and compiled statistical military information pertaining to China and foreign countries. The education and training department supervised military training and schools, drew up schemes, and regulations and prescribed textbooks for military students. Each department had a director *(zongban)*, an associate director *(huiban)*, three or four inspectors *(tidiao)* and a number of orderlies and secretaries.[13] In effect the Tientsin war board was a sub-office of the commission as Yuan had management of both bodies.

Provincial war boards

In each province, as soon as one brigade of standing army had been raised, a local war board known as *dulian gongsuo* was to be established, with the usual three departments as in Tientsin. Normally the viceroy or governor was the director-general *(duban, or duban dachen* in the case of the metropolitan province) and nominal commander-in-chief of the troops under his jurisdiction.[14] Some provinces were slower than others in setting up local war boards. In Guangxi, for example, the war board was reorganised from the old *yingwuchu* (military office) and in 1906 only two departments, namely administration and education and training, had been formed.[15] In Zhejiang the war board was not yet properly organised by 1907. Since it had less than one division, the three departments, as a rule, were in the charge of one director only, who was assisted by an associate director each for administration and general staff, but none for education and training.[16] In Manchuria which consisted of three provinces, there was only one war board located at Mukden, with branch offices in Jilin and Qiqihaer. One of the Tartar-generals served as the *duban* until 1907 when a new Manchurian viceroyalty was created.[17] The old-style military offices which administered the provincial troops were not abolished until 1909.[18]

Shandong was a unique case in that there was no local war board and the governor had no authority over the 5th Division stationed at Tsinan. This was because Yuan Shikai had charge of the division and was represented by the old *yingwuchu*, which was presided over by a local magistrate. When Yuan lost command of the division in November 1906, it was brought under the direct control of Peking's new Ministry of War, and was administered by General Fengshan, who was assisted by a war board of his own until the end of 1910.[19]

Military affairs at the provincial level were managed by both civil officials and military officers with some sort of divided authority. On the civilian side, the viceroy or governor was assisted by the provincial judge and the provincial treasurer. Subordinate to them were four or five magistrates or intendants of circuit *(daotai)* with the military rank of commandant *(tongling)*. The military officers were headed by the provincial general *(tidu,* or *titai)*, and under him were a few lieutenant-generals *(zhentai)*, who in turn were superior to the commandants, each of whom commanded a district.[20] The Tartar-general who had previously been a regular agent of military command had control of the provincial detachments of the old-style Manchu forces only.

It is difficult to tell how much divided authority each side possessed Viceroys and governors, as in the past, had certain military functions, being provincial commanders-in-chief. On the other hand, military officers seemed to enjoy the power of local military command. This marked the continuity of the administration-command dichotomy in imperial China. However, because military administration of a modern type required new administrative skills, officers who assisted in the work of the civil officials must have been educated in a modern school. The fact that they were subordinate to the civil officials who acted as a check on the military authorities and who had little knowledge of military science sometimes generated mutual jealousy and distrust. Fortunately, this situation was partly rectified by a tendency on the part of the civil officials to delegate much of their authority to their military colleagues. In Hunan, for example, the magistrate of Hengzhou had control of thirteen camps, but he left the management of affairs to the local commandants, only retaining control over the movement of troops from one quarter to another.[21] Nevertheless, it was still customary for civil officials to hold the most senior positions in the war boards. Most of the department heads were civilians with the rank of *daotai* or above, usually surrounded by a staff of youthful lieutenants who were mainly returned students from Japan and who actually ran the war boards.[22] The case of Nanking, where the 9th Division was garrisoned, seemed to be an exception. All the three departments of the local war board in 1907 were headed by military officers with the rank of brigadier-general. They were all natives of Zhejiang who had graduated from the Nanking Military School and subsequently been trained in Japan. Apparently they had great influence with the viceroy.[23]

Since the viceroy or governor was the director-general of the provincial war board with financial responsibility for the troops in his province, army reorganisation in the country as a whole in fact operated within a decentralised framework, the efficiency of the troops being dependent to a great extent on his performance and actions. The Commission for Army Reorganisation had not been very successful in placing the organisation, training and armament under one system. So the new Ministry of War after 1906 endeavoured to establish more effective control over the provinces, as a result of which the provincial war boards were reorganised in January 1911, as will be seen later.

The new Ministry of War

In the autumn of 1905 a five-man official mission visited Japan, Britain, France, Belgium, the United States, Germany, Austria, and Italy for a study of foreign constitutional governments. In its report on the foreign political systems, it recommended that the Japanese constitution be a model for China, and this led to the Throne's adherence to the principle of constitutionalism on 1 September 1906. No date was yet fixed for the promulgation of a constitution, but initial steps were immediately taken towards preparing the country for constitutionalism. A decree of 6 November ordered wide-ranging reforms to be instituted in the central administration. It established a new Ministry of Posts and Communications, reorganised the old six boards into ministries (although the designation *bu* continued to be in use). There was now a total of eleven ministries, including Foreign Affairs (formed in 1901), Agriculture, Industry and Commerce (1903), Education (1905), and the Interior (1905). Various changes were introduced in the ministries, except for Foreign Affairs and Civil Appointments. Other areas which were not affected by the decree were the Grand Council, the Grand Secretariat, and the Hanlin Academy, where opposition to change was extremely strong.[24]

The Board of War was transformed into the Ministry of War *(Lujunbu)*, in which were merged the Commission for Army Reorganisation and the Court of the Imperial Stud *(Taipusi)*. Until a General Staff Office *(Junzifu)* was established, all staff matters were managed by the General Staff Council *(Junzichu)*, which was attached to the new ministry. There was also a Naval Council *(Haijunchu)* dealing with naval affairs pending the formation of an independent Ministry of the Navy. The War Ministry now administered all the land forces of the Empire, military schools, ordnance, stores and arsenals, and so on. It was divided into two bureaux *(ting)*, namely, general secretariat *(chengzheng)* and the councillor general *(canyi)* and ten departments *(si)*.[25]

Tieliang was appointed President of the Ministry, with two other Manchus, Shouxun and General Yinchang, as his deputies. His appointment was bitterly criticised by the native press which called him the greatest exponent of the doctrine of Manchus versus Chinese.[26] Later in May 1907 Prince Qing was appointed Comptroller of the Army, a position senior to Tieliang's. Since the prince's appointment was not originally intended, Lieutenant-Colonel Pereira, the British military attaché, suspected that he was put there as a counterweight to Tieliang, who was becoming extremely powerful in army matters.[27] Sir John Jordan, the British minister in Peking, believed, however, that the appointment of a feeble seventy-year-old man to such a senior position was designed 'to consolidate Manchu control of the Army', in direct contradiction to the principles established by the reform edict of 6 November 1906 that distinction between Manchus and Chinese in the making of appointments was to cease and that the old system of having two presidents and four vice-presidents of each board was to be abandoned except in the Ministry of Foreign Affairs.[28]

These appointments revealed a power struggle between the conservative Manchu clique led by Tieliang and the Chinese reform group headed by Yuan Shikai. Tieliang, who had once been Yuan's ally, was extremely jealous of the latter's influence and control of the Beiyang Army. Yuan's power had increased tremendously since 1901, with many of his long-time associates being placed in important army positions. He appeared to be the most powerful provincial satrap controlling a considerable military force. Moreover, he struck the foreign diplomatic corps in Peking as the most progressive official in China as well as the real moving spirit in the modern army. No Manchu could probably have viewed his increasing power with equanimity. Tieliang himself was extremely ambitious, advocating a policy of centralisation in order to curtail the political and military powers of the governors and viceroys, particularly Yuan Shikai. He was believed to have had the support of the Empress Dowager in this respect.[29]

On 30 September, 1906, Tieliang had already clashed with Yuan over some proposed administrative reforms.[30] Following the reform edict of 6 November, Yuan was stripped of his control of four divisions of the Beiyang Army, leaving only the 2nd and 4th in his charge. The 2nd Division had been the Left Division of the Zhili standing army, and the 4th was originally Yuan's Right Division. The other four divisions, the 1st, 3rd, 5th and 6th, were now placed under the Ministry of War. General Fengshan, commandant of the Peking Banners, was appointed general-in-chief of these four divisions. An incompetent man, Fengshan had been a minor police officer for some years, and apparently owed his present appointment to court favouritism. It was only natural that Yuan should feel 'so much annoyed at seeing his troops pass into the hands of such an unworthy successor that he asked leave to hand over charge direct to the Board of War'.[31]

This state of affairs was watched by British diplomats in China with some concern. Pereira believed that the Chinese army should be reformed with the service of a strong man like Yuan through a process which started in a small way in one province and then gradually spread out to the rest of the country. The Commission for Army Reorganisation had the advantage of being directed chiefly by Yuan, whose absence from the Ministry of War would be detrimental to the interests of the army.[32] Sir John Jordan agreed with him, seeing that under Yuan's direction army reorganisation had been 'the one department in which the Chinese have received credit from foreign observers for having made substantial progress'.[33] The British Foreign Office, on hearing the appointment of Fengshan, commented that it was 'extraordinary folly on the part of the Chinese [government]'.[34]

The Chinese themselves were increasingly disturbed by Tieliang's anti-Chinese policy. The *Universal Gazette* (a native newspaper) of 31 January 1907 had a leading article on the dangers of Tieliang's attitude, pointing out that he had long looked askance on high Chinese officials being in control of military affairs, and that for this reason he had forced Yuan to apply to be relieved of the control of the four divisions as well as of various other military duties. He was an ambitious man, the paper added, aspiring to equal the late Ronglu. But while Ronglu was more anti-foreign than anti-Chinese, Tieliang was determined to dominate the Chinese with his newly acquired military and financial power.[35]

The rise of Tieliang must be seen in the context of rapid Manchu predominance in the official hierarchy. The decree of 6 November had ordered a single president and vice-president, irrespective of race, for all the ministries. The government seemed to be moving in the direction of racial equality for the Chinese, but before long the Manchus were seen rising rapidly to senior positions, while the Chinese held most of the less important posts. This strengthening of Manchu power in the capital coincided with the growth of revolutionary activity in the provinces. The assassination of Enming, the Manchu Governor of Anhui, on 6 July 1907, by Xu Xilin, an assistant director of the local gendarmerie school, alarmed Peking. This was followed by the revolt of 13 July, led by Qiu Jin, a lady teacher at Shaoxing. Manchu officials throughout the country were worried about their personal safety and the security of the dynasty. They lived closely guarded in their offices, and the existence of a revolutionary movement was frankly admitted in Peking.[36] In these circumstances the Throne sought to restore the confidence and loyalty of Chinese officials by issuing a decree on 10 August, promising equality to the Chinese in public appointments to official ranks of all grades, as well as equality before the law.[37]

Yet in spite of this promise, the Manchus continued to increase their control of the government. In 1908 they obviously monopolised most of the high offices of state. Members of the imperial clan were placed in many ministries. Of the fifty-two high offices in Peking (including five Grand Councillors, five Grand Secretaries, and the Chairman, but not members, of the Political Consultative Council), twenty-seven (51.92 per cent) were held by twenty-three Manchus. There were equal representations on the Grand Council and the Grand Secretariat until Prince Chun became the Prince Regent at the end of the year. Of the fifteen senior positions of comptrollers, associate comptrollers, and presidents of boards, ten (66.67 per cent) were occupied by nine Manchus. There were twenty-two vice-presidents, half of whom were Manchus. Prince Qing, old and feeble, held several positions in spite of the government's earlier condemnation of pluralism.[38] Consequently, the Chinese were obliged to content themselves with the lower positions.

Obviously, the Manchu regime was incapable of expanding political participation. It failed to absorb more ardent Chinese reformers into its system in spite of the administrative changes. This inability to adapt itself adequately to the demands made on it and to absorb them in terms of policy-making was bound to create serious problems for the reforming regime.

Changes under the Prince Regent

The deaths of Emperor Guangxu and the Empress Dowager in November 1908 precipitated a succession crisis, which was quickly resolved by the appointment of the late Emperor's brother, Prince Chun, as the Prince Regent. Young (aged twenty-six or twenty-eight) and reasonably well informed about some Western countries, Prince Chun appeared to be more progressive than most of the Manchu princes. In 1901 he had been to Berlin as head of the mission that was sent to apologise for the murder of the German minister, Baron von Ketteler, in the Boxer uprising. After presenting the apology, he received an exceedingly warm royal welcome, and was shown the military and commercial resources of the German empire with which he was deeply impressed. Since his return to China, he had been politically active. In anticipation of the high destiny in store for him, he had completed a course of military training in the Nobles' College and had, more than any Manchus of his class, qualified himself for entry into an active political career. When he assumed the reins of power, public opinion in Peking generally endorsed him in his high office. All the princes and ministers were said to have promised him their whole-hearted support. Foreigners in China who appreciated his previous visit to Europe and his general disapproval of anti-foreign outbursts welcomed his accession to power. The Chinese Ministry of Foreign Affairs was hopeful that under his regency many of the outstanding foreign issues would be settled amicably. The native press, too, saw in the new regime the dawn of another reform era.[39]

The Prince Regent had some old grudges against Yuan Shikai because of the latter's 'betrayal' of the late emperor in the Hundred-Day Reform. On 2 January 1910, Yuan, who had been 'promoted' to the Grand Council and appointed President of Foreign Affairs in September 1907, was forced to resign from all his offices and retire to his native town in Henan to 'convalesce' from his 'ailing foot'.[40]

The Regent was determined to uphold Manchu ascendancy in Peking and its vicinity. In July 1909 Xiliang, a Mongol, was appointed to the Manchurian viceroyalty, while Duanfang replaced Yang Shixiang as Viceroy of Zhili. The latter post had always been held by the most prominent Chinese officials like Zeng Guofan, Li Hongzhang, and Yuan Shikai. Its loss to another Manchu further weakened the Chinese influence in the government. After the death of Zhang Zhidong on 4 October, 1909, the Comptrollership of Education was allowed to be vacant. Dai Hongci gave up his law portfolio and became a Grand Councillor. Ge Baohua succeeded Puliang as President of Ceremonies, but this was cancelled out by the appointment of Tingjie as President of Law.[41]

Probably owing to his German experience, the Regent was serious in seeking to strengthen the martial spirit of the nation. An edict of 15 July 1909, proclaimed the Emperor the supreme commander-in-chief of the military and naval forces of the Empire and declared the creation of a special advisory council to study and advise upon the reorganisation of the army and the navy. It was the government's objective 'to stir upon our army to value the profession of army and to aim at a strong army'.[42] The Emperor was now restored to the position which the earlier Emperors Taizu and Taizong had held in regard to the command of the imperial army. While the edict was intended 'to keep the question of the improvement of China's defensive forces before the public, and to educate opinion upon the importance of efficiency in that direction',[43] the Regent stood to gain from the fact that he was to discharge the duties of the three-year-old Emperor Xuantong during his minority.

The special advisory council referred to in the decree was the

General Staff Council, which was now independent of the Ministry of War. Its position was further enhanced by the appointments of Prince Zaitao and Prince Yulang as Comptroller and Deputy Comptroller, respectively. Another prince, Zaixun, and a Chinese admiral, Sa Zhenbing, were appointed High Commissioners to reorganise the navy. Both Zaitao, aged twenty-five, and Zaixun, aged twenty-six, were brothers of the Regent, and had attended the Nobles' College for two years. But because they were young and inexperienced, their appointments excited widespread dissatisfaction and severe criticism in Peking's native press.[44]

The General Staff Council served as a consultative and executive body and was expected to evolve into a General Staff Office in the near future. An imitation of the Japanese staff organisation, its main functions were to make recommendations in all questions relating to defences, general military preparations, military command, planning of operations, and nomination of generals, admirals, and staff officers. The Comptroller, corresponding to the Chief of Staff in Japan, was directly responsible to the Emperor, or the Prince Regent for that matter, and enjoyed direct access to him. His recommendations, after receiving imperial sanction, were transmitted to the Ministry of War or the naval section, if appropriate, for execution. In 1910, the General Staff Council took over complete control of the Staff College (yet to be founded), the surveying schools, the appointment and assignment of staff officers to the divisions, the military information bureau and the translation bureau, and military attachés to Chinese legations overseas. An inspector-generalship controlled by the General Staff replaced the Ministry of War in the supervision of military education.[45]

The emergence of an independent General Staff represented a forward step in the direction of structural differentiation. There seemed to be a gradual shift of military administration away from the general administration. This would help to promote military professionalism which had failed to develop in imperial China. Unfortunately, the General Staff inspired little confidence from the very beginning owing to the inexperience of its personnel. The somewhat injudicious appointments of very young and inexperienced men to responsible positions caused inefficiency and sometimes friction among its own staff.[46]

In March 1910 Prince Zaitao led a military mission to Japan, the United States, France, Germany, Italy, and Russia for the purpose of studying the army systems, arsenals and gun factories of the different countries. The mission had been most rewarding for him. Upon his return to China, he called for a further strengthening of the central administration and the improvement (and thus expansion of the power) of the General Staff. He met with the viceroys and governors and various commanding officers of the divisions on a number of occasions to formulate more detailed regulations for the management of the New Army within a centralised framework. He was in full control of the General Staff, after Prince Yulang, his deputy, had been appointed to the Grand Council in October and was devoting most of his time to the discharge of his new duties.[47]

Prince Zaitao was assisted by able counsellors, chief among whom was Lieutenant-General Feng Guozhang, who had been head of the department of military education, Commission for Army Reorganisation, and director of the Nobles' College. There were two brigadiers, Ha Hanzhang, who accompanied Zaitao on his mission abroad, and Liangbi, a Manchu, both of whom were educated in Japan. Each of the six sections of the General Staff was in the charge of Japanese-educated officers.[48]

The Ministry of War under Yinchang
The Ministry of War had now lost control of the General Staff, supervision of the Staff College and the provincial general staff. The naval section attached to it had also gained its autonomy under the new name of Naval Reorganisation Council, which was expected to become an independent ministry before too long. However, the War Ministry yielded very slowly to the General Staff, clinging tenaciously to the duties which had been within its realm. This was made possible by the inefficiency of the General Staff, which created a situation whereby all important memorials relating to military affairs were jointly submitted by them.[49] In March 1910 Tieliang fell from imperial grace, and Yinchang was installed as the new President of War.[50]

Yinchang was a graduate of the Imperial University (later renamed the National University of Peking), and was subsequently educated in Austria and Germany. For some years he had been head of the Tientsin Military School. From 1901 to 1905 he was Chinese minister to Germany, where he had enjoyed the personal favour and instruction of the able Wilhelm II in army matters. Since his return to China, he had served as commander of the 7th Division, Vice-President of War, and again Minister to Germany in 1909. He was married to a German wife, spoke German fluently and had great admiration for the German army and the House of Krupp, and was believed to have pro-German sentiments. Experienced, able and energetic, he was considered by foreign military experts to be the best man for the post. At the time of his appointment, he was still serving in Germany, and did not assume duty until September 1910. In December of that year when the titles of president and vice-president were replaced with minister and vice-minister, he became the first Minister of War.[51]

Yinchang set out to achieve three objectives: greater efficiency and economy in his ministry, improvement of the profession of arms, and military centralisation. To attain the first goal, he reorganised the ministry and reduced the number of its sections from twelve to eight, doing away with those which were not properly within its realm of responsibility. For example, the control of the old post roads and post stations was turned over to the Ministry of Posts and Communications, as it was no longer necessary to escort the mails by the army. A program of house cleansing was initiated, whereby examinations were held for a great many officials and clerks. As a result, about two hundred of them were found to be worthless and subsequently dismissed. It was also announced that in the future no one would be appointed to an army post without having received a modern military education. Yinchang also insisted that officials in his ministry should not hold posts elsewhere. This aroused a great deal of hostility from the senior officials whose patronage had been responsible for many previous appointments.[52]

Given his military background, Yinchang naturally took much pride in the military profession and expected all his subordinates to share his sentiment. Even before he took up his new appointment, he had announced that he would attend office in uniform.[53] As soon as he assumed office, he directed all officers on duty to salute each other in a military manner instead of the traditional civil practice of holding the hands together and raising them up and down a couple of times. This rule applied whether the officers were in civilian clothes or military uniform.[54] In December 1910 he ordered that from the beginning of the Chinese New Year all officers belonging or attached to the ministry should wear uniforms while on duty.[55]

In November 1910 a new code of military law provided for a system of military courts to which the soldier would be subject for trial in the future.[56] This meant that the civil administration would have to give up jurisdiction over the military which it had traditionally exercised. It represented a step towards achieving the separation of power between military and civil authorities in judiciary matters. The result would be to improve further the status of the soldier.

Military centralisation underlined Yinchang's relationships with the viceroys, governors and the divisional commanders. It will be remembered that Tieliang had gained control of four of the Beiyang divisions from Yuan Shikai. Yinchang went further than that. An edict of 26 September 1910, withdrew the 2nd and 4th Divisions from the control of the Viceroy of Zhili, and turned them into metropolitan *(jinji)* divisions directly managed by the Ministry of War. It also reduced the Tientsin war board to one department, namely, administration. General Fengshan was relieved of command and appointed Tartar-general at Jingzhou in Hubei. This meant that Yinchang now had control of the Beiyang Army and the Imperial Guard Corps, of which he was acting commander-in-chief. Furthermore, he appeared to enjoy the confidence and trust of the Prince Regent, to whom he owed his present rise to prominence, and this helped to strengthen his hands in dealing with his political opponents.[57]

In the meantime, Yinchang desired a reduction in the military powers of the viceroys and governors. The provincial high officials had traditionally enjoyed some sort of local autonomy, having almost complete jurisdiction over the civil and military administration of their own provinces. Central control over the provincial forces was a prerequisite to the development of a strong, unified national army, but this would require the viceroys and governors to give up much of their powers to Peking. Earlier, the General Staff under Prince Zaitao had arrogated to itself the duty of appointing divisional commanders and provincial staff officers. Here again, Yinchang went a step further. He stripped the provincial high officials of their power to transfer military officers from one province to another and made it his responsibility to assign them to the provinces where they were needed. Any officer who had resigned from one division was not permitted to apply for a position in another. The provincial armies were now brought under closer central supervision. Hitherto it had been the duty of the local authorities to fill the soldier quotas. Yinchang now demanded that all vacancies in the ranks should be filled at once, or else the officers concerned would be held responsible. Deputies from the ministry were sent to investigate local military organisations, and they were punishable by military law in the event of false reports.[58] In December 1910 the honorary rank hitherto granted to viceroys and governors as presidents and vice-presidents of the Ministry of War was abolished.[59]

There was co-operation between the War Ministry and the General Staff in their efforts to control military officers in the provinces. The fact that Yinchang was on good terms with Prince Zaitao improved relations between the two bodies and cleared the way for the formation of a War Council composed of their respective heads plus other senior government officials. The council's policy on the question of military officers was that those of the first and second rank, that is generals and lieutenant-generals, should be solely under its control, while other commanders and field officers were to be responsible to the Ministry of War alone.[60] This left the provincial high officials with the power to appoint, promote and dismiss company officers only, but even this power was weakened by Yinchang's directive that the commanding officers who usually recommended such appointments, promotions and dismissals to the viceroys or governors should submit quarterly reports to him. 'Apart from this', the directive added, 'the Ministry will send delegates from time to time to make secret investigations and commanding officers will be held responsible that prompt and accurate reports are sent in'.[61] It was obvious that Yinchang desired to exert his influence in matters that were supposed to be the duties of the provincial authorities.

Added to this was the insistence on Peking's right to appoint directors for the department of education and training in the provincial war boards, which had hitherto been a provincial prerogative. The actual training and maintenance of the armies remained the responsibility of the provinces, but the question of the ultimate station of these troops was to be decided by the War Council. The provinces could make recommendations, which the council was under no compulsion to accept.[62]

Following this was the reorganisation of the provincial war boards. On 24 April 1911, a proposal from the Ministry of War led to the formulation of new regulations, under which the director-general of each provincial war board was to be the viceroy or the governor, the Tartar-general or the lieutenant-general. Each war board was to have a councillor who supervised the various departments, the training of the old and new troops, the recruitment and disbanding of soldiers, general military preparations, and the supply of provisions, stores and munitions. There were now four departments in each war board, instead of the usual three, namely, the administrative department, commissariat and supplies, equipment and munitions, and the topographical department. Each department was to be staffed by assistants, juniors, secretaries and clerks working under the councillor. The functions of each department were clearly defined. The number of officials in each war board was to be determined by the number of divisions maintained in the province concerned, and where there was less than one division it was to be decided by the Ministry of War. Under these new arrangements, although the viceroy or governor was still the titular chief of the troops in his province, his power over them was considerably curtailed, while the councillor, an officer of substantial rank appointed by the Ministry of War, was directly responsible to and under the absolute control of Peking.[63]

The question may well be asked: how successful had Yinchang

been in attaining his policy objectives? On the positive side, he had achieved some economy in the administration of his ministry with a reduced staff, and had also gained more control over the provincial military officers. He was better informed about the provinces than his predecessors. When he was not satisfied with the local conditions reported to the ministry, he was keen to inspect the troops in person, so as to find out the true state of affairs. He liked to summon commanding officers to Peking for consultation on the conditions of their troops and certain strategic problems.[64] He had succeeded in curtailing the powers of some viceroys and governors in military matters.[65]

However, there were serious limitations to his achievements.[66] His house cleansing met with much animosity from high officials who sought sinecure posts for their henchmen. The ministry had been reorganised, but it was difficult to see where improvement had actually been made. The eight sections into which it was divided were charged with so many conflicting duties that the jurisdiction of each defied definition.[67] Added to this were the differences between Yinchang and the Ministry of Dependencies over the question of the control of troops in Tibet and Mongolia.[68]

Another factor contributing to the limited success of Yinchang was the hostility of his own deputy, Vice-Minister Shouxun. A man practically without any modern military training, Shouxun had been a Tartar-general in Jilin for two or three years. His lack of modern training was evidenced by his inspection of the 1st Division in October 1910, after which he recommended 229 civil and military officers for special awards, even though it was common knowledge that the division was in fact in a worse condition than it had been two years before. Yet he had great influence in court circles and was able to control much of the ministry and to act arbitrarily in many matters without Yinchang's knowledge.[69]

Furthermore, it must be emphasised that centralisation was an impossible task because of resistance from the provinces, which furnished the funds necessary for the New Army scheme (see the following section). The last three years of Manchu rule were a period in which the central authority could not have been weaker. The Prince Regent's lack of strength of character and breadth of view, the predominance of a cabal of young and inexperienced Manchu noblemen, the intrigues of the New Empress Dowager Longyu and other ladies in court – all contributed to a decided weakening of the central authority. The Prince Regent gradually allowed the reform of his government to pass from his control.[70] There was no leader in Peking who had the vision and strength of character to inspire confidence. Indeed, no officials dared take the initiative and responsibility. The Chinese Foreign Affairs Ministry was candid about this. In August 1909 its president, Liang Dunyan, told a British business manager that neither he nor any other high official would sacrifice their private interests for the public good by assuming any responsibility which they could evade.[71]

Parallel with the weakening of the central authority was the growing independence of the provinces. The viceroys and governors, though in many respects under Peking's control and liable to transfer and recall, were bent on doing things their own way. If Peking's policy did not coincide with their interests, they would furnish all sorts of excuses and suggestions to avoid putting it into effect while not openly defying the order. On the other hand, if they wished to do something in their own interests, they would do so in spite of Peking. They grew more and more suspicious of Peking, more and more restive under its financial exactions and political control. The extent to which they were determined to retain their powers can be gauged from a joint memorial of January 1911 stating three principles which Peking was asked to follow in its relations with them. First, all the viceroys and governors should be consulted in the formation of the new cabinet under the constitutional program. Second, they should have full powers to employ subordinate officials before they could be held responsible for them. And third, the old-style provincial troops should not be abolished before the modern police force had been completed.[72] If all these propositions were met, the new cabinet about to be formed would have little power in controlling the provinces.

The question of the old-style provincial troops illustrates the vested interests of the provincial leaders. The newly formed National Assembly recommended that these troops be abolished at once or as soon as possible, and in January 1911 made drastic cuts (by two-fifths) in the proposed budget for their maintenance. Both the Prince Regent and the Ministry of War seemed to favour the recommendation, but the provinces reacted to it with vigorous protests, arguing that without those troops it would be impossible to maintain local peace and order, as the New Army was not yet ready to take over their duties. The old troops could do a better job as they were scattered all over the provinces in small detachments and composed of men who could serve for as long as they wished. There was also the question of 'squeezes'. It was impossible for Peking to find out exactly how much was expended on the old troops and how much was appropriated by corrupt officials. Lastly, the indiscipline and mutinies in some divisions of the New Army in the previous year had given rise to doubts about the reliability of the modern troops.[73]

The position of the provinces in relation to the centre was strengthened by China's military geography. As one author has pointed out, the geophysical, political and economic aspects of China have always combined to create a situation conducive to 'military regionalism'.[74] China's sheer size presented a problem which was compounded by the poor system of communication between north and south. This rendered it difficult to maintain a vertical cohesion between north and south, thereby contributing, as it often did, to political division and fragmentation.

In view of these problems, it would have required a man of far greater ability, influence and ingenuity than Yinchang to remove the obstacles to military centralisation. This situation, in the meantime, was complicated by financial problems to which we shall now turn.

Military finances

The implementation of the New Army scheme hinged on the all-important question of finance. The number of divisions assigned to each province was determined by local resources as well as by political and strategic considerations. Zhili had more divisions than any other province because it was the centre of imperial power. Sichuan, a province of great strategic importance, had three divisions, while Jiangxi and Henan, for example, had one division each on account of their scarce resources. Nearly all the divisions were under strength owing to lack of funds, and the provinces were constantly under pressure from Peking to bring them up to size.

With the exception of Xinjiang, Guangxi, Gansu and Manchuria, all the provinces were required to contribute towards the financing of the Beiyang Army and the divisions assigned to the poorer regions. These contributions were of two kinds. The first was known as *jiexiang*, a regular annual contribution made to Peking for the use of the central government. The other kind was called *xiexiang*, paid in addition to the *jiexiang* in the form of grants-in-aid to assist the poor provinces in military reforms. Most of the provinces had to finance not only their own troops, both new and old alike, but also the Beiyang Army and the divisions in the poor regions. They tended to make every endeavour to forward the *jiexiang*, either in full or in part, but were invariably slow or in fact unable to forward the other, as they were hard pressed enough trying to finance their own armies.[75]

The maintenance of the Beiyang Army depended largely on the funds provided by the Board of Revenue. As Stephen MacKinnon has shown, this army was far from being a personal and regional army in spite of Yuan Shikai's care and influence, and from the very beginning was subject to Peking's financial and administrative control.[76] Its annual expenditure was normally submitted to Peking for imperial sanction one year in advance, so that the Board of Revenue could make necessary arrangements for the funds to be made available fully or in part. The Commission for Army Re-organisation was entrusted with the task of exploring all possibilities of increasing the government revenue. Yuan recommended that a stamp duty and additional taxes be levied on native wine, tobacco, opium, tea and salt throughout the country, as well as new land and real estate registration taxes, customs revenues and profits from minting. Accordingly, the Board of Revenue issued a directive to the provinces to that effect, and expected to collect a total of 8,100,000 taels from fourteen provinces in 1904. If this amount was not forth-coming in full, the balance would be met by compelling the district magistrates and other provincial officials to subscribe part of their incomes from the land tax. Meanwhile, the provinces were ordered to practise economy and to make every endeavour to meet the quotas required. Severe punishment was threatened to dishonest officials and gentry who attempted to hamper the fund-raising campaign.[77]

New taxes alone would not suffice to defray the high military cost. The expenditure of government departments also needed to be reduced. The Board of Works was ordered to stop all unnecessary public works. The imperial household, too, was told to spend less. Wealthy merchants and landlords were encouraged to assist with funds, in return for which they would receive official rank and other rewards.[78]

In April 1904 Wang Wenshao, Comptroller of the Board of Revenue and a Grand Councillor, sent a memorial to the Throne advising that apart from increasing the taxes already levied on native wine and tobacco, the land tax throughout the country should be tho-roughly revised, the salt tax raised, the opium tax in Sichuan increased, and all arable public land sold to Chinese peasants. To relieve the burden of the southern provinces, the annual rice tribute to Peking should be discontinued. All public works should be stopped tem-porarily, and civil officials holding lucrative posts should be made to contribute part of their perquisites to the military funds. It was estimated that this would raise about 12,555,000 taels annually. His proposal received imperial sanction.[79]

The Chinese government sought no foreign loans for fear of foreign control of its army. It rejected Acting Viceroy Cen Chunxuan's proposal to raise a foreign loan of one million taels to meet the mili-tary expenses in Guangxi. Rather, it complied with Cen's other request for permission to sell official rank, titles and decorations in Guangdong. Temporary offices were to be set up for this purpose, but they were to be closed as soon as one million taels had been collected.[80]

Peking's demands placed considerable strains on all the provincial treasuries. Earlier in 1904 the Governor of Shaanxi had pointed out that he was unable to meet his quota, as he had enough difficulties dealing with the local problems resulting from the famine of 1900-1. The province had been impoverished, and the living conditions of the people were 'deplorable and pitiable in the extreme'. Standing armies were being formed only by drawing on the old-style troops.[81] Later in the year, the governor reported that even if provincial officials were retrenched and government expenditure reduced, it would still be extremely difficult for him to fill the quota.[82] Similarly, Governor Zhou Fu of Shandong complained about shortage of funds. He needed a minimum of 200,000 taels a year for the maintenance of four new battalions plus equipment costs.[83] He requested that Shandong be exempted from the rice tribute to Peking and that the sale of official rank and titles be permitted (as in Guangdong).[84]

Even wealthy provinces had difficulties. Jiangsu was apportioned one million taels annually, but as Viceroy Wei Guangtao complained, his province was already short of funds for the training of a new standing army at Nanking. To raise another million taels would add to the impoverishment of the local population and possibly force them to join secret societies and engage in rebellious activity.[85]

Zhili, probably because of Yuan Shikai's special efforts, was one of the very few provinces which were not slow to forward the funds required. Hubei was another. But in the case of Hubei, which sent 100,000 taels to Peking in May 1904 as part of the annual contribution, a loan had been raised from a native bank in Hankow. It was with immense difficulty that Viceroy Zhang Zhidong managed to forward the rest at the end of the year.[86]

When the 2nd and 3rd Divisions were completed in August 1904, their total cost was estimated at 4,230,000 taels, including pay and allowances, purchase of arms and ammunition and miscellaneous expenditure. The estimate for 1905 was slightly less, only 3,600,000 taels, because of a lesser need for the initial outlay. They were funded by the Board of Revenue, while Zhili paid for the 1st Division. By then Peking had received from the provinces a total of 2,920,000 taels, which was hardly enough for the 2nd and 3rd Divisions combined.[87]

It was the poor response of the provinces that led to Tieliang's visit to the central and southern provinces in August 1904. The trip was, on the surface, designed as a special tour of inspection of various arsenals, armouries, and powder factories. But it was generally believed that Tieliang was charged with the more important duty of investigating the financial state of the provinces, in the hope of collecting more funds for military purposes. The native press, commenting on the trip, drew a parallel with the mission of the late Gangyi, who had been sent in 1898 to inspect the Yangzi defences and to raise funds from the provincial treasuries.[88] According to the British acting consul-general at Shanghai, Tieliang, after a searching inspection of the Jiangsu arsenal and the Longhua powder factories, had succeeded in collecting from the local magistrate the sum of 800,000 taels.[89]

This search for funds was an encroachment on the preserves of the provincial administrations which became so resentful that the Throne was obliged to issue a decree in November ordering Tieliang to limit his duties to matters concerning the arsenals only. He could study military operations in the provinces he visited, but he must refrain from inquiring into the provincial finances. Obviously the provincial governments were resolute in resisting Peking's attempt to interfere with their financial administration. Peking, too, realised the implications of Tieliang's trip and found it necessary to conciliate the provinces.

In 1905 each Beiyang division cost an average of 1.5 million taels. The 1st Division was financed by Zhili, the 2nd, 3rd and 6th were funded by the Board of Revenue. The 4th Division was paid for principally by Shandong and partly by Hubei, while the 5th Division was jointly maintained by Shandong and the Board of Revenue.[90] Table 2 shows the quotas distributed to the seventeen provinces for the financing of the Beiyang Army and troops in the poor regions. Three provinces (Jiangsu, Hubei and Zhejiang) were able to forward in excess of the quotas required in 1905. It was obvious that because they were relatively resourceful, they had been compelled to furnish more, and consequently their quotas for 1906 were increased. Three other provinces (Zhili, Hunan and Gansu) made full payment in 1905, and the rest all failed to do so. Their quotas for 1906 remained unchanged, while Yunnan and Guizhou, on account of their poverty, were allowed a large decrease.

The Board of Revenue received contributions from the provinces and other sources of income and then handed a large portion of them to the Commission for Army Reorganisation, which in turn distributed the money to the Beiyang divisions through the paymaster-general. The transfer of funds from Peking to Tientsin could be assured if there was co-operation between Revenue, War, and the commission. Such co-operation was well effected when Yuan Shikai had control of the commission and his allies and protégés were at the same time holding senior positions in War and Revenue.[91]

If the President of Revenue was a member of the Grand Council, he had the authority to force the provinces to make contributions. Between 1902 and 1904, the Board was headed by Lu Chuanlin, who was a Grand Councillor. In 1904 Rongqing, another Grand Councillor, became President of the Board. In August 1905 Tieliang was appointed to the Grand Council, while concurrently serving as Vice-President of War. Thus there were extremely influential officials in high places who were willing and able to acquire millions of taels for the maintenance of the Beiyang Army.

Table 2. Quotas of military contributions for 1905 and 1906

Provinces	Quotas for 1905 (taels)	Actual amount forwarded in 1905 (taels)	Quotas for 1906 (taels)
Jiangsu	850 000	1 610 000	1 610 000
Hubei	500 000	1 030 000	1 030 000
Zhejiang	500 000	914 400	914 400
Zhili	1 100 000	in full	1 100 000
Hunan	400 000	in full	400 000
Gansu	100 000	in full	100 000
Sichuan	800 000	only in part	800 000
Guangdong	850 000	150 000	850 000
Henan	400 000	200 000	400 000
Shandong	550 000	192 000	550 000
Shanxi	500 000	100 600	500 000
Anhui	350 000	100 000	350 000
Jiangxi	500 000	200 000	500 000
Shaanxi	300 000	150 000	300 000
Fujian	400 000	20 000	400 000
Yunnan	200 000	120 000	120 000
Guizhou	60 000	10 000	10 000
Fengtian	temporarily	—	temporarily
Jilin	exempted	—	exempted
Guangxi		—	
Heilongjiang	exempted	—	exempted
Xinjiang		—	

Source: *Dongfang zazhi*, II, 10 (November 1905), *caizheng*, pp. 240-3.

In November 1906, the Board of Revenue, now known as the Ministry of Finance, was charged with the maintenance of the 1st, 3rd, 4th (in small part), 6th, and half of the 5th Divisions. Zhili paid for the whole of the 2nd Division and the largest part of the 4th. In that year five million taels had been collected for the army. About half this amount came from profits on the mints or other sources, and the other half by special contributions levied on the provinces, in unequal shares. Yuan's money for his divisions came partly from profits on the imperial railways of north China, salt, and wine duties, and the rest from provincial sources. Funds were always in short supply, and this sometimes resulted in large arrears in the soldiers' pay.[92]

In 1906 Puting, a Manchu of no great mark, was appointed President of Finance, and was succeeded in the following year by Zaize. Neither of them was on the Grand Council, so the ministry seemed to have lost the authority to exact contributions from the provinces. In fact, however, the provinces continued to be forced to pay. They were in addition asked to subscribe to a special military reserve fund established in 1906 for the Ministry of War, the poorer ones being temporarily or permanently exempted. The provinces, as usual, had year by year evaded paying, wholly or partly. In June 1909 this reserve fund amounted to about five million taels.

For the year 1909 the total cost of the New Army in the eighteen provinces and Manchuria, excluding the Imperial Guard Corps, was estimated at 60 million taels. There had been completed ten divisions and twenty-one mixed brigades. As each division cost about 1.5 million taels, the cost of paying all the troops was little more than 30 million taels. This meant that the other half of the 60 million taels represented the administrative expenses of the Ministry of War, the cost of arms and ammunition, the construction of barracks and other military works, the maintenance of military schools and arsenals, and the running of the provincial war boards.[93] Nobody could tell exactly how much military funds Peking could collect annually, since it had little effective control over provincial finances. Thus, no great advances in the army could be made until a thorough reform of China's financial system and a more thorough control of Peking's revenues was effected.

It was not until late in 1910 that there was something of a military budget. As part of the preparations for a constitutional government, a national budget for 1911, the first one ever made in China, was submitted to the National Assembly in November. The original estimate for the expenses of the New Army was 58,760,235 taels, but the National Assembly cut it down drastically to 28,692,680 taels. Other military expenses were also severely reduced; still others were wholly disallowed. Overall more than half the total national budget reductions were made in the estimates for military expenses, while the reductions made under the latter heading were in excess of one-third of what was asked for. The policy of the National Assembly was not to expand the army for the time being, but to improve the instruction and equipment of the existing establishment and to achieve self-sufficiency in military supplies.[94]

The national budget revealed for the first time the military expenditure in the country. The Ministry of War made an estimate based on the expenditure incurred in 1910 plus expected expansion in the following year. The total estimate, according to Chinese sources, was 109,534,895 taels (including both new and old troops alike, military schools, arsenals, transport, forts, horse breeding, and office running cost, but exclusive of the navy). The New Army alone was to cost 54,361,901 taels, or 49.62 per cent of the military budget. The Green Standard troops and parts of the Patrol and Defence Force would be disbanded, thus effecting a saving of over 13,000,000 taels, half of which would be spent in pensions and other provisions for the disbanded soldiery, and the other half on the New Army. This, in fact, would have increased the New Army budget to over 50 per cent of total military expenditure.[95]

Table 3 shows the New Army budgets prepared individually by the major provinces, excluding some outlying regions where the New

Table 3. Estimated military expenditures for 1911 in the major provinces

Provinces	Estimated total revenue (taels)	Estimated total expenditure (taels)	Estimated New Army expenditure (taels)	Percentage	Remarks
Fengtian	16 183 311	15 521 927	5 294 054	34	Surplus
Jilin	8 488 606	9 342 715	1 638 677	17	Deficit
Heilongjiang	5 400 169	5 513 421	1 428 421	25	Deficit
Zhili	25 335 170	21 978 682	3 554 287	16	Surplus
Jiangsu	9 834 751	10 450 471	3 388 895	32	Deficit
Jiangbei	1 507 014	1 565 794	3 041 604	200	Deficit
Anhui	5 195 863	6 735 864	4 704 776	70	Deficit
Shanxi	8 230 884	9 059 828	2 338 638	25	Deficit
Shandong	9 764 848	9 755 823	2 329 217	24	Surplus
Henan	9 900 096	9 840 305	4 141 604	43	Surplus
Shaanxi	5 035 455	6 207 290	1 801 048	29	Deficit
Gansu	3 805 956	4 317 879	4 295 884	99.4	Deficit
Xinjiang	3 567 885	3 473 772	1 486 262	41	Surplus
Fujian	5 417 396	6 565 775	1 957 967	30	Deficit
Zhejiang	11 850 488	13 380 352	3 508 260	26	Deficit
Jiangxi	7 073 278	8 478 381	3 127 475	37	Deficit
Hubei	13 534 251	14 510 681	5 064 904	34	Deficit
Hunan	7 661 553	9 488 703	3 733 739	40	Deficit
Sichuan	22 686 637	26 413 232	10 306 636	40	Deficit
Guangdong	23 201 957	20 262 273	5 618 158	27	Surplus
Guangxi	4 476 002	5 782 331	3 083 513	53	Deficit
Yunnan	5 536 793	7 469 703	4 208 659	56	Deficit
Guizhou	1 842 821	2 749 574	1 248 338	45	Deficit

Source: Shen Jian, *Xinhai geming qiangxi woguo zhi lujun jiqi junfei*, pp. 400-1.

Army was being planned or in the process of formation. It can be seen that Sichuan had the largest budget, followed by Fengtian (where a new division was being created), Guangdong (where the mixed brigade was to be expanded to division strength), Hubei, Anhui, Gansu, Yunnan, Henan, Hunan and Zhejiang. Zhili did not need as many funds because the Beiyang Army had been well established. On average 40-50 per cent of the total expenditure in each province was on the New Army.

The total budget of the Ministry of War accounted for 35 per cent of the total national expenditure and 36 per cent of the total national revenue. The Ministry of Finance reduced it to 91,358,035 taels, or 30 per cent of the total national expenditure.[96] According to the American military attaché, the total national expenditure estimated by the Ministry of Finance amounted to 338,652,295 taels, of which 126,843,333 (31.45 per cent) were for the Ministry of War (excluding the navy). The advisory National Assembly reduced the Ministry of War budget to 77,915,890 taels, or 29.88 per cent of the total expenditure, which was now cut down to 260,745,003 taels.[97]

As an indication of the cost of the New Army scheme, the estimate of the Ministry of War would appear more realistic, that is 36 per cent of the total national revenue, which was not excessive compared with the spending in the European powers or Japan. But in China's case the New Army was an extremely heavy burden on an agrarian economy which had yet to support other necessary reforms. In 1911 the military expenses in many provinces were in fact well above 50 per cent of their total expenditure (see later chapters). It was only natural that they should resent being compelled to contribute to the financing of troops other than their own.

The system of finance, then, enabled the provincial authorities to retain much control of their military organisations. This control extended to the arsenals which they funded. Neither the Commission for Army Reorganisation nor the Ministry of War succeeded in bringing armament under one system administered by Peking. There was some sort of armoury or magazine in every provincial capital where surplus arms and the supply of ammunition on hand were stored. These, too, were under the direct management of the viceroys or governors.[98]

To summarise, significant changes were instituted in the military administration at both the national and provincial levels. A new Ministry of War, a new General Staff Council, and provincial war boards had been set up. The reform efforts of the late Empress Dowager Cixi were followed up by the Prince Regent and his Minister of War, particularly in their attempts to standardise the armies throughout the country and to achieve central control over the provinces, both militarily and financially.

Political intrigues in Peking, the Manchus' desire to increase their influence in the government, the weak central leadership after 1909, the incompetence of the Manchu dignitaries who controlled military affairs, the haphazard manner in which the New Army was financed, and the growing independence, both political and financial, of the provinces, all combined to hinder Peking's efforts at military development. With the possible exception of the Beiyang divisions, a national army existed more on paper than in reality. The southern divisions, although they had achieved some degree of standardisation, were organised, financed and managed by the provinces, and were therefore not truly unified in command. The regulations and guidelines emanating from Peking could be tampered with, if necessary, with relative impunity. Thus, the New Army, though centrally inspired, remained largely territorial in character.

THREE

Military education and nationalism

ONE OF the major problems in the development of Chinese military power was the incompetence of the officers. A soldier could be made in three years, but an efficient officer was the product of many years' training and study. Until about 1910, the Chinese army was seriously handicapped by unqualified officers of four major types. There were those who had been officers of the old-style troops, or of the Banner forces and other similar antiquated organisations and who were old, worn out and ignorant. A second type consisted of former naval officers who were brought into the army through influential connections. Others were civil officials who held military rank because of their administrative ability rather than their knowledge of military affairs. Still others were young students who had been abroad for just a few months or more, including some who had not studied military subjects.[1]

When a new young officer corps emerged in the last few years of the dynasty, it was small in numbers but significant as a new social group. Mainly in their twenties, these officers came from fairly good family backgrounds and were reasonably well educated by Chinese standards. Their modern education gave them a new outlook, a desire to make a career success and a growing sense of national identity.

Modern training, too, contributed to the growth of nationalism in some sections of the officer corps, a nationalism which reflected a sense of urgency to ensure China's national survival and which was fostered by the Peking government both directly and indirectly. The Chinese were anxious to achieve military independence. They needed to learn from foreign expertise and technology, but they wisely restricted foreign tutelage to the hiring of instructors and technicians in the schools and the arsenals. Where Chinese officers were available, foreign experts were dispensed with in a spirit befitting an independent national army.

Military schools in China
Before 1905 there had been established a number of military pre-

paratory schools *(wubie xuetang)* and schools for commissioned officers *(jiangbian xuetang)* on a provincial basis. They varied from one another in supervision, course structure, student numbers, entrance requirements and standards. The training was invariably short and inadequate, turning out officers who were far from efficient and who lacked the initiative essential to technological change.

In September 1904, the Commission for Army Reorganisation recommended for establishment over a period of seven to ten years a hierarchy of military schools and staff colleges run on the same basis as those in Japan. There were to be established primary schools *(lujun xiaoxuetang)* in all the provinces and Manchu garrisons (one in each), four provincial secondary schools *(lujun zhongxuetang)*, one officers' school *(bingguan xuetang)* and one staff college *(canmou daxuetang)* (the last two to be opened in Peking). A quick-course normal school *(sucheng shifan xuetang)* was also recommended for the training of instructors who would teach in the secondary schools scheduled to open in 1908.[2]

The recommendation was sanctioned by the Throne and put into effect in 1905. Detailed regulations were drawn up for the establishment and management of the primary schools.[3] The commission expected a total of 2000 foundation students and a total of 6000 enrolments over a period of three years. It was assumed that 90 per cent of the foundation students would complete the three-year course successfully and proceed to the secondary schools for another two years. After a total of five years, the graduates would serve for four months as first-class privates and sergeants with the title of military cadets *(lujun ruwusheng)*. Afterwards, they would attend the officers' school for one year and a half and then return home to a regiment as probation officers *(xuexiguan)* or trainee officers *(lianxi guanbian)* for another six months. An examination would then be held for them. Those who attained a high rating would receive commissions as company commanders. After two years' service, outstanding officers would attend the staff college for two years leading them to qualify for staff appointments. From primary school to the staff college, it would take almost ten years.

The primary schools were to be opened in 1905 or as soon as possible thereafter. In Zhili, Jiangsu, Hubei, Fujian, Guangdong, Yunnan, Sichuan, and Gansu, which had viceroys in the capital cities, each primary school was to enrol 300 students over a period of three years. In Shandong, Henan, Shaanxi, Anhui, Jiangxi, Zhejiang, Guangxi, Guizhou, Hunan, Shaanxi, Xinjiang, which had governors, each school would have 210 students, or 300 if they liked. In the Manchu garrisons at Jingzhou, Fuzhou and Chahaer, each school would admit ninety, whereas the number was not decided for those in Fengtian, Jilin and Heilongjiang. Admission was by examination. Students were to be recruited principally from the provincial senior (civil) primary schools and partly from the existing military schools established before 1905. The entrance qualifications were as follows: applicants were to be aged between fifteen and eighteen, or twenty in the case of those selected from the existing military preparatory schools; they were to be of good character, honest and with no criminal record; they were to be the sons of decent families *(liangjia zidi);* they were to have a genuine interest in military studies and have no bad habits; they were to have received some education and gained some proficiency in essay writing. The other requirements related to physical fitness regarding height, weight, eyesight, chest dimensions, and the like. The place of birth was relatively unimportant. The fact that the students were to be drawn from the senior primary schools would suggest, as Hatano Yoshihiro writes, 'that even at the lowest level, officers would be drawn from landlords, rich farmers, and prosperous merchants, because only these could afford to send their sons through senior elementary schools'.[4] This would significantly alter the class composition of the officer corps and bring some of the country's best intellects into a hitherto despised profession.

The school curriculum was to consist of ethics, Chinese (language and literature), foreign languages (a choice of Japanese, English, Russian, German and French), history (Chinese and foreign), geography (Chinese and world), mathematics (arithmetic, geometry, algebra, and trigonometry), general science (physics, biology, zoology, hygiene and geology), and drawing. Other subjects included military ethics, general military studies and gymnastics. The students were to pay no tuition fees. Rather, they were to receive a small living allowance in addition to all rations, clothing, uniforms, textbooks and stationery. They would attend classes six days a week, and five periods a day. All lectures would be one hour each, while practical work and gymnastics would be longer. Every week there would be two periods each in ethics, history, geography, drawing, general science and military subjects, four periods each in mathematics and gymnastics, and five periods each in Chinese and foreign languages.[5]

Significantly, emphasis was placed on training the mind as well as the body; for instance much importance was attached to mathematics and also to foreign languages. The fact that military studies would be taught at an elementary level, receiving no more attention than history and geography indicated a recognition of the value of general education as a prerequisite to military efficiency.

Peking's policy of creating a respectable officer corps received the support of the provinces generally. Zhang Zhidong, for instance, had been seeking for years to recruit local degree holders *(juren, gongsheng* and *shengyuan)*, expectant officials, scions of official and gentry families, and men with varying degrees of literary proficiency. Those who intended to enrol in the military preparatory school were required to pass a written examination. Even though it was difficult to fill the quota of 120 such students, he insisted on choosing the best men for the vacancies. In 1901 when the school for commissioned officers was opened, the students were selected from those who had demonstrated a proficiency in literary and military pursuits.[6]

By 1907 military primary schools had been started in all provinces except in Xinjiang, Heilongjiang and some Manchu garrisons. There were two of these in Zhili (one in Peking and the other in Yaocun).[7] Most of them had been converted from the existing military preparatory schools, and conformed with Peking's regulations. The training and instruction in these schools throughout the country appeared to be quite uniform, except in the matter of foreign languages. For example, in Manchuria, Russian and Japanese were taught; in Yunnan and Guangxi, French came first in importance; and in Shandong, German.[8]

Owing to different local conditions and financial constraints, some schools had their own peculiar features. The most notable one was the Hubei school which had a capacity of 3000 places. Since its inception in early 1906, it had recruited 1000 pupils each year because of a great demand for officers. Zhang Zhidong intended to double the intake by having two batches of pupils attending school alternately, one day in school another in the battalion. As well as increasing their numbers, this would promote good communication between pupils and existing officers. In five or six years, there would be 6000 graduates, if all of them completed the course successfully. The pupils were all *bona fide* soldiers in the various commands around and in Wuchang, and were selected by examinations. This was a departure from the Peking's regulations, and the reasons for doing this were, first, Zhang found the sons of decent families mostly unable to bear the hardships of military life, and second, the pupils of the local senior (civil) primary school had not yet finished their courses. In the meantime, Zhang increased the military content of the school curriculum. No change was made to the first year. But for the second and third years, more military subjects, like fortifications, topography, military organisations, weaponry, pure and applied strategies, cavalry and artillery practice, and hygiene, were introduced. The ratio between general studies and military subjects was 3 to 1 in the first year, 2 to 1 in the second, and 1 to 2 in the third. Attached to the school were a cartography class, a military administration section, a medical division and a naval department, each of which had sixty pupils.[9]

Another feature of the Hubei special primary school was that the age requirement was not strictly enforced. The stress was laid on literary standards and physical fitness. Consequently, there was a number of mature students who were in their late twenties, literate and healthy.[10] This provided them with a modern education which otherwise would have been denied them. Zhang's innovations reflected the varying needs and circumstances of different provinces. Contrary to his earlier insistence on local degree-holders and upper-class elements, he was forced by local conditions to choose pupils from the ranks. But this did not lower the standard of the school because his troops consisted of a large number of literate men who could be trained to be good officers.

In 1908 Zhili had a third military primary school opened at Baoding. The one in Peking, which was directly under the Ministry of War, was the best established, with an attendance of 404 pupils, of whom about 300 were Manchus. Because of the high cost of running it, the pupils had to pay school fees, 3 taels monthly for Manchus and 4 taels for Chinese, while sons of officers paid half rate. French, German, and Japanese were taught, but not English. Upon graduation, they would be posted indiscriminately to any one of the first six divisions. The other two Zhili schools, at Baoding and Yaocun, had fewer pupils, about half as many as Peking's. It is worth noting that these pupils were sons of officials and merchants.[11]

Contrary to Peking's rule, pupils in many schools received no pay or living allowance owing to shortage of funds; but they were adequately quartered and provided with rations, clothing, textbooks, and stationery. The regulation that entry was by examinations seems to have been followed everywhere with the exception of some Manchu garrisons. In some provinces pupils were selected by district magistrates who checked their qualifications very carefully.[12]

While each province had its own primary school to meet the local needs, those for the first ten divisions were not divisional schools, and graduates from the schools in Zhili, Wuchang, Nanking, Tsinan, Foochow and Manchuria could be sent to any division where their service was in demand.[13]

The military secondary schools appeared to be more elitist, the original plan being to have only four, namely in Baoding, Wuchang, Nanking and Xi'an. The Baoding school would admit students from

Peking, Zhili, Shandong, Shanxi, Henan, Anhui, Manchuria and Chahaer. The Wuchang school was to cater for the needs of Hubei, Hunan, Yunnan, Guizhou, Guangxi, and the Manchu garrison in Jingzhou. The Nanking school was to serve Jiangsu, Jiangxi, Zhejiang, Fujian, Guangdong and some Manchu garrisons, while the one in Xi'an was to be open to those from Shaanxi, Gansu, Sichuan and Xinjiang.[14] The plan for the Baoding school was later cancelled in favour of one in Peking.[15] In late 1905 there was a proposal from the viceroy of Liangguang for a fifth school in Canton. In October 1909 three of these, one each in Peking, Wuchang, and Nanking, had been established. In the autumn of 1910 the fourth school in Xi'an was also opened, while the fifth one was being planned.[16] The subjects taught in these schools were an expansion of those in the primary schools.

The small number of secondary schools reflected a tendency towards producing a relatively small but well-trained professional officer corps. The four schools could not admit all the graduates from the primary schools; only those of sufficient calibre, with over two years' practical experience, were assured of entry. It is also interesting to note that these schools were located in strategically important provinces, Zhili, Hubei, Jiangsu, Shaanxi (and Guangdong when the fifth school was opened). Yet, strangely enough, Sichuan, which was expected to establish three New Army divisions, did not have a secondary school for itself.

Pending the opening of the secondary schools, temporary arrangements were made for the training of officers. The imperial plan was to establish a military quick-course school *(lujun sucheng xuetang)* in the metropolitan area. The students, 800 in all, were to be selected from those of the existing military preparatory schools in the provinces. The course was to last two years, after which graduates would be on probation for six months before being appointed as battalion officers.[17] This school was subsequently established at Baoding, with students coming from all parts of China, except Xinjiang and Tibet. There were two courses: a general one for two years and a half, with 1140 students, and a special one for one year and a half, with fewer enrolments. The general course offered subjects of general education for one year and military science for the rest of the time. The special one was concerned with the study of military science throughout the entire course. Most students were instructed in infantry, others in artillery or cavalry, and the remainder in engineering and transport. Because of the shortness of the courses, insufficient attention was given to foreign languages, though Japanese, English, French and German were taught to some students. On completion of the courses, the graduates served in the ranks for three months as trainee officers. By 1908 five other similar schools had been opened in different parts of the country. All of them were to be discontinued in 1911.[18]

Another temporary measure to train officers was to set up a series of regimental schools *(biaojiangtang)*, which had started in each of the first six divisions. The course lasted a year, after which the best students were sent to the divisional schools *(suiying xuetang*, literally follow-the-camp school) for another two years, before being commissioned. Most of these schools were abolished late in 1909 when three of the secondary schools were opened.

The opening of the military secondary schools was delayed for a variety of reasons, the most important of which was the shortage of qualified instructors. The quality of Chinese instructors was indeed a serious problem, for they were 'more or less ignorant', able to give their students no more than 'a smattering of education'.[19] Foreign instructors were employed, but it was imperative that China should try to turn out her own instructors. To this end, a military normal school *(lujun shifan xuetang)* was opened in the spring of 1908 at Boading. The course was for two years (or eighteen months if necessary), with 140 students specially selected from graduates of the military primary schools who were instructed only in the subjects which they would afterwards teach, for example mathematics, drawing, physics, history and geography.[20] In 1910 this school was discontinued (probably because it had outlived its usefulness).[21]

Before the Staff College was opened in 1916, temporary staff training colleges *(jiangwutang*, literally, schools for military lectures) were instituted at Tientsin, Mukden, Wuchang, Nanking and other provincial capitals. The most outstanding of these was the Hanliushu Military School (near Tientsin) opened in May 1906. It was divided into two sections, one for commissioned officers and the other for non-commissioned officers. The latter section was formed as a battalion, 540 strong, selected from the first six divisions: ninety from each, all for instruction in infantry only. After completing the one-year course, they were appointed sergeant-majors, sergeants, or corporals, or company-quartermasters. To be eligible for attendance, candidates must have served more than six months in the army, must be diligent, of good character and highly motivated. In the other section there were 150 to 160 officers, all coming from the first six divisions, detailed by the Ministry of War for a six-month course. Each division sent one colonel and two lieutenant-colonels, and others ranging between majors and quartermasters, in order to update their military knowledge and to insure uniformity of instruction.[22]

Hubei had its own staff training college called *jiangxiao jiangxisuo*, which instructed company officers (below regimental commanders) in staff duties for three years. These officers went in alternate batches for six months and returned to duty for one year and then repeated the same process until the course was finished. In 1907 there were about 800 officers taking the course, of whom fifty were being instructed in staff duties. In Nanking there was a similar college designed for regimental officers, but its course was much shorter, lasting six months, or three months if necessary.[23]

In addition to these, there was established at Baoding a preparatory staff college *(junguan xuetang)*, which offered two separate courses, one for officers commanding battalions or squadrons and the other for company officers. The former course lasted one year and a half, and the latter three years. All the officers were from the Beiyang and the 8th and 9th Divisions. The college was run on the same lines as the Hanliushu school, except that its courses were longer and were meant for the higher training of officers who had been through the quick-course schools. In 1910 there were 120 students. There were plans to expand the school and move it to Peking in the following year.[24]

Preparations were made in the summer of 1911 for the opening of the officers' school. By then, apart from the institutions so far described, there were a gendarmerie school at Dagu (later moved to Peking) and about two dozen schools for special services, such as engineers, telegraph, military survey, ordnance, veterinaries, medical and supply.[25] According to Major Swift of the General Staff, US Army, the total number of students in the Chinese military schools in 1910 (not including those in the schools for special services) was about 7000, a figure which was expected to double in 1912.[26] The United States military attaché put the figure at 7600, of whom 5500 belonged to the twenty-four primary schools.[27] At the time of the Wuchang uprising, according to Powell, there was a total of seventy military schools of all kinds, while *The China Year Book (1912)* pointed to the existence of twenty-seven primary schools (not twenty-five as Powell reported) fifteen surveying schools and four secondary schools, in addition to the preparatory staff college and the Nobles' College.[28]

Finally, it is worth mentioning the Nobles' College, which was opened in Peking in 1906. Its students, aged from 18 to 25, were members of the imperial clan and the sons or other relations of the highest officials like viceroys, governors, presidents or vice-presidents of boards, and provincial generals. Prominent among them were the sons of Prince Qing, Tieliang and Songshou,. Viceroy of Fujian. Prince Chun, Prince Zaitao and Prince Zaixun had attended the lectures regularly. The students studied general subjects for three years, followed by two months practice in the army. They then returned to the college for another year and a half to study military science. After that they went to the ranks again for a few months, before receiving commissions as lieutenants.[29]

The first director of the college was Lieutenant-General Feng Guozhang, formerly director of the Baoding Military School. In 1908 there were a hundred and twenty students, seventy of whom belonged to the imperial family, twenty-three were sons of Manchu officials, and twenty-seven were sons of Chinese officials. The Manchu students were said to be quick at learning and sharper than the Chinese. Besides English, German and Japanese languages, they learned European and Chinese history, geography, military tactics, foreign military organisations, and military drill. No foreign teachers were engaged. The students were generally well behaved. The Empress Dowager had urged the imperial princes and high officials to send their sons to the college; so if any one of the students was dismissed, not only the culprit but also his parents would be in trouble. Timothy Richard, the well-known missionary educationalist in China, visited the college in 1908 and found the whole teaching system bad.[30] It was not clear what measures had been taken subsequently to improve it.

Overseas military studies

In addition to training at home, Chinese cadets were sent to military schools in Japan, Europe and the United States. The majority of them went to Japan, and with good reasons. Geographically Japan was close to the mainland; the Japanese language was easier to learn than Western languages; the cost of living there was lower than in the West; the Japanese social system was similar to the Chinese in many respects.[31] Above all, Japan was becoming a model for emulation by China, especially after her victory over Russia.

Since the Sino-Japanese War, a few provinces, notably Hubei, Hunan and Sichuan, had taken the initiative to send small numbers of young men for overseas studies. In 1900 there were forty Chinese students doing military subjects in Japan. In September 1901 the Chinese government urged the other provinces to follow suit. Yuan Shikai was particularly interested, and in early 1902 sent fifty-five students from the Right Division and the Tientsin Military School to undergo a military course in Japan.[32] In 1903 there were 185 Chinese students in the *Rikugan seijo gakko* (Seijo Army School) in Tokyo. Forty-four of them were private students, the remainder being sponsored by the governments of Hubei, Fujian, Sichuan, Hunan, Zhejiang, Yunnan and Zhili. Twenty-four of them were attached to the Japanese army to gain practical experience.[33] In 1904 the enrolments rose to over two hundred.[34]

The Japanese Ministry of War made a special effort to assist the Chinese students by building new school premises and appointing additional instructors and administrative staff. Because the number of students arriving in Japan varied from year to year, there were difficulties in accommodating them and supervising their studies. The Japanese Ministry of War thus proposed to the Chinese legation in Tokyo on more than one occasion that a system be instituted whereby students came to Japan regularly. The proposal was communicated to Peking by the Chinese minister, Yang Shu, who recommended that an annual quota be set and that viceroys, governors and provincial generals be urged to recruit students from the sons of official and gentry families. The matter was referred to the Commission for Army Reorganisation, and regulations for overseas studies were subsequently drawn up and sanctioned by the Throne in May 1904.[35]

A few aspects of the regulations are worth mentioning. The annual quota was fixed at one hundred, subject to change at the end of four years; six from each major province (Zhili, Jiangsu, Hubei, Sichuan, Guangdong) and Peking; four from each medium-size province (Fengtian, Shandong, Henan, Anhui, Jiangxi, Zhejiang, Fujian, Hunan and Yunnan); three from small provinces (Shanxi, Shaanxi, Gansu, Guangxi and Guizhou); and one from each Manchu garrison (thirteen in all). The students were to be selected from those already attending local military schools, or from sons of official and gentry families in provinces where military schools did not yet exist. All of them were to have good family backgrounds and be physically fit, intelligent, highly motivated, and without bad habits. They were to have a good grounding in Chinese learning as well as a basic knowledge of military subjects. The age limit was between eighteen and twenty-two. In places where there were no military schools, the students were to be excellent in Chinese classics and history. They were all to be government students, financed jointly by Peking and the provinces. No private students were to be allowed in the future. Those who were currently studying in Japan would be examined by the Chinese minister in Tokyo with a view to converting them into government students. After completing their courses, they were to serve as trainee officers in the Japanese army for a short period of time. Subsequently, some of them would enter the Japanese Staff College or other schools for specialised studies, while the rest returned to China. All returned students would be considered for suitable employment. The best of those who had not yet been through the Staff College or any special schools were to be appointed as battalion commanders. The second best were to be appointed as lieutenants and the third best as company officers. Graduates from the Japanese Staff College and the special schools would receive commissions of a higher rank depending on their qualifications and experience. Others would serve as military instructors.

Here again, the most striking feature of the recruitment policy was Peking's insistence on selecting students from the upper class. There was a firm conviction that only when the country's best intellects and men from decent families adopted a military career could the officer corps improve itself and gain respectability.

The students who were sent to Japan came largely from Zhili, Hubei, Hunan, Zhejiang and Jiangsu, which indicated that the provincial quota was in fact more flexible than was required under the rules. The reason why these five provinces had more students studying overseas was partly because of their richer resources and partly because of the attitudes of their viceroys. Besides Yuan Shikai and Zhang Zhidong, Duanfang, Viceroy of Liangjiang (1906-9), was also a man of progressive tendencies who was equally enthusiastic about sending students for overseas studies.[36]

The Japanese government, in response to the Chinese needs, opened a new military school called *Shinbu gakkō*, specially designed for the Chinese students. Both this and the *Rikugun seijo gakkō* were preparatory schools, entry into which was restricted to students endorsed by the Chinese minister in Tokyo. Under the regulations of the Japanese military authorities, graduates of a preparatory school were required to serve in the ranks for six months to a year as privates or subalterns. Afterwards they entered the prestigious *Rikugun shikan gakkō* (Army Officers' School) for one or one and a half years. Upon graduation they were attached to a regiment on probation for another three to six months before being commissioned. The Chinese students in Japan followed the same rules.[37]

From 1904 the number of Chinese military students in Japan had increased by about one hundred every year. By 1907 the total enrolments, according to a Chinese source, were over five hundred and twenty.[38] This tallies with the figure provided by the Japanese assistant military attaché in Peking, who reported seventy-seven Chinese students in the *Rikugun shikan gakkō*, two hundred and twenty-three attached to the Japanese army (they had been in the preparatory school the year before), and two hundred and twenty-four in the preparatory schools.[39] In early 1910 Major Brissaud-Desmaillet put the figure for that year at five hundred.[40] (The decrease can be explained by the fact that the previous year's graduates had returned to China.) Major Swift estimated it to be seven hundred (probably including those studying subjects on the manufacture of arms, observing Japanese manoeuvres, and taking courses on army administration and general staff duties), and it would be reduced by fifty each year.[41] By 1911 there were about eight hundred officers in the Chinese army who had graduated from or studied in Japanese military schools, six hundred and thirty of whom had been trained in the *Rikugun shikan gakkō*.[42]

There were comparatively few students going to Europe and the United States. Germany and Britain were held in high esteem for their respective pre-eminence in army and naval development. In 1903 eight students from Hubei were sent to Britain to study naval affairs and another eight to Germany to study infantry, cavalry, artillery and engineering.[43] Early in 1904 Duanfang, then Acting Viceroy of Huguang, dispatched another ten first-class students from the Wuchang military schools to Germany and thirty others to Belgium to study railway, mining, agriculture and other industries.[44] Zhou Fu, Viceroy of Liangjiang in 1905, was in favour of Austria, and wanted to send ten students there. He also urged more students to go to Britain and Germany to study the manufacture of arms, munitions of war, mining, and other military industries.[45]

The provisional regulations governing overseas studies in Europe and the United States were similar to those for studies in Japan. There was, however, no annual quota, and permission had to be sought from the Commission for Army Reorganisation before students could be sponsored. Students, aged between fifteen and twenty-four, were to be, as usual, selected from decent families, and should have attained a good standard of Chinese classics and history plus three years' experience in the languages of the countries to which they were going.[46]

In 1908 the Ministry of War ordered that students who had returned without completing their studies were not to be employed. Rather they must refund the government all the expenses which they had incurred during the course of their studies.[47] With a steady supply of graduates, the ministry could now be more selective. Examinations were thereafter held in Peking for all returned students before they could receive commissions.[48] Such examinations seemed to work against the non-Japanese-educated graduates, for the new military nomenclature of the Chinese army had been borrowed from the Japanese. But in fact this was not the case, since the Japanese nomenclature itself was based on the translation of the Western military terms. The Western-educated officers needed only to have spent some time studying the Chinese translations in order to avoid any real cause for complaint.[49]

Evaluation of the school system and the officers

By the end of the decade the new educational system had succeeded in gradually improving the quality of the officers. This was evidenced by the changing opinions of foreign experts who had previously been extremely critical. In 1908, for instance, the British annual report on China described the Chinese officers as 'still very backward, and behind other countries', in spite of some progress in education. There were large numbers of officers still of the old uneducated type, even though there was a movement to replace them by graduates from Chinese and foreign military schools. Even those who had been educated abroad seemed to have acquired less than a sound military education owing to the shortness of their training period. While senior positions like divisional commanders usually belonged to the old, uneducated class, those returning from Japan were appointed as brigadiers and staff officers and thus could not help feeling themselves competent. As the British report stated, 'It will be a long time — ten years at least, probably more — before Chinese officers are really efficient.'[50]

A United States report on the Chinese army in 1908 equally criticised the 'inadequate and methodless' training of officers, which was attributed to the Chinese assumption that the science of war could be mastered in a few months or a year. Many cadets were commissioned even though they were deficient in knowledge and had no practical experience. Many colonels and some generals were young men in their twenties, while company officers were frequently old people.[51]

The following years saw some noticeable improvement. In 1909 British diplomats reported that the Chinese military education was making 'steady progress', with more new schools opened in various provinces, and that the supply of graduates was increasing out of all proportion to the formation of divisions and brigades.[52] In early 1910 the French military attaché, Major Brissaud-Desmaillet, was impressed by the Chinese program of military education, which was 'being executed with remarkable efficiency and thoroughness'.[53] At the end of the year his American counterpart in Peking, Captain Reeves, was of the opinion that education was 'a better organization than any other branch of the military establishment', and that the graduates it produced were 'of a better grade than those serving with troops'.[54]

On the other hand, some deficiencies in the system were still obvious. One of these was the absence of schools which offered courses on applied instruction for junior officers. The officers, superior and subaltern alike, learned the method of instruction at ad hoc divisional classes where lectures were given both periodically and in series.[55] Another defect was the lack of adequate Chinese teachers. The locally trained instructors from the normal school were not of a high order. This problem could have been solved, at least in part, by recruiting those who had graduated from foreign military schools; each year there was a number of them. But until the end of 1910 the demand for their services in the army was so great that only a small proportion of them were put to teaching. In earlier years foreign instructors, especially Japanese and German, had been appointed to supervisory positions in the schools, but later the Chinese felt that they had learned how to run the schools themselves and wanted to make no more use of them.[56] There was yet a third problem: that many cadets had become officers as soon as they left the military primary schools.[57] This was made possible by the great demand for officers in earlier years; subsequent efforts to replace them with better trained officers had not been very successful.

By 1911 the new educational system had been in operation for six years and was beginning to show its impact with its first batch of graduates from the secondary schools. Considering their inexperience, it was no surprise that they were not as efficient as British, French or American officers. But the system did represent a major step towards achieving military professionalism. Also, imperfect as it was, it furnished the troops with an opportunity for self-improvement. F.A. McKenzie, who visited the Beiyang divisions in late 1906-early 1907, was very impressed by the fact that every soldier went to school. After examining 'with considerable astonishment' the exercise books in the classrooms for non-commissioned officers, he was of the opinion that:

> The geometrical plans, the neat drawings of entrenchments, the diagrams for land-surveying, and the advanced mathematical work were proof enough that the brain as well as the body of Yuan's soldiers is receiving full attention.[58]

What was true of Yuan's army applied to many other divisions. Generally the school was 'one of the most important parts of the solider's life'. The private was required to attend it for two hours every day, besides his four hours' drill, learning Western methods and values.[59] Alternate batches of privates, selected by examinations, were sent to the school. Literate soldiers in the ranks were encouraged to form student-solider battalions *(xuebingying)* among themselves. The outstanding ones had the opportunity for quick promotion to corporals or sergeants.[60]

The military graduates often served in their native provinces because of a virtually decentralised framework (in spite of Peking), in which viceroys and governors could make their own appointments. This tended to strengthen the basis of a territorial army, and encouraged both officers and men to develop an interest in provincial matters.[61] On the other hand, officers could be transferred to another province upon request or on the order of the provincial authorities and the Ministry of War. Furthermore, owing to the inferior quality of some schools in the south, officers from the north were often appointed to senior positions in the southern armies. In provinces like Guangxi, where the New Army was a late development, the officers were mainly from outside provinces.

The foreign-educated officers were more highly prized. A few of them rose quickly to the rank of divisional and brigade commanders. Others were installed in staff positions or as directors and supervisors of military schools. They, too, often returned to their native provinces for service, and were subject to transfer.

By 1911 there had emerged, in a professional sense, a new class of young, modern-educated scholar-officers, a good many of whom were from good socio-economic backgrounds and held a traditional degree. The products of a reform era and a blending of Confucian culture with the technological learning of the West and Japan, they constituted a new military elite which, in terms of social origin, may be described as an extension of the lower gentry class.[62] (The gentry class will be discussed in chapter 4.) They were not an independent elite like the Japanese army officers after the Meiji period. They earned their improved status by virtue of the education and the social background which distinguished them from the traditional army officers. In other words they were not markedly differentiated from the civil elite. Indeed, they shared with them common social ties, common political experiences of the assault of foreign imperialism, a common concern about China's need for revitalisation, and a common belief in the value of new learning.

Like the civil elite, this new corps of officers had divisions and differences within itself. There were at least three cliques. Graduates of the *Rikugun shikan gakkō* formed the so-called *Shikan* clique as distinct from the Beiyang clique, those who were trained in the Beiyang military schools. There was also a third broad category of officers who graduated from schools in central and south China and who had to deal with both the *Shikan* and the Beiyang cliques. There were rivalries and mutual jealousies among them.

The modern-educated officers, too, persisted side by side with a diminishing number of old-style officers, some of whom were in senior positions. Efforts to weed out the worthless elements had caused considerable animosity in some quarters, as Yinchang's experience showed. Until all the old ones were replaced and the new ones became more experienced, the Chinese officer corps would remain inefficient.

Nationalism in the New Army

It has been pointed out by some political scientists that rapid changes in military education and technology are often a politicising experience. These changes provide both officers and men with some form of training in citizenship, even if they receive no formal and explicit training in political matters. The new military, learning about the new technological world and the systems on which a modern state is based, tended to develop a particular awareness of the relative weaknesses and political dimensions of their own society and of their special role in its development.[63]

The contents of the new Chinese military educational system proved important in changing the outlook of the soldier. He was now trained in modern (therefore foreign) technology in the defence of the motherland. He became more informed of what was going on in the outside world as well as in China. He read books on the geography and history of foreign nations, on the expansionism of the imperialist powers and their encroachments on weak countries, including China. He learned about the nations where modern weapons were manufactured and where he acquired his technological skills. He was drilled along lines similar to the soldiery of countries which had seized 'spheres of influence' and concessions of all kinds from China. All these factors could hardly fail to instil a sense of patriotism among some sections of the soldiery.

Overseas training brought a large number of cadets to a new environment where they were exposed to a new system of values. A year's or a few months' stay abroad was sufficient to give them an awareness of the deplorable differences between China and the foreign country. Many of them quickly became imbued with radical ideas and joined the Tongmenghui or some other revolutionary society back home. More often than not these cadets returned to China with a reformist or revolutionary zeal, wishing to be party to the movement to build up a strong, independent China.

There is ample evidence that a new sense of nationalism was developing in the Chinese army. It manifested itself in the form of a military spirit which was becoming a national virtue. The English journalist, Edwin Dingle, was much struck by it while travelling in Yunnan in 1909. Many of the officers he met had been trained abroad or drafted from Peking, with their queues discarded, and exhibiting good discipline and a tough appearance. In many places temples had been transformed into barracks, in others huge arsenals and modern barracks had been erected, and everywhere drill went on all day.[64] Similarly, a vice-president of a Christian college in Canton found that there was an increasing martial spirit in the army and that the soldier began to have patriotic sentiments and take pride in his position of importance.[65]

The spirit of patriotism was assiduously fostered in the Chinese army as evidenced by the rapid growth of self-respect and pride in the military profession. No foreigner could help being impressed by the absolute refusal of both Chinese officers and privates to accept any gratuity for services rendered. This particular form of pride was the more striking because the soldier's pay was small and the acceptance of presents was a generally acknowledged part of Chinese life. There were certainly many people who enlisted in order to make a living, or for want of anything better to do, but there were also large numbers of those who chose a military career out of patriotic motives.[66] In the military schools considerable attention was given to 'cultivating ideas of patriotism and honor'.[67] The troops of the 8th Division were well known for singing patriotic songs when marching.[68] In May 1911 Zhang Biao, the divisional commander, issued a book entitled *The Country's Disgrace*, and distributed it to the troops to stimulate their ardour on the battlefield. It dealt with such topics as the miseries suffered by China in the Boxer war; the indemnities and territories extorted as a result of the war; the 'occupation' by the powers of the treaty ports; the outrageous treatment of China by foreigners; the great value of the soldiery to their country and people; and the way in which soldiers should sacrifice their lives for the country.[69] Yinchang, too, was well known for directing all divisional commanders to pay more attention to 'spiritual teaching' in the army, with the aim of promoting 'a spirit of patriotism and love of country, devotion to duty' and such similar national values and virtues in which the soldier was previously deficient.[70]

It was this new nationalism that led some officers to be involved in the railway issue. In 1910 a few provinces strongly opposed Peking's attempt to nationalise the country's trunk railways through a foreign loan. They demanded the right to build their railways with their own funds. The section of the railways which caused the most trouble was the Hankow-Sichuan line (see chapter 8). In Hubei the people, led by students who had returned from Japan, held mass meetings and sent representatives to Peking to express their protests. The provincial gentry and members of the New Army also participated in the meetings. At one of them, a Wuchang military officer chopped off his finger in anger, an act which appealed to the Chinese as it would not to Westerners.[71] At another meeting a private bit his finger and wrote a letter in blood to the railway company asking that they raise funds to buy back the railway rights.[72] At yet another meeting

Li Yuanhong, commander of the 21st Mixed Brigade, was unanimously elected as the Hubei representative to go to Peking.[73] It was reported that the Hubei troops were taking an active share in the agitation with the consent of their officers.[74]

The movement for the cutting off of the queue ('pigtail') was another expression of Chinese nationalism. There could hardly be a more awkward sight than that of a modern soldier, dressed in a khaki jacket and trousers, a forage cap, foreign boots, but with his hair still braided in a queue. The encumbrance it placed on the drill and physical training of the troops was only too obvious. The movement to cut it off gathered momentum in the military schools. In Hangchow in 1907, many cadets and instructors had cut off their queues, but no officers and privates in the army units had done so. In Anqing a couple of soldiers had done away with theirs too; others had their hair coiled inside their caps and allowed the rest of it to grow long, so that with their caps on, they looked as if the queues had been discarded. In Canton 25 per cent of the students in the military primary schools had cut off theirs.[75] No case was reported of a cadet or a soldier severely punished for having discarded his queue, which indicated that the military authorities were sympathetic to the movement.[76]

Peking's attitude was equivocal but conciliatory. Although no official permission was given for the queue to be abolished, the government did not take any action against those who had done so individually. Prince Zaitao, after his European trip, favoured its total abolition in the armed services. In September 1910 the Ministry of War, the Naval Board, and the Ministry of Foreign Affairs were advised that their officers might discard their queues if they liked, but this did not apply to other ministries. As a result, the Minister of War and many senior officers did so, followed by thousands of soldiers and cadets. It was expected that by the end of 1911 the queue would have been abolished altogether in the military service.[77]

From the Chinese point of view, this was a matter of much greater import than it appeared on the surface. Military reform had rendered the queue an ugly appendage. The cadets and officers who set an example in cutting it off were motivated by a sense of shame and nationalism. Their success would encourage them to participate in a broader movement for more social change. The queue was more than a hair-style, for it had significant political implications for the Manchu ruling class.

Some foreigners, however, expressed concern about what they saw as the conceit, arrogance and overconfidence of the Chinese officers.

Those who had been educated overseas returned to China with great expectations and a reforming zeal which could only be matched by their inexperience. In foreign eyes they were 'swollen heads', with inflated views of their own importance. It was alleged that this new generation of officers, from a spirit of pride and sensitiveness, were reluctant to learn from foreigners properly and were too eager to assert themselves and to dispense with outside assistance and instruction. '[U]nfledged babies bloom into Brigadiers', as a British military expert remarked with sarcasm.[78]

The exuberance of the New Army officers led others to believe that they were overbearing in their attitudes towards foreigners. The following comment by Lieutenant-Commander Mulock, a British naval officer serving in China, shows his disapproval of them:

> It would appear that the army is no longer a despised profession in these parts, but it is not certain that the cultivation of a 'Professional Pride' which is justified by efficiency in the Japanese army has not been confounded with the cultivation of 'Conceit' by the Chinese who have been trained in Japan . . . the bearing of the army in these parts towards the foreigner is accounted for by an overestimation on their part of their present knowledge and experience.[79]

Weiss, the German consul in Chengtu, also complained about the 'bad bearing' of the Chinese officers. According to Mulock again,

> . . . he [Weiss] had had occasion to complain to the [Chinese] officials twice during last year [1909]. Once when his Assistant, Herr Fischer, was riding in the city, he met a long train of army mules, and wishing to cross over the road, he passed through a gap in the train. His bridle was seized by one of the men and his horse turned around, and he was made to wait till the whole train had gone past. The other occasion was when he met a squadron of cavalry at a corner. As a measure of safety he got out of his chair and walked, and as one of the officers passed his colleagues, he struck them with his whip though they were in the consular uniform.[80]

While there was a general feeling on the part of the foreigners about the conceit of the Chinese officers, the bad bearing alleged by Mulock and Weiss was disputable. The German assistant acted improperly in the first place, for he should have given way to the military mules. As regards the latter incident, the information was insufficient for one to make a fair judgment. In fact, the British military attaché, Lieutenant-Colonel Willoughby was sceptical about the story, which did not accord with his own personal observation, or that of his predecessor, that Chinese officers were generally friendly to foreigners.[81]

Edwin Dingle offered some insight into the subject. While in

Yunnan in June 1909, he observed the troops undergoing their daily drill and wrote in his diary:

> Whilst I was on the field gazing in anything but admiration on the scene, I was ordered out by one of the khaki-clad officers in a most unceremonious manner. Seeing me, he shouted at the top of his thick voice, 'Ch'u-k'u, ch'u-k'u' (an expression meaning Go out! — commonly used to drive away dogs), and simultaneously waved his sword in the air as if to say, 'Another step, and I'll have your head.' And, of course, there being nothing else to do, I 'ch'u-k'ud,' but in a fashion befitting the dignity of an English traveller.

> The reorganisation of the army, with the acceleration of warlike preparations, has the advantage that it appeals to the embryonic feeling of national patriotism, and affords a tangible expression of the desire to be on terms of equality with the foreigner. That officer never had a prouder moment in his life than when he ordered a distinguished foreigner from the drilling ground, of which he was for the first time the lordly comptroller. And it may be added that the foreigner can remember no occasion when he felt 'smaller', or more completely shrivelled.[82]

Generalisations about a large country like China are dangerous. When we say that nationalism was developing in the New Army, it must be emphasised that only certain sections were imbued with it. These were the young, proud, sensitive, modern-educated officers and the privates who enlisted out of patriotic motives — people who were learning the national and military values essential to national regeneration. On the other hand, there were many sections where the officers were still unqualified, physically weak and addicted to opium-smoking, and the privates were illiterate and ignorant. The military spirit that Dingle and other foreigners described was found in some divisions, but not in others. The extent to which patriotism was whipped up in the troops no doubt varied greatly from unit to unit.

Chinese attitudes towards foreign tutelage

Nationalism in the Chinese army found yet another expression in the government's attitude towards foreign guidance and instruction. The Chinese displayed a determination to achieve military self-sufficiency as soon as their own graduates were available for service. This meant, among other things, employing every well-educated officer as far as possible, thus increasing his awareness of his special role in military development.

Unlike the leaders of the Tongzhi period (1862-74),[83] the military reformers of the post-Boxer decade did not appoint foreigners to organise Chinese troops or to hold a Chinese rank. There was no

Frederick T. Ward or Charles G. Gordon, no Paul d'Aiguebelle or Le Brethon de Caligny, no Roderick Dew or August Protet, who had accepted commissions in the nineteenth century. Now the foreigners in the Chinese employ were private individuals having no official connections with their own governments and were entirely limited to instructional or supervisory appointments in the military schools, arsenals, gunpowder factories and armouries. Their contracts varied between one and three years. None of them was allowed to interfere, directly or indirectly, with China's internal affairs, whether civil or military.

The foreign instructors were predominantly Japanese and to a lesser extent German. The Japanese were cheaper to hire, their military system and nomenclature had been adopted in China, and socially they could mix with Chinese officers more readily than Europeans. Furthermore, many Chinese officers themselves had been educated in Japan and had some affection for that country.

Since 1903 it had been China's policy to train the New Army largely on Japanese lines and to manufacture Japanese-type arms and weapons, and this necessitated the employment of more Japanese experts. In 1904 Viceroy Wei Guangtao was prepared to dismiss the German instructors serving in the Nanking Military School at the end of their contracts and to employ Japanese exclusively in the future.[84] His policy was subsequently carried out with partial success. In 1907 there were two German gunners, Count Praschma and Bleyhoffer in the school. This contrasted with a much larger number of Japanese: two officers, Lieutenant Sakata and Lieutenant Amano, besides five non-commissioned officers. The veterinary school was also in the charge of a Japanese expert, while two others instructed the Chinese in the working of guns.[85]

In 1906 the Japanese instructors in the Guangdong army consisted of four officers, one sergeant-major and six sergeants. There were, in addition to these, one Japanese captain and three or four non-commissioned officers in charge of the military school at Huangpu (Whampoa). They had some supervisory control over the regiments stationed near the mint. But all of them were purely instructors while the regimental officers were all Chinese.[86]

Japanese influence was also paramount in the central Yangzi provinces. A Major Ikuta had important duties in a Changsha military school; others were in force to a lesser extent in other Hunanese cities.[87] The Hanyang arsenal was developed with much Japanese guidance. A British naval officer who inspected it in July 1906 found fifteen Japanese employed, two of whom were officers in the Japanese army, the remainder being technicians. They had superseded the

Germans who were formerly employed.[88]

Sir John Jordan neatly summed up the situation in 1908:

> Everything in the army is borrowed from the Japanese, who are not loved by the Chinese. Foreign instructors have no authority over regiments or battalions, and are confined to the schools. At present, there are probably about seventy Japanese (officers and non-commissioned officers) employed, and, I believe, only five Germans (all in the schools of the 8th and 9th Divisions on the Yang-tzu). In addition, two Germans act as confidential advisers on questions of forts and arsenals, and it is not therefore surprising that German firms get the chief trade in the sale of guns, rifles, and arsenal machines.[89]

While foreign officers did not train the Chinese army, they were sometimes called upon to assist in the manoeuvres. The Chinese had their first grand manoeuvres in 1905, and were anxious to impress the foreigners who were invited to observe them. The manoeuvres were held at Hejian (in Zhili) in October, involving the Beiyang Army only. The movements had been rehearsed with the assistance of ten Japanese 'translators', who organised the scheme and orders, and practically did all the staff work, while being kept well out of sight.[90] In the manoeuvres of the following year, both the Beiyang and the southern divisions were involved, the latter including the 8th Division commanded by General Zhang Biao. Once again, the Chinese were dependent to a great extent on Japanese advisers for the planning and the execution of their movements. The Japanese took part either as officers or umpires. Prominent among them were, on the northern side, Colonel Banzai, an important military adviser to Yuan Shikai, as chief umpire, Colonel Teramishi, director of the military school at Baoding, and Major Kayetsu, head of the Hanliushu Military School. On the southern side were Colonel Igata, chief of the staff to General Zhang Biao, and Major Kojima, who was reported to have led the southern cavalry. The commander of the southern artillery also appeared to be a Japanese. Indeed, it was no secret that Japanese instructors, both regimental and on the staff, had the main share in organising and executing the shows.[91] This indicated that an efficient corps of regimental officers and staff officers had yet to evolve.

Owing to lack of funds, there were no grand manoeuvres in 1907. Only some local divisional ones took place. In 1908 the Chinese were prepared to do it again, this time at Taihu district, in south-west Anhui, near the Hubei border. There appear to have been no foreign instructors with either the northern or the southern army. Either the Chinese thought they were good enough to do it all by themselves, or they wanted to try it on their own in any case. Yinchang and Viceroy Duanfang were joint imperial commissioners, with Lieutenant-General Feng Guozhang, chief of staff, and Major Ha Hanzhang, assistant chief of staff, as directors. There was a large body of umpires, but they appeared to have done nothing. Probably because of their independent efforts, the manoeuvres were not a great success.[92]

The absence of Japanese advisers in the manoeuvres of 1908 reflected a strong desire on China's part to dispense with foreign experts. Rightly or wrongly, the Chinese now felt that they had acquired enough experience and expertise to build their own arsenals and train their own officers. Indeed, the Chinese government was sensitive on the question of foreign assistance and direction, and was always quick to deny reports of predominant Japanese influence. Its policy was to use the Japanese and then to remove them in the same way that the Japanese themselves had done with European instructors. The Japanese were keen to establish their influence as widely as possible, and diplomatic pressure was said to have been brought to bear on Peking. However, China had no cause for allowing herself to be under exclusive Japanese influence. She had no particular affection for the Japanese. Rather she tended to see Japan as a potential enemy and recognised, too, that the Western powers would not like to see a Chnese army under Japanese sway.[93]

The policy of replacing the foreign experts was carried out with moderation. Contracts were normally allowed to expire. Some foreign employees, as soon as their contracts expired, left of their own accord for personal reasons, or because of unsatisfactory working conditions and the 'unco-operative attitudes' of Chinese officials. Others stayed for one or more terms where their services were earnestly sought. In one or two rare cases, they were dismissed for acting independently of the Chinese authorities.[94]

The tendency to rid China of foreign tutelage was so marked that even Yinchang, for all his pro-German sentiment, could not reverse it. Before he returned to China from Berlin in September 1910, he was reported to have arranged with the German government for the dispatch of a military mission to give instruction to the Chinese army. That report was never confirmed and the mission never sent. But obviously Yinchang was a little out of touch with the prevailing mood in China. In that year the schools in north China were almost entirely taught by Chinese instructors, even in the teaching of foreign languages. In the Yangzi provinces, there were still some foreign experts in Wuchang, Nanchang and Nanking. A few Japanese were employed in topographical instruction, while some officers of the German army taught military science as well.[95]

In the meantime a serious problem arose concerning the employment prospects of the graduates from the modern military schools. There were more graduates than could be provided for in the commissioned ranks of the Chinese army, and herein lay a serious source of danger to the government. To dispense with the foreign instructors would help to ease the problem. Furthermore, the foreigners were in any case more expensive to hire, and Chinese officers were jealous of them. Shortage of funds furnished another good reason for employing Chinese graduates who were anxious to secure their billets. Finally, some concern was expressed in Peking that the use of foreigners might cause security leaks.[96]

However, the Chinese government did not pursue its policy doggedly, for it realised that in some important areas the service of foreign experts was still necessary. This was evidenced by the employment in July 1911 of three German officers on the educational staff of the Peking Officers' School, which was expected to open in a few months. They were Major von Dinkelmann (infantry), who had just given up the command of the German legation guard in Peking; Captain Bleyhoffer (artillery) who had previously been employed in one of the military schools; and a captain of pioneers to be selected in Germany. Their contracts were all for two years. They were not to teach the cadets directly but to serve as advisers and supervisors and be responsible for the instruction of the Chinese teachers. The Peking government had originally intended to have only Chinese instructors in the Officers' School as in other schools, but it later appreciated that for this highest military cadet school, the knowledge and experience of Chinese instructors was insufficient.[97]

On the eve of the revolution, *The Times* reported that there were only seven Japanese instructors in China: one in Canton, one in Wuchang, and five in Baoding. Two of them subsequently returned to Japan before the end of 1911. There were three or four German instructors, but no British or American. Nearly all the teaching in the army and in the military schools was the responsibility of Chinese graduates who had been trained in Japan.[98]

To conclude, a new military educational system had been established and was producing its results before the end of the dynasty. The schools operating in the provinces were very popular, and there was a great deal of competition for admission. By 1911 there was an adequate supply of military graduates who were 'better turned out and more military in bearing and show[ed] more confidence in themselves'.[99] Owing to their inexperience and shorter training, they were no doubt far behind their European and American counterparts in knowledge and efficiency. But they represented a new political force in China and quickly assumed an importance out of all proportion to their numbers.

The growth of nationalism in some sections of the New Army was significant. It was the result of a response to the foreign threat and of modern military training. It was fostered by the government, even though there was no program for ideological indoctrination like that in the Guomindang's National Revolutionary Army or that in the Chinese Red Army. Foreigners in China who criticised the bearing of the young officers and the Peking government's policy of dispensing with foreign instructors missed the point that the Chinese felt a sense of urgency to put their military house in order, for China would have no hope of being truly independent until she had a Chinese-controlled army, well officered, self-sufficient and strong enough to defend her national sovereignty.

FOUR

Social attitudes

THE MILITARY reforms described in the previous chapters had a profound impact on Chinese society, contributing to a new social attitude
towards the soldier and his profession. That military status was being
considerably raised was testified by every well-informed foreigner in
China. Referring to the 3rd Division, Lieutenant-Colonel Pereira
remarked in 1908: 'The men are well treated, and paid regularly,
and there is no doubt that the army, here as elsewhere, is becoming
more popular.'[1] The New Army was no longer a place for a sluggard.
A good class of soldiers, healthy, young and interested in their work,
was emerging. 'The gradual rise in the status, officially and socially,
of the officer and soldier', asserted Captain Reeves, 'may tend to
make the army popular and cause a good class of men to seek service
therein.'[2] Lieutenant-Commander Mulock, who was always critical
of the bearing of the new troops, also conceded that 'the new army
is no longer a despised profession . . . great progress has been made
in instilling a military spirit and that the power accruing to a nation
proficient in military knowledge is fully appreciated'.[3]

In early 1910 George E. Morrison of *The Times* reported from
Peking:

> Probably the greatest change observable in modern China is the
> honour shown now to the formerly despised military profession . . .
> Military rank may come to supersede civil rank in the aspirations
> of the ambitious. Soldiers now are proud of their uniforms, they
> keep their rifles clean, they are smart and respectful — always, of
> course, comparing them with the Chinese soldiers we knew a few
> years ago. Soldiers now demand that they be treated with con-
> sideration by their own authorities. Officers travel on the train first-
> class; the rank and file will not suffer themselves to be herded as
> before like cattle in open trucks; they now require covered carriages
> in which they can sit with comfort. It is a noticeable change.[1]

It was an exaggeration to say, as Morrison did, perhaps intention-
ally, on another occasion, that the 'relative ranks of civil and military

have been reversed. The military now takes precedence over the civil'.[5] But there was no doubt that the introduction in November 1909 of a table of precedence for civil and military officials, whereby the latter were accorded surprisingly high comparative rank (see Table 4), had resulted in appreciably enhancing the standing of the military profession. It put an end, at least officially, to the civil mandarins' traditional contempt for military officials and placed the latter in an equally privileged position.

Table 4. The new relative ranks proclaimed in November 1909

Military ranks	Relative civil ranks
Field Marshal *(da jiangjun)*	Grand Secretary
General Commanding an Army Corps *(zheng dutong)*	Viceroy, also holding appointment of Censor
Lieutenant-General *(fu dutong)*	Viceroy or Governor holding brevet appointment of Vice President of War
Brigadier-General *(xie dutong)*	Governor or Provincial Treasurer
Colonel *(zheng canling)*	Provincial Judge
Lieutenant-Colonel *(fu canling)*	Salt Controller
Major *(xie canling)*	Intendant of Circuit
Captain *(zheng junxiao)*	Prefect
Lieutenant *(fu junxiao)*	Subprefect
2nd Lieutenant *(xie junxiao)*	Assistant Subprefect
Sergeant *(zhengmu)*	Secretary to the Subprefect
Corporal *(fumu)*	Police Inspector

Source: *Qingshilu* (Xuantong), 22, pp. 20b-24b; Brissaud-Desmaillet, p. 1183; FO 371/845, encl. in Jordan to Grey, No. 463, 13 December 1909; Brunnert and Hagelstrom, pp. 290-2.

For any Chinese officials who still had doubts about the imperial government's commitment to military reform, the following edict of 3 April 1911, served as a reminder:

We are of the opinion that militarism is the first essential thing for the building and preservation of a nation and national harmony to the prevention of disorder . . . For our first Emperor Taizu there was not a single army, but the Dragon made its appearance in the Liao River, and the capital was founded at Shenyang. Our Taizong, being the successor, solemnly followed the programme of aggrandisement, and extended his influence throughout the country. These imperial meritorious deeds were attained by our imperial ancestors through their fighting in arms and travelling in the field. Soon after the mandate of heaven was won over to our Shizu, the founder of the present dynasty, our Shengzu, ascended to the Throne at a young age . . . His fame was so great that all nations paid him respect. This is an instance of the military spirit of our ancestors and people. From that time on, able rulers succeeded one after another . . . Military spirit was at its height until the reigns of Qianlong and Jiaqing when internal troubles repeatedly arose . . . It must be said that the ancestors of our soldiers who had followed the various expeditions heart and soul had played a great role in the building up of this glorious Empire . . . At present foreign aggression is found in all directions. *A nation cannot go without militarism. Our soldiers . . should know this well and need no reminder.* As we dare not be idle and ignore the will of our ancestors and ancient soldiers, our present soldiers should follow their example. Let us mutually strive for the safety of our Empire so as to make China into a military power and her constitutional government a great success. Then every citizen, high and low, will enjoy peace and prosperity to the wishes of our ancestors and ancient soldiers . . . [Emphasis added].[6]

How did the public respond to the government's military policy? How was the idea of militarism received by the modern-educated scholars? Was the gentry class well disposed towards the New Army? What were the attitudes of the civil population? What kind of support did the different social strata give the reforms, and how did they gain or lose from them? These are interesting questions which this chapter attempts to answer in order to show the relationship between the New Army and the social order, and thereby to promote a better understanding of the social implications of the military reforms in a wider context.

Modern Chinese views of militarism

Chinese disdain for the soldier in traditional times stemmed from two sources: the pacifist attitude of the imperial Chinese civilisation and the recruitment of soldiers from among landless labourers and other drifting elements who were too poor and too uneducated to fit into any one of the recognised social classes. The first point is of particular interest to the discussion in this section. Military rule and territorial expansion by military means has not been an important feature of Chinese history. The Confucian ideology had a strong pacifist effect on the values and psychology of the Chinese people generally. The stress on righteousness, benevolence, social harmony, moral values and the Golden Mean could hardly fail to produce a general aversion to war. Conflicts between states, and between people, were often resolved through negotiations and compromises; war was merely the last resort. In the event of war, pacification was preferable to total destruction of the enemy. A general who captured a city without sacking it was more respectable than someone who engaged in a bloodbath. The ultimate aim of war was to force the enemy to submit to the imperial authority. Once that had been achieved, the enemy would be allowed to escape total defeat by negotiating a sort of 'conditional surrender'. This concept of 'limited war' as opposed to 'total war' was an important feature of Chinese military thinking.[7]

The pacifist theory should not, however, suggest that the rising military status in the late Qing period was incompatible with the Confucian ideology and the traditional order. There is ample evidence that military virtues were sometimes highly appreciated and encouraged by the emperor. In the long history of imperial China, there had been many periods of political fragmentation when large parts of the Empire were dominated by military commanders. There had also been times when the founding emperor of a new dynasty enhanced the prestige of his regime by military conquests. The military exploits of Emperor Tang Taizong are a classic example. The early Qing emperors, as the edict described in the foregoing pages shows, also had achieved 'meritorious deeds' through fighting on the battlefield. The available histories of China are not without the details of wars, battles and military intrigues.

There are Chinese proverbs which stress that military qualities are as important as civil virtues. One of these says: 'Literary and military qualities combine to make complete talents' *(wenwu quancai)*. Another speaks of 'the literary longitude and military latitude' *(wenjing wuwei)*, which unites civil and military talents to make the perfect man. A third, with the words 'civil administration and military services' *(wenzhi wugong)*, attaches equal importance to government and military armament. Other proverbs exalt military prestige; for example 'a general leads a hundred thousand mounted troops' *(jiangshi wanqi)*; 'a great general has an awe-inspiring reputation' *(dajiang shengwei)*. The continuity of military tradition within a family line is reflected in the saying, 'from a general's family come more generals' *(jiangmen youjiang)*.

Chinese literature is not without its stirring war songs which portray the suffering of those at home and the sacrificing patriotism of the soldiers. The following is a poem from the *Book of Odes:*

> I climbed the barren mountain,
>   And my gaze swept far and wide;
> For the red-lit eaves of my father's home,
>   And I fancied that he sighed.

I climbed the grass-clad mountain,
  And my gaze swept far and wide;
For the rosy light of a little room,
  Where I thought my mother sighed.

I climbed the topmost summit,
  And my gaze swept far and wide;
For the garden roof where my brother stood,
  And I fancied that he sighed.

My brother serves as a soldier,
  With his comrades night and day;
But my brother is filial and may return,
  Though the dead lie far away.[8]

Another old poem describes a battle between the ancient Chinese tribe of Wei and the Northern Mongols:

Many men with but one heart;
Many lives to sell as one.

Foes and Nature interlock;
Sands arise; hills join the shock.

Rivers, death fills like a flood;
Red, Wei's Great Wall too with blood.

Slaves ye shall be if ye yield;
Dead men if ye fight the field!

Fled no warrior; name on name,
Ghosts approach me, starred with fame.[9]

Portrayals of military situations and characters can be found in such popular novels as *The Water Margin (Shuihuzhuan)* and *The Romance of the Three Kingdoms (Sanguo)*. Mention must also be made of *The Art of War (Sunzi bingfa)*, the oldest military treatise in the world.

Chinese tradition includes both pacifist and warlike elements, although the former were often more dominant. In eighteenth- and nineteenth-century China, the pacifist was obviously dominant, and it was a tremendous handicap. But it was not impossible to change this. The modern scholars of the early twentieth century who urged rapid development of Chinese military power tended to ignore, deliberately perhaps, the military aspects of Chinese history and culture. Rather, they emphasised, even exaggerated, its pacifist features to show how they had prevented China from becoming a strong nation. They found it necessary not only to update the defence system but also to reorientate the psychology of the Chinese people towards military values.

Before the New Army was well under way, modern scholars had already urged the Chinese government to build up its national defence and the Chinese people to contribute to it. Their writings on this subject were serious, reflecting their concern about the relationships between army, state and society. Those discussed below were mainly students studying in Japan in the period 1903-5, and some later served in the Chinese army. Liang Qichao, though not a young student like the others, had also written on the military in China, and therefore references to his work will also be made.

Most of these scholars appear to have been influenced by the idea of social Darwinism which was being popularised in Japan by Katō Hiroyuki. Katō had translated some important Darwinist works into Japanese, with his own interpretations. He gave much attention to the laws of 'the struggle for existence' and 'natural selection', which were applicable to the human society in an era of imperialism. Much emphasis was put on the idea of *kyōken (qiangquan* in Chinese, literally, rights of the strong) which replaced the doctrine of *tenpu jinken (tianfu renquan* in Chinese, literally, natural rights) in the world of the jungle. Assessing Japan's position in the new world order, Katō found in social Darwinism a justification for Japan's development as a new imperialist power.[10] Such rationalisation had a strong appeal to the Chinese scholars who felt that the same could be used to justify the creation of a new militant China. As well as attributing China's plight to the onslaught of foreign imperialism, they displayed a distinct introspective attitude which sought to explain China's problems in terms of her own inherent weaknesses.[11]

One major weakness was that the Chinese had traditionally shown little social appreciation of the role of the military. It was a common view among the scholars that unless the soldier's role was well defined and appreciated, the Chinese army could not be truly improved. In an article entitled 'The meaning of the military', Lan Tianwei, a Hubei military cadet who was later to become commander of the 2nd Mixed Brigade in Manchuria, defined the soldier as the most righteous and civilised, yet at the same time the most savage and uncivilised, man on earth. The soldier was savage and uncivilised because he was ruthless in dealing with enemies; he seized foreign lands, and sought to dominate, even enslave, other peoples. He belonged to an unjust world in which problems of war and peace were resolved by brute force. Yet he was the most righteous and civilised because he defended his country, protected its people, and promoted the national interest.[12]

Lan saw the world in terms of comparative military power. For him, military power was 'the wall and fortress which surround the state, the air which inflates the nation, and the mother who gives birth to and nurtures civilisations'. The degree of civilisation achieved by a country was in direct proportion to its military prowess. The European powers had reached a higher level of civilisation than China precisely because of their military strength which had enabled them to expand overseas, spread their religions, conduct international diplomacy, and establish colonial empires.

The barbaric-civilised rationalisation offered a new perspective on the soldier's role and behaviour. The traditional moral values which had influenced Chinese military actions were simply inadequate as pacifism no longer served China's interests. The new soldier should have a civilised mind and a savage body; barbarous actions towards foreign enemies, and righteous behaviour towards fellow countrymen.

There was a consensus of opinion that the soldier's external functions should take precedence over internal ones. Armies were maintained not only to defend a regime from domestic challenge but more importantly to defend it and the people against foreign invasion. Traditional armies, wrote a Zhejiang student, were either private armies or armies of the ruling class, their functions being those of a constabulary force. What China needed was a national army committed to the maintenance of her national sovereignty and territorial integrity. It was to be distinguished from the police force. The soldier was to love his country, defend it and make sacrifices for it. He was to be militant, enterprising, and to regard the nation as the only focus of loyalty, to which his private interests were to be subordinated.[13]

The commitment of a militant army to national defence and the advancement of the national interest could easily lead China to war. But war was not to be feared, said Lan Tianwei. On the contrary, it should be regarded as a means of nation-building.

> Countries that are militant are sure to enjoy the fortune of war. Countries that fear war will inevitably fall victims to it. Those who delight in killing glorify their countries. Those who abstain from killing will find their countries plundered. The object of a militant citizenry is to forge a national character bent on killing, for the sake of defending the country and thereby to maintain peace. Countries that despise the soldier but exalt letters cannot inspire awe and respect. Nor can they be entrusted with the duty of protecting the people.[14]

Lan believed that war was inevitable in an age of imperialism. It would be necessary for the Chinese people to be prepared for it both militarily and psychologically. In a Bismarckian frame of mind, he argued:

> What one can rely on in the world is iron and blood. All the mono-

polies and privileges of the state are increased and sustained by application of its armed forces.[15]

Lan was not alone in lauding war. Another scholar, writing anonymously, considered it to be a universal truth that 'there is war in the world before there is happiness'. He quoted Katō Hiroyuki as saying that 'war is the vanguard of civilisation . . . Civilisation is something everyone wants. But one has to pay a price for it. The price is war'.[16] The price was worth paying, for without war world civilisation would not have advanced to its present stage.

According to Lan, the relationship between the military and the state was twofold. First, it was 'naturalistic', manifesting itself in the form of a national sentiment and martial spirit; it engendered the concept of racial nationalism and the hero cult. The Germans and the Japanese were patriotic because they were proud of their own races. The Chinese, by contrast, did not believe in racial nationalism, but allowed themselves to be ruled and killed by alien races and even fought among themselves. Unlike the Americans who lauded George Washington, and unlike the Russians who adored Peter the Great, the Chinese had no hero cult. There was no lack of eminent figures in Chinese history who had fought valiantly in defence of the Chinese race. Some of them, Lan urged, should be honoured as national heroes, to set an example for the Chinese soldier.[17]

Second, the soldier's relationship with the state was 'positional'. This meant that he had a right to participate in all spheres of the national life, which not only brought him closer to the people but also enabled him to advance the national interest in all fields of activities. In the United States, Lan believed, universal conscription was in force and military drill taught at school. In Germany every man was a soldier, the country was virtually a military school on a grand, national scale, and society was the macrocosm of a military educational organisation. Lan was convinced that this 'positional relationship' was instrumental in national expansion and empire building. It enhanced national prestige, thus increasing the pride of the people.

Lan pointed out that the state, the military, and the people were mutually dependent. The survival of the state, he maintained, depended entirely on its armed forces, and the duty of organising the armed forces rested with the people. The desire of the state to extend its influence, therefore, depended not so much on the government as on the people who alone could transform their country into a military power. Going to war involved the mobilisation of the whole population who provided the manpower, funds, and whatever constituted war efforts. The people were protected by the state. The state, on the other hand, owed its survival to the people who formed the soldiery. The idea of a private army fighting a dynastic war had no place in the modern world.[18]

Lan's stress on the inevitability of war and the need for military expansion reflected his anxiety to meet the challenge of foreign encroachment on the sovereignty and territorial integrity of China and a desire to imitate the imperialists and to deal with them on equal terms. The best defensive strategy was to be ready to take the offensive. China was to be adequately equipped and prepared to go to war, for only then could foreign imperialism be held in check and the role of the soldier be truly appreciated.

Other scholars attributed China's military weakness to the pacifist tradition. Liang Qichao lamented the fact that whereas Japanese poets spoke of war's joys, Chinese poets spoke of its bitterness. In his opinion, the Chinese were cowards who prized no military virtues.[19] In the same vein, Cai E, a Hunanese military cadet, noted that Chinese war literature was given to the sufferings of armies and the sorrows of war, and that there was hardly any piece of work that extolled the satisfaction of war and military life. Cai also condemned the traditional education system for its lack of a nationalistic content. Traditional scholars were wanting in youthfulness. Even when they were young, they appeared like an eighty-year-old 'with the body of a dried stick and the heart of cold ashes'. There was no Chinese religion which inspired activism and aggressiveness. Confucianism was originally a progressive philosophy encouraging activism, advancement, endurance, duty, and struggle, but true Confucianism, Cai asserted, had long been perverted and become a conservative orthodoxy.[20]

Both Liang and Cai deplored the fact that Chinese people gave little attention to physical exercise. In spite of a population of four hundred million, healthy and strong people were few. The scholar class despised physical prowess. There were many opium smokers, handicapped and invalid people. Only one-tenth of the population had no physical disabilities, and among them few had the appearance and strength of a foreign warrior.[21]

There was a general feeling that if there was one thing China needed badly, it was a national spirit. For China to survive, it was not enough simply to drill the troops, to equip them with modern weapons, and to educate them in modern military science. It was recognised that every military power had a national spirit. In Japan it was the *Yamato-damashii*; in Germany it was 'iron and blood'; in the United States the spirit of the Monroe Doctrine; in Russia Pan-Slavism. In China there was none. The rise and fall of Chinese dynasties was often the result of a power struggle between one ruling clique and another. The Chinese could neither boast of a revolutionary spirit nor claim to be united in fighting foreign invasion. Rather they had been submissive to alien rule for most of the last thousand years.[22]

The national spirit that China needed was to have a strong military orientation which constituted what the modern scholars called the *shangwu zhuyi* (the military cult). In an eassay on *shangwu*, Liang Qichao defined it as 'the national ethos of the citizen with which the state is formed and by which civilisation is sustained.' He quoted Bismarck as saying that a country depended for its survival not on international law but on iron and blood. A nation without a *shangwu* citizenry and an iron-and-blood ideology could not stand on its own. The classic example of a *shangwu* state was Sparta, the ancient Greek city-state. A more recent one was Bismarck's Germany, which had emerged as a strong military power in the space of but a few decades. Japan, with its warrior tradition *(bushidō)* was another. To promote a military cult in China, the Chinese people needed to strengthen their will-power, their courage, and their body. Only then could they overcome their cowardice. Liang criticised that although China had been reforming her military system for a few decades since the mid-nineteenth century much attention had been given to the form of change and little to the spirit of it.[23]

Another scholar expressed the view that *shangwu* was manifested in two ways. First, it was materialistic, represented by the technological change in the army. Second, it was spiritual, consisting in such attributes as fearlessness, adventurism, independence, calmness, endurance and the like which asserted themselves most clearly in adversity. Both types were important, one complementing the other. The *shangwu* spirit could be nurtured by raising the status of the soldier, introducing military national education *(junguomin jiaoyu)*, and fostering a kind of Chinese *bushidō*. The Chinese people would then feel an obligation to the state and regard it as their 'heavenly duty' to serve it. This spirit, once it had become part of Chinese life, would be an important force in the preservation of the Chinese people and state.[24]

Military national education was meant for the entire population and aimed at training a new militant citizenry *(junguomin)*. Such military virtues as patriotism, independence, hard work, and discipline, were useful to the civil population, and should be taught at school, in the family, and in society. Jiang Fangzhen, a military cadet from Zhejiang, recommended that school curricula should include physical exercises, military drill and general military studies. He viewed the school as a microcosm and the state a macrocosm of the army. All schools were to maintain close connections with the military organisation. Some of the teaching staff were to be drawn from active army officers, or competent retired officers, for varying periods of time. In this way the school would become a training ground for citizenship, preparing students for national service. Such education, Jiang urged, should begin at home, and parents should co-operate with the school in the education of their children. Outside the school and the family, military national education was to be achieved through a reorganisation of society. Like Liang Qichao, Jiang was interested in a Spartan-type society, and anticipated the birth of a new people, when all the government departments, executive, legislative and judiciary alike, had been reorganised in a military spirit.[25]

The creation of a new type of soldier was the ultimate goal of military education. In a way similar to Liang Qichao's call for a new citizenry *(xinmin)*, one military cadet strongly advocated a true soldiery *(zhenjunren)* which was to be patriotic, devoted, and possessed of all the good qualities of a Western soldier. Universal conscription was to be in force in order that every citizen honoured his obligation to the state. When a true soldiery was created, the Chinese army could be truly revitalised.[26]

Not only was a revitalised army to be an instrument of national defence, but it was to have a significant social role as a moral symbol and public morale booster. China had become so decrepit, corrupt and demoralised that it was necessary to use the army to restore the people's confidence in their ability to save themselves and their country. Indeed, many scholars wanted the army to be a model for emulation by the people, in order to cleanse society by showing the ways in which they could work diligently and aggressively with a goal in life and in the public interest. One scholar pointed out that the Chinese had long lost their moralistic concern for the public good *(gongde)*. 'The army', he asserted, 'is the fountain of public virtues and the embodiment of the community spirit.'[27] It engendered a sense of community, serving as a nexus between the individual and society. When it collapsed, both individual and society would go down with it.

Obviously some modern scholars desired to use the army as a device for developing a sense of national identity and a social psychological element of national unity and public purpose. This meant making the army into an agent of social change. In the end what they wanted to see to develop in China was militarism. But what did they mean by militarism? To answer this question, let us digress for a moment to see how the term is defined in modern Western scholarship.

According to Laurence I. Radway,

Militarism is a doctrine or system that values war and accords primacy in state and society to the armed forces. It exalts a function — application of violence — and an institutional structure — the military establishment. It implies both a policy orientation and a power relationship . . . A fully militarized society also confers a privileged position on warriors. In the extreme case, the armed forces unilaterally determine the nature of basic institutions, the choice of regimes, the rights and duties of citizens, and the share of national resources allocated to military functions.[28]

For Stanislav Andreski, militarism is the compound of militancy ('aggressive foreign policy involving the readiness to resort to war'), militarisation ('the extensive control by the military over social life, coupled with the subservience of the whole society to the needs of the army'), militocracy ('the phenomenon of preponderance of the military over the civil personnel'), and militolatory ('an ideology propagating military ideals'). 'Where all four components are present to a high degree (e.g. Japan under Tojo), we have a clear case of militarism'.[29]

Andreski's definition of militarism is useful to our understanding of Chinese militarism. The Chinese scholars favoured militancy in dealing with the imperialist powers. They desired militarisation, not in Andreski's sense, but in the sense of modernising and building up the army and organising society in a military spirit. They showed a preference for militolatory in the sense of exalting military ideals which had good civil values. But they wanted no militocracy. There was no desire for military rule or military ascendancy over the civil establishment. Their demand was for a civil-military polity in which the military received social appreciation and played a specific role in national defence, in militarising the people and a moralistic role in cleansing society. Militarisation could occur without militocracy. Chinese militarism was a means to an end, not an end in itself.

The concept of nation-in-arms, which is often associated with the city-states of Sparta and Athens, is also relevant here. The Chinese scholars made frequent references to Sparta,[30] whose strength and stability had been based on a citizenry of warriors. Every act of the Spartan was weighed with reference to its probable effect upon the state; the entire educational system was but a formal training for effective leadership. Spartan children from the age of seven to eighteen resided at public barracks, where they learned to read and write and received military drill. At eighteen a boy became a 'cadet' for two years, after which he spent his next ten years on active service to qualify for citizenship. The Chinese scholars believed that they could learn from these ancient Greeks. The Prussians had done so, and were in turn copied by the Japanese. Germany and Japan thus provided a model for Chinese military development.

The form of militarism which these scholars advocated was a new phenomenon in China. It was neither the 'centralised militarism of dynastic founders' nor the 'regional militarism of the periods such as the early Republic', about which Diana Lary writes.[31] It was a form of positive, national militarism, where the dominant desire was to strengthen the national polity through a military and psychological reorientation of the entire population as well as through an updating of the defence system. To be militaristic was to be modern. It would involve an ideological movement to change the pacifist tradition of the Chinese people so that they would become more militant and aggressive towards their enemies, both real and potential.[32]

The call for military national education
Military national education was an important feature of this form of militarism in the late Qing period; the call for its introduction struck a responsive chord in government circles. It was, in fact, Peking's policy to connect the New Army scheme with the new civil school system, which stipulated in 1903 that students should wear uniforms and that military drill should be taught in all schools, including mission schools. It was also decreed that in schools of higher levels military organisation, history of war and military art should be taught, while foreign military and naval sciences should be added to the curricula of political science departments in the universities.[33] The school textbooks published between 1903 and 1906 emphasised patriotism, the importance of military valour, China's defeats and humiliations and territorial losses, the unequal treaties, the presence of foreign missionaries in the interior, and the importance of racial conflict and national struggle. A lesson in the *New National Reader* stated: 'soldiers are the foundation of a strong country'. It taught the students that bows and arrows were no longer in use, but guns and cannons. There were also lessons on national geography, on the defence of a city, on the Boxer catastrophe and on the nationalists' reactions to the foreign attempts to build railroads and operate mines in China.[34]

In 1906 an imperial decree stated the aims of education as follows: 'To inculcate loyalty to the Emperor, reverence for Confucius and to promote the public spirit, *the military spirit*, and the realistic spirit'.[35] The cultivation of the military spirit was obviously a nationalistic aim which marked the beginning of education for a new militant citizenry in China.

Significantly, the civil schools had taken on the military air. Henry B. Graybill, acting president of the Canton College in 1911, wrote:

There are organisations and drill, marching through the streets with fife and drum, uniforms, guns, swords and flags; military drill and gymnastics are given even in the elementary schools. Physical education has suddenly become very popular. At Cheefoo an athletic meet and drill and contest was held together last year [1910] . . . Patriotic songs in chorus are frequently heard.[36]

The most popular song in Canton schools ran like this:

The yellow dragon signals flying, China's banner gay;
Ten myriad swords flash light athwart the breasts that burn to slay;
New songs of war accompany our army marching forth;
Behold amid the war clouds their terrible array!
Our ninefold land is filled with fumes of foreign war and woe,
Our people chant their battle-songs today against the foe.

The soldier's blood of sacrifice is daily flowing free;
Forsake not now the liberty beloved from of yore!
With guns upon right shoulder, and with belted knife at side,
We desert the royal audience, the decree goes far and wide;
Father, mother, wife and children march beside to bid farewell,
Encouraging their solders with jests on as they ride![37]

When Yinchang became Minister of War, he was most interested in educating the whole population on the question of general militarism throughout the country. In March 1911 he proposed that primary military instruction should be given in all middle schools. This was approved by the Throne, and accordingly plans were made to open more military primary schools and to teach military science in the civil schools. The Chancellor of the Imperial University was ordered to add a military course to the curriculum. Meanwhile, the government had also given sanction to the joint recommendation of the Ministry of Education, General Staff, and the Ministry of War in favour of a memorial of Xiliang, Viceroy of Manchuria, proposing that military instruction, tactics, drill and musketry practice should be included in the curricula of the civil middle schools in Manchuria. The object of this, Xiliang emphasised, was to promote the *shangwu* spirit.[38]

This set the stage for more military subjects to be taught in the civil schools. On 28 April 1911 the All-China Education Association held an inaugural meeting in Shanghai, with representatives from twelve provinces. Five resolutions were made, one of which was that the Ministry of Education should be asked to formulate a policy on military national education. Each province, in the meantime, was to study its feasibility and implementation. Subsequently, a Central Education Conference was held in Peking from 15 July to 11 August, with an attendance of 138 representatives from various parts of China.

It resolved, among other things, that the Minister of Education should be urged to introduce a bill on military national education in the Naitonal Assembly.[39] Meanwhile, the provincial education authorities had jointly drawn up a proposal which embodied the following points. First, an imperial edict should be proclaimed to announce the principle of military national education. Second, emphasis should be placed on military drill in all senior primary schools and above. Third, musketry practice and general military studies should be introduced in all senior primary schools and above. Fourth, these new changes should apply to all registered private schools. Finally, physical exercises should be a major subject in all schools.[40]

It is not clear how the government reacted to this joint proposal, but presumably the official response was not bad. In any event the dynasty came to an end before substantial progress in military national education had been made. But the trend towards militarism had been set, and it continued into the post-1911 era. Unfortunately, what was intended to be a positive, national militarism soon degenerated into the divisive, regional militarism of the later decades.

Gentry and merchant relationships with the New Army
In studying gentry attitudes towards the New Army, it is necessary to discuss the metamorphosis of this class after the turn of the century. The gentry had traditionally been the social elite from which the bureaucracy drew its administrators. According to Chang Chung-li, it was composed of all degree holders, hence the upper gentry (those with *jinshi, juren* and *gongsheng* degrees) and the lower gentry (those with *shengyuan*, and purchased titles). The higher degree holders were appointed to official positions in the capital or in the provincial administrations, whereas the lower gentry held no official posts, and lived in their home communities, dominating local affairs by virtue of their academic standing, status and connections.[41] The *shengyuan* did not enjoy as much influence, power, and status as the *juren* and *jinshi*, and on this ground Ho Ping-ti has suggested excluding the former from the gentry class.[42] Philip Kuhn, defining the Chinese elite in terms of power and prestige on various scales of organisation, has divided the gentry into three groups. The first group was the 'national elite' which 'had influence that transcended its regional origins, and connections that reached to the apex of national political life'. A second group comprised the 'provincial elite' which 'had close links to the former group, but its interests and influence were more narrowly defined'. A third group was the 'local elite' which 'lacked the social prestige and powerful connections of the former two groups but might still wield considerable power in the society of village and

market town'. The lower degree holders belonged to this last group.[43]

The traditional gentry enjoyed a wide range of privileges and certain legal immunities by virtue of their academic standing. On the other hand they shared with officials the responsibility for local government, performing under official supervision many important functions such as welfare activities, publishing books, school and temple maintenance, Confucian worship, arbitration and public works. At times they also organised local militia and helped collect taxes. They acted as an intermediary and mediator between populace and officialdom, assisting local officials in carrying out government policies and maintaining law and order on the one hand, and protecting local interests against the impingement of corrupt officials on the other. Gentry leaders were sometimes seen inciting riots against specific officials who attempted to encroach upon gentry privileges.[44] But, as a privileged class established by the state, the gentry had traditionally been part of the ruling class, generally sharing the desire of the established authority to maintain the existing social order.

Gentry participation in local affairs was by invitation, and not through formal institutions or regular political mechanisms in their local communities.[45] It was essentially one of active involvement without political initiative and formal political power. The gentry formed no political organisations and did not function as a distinct political group. Its activities were sanctioned by custom and recognised by the central government within the framework of a decentralised administration. Its members were neither government functionaries nor members of any local representative institutions which did not exist in traditional China. It was this lack of formal political power that prevented them from initiating political actions whether or not such actions might conflict with government interests. While they exercised their influence in the local communities, they had no legal right of participation in the process of policy making, even in matters which directly affected their interests or those of their localities. Gentry relationships with local officials had traditionally been based on co-operation and mutual non-aggression. Any attempt made by one side to encroach upon the province of the other would upset the scheme of things in rural China, where everyone's role and position were defined.

To the extent that it tended to resist any social change which threatened to jeopardise its privileged position, the traditional gentry was a conservative class. It was also a stabilising social force, in that its commitment to Confucianism and the imperial system precluded the possibility of the sort of radical change which European elites in the eighteenth and nineteenth centuries had demanded. Its conservatism was deep-rooted in tradition, and could not be significantly changed without some new forces at work. Such new forces were generated by the advent of modernity represented by the Western powers and Japan in the nineteenth century. Foreign impingement on China created an array of new problems which were compounded by the internal challenge typical of a declining dynasty. China's response to the foreign challenge called for a reappraisal of her traditional values. The reform movement in the latter half of the nineteenth century represented the first phase of China's encounter with modernity, which prepared the ground for changes in the traditional role of the gentry.

Long before the close of the nineteenth century there had already been a gradual shift in the focus of gentry activities from the rural areas to the market towns and capital cities.[46] This was not a new process: the gentry had always been drawn to the city because that was where the officials, whom they were privileged to advise, worked and lived.[47] What was new was that the capital cities were becoming more and more commercialised and urbanised as a result of the opening of the treaty ports and the expansion of foreign trade. The new urban life had much attraction for the gentry who had the capital to invest in new lines of commerce and industry. Many gentry families thus migrated to the city, where modern enterprises provided new sources of income, leaving their land to the care of agents, whose sole duty was to collect rents from the peasants.

After 1900 the process of gentry migration and urbanisation had been accelerated by the formation of chambers of commerce *(shanghui)*, agricultural associations *(nonghui)*, school boards and various kinds of semi-official bodies designed to promote commerce and industry. As one would expect the gentry dominated these organisations, especially the chambers of commerce. For example, the Canton Chamber of Commerce was 'evidently a creature of the wealthy gentry-merchants', who were 'all closely identified with the world of the gentry officials'.[48]

Another factor which undermined the foundations of the traditional system was the evolution of democratic political institutions which provided new opportunities for the gentry to exercise their power and influence in a more formal political manner. One such example was the Shanghai City Council formed in 1905, which was a fusion of various bodies of merchants and mandarins. The council's leaders were predominantly of gentry origins; they were well acquainted with foreign ideas and customs and were at home in commerce. All the members seemed to hold official rank, acquired largely by purchase.[49] The lines between the newly migrated gentry and the urban-centred merchants were becoming blurred. Indeed, the newly emerging bourgeoisie was a gentry-merchant combination, even though the gentry and merchants as separate classes 'remained self-consciously distinct' as in the case of Canton.[50] With the increase of fluidity in social status and overlap of roles, the term *shenshang* (gentry-merchant) came into general use.[51]

The abolition of the examination system in 1905 added considerably to this process of change. It altered the basic source of gentry status and power, and destroyed one of traditional China's most cohesive stabilising forces. Dealing a hard blow to Confucianism, it removed much of the premium on classical studies, thereby changing the fundamental system of values. The gentry class was now undergoing a more profound change than ever before. Before 1905 it had already broken up into what Arthur Rosenbaum has described as the conservatives, the moderates and the progressives, in terms of their socio-political attitudes. After 1905 this division was sharpened. The progressives, as in the case of Hunan, consisted of constitutional reformers who desired to dominate the democratic institutions which were being formed in the province. The conservatives opposed the administrative and constitutional reforms introduced by the government, and were interested in maintaining the status quo. The moderates supported some of these reforms but refrained from either serving in the new institutions or participating in the constitutional movement.[52] To these may be added a fourth category, namely the recluses, who could not accept innovations and therefore withdrew from active roles in either provincial or local life, and retreated into nostalgia or bitter regret, spending their time on traditional scholarship.[53]

It was the progressive group which concerned itself with the great national issues of the day, and shared the outlook of another type of new elite, the modern-educated scholars who had no traditional degrees. The abolition of the examination system immediately laid before the progressive gentry the question of how to secure the influence and power which they had acquired previously. It was possible for them to enter into new careers, like commerce and industry. But what concerned them most was the expansion of political participation and a more positive political voice in the management of provincial and national affairs. They were anxious to establish local self-government bodies and provincial assemblies in which to formalise and expand their political power. The opportunity presented itself in 1909 when these institutions were established. From the election results of five provinces on which materials are available, Chang P'eng-yüan has shown that a large proportion of the members of the provincial assemblies were of gentry origins — 50.5 per cent held *jinshi, juren,* and *gongsheng* degrees, 39.5 per cent held *shengyuan* degrees.[54] In the meantime, other *shengyuan* degree holders ran for local elections and many succeeded in occupying the important posts in the self-government bodies at the sub-county level — in cities, towns, and rural areas.[55] Thus the gentry had not only regained their status and influence, but also increased it through the formalisation of their political power.

It must be pointed out, however, that the majority of the lower gentry members did not hold any posts in the local self-government bodies or in the provincial assemblies, and had to seek new avenues of advancement. Some were quick to see the reality of the situation and adjusted to it by preparing themselves for new careers in business and other professions. Others enrolled in the newly founded modern schools. However, these schools were far more expensive than the traditional colleges, and not very many families could afford to send their children through them. Consequently, large numbers of young men were attracted to a military career which promised a new ladder to success. This appeared to be a general phenomenon in the country, particularly in Hubei. In late 1905, for example of ninety-six new recruits from Huangpi prefecture, north of Wuchang, twelve were *lingsheng* and twenty-four were *shengyuan.*[56]

For those lower gentry members who failed to obtain a place in the new schools, the army and the military schools were an alternative route to social mobility. Once they had joined the ranks, they were likely to be quickly promoted to corporals or sergeants. One ex-soldier knew of at least forty *shengyuan* and four others with equivalent qualifications in the 29th, 30th, 31st and 41st regiments of the Hubei army.[57] Lower gentry members enlisted in growing numbers towards the end of the the decade, and it was not uncommon for the men of letters to give up their pens in favour of a gun.[58]

The lower gentry's inroads into the military profession were accompanied by two important groups of non-gentry scholars. First, there were those who had received a traditional education, but for various reasons had not acquired a degree and were therefore not members of the gentry class, though under the old system they might have become so. They had prepared for many years to take the examinations and now suddenly found themselves left in the lurch. Since there was now a premium on Western learning, rich students flocked to Japan in large numbers, and to Western countries to a smaller extent. Others stayed at home and entered the new schools. Still others who could not afford to go overseas or study locally gravitated to the army or the military schools.

Capital cities were centres of new learning and military training.

Many promising young men coming from the hinterland with the intention of taking a course of study in the city found on arrival that the entrance examinations were not held regularly, and that even if they passed the examinations they would have to wait for a long time before actually being admitted. Those who were unemployed and did not have enough money to tide them over the period were often inclined to switch to a military career. Others who were interested in teaching were discouraged by the length of training (six years in the secondary school) before they could become qualified teachers.[59] By contrast, it took the pupil of a military primary school only a few years to become a non-commissioned officer, with the possibility of further advancement.

A second group of non-gentry scholars who showed a keen interest in the army were the modern-educated students. Many of them were nationalistic, seeing military training as a prerequisite to China's regeneration. After the Russo-Japanese War, which almost coincided with the abolition of the examination system, an increasing number of them gave up their studies and joined the army. Some did so after a period of frustration in other careers like teaching and journalism.

A military career was not considered to be a first choice for those who could find a more satisfying civil position, but it represented a strong career choice for those who could not. By a strong career choice is meant a career decision which represents strong ambitions, high ideals and a sense of personal self-confidence. Among these were those who believed that the army provided the opportunity for modernising the country and thus emancipating it from foreign control. For them, a military career reflected a long-term, realistic outlook as well as an immediate career interest.[60]

A measure of just how widespread the idea of educated men joining the army was could be seen in the memorial of one conservative censor who attributed the indiscipline of the new troops in Anhui, Jiangsu and Guangdong in 1910 to the sizeable entry into the profession of 'feeble' but 'arrogant' scholars and students who were allegedly as unruly as the riff-raff in the market place.[61] Yet, it was precisely this change in the class composition of the army that influenced gentry attitudes towards the new soldier and his profession. A modern army was more than a defence system; it was a symbol of nationhood, to which all progressive Chinese would have aspired. The gentry class, with the possible exception of the conservatives and the recluses, were in tune with the scholars and students who had chosen an army career. Without their support it would have been almost impossible to establish and operate the military schools, the barracks, the arsenals, the armouries and the like.

The favourable attitude of the gentry can be illustrated by their reaction to the revolt of the Canton army on 10 February 1910.[62] Public opinion was extremely sympathetic to the soldiers concerned. The local gentry brought much pressure on the government to treat the mutineers and deserters leniently. They gave the main reasons as follows. First, the revolt stemmed from a trivial matter which would not have developed as it did had it not been for the mishandling of the situation by the officers. Second, the soldiers involved all came from good family backgrounds, enlisting for the first time out of patriotic motives. Third, they had never molested the local population and were in fact on very good terms with them. The authorities eventually yielded to public pressure. The significance of this lay in the fact that the New Army in Canton had been accepted as a respectable section of the community by virtue of its specific role, its improving quality and above all the presence of large numbers of educated youth in the ranks.

The gentry-merchants and the chambers of commerce were sympathetic to the military cause advocated by the government. Apart from making financial contributions, they were interested in participating in the military movement, albeit in a modest way. In 1907, for example, some wealthy Shanghai merchants founded the Merchants' Volunteer Corps. By the end of 1910 the corps numbered 350 men, and by early 1911, the membership had risen to 650 and was expected to rise to 1000 before long. The members were respectable people from various societies and guilds. Similar corps had been formed in Hankow, Suzhou, and Foochow, under the auspices of the local chambers of commerce. The drill was usually modelled on Japanese lines with a tincture of German; the drill masters were Chinese who had graduated in Japanese military gymnasia or academies. These corps had professed themselves ready to lend their aid to the government if called upon to do so, for they took the view that it was the duty of the people of China to render military service to the country.[63]

But the gentry and gentry-merchants' support for army reorganisation had limits. The New Army, as we have shown, was the most expensive reform item in the provincial and national budgets. Much concern was expressed by the merchants, the local gentry and the provincial assemblies at the huge amount of funds expended on the army at the expense of other reforms. On the national level, the sentiments of the gentry leaders were clearly expressed in the budget debate when the National Assembly recommended substantial cuts in Yinchang's proposed military expenditure. They realised that military expansion would lead to further increases in tax, which in

turn would result in revolts of the poor masses who had been impoverished by years of natural disasters.

John Fincher finds that by 1911 protests over Peking's military
expenditure had reached a new stage. Student agitation on the issue of
military reform prompted the central government to ban unauthorised
meetings and to censor student writings. In May and June a Conference of the United League of Provincial Assemblymen was held
in Peking to discuss the question of military reform. It was proposed
by some delegates that the nineteenth-century militia *(tuanlian)*
should be revived and strengthened, but this was rejected because
it was obviously unrealistic and inadequate to meet the nation's needs.
Finally, a new proposal was adopted that a system of reserve forces
(virtually consisting of the majority of the male population) should
be raised in the localities, in order to reduce the cost of the existing
New Army system and the financial burden on an already overtaxed
population. Furthermore, it was believed that the reserve system
could ensure that conscripts came from settled families and already
had a regular occupation to which they could return after completing
their service.[64]

In short, the gentry shared the central government's stand that
Chinese military power must be developed to meet the foreign challenge, and supported Peking's policy of improving the status of the
soldier. But the problems of finance were so serious that leading
members of the provincial and national gentry were obliged to curb
the military growth for fear of more mass revolts against overtaxation.

Attitudes of the civil population

In spite of the government's efforts to recruit the educated men, the
majority of the soldiers of the New Army were originally bankrupt
peasants, unsuccessful tradesmen, craftsmen, and the unemployed
city-dwellers.[65] These peasants had mainly migrated from the countryside in search of a better living. The natural disasters which occurred
almost every year had contributed to this migration and prompted
the poor peasants to join the army, where food and lodging was
assured. The craftsmen and the urban poor enlisted for the same
reason, for in such times of extreme poverty, there were very few
places where a decent living could be made. The literacy rate in the
country was so low that even though large numbers of educated men
enlisted, there were still thousands of vacancies in the ranks that had
to be filled by illiterate people from the other social classes. Thus the
New Army was predominantly a peasant army as far as the rank and
file were concerned. Nevertheless, they appeared to have a better
image than the traditional ones who had been mostly criminals,

vagrants, opium-smokers and social dregs.

While the rising military status contributed to improving the attitude of the civil population towards the New Army, there were two other important factors which influenced civil-military relations. One was the discipline and behaviour of the troops; the other was the tax increase due to military expenses.

Earlier studies in this field have noted good discipline and behaviour in the best sections of the New Army, which contrasted markedly with the actions of the traditional soldier.[66] There is adequate evidence to confirm this impression. When Yuan Shikai assumed control of the Newly Created Army, one of his 'military commandments' was to protect the good people *(weiliangmin)*. He stressed that everything the soldier possessed came from the people. It was his duty to protect them, not to molest them. Every soldier had a family which formed part of the people. How would he feel if his family was molested by another soldier? To molest the people would be to molest one's own family, one's own parents and one's own brothers. In dealing with the people, Yuan ordered, the soldier should not resort to violence, and in the event of dispute, should put the matter before a civil judge.[67]

The order to treat the civil population well was in force in many armies, and at least part of the soldiery appeared to have acted accordingly. There were few cases of looting and rape which were common among the old troops. This could be seen in the way in which the local population reacted to the first grand manoeuvres of 1905. When they first heard about the forthcoming manoeuvres, they had a lot of misgivings, and Yuan Shikai found it necessary to allay their fears by issuing a proclamation of the good intentions of the army. When the troops arrived, the people were gratified if somewhat surprised to find them well disciplined, paying for everything they bought. By selling them fruit and other things, the local people in fact made a profit. One British military officer on the spot could not help feeling amazed:

A few years ago, had 30,000 Chinese troops visited any part of the Empire, they would have had either to starve or to live on plunder. The country would have [been] deserted and the women would have thrown themselves down wells.
. . . This [the good behaviour of the troops] is a sort of social revolution and the first step towards military strength appears to have been made, contempt for the soldiers if not extinct has diminished.[68]

When the local manoeuvres of 1907 were held in Zhuozhou, about seventy-five kilometres south-west of Peking, the people there had no fears. On the contrary they showed much good feeling for the troops. According to one eyewitness account, the villagers appeared to be very friendly; they brought in supplies of forage, which were weighed and evidently paid for. The soldiers obtained water from the wells in civilian homes, and each well was marked with a notice on a board, stating which unit was to use it.[69]

In 1908 when the grand manoeuvres were about to take place in Taihu, orders were issued for the good behaviour of the troops, forbidding all of them to stroll into the villages. On their approach the local population were alarmed, and most of the women fled to the hills for fear of being raped. But the people were quickly reassured, as the troops were well disciplined and paid for everything they bought and for damages done to civilian property. There were some complaints from the French priest in the locality about a few soldiers taking things forcibly without payment, but on the whole the behaviour of the troops, in the opinion of three British military officers, was 'excellent'.[70]

Until 1910, the discipline of the New Army was, generally speaking, between moderate and good. For a variety of reasons which will be examined in other chapters, it started to deteriorate after that year. Mutinies occurred in some units, and friction with the police was frequent. Nevertheless, relations with the civil population continued to be 'generally good'.[71]

It would of course be wrong to assume that the New Army had the full trust and confidence of the civil population. By and large the people were still wary about having contacts with the soldiers, but they would be happy to express their goodwill and social appreciation if the latter behaved themselves. They were at least willing to listen when local authorities explained the nature and purposes of the manoeuvres and assured them of the good conduct of the troops.[72] Unfortunately, not all the troops behaved themselves. In 1907, for example, there were some complaints about the 7th Division, and one of these was that some soldiers were found to have 'squeezed the wretched inhabitants' during a local famine in that year.[73] In 1909 a section of the Yunnan army stationed in the rural areas showed 'a tendency to bully inoffensive country people and push them off the road [although this] is not noticeable in the city itself'.[74] In 1910 some dissipated officers in the Yangzi provinces caused troubles in the brothels on several occasions. Others, officers and privates alike, were addicted to gambling and were involved in cases of burglary. Still others were found to have molested the local people in various ways.[75] Similar incidents must have happened in other parts of the country. The military authorities did not condone these incidents which appeared to be mostly isolated cases.

Relations between the army and the people were strained in 1910 and 1911. Troops were often used to suppress disturbances and riots caused by excessive taxation and soaring rice prices. One of the serious clashes between troops and villagers took place in Laiyang prefecture (in Shandong). On 13 June 1910 riots broke out following the decision of the newly appointed district magistrate to levy the taxes which the former magistrate had agreed to abolish. The riots were led by the president of a local association of some sort, who had mustered a few hundred angry peasants for his cause. The ensuing clash with government troops caused the deaths of twenty or thirty villagers and many wounded. Some time later, a contingent of new-style troops arrived from Tengzhou. On 15 July rioting broke out again and fighting was renewed. Five or six hundred rioters were reported to have been killed, while the rest fled in all directions. The government troops pursued them, burning down a few houses on their way. The district magistrate, in the face of strong criticisms, claimed that the troops had been ferociously attacked by the rioters and were forced to retaliate. He also reported that only about one hundred people had been killed. However, this was contradicted by the local press, which expressed indignation at the 'crimes' of the troops. The native press outside Shandong also declared its support for the Laiyang villagers and condemned the actions of the troops.[76]

There were other instances where sections of the New Army were called out to assist in the suppression of unrest among the rural and urban poor, and this aroused a great deal of popular resentment. The New Army was supposed to protect the Chinese people against foreign attack and to defend China's sovereign rights and territorial integrity. But instead of fighting foreign intruders, it had become an instrument of political repression. It failed to check the foreign advance. What was the army for? To protect the people or to kill them?[77]

Worst of all, the people were forced to pay excessive taxes to defray the high cost of the military reforms which brought them no tangible benefits. Taxation increased every year in total disregard of the poverty of the rural masses and the urban underprivileged. The people might be gratified to see the creation of a better educated and modern trained army, but they were undoubtedly resentful of the cost and the taxation which the army involved.

Between 1909 and 1911 there were numerous anti-tax revolts throughout the country. The most obvious targets of attack were the new urban-centred schools which did not benefit the rural masses to any significant extent. Others included the modern police force and the New Army. In the Changsha rice riots of 1910, for example, the rioters demanded, among other things, the closing down of the new schools and the disbandment of the modern police and the regular army.[78] In Zhili of the same year a revolt broke out in Yizhou district, resulting in the burning down of the local self-government bureau and a secondary school. The rioters put forward eight demands, two of which were that all new schools should be permanently closed and the police force disbanded.[79] No mention was made of the local New Army. However, the fact that the New Army was the major cause of heavy taxation led the poor people in many places to oppose military reforms.

The late Qing military reforms ushered in a new era in China when soldiers and soldiering had ceased to be relegated to the lowest grade in the social hierarchy. Army reorganisation was welcomed by the modern-educated scholars who saw militarism as the best means of warding off foreign imperialism and fostering a sense of national unity and public purpose. They called for the creation of a new, militant citizenry not only through modern training of the soldier but also by means of military national education. Likewise, the educationalists favoured a kind of military national education that would prepare the people for more far-reaching changes. The gentry class, from which these scholars and educationists came, supported the militarisation of China. For many lower gentry members after the abolition of the civil service examination, the New Army was a new agent of social mobility which tended to reinforce their social position and influence. For others, it was a training ground for citizenship which was essential for China's regeneration. The merchants, especially those with a sense of patriotism, also approved of the new military scheme, and hoped to gain from a strong China which it was supposed to produce in the long run.

Until 1909 or 1910 the civil population took an improving attitude towards the modern troops who appeared much better disciplined and better behaved than the old, traditional troops. Unfortunately, during the last two or three years of the dynasty, the New Army was used more frequently than before to deal with revolts and riots, thus generating considerable popular animosity towards the troops as well as towards the dynasty. The soldiers themselves, because of low morale and a variety of grievances (see Part II), were not so well disciplined and behaved as they were some years before. The image of the soldiery which had taken so much time and care to improve was tarnished once again.

Finally, the question of military finances had an important bearing on public attitudes towards the army. The common people, young students, merchants and gentry leaders, all found the cost of military reforms too high. The ever increasing tax had become so intolerable that anti-tax revolts occurred in many places and the powers of the central government to raise taxes were seriously challenged.

FIVE

Revolutionary movement in the Hubei army

SINCE IT was the New Army which determined the opening phase of the revolution in October 1911, it is of interest to examine the process whereby this army became disaffected and eventually turned against the dynasty. The revolution was not made by the soldiers, but their political attitudes in 1911 were a crucial factor in the abdication of the Manchu emperor. By 1911 the armies in the Yangzi and southern regions had been subverted by both revolutionary and non-revolutionary forces to a much larger extent than those in north China. When the revolution broke out, the republican sentiment was fairly strong in the south, while the north tended to favour, at least for a few months, a constitutional monarchy. But the Beiyang Army, which also had its share of discontent, was not pro-government as such. Before long, it joined the south in urging the abdication of the monarchy.

It is the purpose of this part of the book to study the ways in which military subversion manifested itself in different provinces. The first province to be examined is Hubei, where there was a remarkable revolutionary movement which was both a typical and a distinctive phenomenon. It was typical because, like the revolutionary movement in other parts of the country, it was marked by the forming and re-forming of revolutionary parties, and the comings and goings of revolutionary leaders.[1] In its first phase, 1903-6, it was part of the student movement which was growing apace across China in that radical students provided the revolutionary leadership, organising study groups and societies to carry out anti-Manchu activities. It was a distinctive phenomenon because from the very beginning it was intended to be a movement aimed at 'the struggle for the troops', a strategy which was the first of its kind to be adopted by Chinese revolutionaries. In the early period, efforts were made by a number of students who enlisted in the army to forge an 'alliance' between the soldiers and those in the educated circle *(xuejie)*. During the second phase of the movement in 1907-11, the new-style soldiers fully asserted themselves as the prime movers. Indeed, the distinguishing features of the Hubei movement were the blending of revolutionary leaders and soldiers and the unusual structure of their organisation. In this sense, Hubei was atypical, for nowhere else in China had the new-style troops been subverted so long, so diligently and so successfully.

This chapter focuses on the structural evolution of the Hubei revolutionary societies. It also investigates the conditions in the army which caused widespread discontent and thus facilitated the growth of revolutionary influence.

The Hubei New Army 1904-11

Hubei was one of the earliest provinces to create new-style armies. The Commission for Army Reorganisation initially proposed that Hubei organise three divisions, but later this was changed to two. Subsequently, only one of them, the 8th Division commanded by General Zhang Biao, was fully completed. The other one, the 11th Division commanded by Colonel Li Yuanhong, was never brought up to full strength and became in fact the 21st Mixed Brigade.[2] Zhang Zhidong took an active interest in army reform apparently with a determination to rival his political opponent, Yuan Shikai. Had it not been for financial difficulties, Hubei would have had two full divisions before the end of the dynasty. In 1910, according to Qing official sources, the 8th Division had a strength of 10,502 men plus 802 staff, while the 21st Mixed Brigade consisted of 4612 men and 288 staff.[3] These included a battalion of Manchus who accounted for less than 10 per cent of the new-style soldiery.[4]

The Hubei New Army was among the largest in the country, and nearly all the regular troops were stationed in the Wuhan area. It was also widely known to be the most efficient of all the southern divisions. In 1905 Tieliang, then assistant director of the Commission for Army Reorganisation, after an inspection tour of the Yangzi region, described the Hubei troops as 'the best of all forces along the Yangzi Valley'. He found that all the officers 'had either studied abroad or had graduated from the military schools, and among the privates are many possessing some education'.[5] On military education, he reported that a middle school for special training and general instruction had been opened in 1903. The curriculum included the science of war, foreign languages, history, topography, mathematics, physics, natural history and map-drawing. Half of the instructors had completed courses of study in Japan, and they taught well. In the school for commissioned officers, the students were occupied with studies of a general nature, including physiology, foreign languages, history, topography, mathematics and map-drawing. The special courses included strategy, military administration, equipment, fortification, cavalry drill, physiology and hygiene. Besides these, field work in artillery and infantry drill, as well as calisthenics, were emphasised. Although there was plenty of room for improvement, these schools were 'a nursery for military talents', being 'the most prosperous and well-regulated', and 'giving most careful attention to duty'.[6]

Lieutenant-Colonel Pereira who inspected the army in April 1907 was generally impressed. He found General Zhang Biao, a native of Shanxi, 'one of the most enlightened generals in China'. Zhang's staff had all been to Japan, and they appeared to belong to the young and progressive school. The regimental officers were also young, having either been educated in Japan or in local military schools. The 8th Division had two battalions of field battery and one battalion of mountain artillery, and the 21st Mixed Brigade had one battalion of mountain artillery. The horses of the field battery were Japanese, all appearing in good condition. The barracks for the infantry units were by far the best Pereira had seen in China. Every soldier, the Chinese claimed, could read and write. Three military schools were in operation: the temporary staff training college (mentioned in chapter 3), the military school for general studies *(wuputong zhong-xuetang)* (pending the establishment of a military secondary school), and the special military primary school.[7]

Captain Leonard of the United States Marine Corps made similar observations. He found the men's appearance 'excellent'. They were all very young, aged between twenty and twenty-five. The officers were particularly impressive, appearing 'to have more dignity and being less effusive than is usually the case'. In addition to the three schools mentioned above, he found an engineering school with 560 students.[8] These troops performed extremely well during the grand manoeuvres of 1905, 1906 and 1908, and were regarded as the best of the southern divisions.

In February 1909, another British army officer reported after a visit to the 8th Division that on the whole the men were soldierly in their bearing. There was 'some discipline', in sharp contrast to the troops of Nanking who appeared 'very slovenly'. They were well equipped and their parade movements and drill were 'distinctly good'. The division seemed to have attained a major step towards efficiency in the field, even though it did not necessarily follow that the troops would give a good account of themselves in action.[9]

The Hubei army was supported by a local armament industry in Hanyang. Since its inception in 1895, the Hanyang arsenal had six plants erected for the manufacture of Mauser rifles, cannons, ordnance, chemical cartridges, smokeless powder and quick-firing ammunition.[10] The British consul-general in Hankow, A.G. Major, observed during a visit to it in 1906 that the small arms factory turned out rifles and carbines of the Mauser 1888 pattern taking a clip of five cartridges. These appeared 'to be of very good make and finish'. The gun factory manufactured only one class of gun, a quick-firing 57 mm mountain gun with carriage. There were some Krupp guns of different sizes, and a Hotchkiss Q.F. gun, from which model the Chinese made their mountain guns. In the small arms ammunition factory, Major was struck by the 'amazing rapidity with which sheets of brass, nickel and lead were transformed into finished ammunition'. The machinery was imported from Germany, and it was most intricate and up to date, capable of turning out a million rounds of ammunition per month.[11] In 1908 Chen Kuilong, who succeeded Zhang Zhidong as Viceroy of Huguang (1908-9) reported that the arsenal was operating on such a scale and with such achievements that it was without precedent in any other province.[12] In 1910 it was rated to be the most efficient in the whole of China.[13]

Another distinctive feature of the Hubei army was the high level of literacy of its men. Joseph Esherick has suggested that this was due to 'the inability of the provincial school system to absorb all the partially educated and potentially revolutionary youth of the province', as there were 1200 primary schools in Hubei, which 'represented less than one school, with perhaps two teachers, for every 24,000 people'.[14] This explanation is sound and valid up to a point. Hubei's educational institutions, both in terms of number and in terms of quality would appear to compare favourably with those of many provinces. For example, there were only 542 primary schools in Hunan in 1909,[15] for a population which was more than half the size of Hubei's. Yet, the Hunanese soldiers were generally not as well educated as their Hubei counterparts.

Another factor which accounted for the high literacy rate of the Hubei soldiers was Zhang Zhidong's incessant efforts to improve the quality of both officers and men by recruiting the educated youth into the ranks. When he was transferred to Peking in 1907, the Hubei army had been well established (except for the inability to bring the mixed brigade to the strength of a division) and there had been little substantial increase in its size since then.[16] Zhang's recruitment policy was carried out by the senior commanders. Li Yuanhong, a military graduate himself, was well disposed towards the educated men.[17] Zhang Biao's attitude might have been less obvious. He has often been described by Chinese historians as ignorant and corrupt,[18] although foreign military experts who knew him well had high regard for him. His staff was filled with educated officers and he seemed to be proud of them.[19] There were various charges of corruption brought against him in 1911,[20] and this has led many a Chinese writer to underrate his ability in army matters and to ignore his liking for educated soldiers.

Viceroy Chen Kuilong, in his brief term of office, also gave a great deal of attention to the army, as evidenced by his attempt to open a new military primary school in 1908. It will be recalled that the special military primary school opened in Wuchang the year before did not conform with Peking's regulations. Chen's proposed school would conform with the rules and run parallel to the special one.[21] Had it been opened, which finance did not permit, there would have been an even larger number of educated young men in the army.

It is also worth noting that a fairly large section of the Hubei officer corps was a product of China's own military education system. Neither Zhang Biao nor Li Yuanhong was educated overseas, though both had visited Japan a couple of times, and very few of the commanding officers in 1911 were known to have been foreign-educated.[22] Part of the reason for this was that the Hubei schools were producing a good number of graduates every year. More important was the fact that Zhang Zhidong, in his last years, had become exceedingly critical of the bearing of the returned students. In September 1907, he stated in a memorial to the Throne:

> Less than half of all the military students who have returned from overseas have acquired practical knowledge without developing some ridiculously bad habits. Even those who are employable appear arrogant and overbearing because of their long stay overseas. Having extravagant expectations, they will not be happy with anything short of an exalted position and an attractive salary. They are loath to work under Chinese-educated divisional and regimental commanders. Furthermore, they tend to be fickle-minded, having no qualms about leaving their jobs whenever they like. These students, though well-educated, lack practical experience. It is doubtful whether they could all be entrusted with important duties.[23]

An examination of the list of commissioned officers in 1905 shows that less than 25 per cent were known to have been educated overseas, the rest being locally trained.[25] But Zhang had always supported overseas studies. Where, then, had the Hubei returned students gone? The answer is that most of them had found employment elsewhere. They were obliged to serve in Peking, if their services were needed there, which was often the case. In 1904 only half of them had remained in Hubei. All were subject to transfer, others left their jobs for more attractive positions elsewhere.[25]

The large proportion of Wuchang-trained officers in the Hubei army indicated that there was no fierce competition from the Beiyang graduates or the Japanese-educated cadets. There appeared to be less discontent among those officers than in armies where the commissioned ranks were mostly held by graduates from outside provinces or by those who had returned from training overseas. This largely accounted for the fact that the Hubei officers by and large evinced little enthusiasm in subverting the political order in which they had a vested interest.

The first phase of the revolutionary movement, 1903-6

Following the Boxer catastrophe in mid-1900, an uprising led by a Hunanese scholar, Tang Caichang, took place in Hankow. The object of this uprising was ambivalent, appearing to be a loyalist effort 'to protect the Emperor' on the one hand and a revolutionary attempt to overthrow the government on the other.[26] Many returned students of Hubei and Hunan origins took part in it. The Wuchang authorities, acting promptly, arrested Tang and a number of secret society leaders on whose support the revolt was based. Many of the students who were involved or implicated fled to Japan.

The years 1901-3 saw an upsurge of Chinese student activities in Tokyo, the formation of student organisations, and the appearance of a number of student journals concerned with China's problems.[27] These journals, published by provincial student groups, dealt with a wide range of subjects of educational, political, economic and military interest. One of them was *The Hubei Student Circle (Hubei xueshengjie)*. It was by no means a radical or revolutionary journal, but some of its feature articles and commentary on the state of affairs in China could be politically subversive. Zhang Zhidong banned it from Hubei and recalled its editors, which only served to give the journal the publicity it wanted.[28] Many Wuchang students were said to have read it surreptitiously and vowed to 'fight for the liberty of the Chinese people and to recover China's sovereign rights'.[29]

In early 1903 the Russians refused to evacuate southern Manchuria which they had occupied during the Boxer uprising, unless they were given special concessions in that area. The issue created a sensation in Japan, where Chinese students organised a mass meeting at which a Resist Russia Volunteer Corps *(JuE yiyongdui)* was formed under the command of Lan Tianwei. Over one hundred and thirty students volunteered for action, another fifty expressed willingness to work in the Tokyo headquarters and twelve women students signed up for nursing duties. They wired to Viceroy Yuan Shikai, urging immediate action to resist the Russians, while several representatives were sent to see Yuan.[30] When the news spread to Hubei, Wuchang's students reacted strongly. They requested Zhang Zhidong to send a telegram to Peking to the effect that the Russians should be resisted, and they also suggested that British and Japanese support be sought in case of war. When their appeal was ignored, a meeting of hundreds of students was held to denounce the Russian aggression. They also castigated Peking's appeasement policy and pusillanimity in the face of foreign encroachment.[31]

The return from Japan of some radical students at the end of the year further stimulated the growth of student nationalism. Chief among them were Wu Luzhen and the editors of *The Hubei Student Circle*. Being one of the first Hubei cadets graduating from the *Shikan gakkō*, Wu was offered several senior positions, even though he appeared to have radical tendencies. Indeed, Wu's case is an interesting one. Wu came from a gentry family. His father was a respected *xiucai* and his grandfather had been a local official. At the age of seventeen he enrolled in the Hubei Military Preparatory School. In 1899 he was among the first batch of government students sent to Japan for study. In 1900 he was involved in the Tang Caichang uprising, after which he returned to Japan and became very active in the Chinese student movement. Zhang Zhidong was well informed about him and did not expect him to return to Hubei. So when Wu arrived in Wuchang, he was detained for three days. Subsequently, Zhang granted him audience, and was impressed by his talent and eloquence. As a result, Wu was appointed to various important posts concurrently: chief instructor of the Wuchang bodyguard, chief instructor in the military school for commissioned officers, associate director of the military education department, and finally assistant director of military administration.[32]

Apparently, it was Zhang Zhidong's intention to 'buy off' those whose radical tendencies might otherwise become dangerous to the government. Wu, on his part, seems to have been gratified to see his rapid rise and developed a great deal of respect, even affection, for the viceroy. Even though he continued to be party to the student movement until late 1903 or early 1904 when he was appointed to a senior position in Peking, his revolutionary fervour appears to have lapsed through considerations of his career prospects. Indeed, his commitment to revolution is open to serious doubt.[33]

Most of the recalled editors of *The Hubei Student Circle* were not been 'bought off', probably because Zhang did not consider them to be a serious enough threat. Nevertheless, they were kept under surveillance, and this forced some of them to go elsewhere for employment or for revolutionary action. A few went to Shanghai, where they opened a firm called the Changming Company, which had branches in Wuchang. Its stated objectives were to advise students intending to go overseas, to sell and distribute political pamphlets, and to serve as an information centre for local and foreign news. But under its cover, a propaganda campaign was launched, financed by the proceeds of four volumes of lecture notes compiled by the returned students and published by the company. Slides on world nationalist movements and anti-oppression struggles were shown in Wuhan, and these were sometimes supplemented with lectures.[34]

By then a few secret cells had been set up as the meeting places of radical students. These included the homes of Wu Luzhen and Li Lianfang, one of the recalled editors. Wu's place was used for ordinary gatherings, while Li's was used for political discussion sessions. There was also a cell known as *wuku* (the Arsenal) under the guise of a reading-room, where discussion sessions were held every month.[35] These cells were of a simple and ephemeral nature, and never assumed much importance except as an indication of an indigenous revolutionary ferment which, by 1903, was developing in many major cities in China. Later, with Wu's transfer to Peking, the political discussion group ceased activity.

In May 1904 a group of locally educated young men held a meeting in Wuchang to work out a revolutionary strategy. Several resolutions were made. First, as a source of military power, the secret societies were not to receive first priority on the grounds that they had proved unreliable, unruly and troublesome in the event of revolt. Second, the new-style army which was being created in Wuchang was to be infiltrated. Third, the subversive process was to focus on the common soldiers rather than on officers who had vested interests in preserving the political *status quo*. Finally, great restraint and patience was to be exercised until adequate preparation had been made and the time was ripe for revolution.[36]

These decisions were of profound significance. The emphasis on military subversion reflected the realism of the revolutionary students who were quick to come to grips with the problem of military power. Their lack of confidence in the secret societies was justified by the failures of the earlier revolts, particularly the Tang Caichang uprising. The technical resources and skills of the regular troops made it practically impossible for secret society elements, untrained and poorly equipped, to stand up against them. The secret societies had to buy and collect arms clandestinely; their financial resources were limited, and they often had difficulties in getting large diverse groups to act together.

In pursuit of their objectives, Zhang Nanxian and Hu Ying enlisted in the engineer battalion of the Wuchang bodyguard. Zhang, a native of Hubei, was a schoolteacher. Hu from Zhejiang was brought up in Hunan, where his father once served as a city magistrate. At the age of sixteen, Hu studied in a Changsha school founded by Huang Xing. Under Huang's influence, he took part in revolutionary activities, for which he was wanted by the provincial government. He escaped to Wuchang where he met Wu Luzhen and Zhang Nanxian.[37]

In June 1904 a revolutionary society, the Science Study Centre *(Kexue buxisuo)* was formed with Lü Dasen as the president, Hu Ying as the chief executive, Cao Yabo as the propaganda chief, Shi Gongbi as the treasurer, Song Jiaoren as the secretary, Kang Jiantang as the general affairs manager, and Zhu Zilong as the liaison officer. Both Lü and Cao came from good family backgrounds and had received a blending of traditional and new learning. Song was a *shengyuan*. Zhu, the son of a *lingsheng*, was self-educated.[38] There are few biographical data on Shi and Kang. But one thing is certain: none of them was or had been a soldier. What held them together was not so much their family or class backgrounds as their discontent with the Manchu government and their concern about China's future.

The ordinary members were mainly students from the local civil and military schools. At the time of founding, the centre had forty-eight members.[39] About forty of them were from the Wuchang Civil High School, and they were most active in establishing connections with military students and the soldiery.[40] The secret societies were not entirely dispensed with, since many of their members were already soldiers. Others were asked to enlist in the New Army, and they had an understanding with the centre that they 'would become activists, awaiting an appropriate moment to rise in revolt for the revival of the Chinese'.[41]

Loosely organised as it was, the Science Study Centre represented a first attempt at revolutionary organisation in Hubei under the cover of academic pursuit. It did not have a constitution or any rules for membership, but it inaugurated a local movement focused on the military and the students under the latter's leadership. It also marked the beginning of a strategy which sought to move away from the previous policy of relying on the secret societies as shock troops for revolution.

There was a great deal of co-operation between the Hubei and Hunanese revolutionaries. The Science Study Centre had many Hunanese who also belonged to Huang Xing's Society for China's Revival *(Huaxinghui)*, which was founded in Changsha in 1903. Song Jiaoren, a Hunanese, and Cao Yabo, a Hubei native, frequently travelled back and forth to Changsha, maintaining close contacts with Huang Xing.[42]

Indeed, it was the centre's implication in an abortive revolt in Changsha that led the Wuchang police to raid its premises on 28 October and forced its leaders to flee. As a result, the centre was dissolved and for some months the revolutionary movement came to a halt. [43] The Wuchang government promptly dealt with the radical students by sending them to study in Europe or Japan.[44] Confucian songs were composed for both students and soldiers in the hope of strengthening their loyalty.[45]

Yet, despite this setback, a beginning in the subversion of the army had been made. According to a Wuchang *daotai*, the rank and file of the regular troops were imbued with a sense of their own importance and had no particular respect for their officers who would have little control over them in case of emergency. He said to the British consul-general in Tientsin upon his transfer there that he

> used to live in a house near which a number of them [soldiers] used to pass on their way to and from their parade ground. Having had reason to complain to one of their officers of the men's conduct, he heard them say afterwards one day, as they passed, 'Ah, this is the house where they complained of us. When we rebel, we will take this house first'. He gave this as an instance merely of what he stated — namely, that 'rebellion' is a familiar idea to these troops, and one that they freely discuss among themselves.[46]

Not surprisingly, then, the revolutionary movement was soon revived in 1905 by a local scholar named Liu Jing'an whose name appeared in the Tongmenghui registry as Liu Zhenyi.[47] Liu was steeped in Chinese classics, although he did not hold a traditional degree. When young, he was converted to Christianity. As he grew older, he became concerned with China's future and lost his confidence in the Manchu dynasty. In 1901 he enlisted in the army under the assumed name of Liu Daxiong, and in 1904 was promoted to be Li Yuanhong's secretary. He had attended the May 1904 meeting and was a member of the Science Study Centre. After the Changsha revolt, he resigned from the army when Li Yuanhong became suspicious of him. Liu then took refuge in Wuchang's American Episcopal Church, which was in the charge of the Reverend Hu Lanting, who had earlier also given asylum to Cao Yabo. Liu soon realised that a foreign church was the sort of institution that could be used to cover and protect revolutionary activity. He successfully prevailed upon the Reverend Hu Lanting to turn the church library into a centre for revolutionary activity.[48]

The library was called the Society for Daily Increase in Knowledge (*Rizhihui*), which was originally a newspaper and periodical reading-room. There were similar reading-rooms with the same name in the episcopal churches in Changsha, Hankow and Kiukiang. The Wuchang one did not assume a new character until it was taken over by Liu Jing'an. To cover its revolutionary use, Liu kept its name intact and maintained its usual appearance.[49]

In late January or probably early February 1906, the library was transformed into a revolutionary centre. At its secret inaugural meeting, Liu made a speech emphasising the anti-imperialist and anti-Manchu theme, and calling for a new China. It was also important that he stressed the need for a military-student alliance in the revolutionary movement.[50]

The new society had an executive board divided into four sections: general affairs, administration, secretariat and public relations. There were about twenty members on the board, with Liu as the chief executive. There was also a board of assessors, on which information is scant. The society was self-financed. Wu Luzhen remitted one month of his salary towards its formation, others contributed at their own discretion ranging from one to five yuan each. Sympathisers who had not paid any subscription fees or signed the membership roll were also regarded as comrades.[51]

The membership of the new society was much larger than that of the Science Study Centre. One account listed 118 names of which eighteen were former members of the centre.[52] Another reported two hundred-odd, most of them being soldiers, and the rest students, schoolteachers and journalists. There were only four comrades from the religious circle, which indicated that religious elements were insignificant in the movement. Also admitted were six junior officers who were probably too enthusiastic to be excluded altogether.[53]

Under the protective umbrella of the church, the society tried to influence all those who came to use the library. Public lectures on Chinese political affairs were given every weekend in the Wenhua College, a mission school in Wuchang.[54] The propaganda campaign was not confined to the Wuhan area. In the prefecture of Huanggang, about 175 kilometres east of Wuchang, a clandestine printing house was set up. It reprinted and distributed Zou Rong's *Gemingjun* [The revolutionary army], Chen Tianhua's *Jingshizong* [Alarm to arouse the age], *Menghuitou* [Sudden realisation], *Shizihao* [The lion roars], as well as others written by local propagandists.[55] The theme was invariably anti-imperialist and anti-Manchu. Little mention was made of such doctrines as republicanism, democracy and social welfare. The traditional forces of xenophobia and ethnocentricity sometimes entered into the spectrum of propaganda slogans and had a great appeal. Many soldiers were said to have kept the propaganda tracts under their beds like treasures, and turned them into simple songs for the rural community when they returned to the villages at the end of their service.[59]

A number of clandestine bodies sprang into existence outside Wuchang under the guise of schools, study groups and reading-rooms. It was also in Huanggang that a notable Institute for the Soldiery and the Students *(Huanggang junxuejie jiangxisuo)* was founded by a scholar-soldier, Xiong Shili. Its leading members were graduates of Wuchang's civil and military schools, as well as soldiers. The military comrades formed small propaganda teams of ten men each. What began as a small local body soon developed into an influential centre attracting many people from the neighbouring areas. In May 1906, the local authorities found Xiong fomenting revolution, and forced him to flee. As a result, the institute was closed.[57]

In the summer of 1906 Sun Yat-sen advised the Society for Daily Increase in Knowledge that a high-ranking French military officer had assured him that the French government was sympathetic to the Chinese revolutionary cause, and that seven French officers in Tientsin were ready to help Sun in any possible way. Sun had asked one of them, Captain Ozil, to make a study of the Yangzi situation. On his arrival in Wuchang, Ozil was well received. At a meeting attended by several hundred revolutionary sympathisers, including officers and men from the local garrison, he delivered a speech on the French Revolution, drawing parallels between the overthrow of the *ancien regime* in France and the need for revolution in China. Among the audience were General Zhang Biao and a police constable, both in disguise, and a British employee of the Chinese Imperial Customs. The affair was brought to the attention of the viceroy. A protest note was lodged with the French legation in Peking, but the French minister denied any knowledge of French support for the Chinese revolutionaries.[58] The Ozil affair, while eliciting much response from the audience, aroused official suspicion of the nature of the church library.

The leaders of Society for Daily Increase in Knowledge were not anxious to rise in revolt, realising that patience and hard work were necessary in a subversive process. As Yin Ziheng, who was later apprehended by the police, said during interrogation, they had always thought about revolution but no military action had yet been contemplated.[59] In fact, the society could have escaped government prosecution had it not been for the Ping-Liu-Li uprising on the Hunan-Jiangxi border in November 1906. The uprising was staged by the secret societies with the support of the peasants and miners following a Yangzi flood which had caused a great deal of disturbance.[60] The Tongmenghui, though having no prior knowledge of it, decided to take advantage of the situation and sent three of its members, Hu Ying, Zhu Zilong and Liang Zhonghan, to Hubei. Their arrival in Wuchang forced the society to decide what action to take. But before it reached its decision, a man named Guo Yaojie reported to the police that the society was a revolutionary body in disguise, and that Liu Jing'an was the same as Liu Jiayun, a secret society chief wanted by the police in connection with the Ping-Liu-Li uprising. The police stepped in quickly, arresting Liu, Hu Ying, Zhu Zilong, Zhang Nanxian, Liang Zhonghan, and four others.[61] The Reverend Hu Lanting was then on leave in Japan. He immediately sought their release with the assistance of the United States legation in Peking. The men, saved from execution, were sentenced to varying terms of imprisonment. Zhang Nanxian was released in 1907 on a bond of good behaviour, and later took up a teaching post in Wuchang. Liu Jing'an suffered tremendous torture and died in prison three months before the Wuchang uprising.[62]

Zhang Zhidong was alarmed at the activity of the revolutionary bands in the Yangzi Valley. What really worried him was not so much the student movement as the fact that the movement was associated with the secret societies which had their members in many army units. On 15 December 1906 a local newspaper, the *Nanfangbao*, published Zhang's instructions on the subject of rebellious societies, giving particulars as to their strength, methods and organisation. The viceroy, particularly concerned about the smuggling of munitions of war into the Yangzi region, instructed all customs and *likin* stations in Hubei and Hunan that whenever goods of suspicious appearance were seen, they must be examined as a precautionary measure. Orders were also given to all officials, both military and civil, to take stringent and secret precautionary measures against the secret societies.[63]

The officials were ruthless and unscrupulous in their determination to crush the revolutionary movement. Hundreds of people were implicated, and many lost their lives. The Society for Daily Increase in Knowledge was dissolved, and many of its members fled Hubei. The few army officers who belonged to it were frightened and receded into the background. The local revolutionary movement was at its lowest ebb.

Thus ended the first phase of the Hubei revolutionary movement. Before the setback of 1906, there had been a noticeable increase in the number of revolutionary sympathisers, of whom substantial proportions were common soldiers and secret society elements. Cao Yabo's claim that the highest number on record, civilians inclusive, was 10,000[64] is certainly an exaggeration. On the other hand, the claim of another writer that about 2000 soldiers belonged to the Society for Daily Increase in Knowledge[65] seems a reasonable estimate, since this represented only ten per cent of the Hubei new-style soldiers. Although the majority of the troops were either indifferent or unsympathetic, the achievement was notable, considering the fact that Hubei was the first to undertake a process of army subversion of this kind.

The weaknesses of the student-soldier revolutionaries were also remarkable. The Science Study Centre was a primitive rebel organisation, experimental and temporary in nature. The Society for Daily Increase in Knowledge, though an improvement on its precursor, was also loosely structured. Both were too short-lived to improve themselves. From the very outset, revolutionary subversion was to all intents and purposes centred on Wuchang. The Society for Daily Increase in Knowledge had established no hierarchical relationships with the small independent bodies which had sprung into existence in various places. There were no regulations. Membership was open to all; the only requirement was sympathy to the revolutionary cause, hence the lack of a system whereby interested people could be politically screened. The subscription fees were not fixed, each member contributing of his own accord. Nor was there a chain of command over different groups of revolutionary soldiers. Furthermore, although the propaganda campaign had made some headway, it reflected the inexperience and amateurism of the revolutionaries who easily exposed their subversive ideas to the authorities. The lectures, slide shows and meetings held by them were to some extent open to the public; and photographers were light-heartedly engaged to take pictures as they met. Consequently, government agents could mix with the audience. As soon as suspicion was aroused and one or two people caught, the authorities, by getting hold of the whole stock of the pictures, had most damning evidence against all those concerned.[66]

The second phase, 1907-11

The year 1907 saw considerable unrest in the Yangzi provinces, arising partly from shortages of rice and partly from a feeling of Chinese sentiment against the Manchu dynasty.[67] In Wuhu many Chinese officials were found to be in sympathy with the movement, which partly explained why so few of the revolutionary adherents had been discovered and punished.[68] Indeed, 1907 was a year of revolutionary putschism. There were more than ten uprisings; five in Guangdong, two in Guangxi, one each in Anhui and Zhejiang, and a few sporadic outbreaks in Sichuan. Since May, not a month had passed without a revolt. Each of these uprisings was intended to be the signal for a nationwide revolution. But all turned out to be isolated incidents through lack of co-ordination, poor leadership, bad organisation and inadequate military support. [69]

The putschism of 1907 reflected an overestimation of the revolutionary strength and the extent of popular support. The anti-dynastic movement, though on the increase, was fragmented and loosely organised. A successful revolution was out of the question until the insurgents had adequate military support from their allies or from the government forces, and until the new elite group, the ardent reformers, were irrevocably alienated from the authorities.

There was no uprising in Hubei in 1907. The Wuhan revolutionaries, under the government's vigilance, had to be very cautious. Some of them retreated to the rural town of Anlu in central Hubei, where a welfare society was used as a liaison centre. They met from time to time, and took care of the families of those comrades who were serving sentences in prison. [70] The prisoners in Hanyang formed themselves into a body known euphemistically as the Chinese Iron and Blood Corps *(Zhonghua tiexuejun)*. With the sympathy of the prison officer, they were able to maintain contacts with their associates outside. Hu Ying was often consulted on matters of general interest. Li Yadong, another prisoner, regularly contributed under a pen-name to a small local vernacular newspaper published by a revolutionary sympathiser in Hankow. [71]

On 5 September 1907, Zhang Zhidong was appointed Grand Councillor. Five days later, Li Minchen, the treasurer, became the acting viceroy. On 11 September Zhang departed for Peking. It was not until 5 May 1908 that Chen Kuilong arrived in Wuchang to assume duty as the new viceroy. [72] During this interval, official vigilance seems to have relaxed, thus affording an opportunity for the revival of revolutionary subversion.

In the spring of 1908, a Hubei member of the Society for Daily Increase in Knowledge named Ren Zhongyuan returned from Sichuan. He was then recommended by another comrade, Li Changling, to join the 3rd Battalion of the 41st Regiment in Wuchang. Both Ren and Li were critical of the Tongmenghui strategy of waging uprisings in the outlying provinces, and they held the view that a revolution in the heart of China would be most fatal to the dynasty. They then initiated action to bring together four hundred soldiers at a meeting on 26 July, which saw the formation of a new society known as the Hubei Military League *(Hubei jundui tongmenghui)*. There were divided opinions as to the appropriateness of this name. Some felt that under such a name, the society would appear to be a purely military organisation, thus discouraging civilian participation. Others argued that since most of the comrades were soldiers, a military league was precisely what they wanted. The debate was not resolved at the meeting.[73] But the fact that the new society ultimately assumed the name it did proved that the military comrades were in the ascendant.

Unfortunately, the Military League was disrupted towards the end of the year partly because Ren Zhongyuan had been transferred to Sichuan, and partly because the authorities had discovered some revolutionary activities and stepped up security measures. The vernacular newspaper with which Li Yadong was associated was ordered to close, while activities in the barracks were watched. The Military League became defunct, after a period of five months. No notable achievement had been made.

Yet the founding of the league was significant in two ways. First, it reflected a desire on the part of many comrades to set up an exclusive, military body. Although there were still civilian members, the trend was set for military domination. This distinguished the league from the earlier societies, and foreshadowed the emergence of the military to positions of leadership in the revolutionary movement. Second, despite its ephemeral nature, it was the only notable society which revived the anti-dynastic movement and re-established the link in the chain of the local revolutionary societies.

At the end of 1908, it was brought home firmly to the Hubei revolutionaries by the Xiong Chengji mutiny in the Anhui army (see chapter 6) that revolutionary subversion was an arduous task requiring good organisation more than sheer enthusiasm for military action. More party work remained to be done, and this raised the question of the future direction of their organisation where recruitment was concerned. Opinions on this question were still divided. Some suggested that a broader organisational structure incorporating both soldiers and civilian students should be established, in the belief that to concentrate on the soldiers alone would greatly restrict the scope of revolutionary work. The majority, on the other hand, favoured an exclusive, military body to be dominated and controlled by the common soldiers. There were, again, criticisms of the leadership of the Tongmenghui on the grounds that its head office was not in China, and that its operation was based on the unpredictable support of overseas Chinese and the secret societies. The Tongmenghui was not closely knit and lacked a modern military force to support itself. Meanwhile, the role of army officers was again disparaged for the same reason as before. To the suggestion that civilian students should be part of the subversive movement, the military advocates replied that Wuchang's schools were full of Hunanese students whose political attitudes were 'complex' (and therefore allegedly unreliable).

Believing that civilian students were incapable of keeping secrets, they attributed the failures of the earlier societies to the incongruous intermeshing of soldiers and students. The best means of achieving a close-knit organisation, and of ensuring secrecy, was therefore to operate among the ranks of the troops alone.[74]

With this rationale, the military advocates won in the end. On 13 December 1908 the Military League was restructured under the new name, Society for the Study of Popular Government *(Qunzhi xueshe)*. Although the name was not military-oriented, it was in fact the first revolutionary society of the common soldiers. It was also the first local society to have a constitution and a set of rules for membership.

The new society consisted of a president, two secretaries, one treasurer, one general affairs manager and several assessors, all of whom were elected. In addition to an initial fee of one yuan, each member contributed one-tenth of his monthly stipend to the society. To step up the recruitment drive, each member was obliged to recruit two new members every month. Membership was more selective than before. Any person intending to join was to be introduced by three old members and subjected to political screening. Another rule stated that 'when members of the society introduce new comrades for admission, no officers were to be considered in order to prevent unpredictable dangers'.[75] This policy had been followed since 1904, but it required the effort of the new society to make it a rule.

There were no standard methods or mechanisms for judging the political attitudes of the new soldiers. The requirement that everyone had to write an essay at the time of his enlistment helped the revolutionaries to decide whom to approach in the first place. But the essays were not reliable evidence, so a practice called *huantie baiba* (exchange cards and become sworn brothers) was adopted. It was customary for Chinese people to exchange cards with acquaintances they admired, giving full personal particulars, thus hoping to become good friends or sworn brothers. The revolutionaries, in exchanging cards with their fellow soldiers, expressed their political views implicitly at first. If cards were returned with a favourable response, then more would be exchanged and the idea of revolution would become more explicit each time. Finally, interested soldiers would be induced to join the society.[76] This process was completely clandestine. Public lectures, films, slides and inflammatory speeches of the type employed by earlier revolutionaries were no longer in use. Instead, each soldier was approached individually. There was nothing new in the language of revolution used to recruit supporters, for it always reiterated the oppression and corruption of the dynasty, its servility to foreigners and the need to overthrow it. When a new comrade was introduced, he was interviewed by two or three old members, and, if admitted, was asked to complete an oath statement written on a loose piece of paper. After the new member was warned that he would be in great danger if he did not treat the activity of the society in strict confidence the oath statement was burnt without his knowledge.[77]

Before long, the Society for the Study of Popular Government spread its influence in the 41st, 42nd and 32nd Regiments. Its activity in the 41st Regiment was facilitated by the fact that Yang Wangpeng, a radical private, had been promoted to secretary in the 1st Battalion, a position which enabled him to observe government actions. Later, he was discovered by Pan Kangshi, a battalion officer, who expressed his support for the revolutionary cause and a strong desire to join the society as a full member. It was difficult to reject Pan's friendly gesture, so contrary to the rule discouraging the membership of officers, he was admitted in these exceptional circumstances. Moreover, there was good reason to believe that Pan was sincere and enthusiastic. He came from a poor peasant family in Huangpi, and had received some private education from a clan relative for two years. In 1906, after passing an officer's examination, he was appointed lieutenant and, two years later, promoted to captain, so obviously he was not one of those frustrated soldiers who were deprived of self-advancement. His claim that in choosing an army career he was motivated by a desire to 'save the country' was highly credible. In fact, he was soon to prove himself a dedicated revolutionary in the 41st Regiment.[78]

The society was now in the charge of Li Liuru, a fairly well educated private in the 41st Regiment. Able and enthusiastic, Li recruited a good many followers in the 8th and 32nd Regiments in the space of a few months. Revolutionary influence was also widespread in the special military primary school.[79]

In addition to distributing anti-imperialist and anti-Manchu tracts, the society sponsored a local vernacular newspaper called the *Commercial News (Shangwubao)*. Originally owned by a Mr Luo, it was sold to a Hubei scholar, Zhan Dabei, who appointed He Haiming as editor. Zhan, a native of Hubei, was an outstanding student from Huangzhou who had been expelled from middle school after a quarrel with the supervisor. Frustrated, he went to Wuchang and became a journalist.[80] He Haiming was a former non-commissioned officer in the 41st Regiment, and used to contribute to various local newspapers.[81] Later, they were joined by two Hunanese Tongmenghui members, Jiang Yiwu and Liu Fuji. Jiang, who had the appearance of a simple-minded country peasant, was first educated in a senior primary school in Lizhou and later in a normal school in Changde. He had been associated with Song Jiaoren and the secret societies. He once wanted to go to Japan, but became ill in Shanghai. So instead of going overseas, he enrolled in a local modern school, and later worked for a vernacular newspaper there. After this paper was suppressed by Viceroy Duanfang for allegedly engaging in anti-Manchu propaganda, Jiang returned to Hunan. In the autumn of 1909 he came to Wuchang, wishing to enlist in the local army.[82] Liu Fuji also graduated from a senior primary school and had been associated with Huang Xing and Song Jiaoren. He had been to Japan and worked with Jiang before joining the staff of the *Commercial News*.[83]

In late 1909 Jiang and Liu were covering a flood in south Hubei when they heard about the Society for the Study of Popular Government. They met a revolutionary soldier who told them all about the society after they had expressed a desire to join the army. Subsequently, Jiang enlisted in the 3rd Battalion of the 41st Regiment, while Zhan and Liu went to see Li Liuru. The *Commercial News* was then in serious financial straits, so Zhan and Liu made a proposition to the society that it take over the management of the newspaper. Li agreed, in order to turn it into a propaganda organ. Henceforth, the newspaper concerned itself with current political affairs, and became very critical of government policies. It also provided the society with some useful contacts with civilians without actually bringing them into the organisation.

Early in 1910 the *Commercial News* was forced to close as a result of the Yang Du incident, which arose over the issue of the nationalisation of the trunk railways. The Hunanese provincial assembly had offered to send a delegation to Peking to protest against the government's policy. When the delegation arrived in Hankow, Yang Du,[84] a supporter of foreign railway loans, attempted to stop it. The *Commercial News* inveighed against him for several successive days. Some revolutionary soldiers invited him to a dinner given in honour of the delegation. When he refused to come, Yang was dragged out of his residence in the British Concession. The British municipal police intervened, and detained the 'trouble-makers' for eight hours. Consequently, in order to avoid trouble, no printer was willing to work for the *Commercial News*.[85]

In May 1910 the Changsha rice riots led the Hubei revolutionaries to believe that the time was ripe for an uprising. Agents were sent to Hunan and Sichuan, and firearms were smuggled into some regular units. When the Changsha situation was later brought under government control, the plan was cancelled. But the authorities had already got wind of it, and instantly swooped down on the 32nd Regiment, where the plot was hatched. The chief conspirators fled to Shanghai and Sichuan. All the important documents of the Society for the Study of Popular Government were either removed or burnt. No arrest was made. But the society could no longer function under the same name. On 18 September 1910 it became known as the Society for the Promotion of Military Studies *(Zhenwu xueshe)*, with Yang Wangpeng as its president.[86]

The new society was structured on the same basis as its precursor, but it distinguished itself from all the others in one respect, namely, its elaborate system of representatives which formed the most crucial part of its cellular structure. Before 1909 there had been a lack of centralised control over diverse groups in the regular units. With the steady increase in revolutionary membership, some sort of structural unity was badly needed. To achieve this, the system of representatives was first introduced by the Society for the Study of Popular Government as a new experiment. It was later institutionalised by the Society for the Promotion of Military Studies. Under this system, a representative elected from the ordinary members in his unit directed the subversion carried out in each regiment, battalion, company, platoon and squad. Representative meetings were held at the regimental level only. If a representative was unable to attend, his battalion counterpart would stand in for him. Significantly, the regimental representatives evolved as the nucleus of the organisation, forming a kind of cadre corps in what would appear to be a central committee, which was in fact the decision-making body. Information and directives were transmitted to the ordinary members through a hierarchy of representatives. To prevent members from becoming well acquainted with their counterparts in other camps, communication between different units was strictly limited.[87] The purpose of this was to minimise the danger of security leaks, although in actual fact communication sometimes occurred.

Another advantage of this system was that in the event of revolution, the representatives, under the direction of the 'cadre corps' would be able to command the men in their own units·the way officers commanded the troops.[88] This was extremely important, because the revolutionary soldiers lacked the standing required to win the respect of their fellow soldiers, or the expertise to conduct military operations as efficiently as the officers. The special status of the representatives was intended to provide a partial solution to the problem of military command.

This cellular structure, which showed some traces of Leninist techniques, was purely an indigenous innovation in response to a difficult situation where large meetings of revolutionary members in the barracks would be impossible. There appeared to be some sort of 'democracy' in the system whereby the representatives were elected by the men in their own rank. There was, too, a certain degree of 'centralism' in that all the operational groups took orders 'from above'.

On 11 October 1910 the first meeting of regimental representatives of the Society for the Promotion of Military Studies was held. Delegates were sent from the 31st, 32nd, 8th (artillery), 41st and 42nd Regiments, out of a total of eight regiments which formed the Wuhan garrison. It reported that a total of two hundred and forty members had been recruited in the previous month. Before the end of the year, revolutionary influence had been asserted in most of the army units to varying degrees. However, no attempts were made to subvert the Patrol and Defence Force, which was much less responsive to revolutionary ideas.[89]

The year 1910, as we shall see in the next chapter, was marked by a number of mutinous outbreaks in various places; so the Wuchang authorities became increasingly vigilant. Colonel Li Yuanhong soon found Pan Kangshi engaged in subversion and discharged him. Pan was succeeded by one of Li's protégés, whose watchfulness led to the dismissal of Yang Wangpeng, Li Liuru and others, thus disrupting the work of the society. Before the end of the year, another vernacular newspaper, the *Yangzi News* was published by Zhan Dabei in the same style as the then defunct *Commercial News*.[90]

The revolutionary movement in the Hubei army so far described showed another outstanding feature: the promptness with which the revolutionary soldiers set up a new society after each setback. Taking advantage of the process of reform which permitted the formation of cultural societies, they changed the names of their organisations, whenever necessary, to guard themselves against government suspicion. There was a marked continuity from the early societies to the Society for the Promotion of Military Studies, each improving on the one which preceded it. In a similar fashion, therefore, the Society for the Promotion of Military Studies was transformed into the Literary Society *(Wenxueshe)* on the Chinese New Year Day, 30 January 1911. The constitution of the Literary Society, which claimed to aim at literary pursuits, was published in the *Yangzi News.* From the very beginning, it was designed to be a large organisation in anticipation of a rapid increase in membership and an expansion in the scope of party affairs. It consisted of a president, a vice-president, a secretariat and a board of assessors. The head of the secretariat was assisted by four secretaries, one accountant and one general administrator. The board of assessors consisted of an indeterminate number of assessors and inspectors. Membership fees and financial contributions were the same as before. Jiang Yiwu, Zhan Dabei and Liu Fuji were elected president and heads of the secretariat and the board of assessors, respectively. The vice-presidency was allowed to be vacant until the society had grown large enough.[91]

The rise of Jiang, Zhan and Liu was due to the fact that the leaders of the previous society had been either dismissed from the army or fallen under government surveillance. Jiang had been in charge of the Society for the Promotion of Military Studies for some time and proved himself an able leader. Liu was a good friend of Jiang's. After enlisting in the 3rd Battalion of the 41st Regiment the year before, he quickly rose to fame through his prudence and tactfulness in dealing with his fellow soldiers.[92]

The position of Zhan Dabei was an interesting one, since he was a civilian and had never been a soldier. His election as head of the secretariat represented a departure from the policy that only the military could join the society. This reflected the greater importance now attached to Zhan's *Yangzi News*, which was virtually the party organ. In an attempt to intensify revolutionary propaganda, the choice of Zhan could not have been better. The *Yangzi News* was oriented towards current political affairs and became more radical in tone; it often exposed the corruption among the army officers and their maltreatment of the men. Financed by the Literary Society, it was distributed free to all interested soldiers, and became so popular that it came to be regarded as a most powerful weapon against corrupt officialdom.[93]

The progress of the Literary Society was spectacular; in less than two months it had recruited members from nearly every regular unit. On 15 March 1911 the first meeting of regimental representatives was held with delegates from the 29th, 31st, 8th (artillery), 41st, and 42nd Regiments. Other representatives who were not of regimental standing came from the 8th Engineer Battalion, the military police and the supply department. This appreciable headway warranted the election of a vice-president. Accordingly, Wang Xianzhang, a platoon chief in the 30th Regiment, which had a predominance of Manchus, was elected. Meanwhile, Zhang Yukun, a private in the 41st Regiment, was charged with a mission to subvert the 8th Cavalry Regiment, where revolutionary influence was not yet established.[94]

On the question of future recruitment, there was a debate as to whether the members should be relieved of their financial obligations. Zhang Yukun proposed that members should not pay at all, and that the society should be financed by its office-bearers alone. He argued that many interested soldiers hesitated to join because of their meagre stipends and family responsibilities. This proposal was finally accepted, despite Liu Fuji's objection that this might cause financial problems. Subsequently, the membership rose remarkably, while many continued to contribute voluntarily whenever they could. On the other hand, Liu's worry was warranted, for the society was soon faced with serious financial problems.

After the Canton uprising of April 1911, government vigilance prevented the regimental representatives from meeting. Worried about the possible breakdown of communication, Liu Fuji resigned from the army and lived inside Wuchang city in order to maintain contacts with various units through regular visits. It was in these circumstances that another meeting of representatives was held on 10 May. It resolved to establish a Literary Society headquarters inside Wuchang city and a new board of general affairs headed by Zhang Tingfu.[95]

On 1 June, a third representatives meeting was held. Following a proposal from Hu Yuzhen, representative of the 42nd Regiment, it was resolved that a branch organisation for Hanyang and Hankow be set up. The 42nd Regiment consisted of three battalions. The first battalion was stationed in Hanyang near the arsenal and the iron-works. The second battalion was garrisoned outside the Hankow railway station, where the regimental headquarters was located. The third battalion was scattered at various points north of Hankow along the Peking-Hankow Line. Hu Yuzhen was elected head of the Yangxia (Hanyang and Hankow) branch, assisted by a deputy.[96]

This branch of the Literary Society provided a useful link between revolutionaries in the three cities, which were separated from one another by the Yangzi or the Han. It was different from the head-quarters in some respects. Owing to its relatively limited scope of activity (confined to just one regiment), all its representatives, regardless of their status, met once a week at the residence of the office-bearers. Financially, its members made 'ordinary contributions' according to their stipends and 'extraordinary contributions' in special circumstances. It kept all the funds, less the monthly contributions of its office-bearers which were forwarded to the Wuchang headquarters.[97]

The degree of success achieved by the Literary Society can be measured by the rapid rise of its membership. From 800 at the time of its founding in January,[98] it rose to between 3000 and 5000 in August,[99] or about 30 per cent of the total military population in Wuhan. There were now a number of civilians who had been admitted as a result of the merging of several small study groups outside the military circle. This merging was desirable as the revolutionary movement had reached a stage where it was no longer necessary to reject civilians out of hand. Nevertheless, the Literary Society remained a military-dominated organisation, its overriding concern being the overthrow of the dynasty. Being managers of violence, the revolutionary soldiers were not interested in political doctrines, and hence there was little discussion of political reform or social transformation. Conscious that their role was a military one, they believed that the establishment of a new form of government was the responsibility of the civilian-led Tongmenghui.[1]

Amalgamation of the revolutionary societies

Apart from the chain of revolutionary societies described so far, there was another stream of the Hubei revolutionary movement represented by the Society for Common Advancement *(Gongjinhui)*. Together with the Literary Society, with which it amalgamated on the eve of the Wuchang uprising, it determined the opening phase of the revolution. I have documented its history elsewhere;[2] so it will suffice here to concentrate on those aspects which had an important bearing on military subversion.

Like other revolutionary societies, the Society for Common Advancement was anti-Manchu in both a racial and political sense. Like the Tongmenghui, from which it stemmed as a splinter party, it regarded the secret societies as an important military instrument. However, in terms of military strategy, it differed from the Tongmenghui in that it intended to use the secret societies as a channel to establish communications with the soldiery. One of the founding members recalled an early meeting at which its strategy was mapped out:

> It was all agreed that to overthrow the Manchu regime, it was necessary to obtain the support of the army all over the country, as well as to achieve the unity of all diverse groups and parties. Since the majority of the armymen were members of the secret societies, it was also imperative that the latter's co-operation be sought. In order to seek their co-operation, it was necessary to adopt their rituals and practices.[3]

The Society for Common Advancement focused its activities on the middle Yangzi region, although agents were also sent to operate in Guangdong and Guangxi. In fact, it was in Hubei that this society developed into a significant conspiratorial body. Sun Wu,[4] one of its leading members, returned from Japan in late 1908 to set up its headquarters in Hankow's French Concession, and various communication centres in Shanghai, Wuchang, Ichang, Yuezhou and Changsha. The new members, predominantly secret society elements from the Elder Brothers Society *(Gelaohui)*, were organised in five military divisions scattered in various parts of Hubei, with Sun Wu as chief commander.[5]

However, the policy of using these elements to subvert the New Army was not seriously put into effect in the beginning. As far as Sun Wu was concerned, the secret societies were a useful military force in their own right. It was not until mid-1909 that events in central China forced him to reappraise their revolutionary potential. In July of that year the Elder Brothers Society in Changsha had prematurely broken out in revolt. In August the second and fourth divisions of Sun Wu's army also went into action without his instructions, and the fourth division had become so unruly that it had to be disbanded afterwards. Meanwhile, the triads in south China, where some Society for Common Advancement forces were at work, proved no better organised or disciplined. In October a revolt was planned in Guangxi, and Sun Wu was asked to be there, but it broke out and failed dismally before he arrived. This convinced him that the secret societies were unreliable allies. Upon his return to Hubei, he immediately turned to the New Army, where he had friends who told him all about the subversion already well under way.

This change gave the Society for Common Advancement a new character, which was reflected in the methods it used to subvert the 32nd Regiment in Wuchang. There were strict regulations.[6] The stated aim of the society was 'to avenge the national disgrace and to restore the Chinese'. It claimed to be essentially a military body, though membership was open also to interested people from the commercial and student circles. Revolutionary representatives elected from each unit were responsible for the execution of policies and, more importantly, to act as commanders in the event of revolution. They had the authority to admit new comrades, who were to be introduced by three old members, sign a statement on oath and vow to abide by all the regulations. It was also the responsibility of the representatives to finance the society, while ordinary members contributed to it at will. The duties of the ordinary members were to recruit new comrades, to help finance the society if they could, and to keep their activities strictly confidential. General meetings were to be chaired by the regimental representative. Every member was to attend with the full right of debate. Extraordinary meetings did not need a quorum, but the minutes were to be subsequently communicated to all other members. Furthermore, there were rules dealing with the reward and punishment of members.

In external affairs the Society for Common Advancement was willing to co-operate with other revolutionary groups. When it was necessary to communicate or exchange views with them, a representative was to be sent whenever possible. In circumstances requiring correspondence, letters were to be couched in a secret language and delivered in person. Correspondence between members was not to deal with confidential matters, except in special cases where such letters were to be censored by the representatives, delivered in person and burnt after reading.

On recruitment, the regulations prescribed that only close friends were to be approached. Some members were assigned special duties to observe government actions, and were required to report to the society regularly. Ordinary reports were to be forwarded to the representatives through the members closest to them, while special reports were to be submitted in person to ensure security. When a member was in danger while carrying out his duty, he was to be prepared to sacrifice himself. The society on its part was to make every endeavour to secure his safety and be responsible for his funeral and the maintenance of his family should he lose his life.

All these regulations were evidence of an elaborate organisation modelled on the Society for the Promotion of Military Studies. There were some differences, however. One was that membership of the Society for Common Advancement was open to civilians as well as to the soldiers. Another was that this society encouraged all its members to attend meetings, at least within the same regiment, and to participate in the decision-making process. An inner core like the regimental representatives committee of the Society for the Promotion of Military Studies did not exist.

The Society for Common Advancement also adopted the practice of exchanging cards with the new soldiers before asking them to join. Each new member was told not to confide his activities to anyone, even his parents, wife, children or relatives.[7] The belief in some quarters that Sun Wu was Sun Yat-sen's brother increased the influence of the society and attracted a large following. Its membership rose from 1700 in May 1911 to about 2000 in August.[8]

Following the abortive Canton uprising of April 1911, the Hubei revolutionaries were more convinced than ever that the time had come for the middle Yangzi region to take the lead in the revolution. It was then imperative that the local revolutionary bodies should combine rather than compete with one another. Accordingly, the Society for Common Advancement at a special meeting held in May adopted a resolution calling for amalgamation with the Literary Society.[9]

There were considerable differences in the family background and life experience of the leaders of the two societies. Most of the Literary Society leaders were locally educated people of Hunan origin who had never been abroad and had almost no contacts with revolutionary groups outside Hubei. The leaders of the other society, on the other hand, were natives of Hubei who had been educated or lived in Japan and were better informed of developments in other provinces. The Literary Society leaders therefore tended to be suspicious of the returned students, fearing that they might be deceived if they joined forces with them. Jiang Yiwu, for example, felt that these people were tricky, arrogant and contemptuous of his society, which was, furthermore, a self-supporting organisation operated by soldiers of humble origins, while some leaders of the Society for Common Advancement were from relatively rich families.[10]

By and large, the ordinary members of both societies were not particularly aware of belonging to one party and not the other. For one thing, they were local recruits brought up in more or less the same environment and had developed a similar outlook; and they did not really mind which society claimed them. In fact, many had dual memberships, hardly knowing where the difference lay.[11]

The leaders themselves were not irreconcilably opposed. Common bonds, however loose, held them together and promoted an easy *camaraderie*. There was a common desire for unity and action which became the dominant theme of the negotiations which followed. The sense of urgency served to sink, temporarily at least, their individual and party differences, and enabled them to merge into a common group.

The merger achieved on 14 September brought the total number of revolutionary soldiers to between 5000 and 6000, or at least one-third of the Hubei modern troops.[12] Another one-third of the soldiery was sitting on the fence, and the remainder was believed to be loyal to the government.[13]

The formula of joint leadership was worked out in a fairly satisfactory way. A military preparatory centre *(junshi choubeichu)* and a political preparatory centre *(zhengzhi choubeichu)* were formed.[14] The Literary Society enjoyed more influence in military affairs, because, as Josef Fass has pointed out, it consisted almost exclusively of revolutionary soldiers. On the other hand, the Society for Common Advancement dominated the political preparatory centre, as some of its civilian leaders had contacts with the Tongmenghui.[15]

A final point about the Hubei revolutionary societies is their resourcefulness and independence. They had developed largely on their own, and their relations with the Tongmenghui were tenuous.[16] This reflected the fragmentary nature of the Chinese revolutionary movement, but what constituted its weakness also laid the foundations for an uprising which was to become the beacon for a successful revolution.

Disaffection in the Hubei army 1910-11

The spread of revolutionary influence in the army could not be attributed entirely to the work of the revolutionaries. Neither the Literary Society nor the Society for Common Advancement could have expanded so rapidly without the disaffection which had become widespread in the army after 1910. The succession to the viceroyalty in Wuchang by two Manchus, Duanfang in 1910 and Ruizheng later, did not augur well for the authorities. Duanfang was looked upon by the soldiers with little respect, as he was a corrupt official lacking the good intentions or abilities of his predecessors.[17] Ruizheng, though more competent, had the misfortune of governing at a time of immense financial difficulties.

October 1910 was a disquieting month in the Hubei army. It saw more than ninety desertions in the 8th Cavalry Regiment, and efforts to fill the vacancies had been unsuccessful. Corporal punishment was enforced with severity. In one regiment a private found gambling in the barracks was flogged to death by an officer, an act which immediately aroused a great deal of resentment among the ranks. In another instance, a soldier received 'a thousand strokes' of the cane for taking one day's leave without permission; some time later he shot dead the officer who had administered the beating.[18]

Troops from Wuhan were often called out to assist in the suppression of riots and disturbances in other parts of Hubei or elsewhere. The soldiers generally hated such duties, which resulted in low morale, poor discipline and desertions. Many spent much of their time gambling; others made trouble in the brothels and occasionally clashed with the police.[19] They were also apprehensive of transfers to Manchuria, where the Russians had territorial designs. Life in the north-east was extremely hard for anyone from central China who was not accustomed to the cold climate and different living conditions. In March 1911, on hearing rumours of such transfers, soldiers of the 31st Regiment started to panic, and many deserted. A similar situation was found in the 41st Regiment, where more desertions were feared. Precautionary measures were taken, but some officers themselves were extremely worried about the threatened transfer.[20] In that month alone a total of 254 desertions was reported from the various units.[21]

The desertion rate continued to rise as a result of rioting in Sichuan in September. Many Hubei troops had left for Sichuan. A large number of those who remained asked for leave on various pretexts. Others simply deserted.[22] There were scores of deserters in every battalion. A recruitment campaign in that month failed to fill all the vacancies. Consequently, the military authorities were obliged to recruit anyone who had good eye-sight and good physique, regardless of his place of origin.[23] Yet, for all these efforts, desertion remained a serious problem.

The financial crisis in the province added to the discontent, since the New Army budget accounted for 50-60 per cent of the provincial expenditure.[24] Early in 1910 there were rumours that the pay of all the troops in Wuchang was to be reduced, but this was denied officially.[25] Towards the end of the year, the Wuchang government announced various cuts in the New Army amounting to a total of 559,614 taels.[26] The native press in Hankow, too, reported the financial straits of Hubei necessitating reductions in the salary of officers of all grades, dissatisfaction at the rate of pay, and desertions with or without arms.[27]

In 1911 it was no longer possible for the authorities to pay the troops fully. It was announced in May that the pay of officers of all ranks was to be reduced by 40 per cent.[28] It is not clear how much the men's pay was cut, but it may have been 20-30 per cent.[29] The 21st Mixed Brigade, which had been ordered to expand to division strength, had been in arrears of pay for some months. To find money for the New Army, it was ordered that all the Green Standard troops in the province should be completely disbanded before July. Drastic cut-backs were also made in civil administration, education, and public works, for it was realised that to withhold the soldiers' pay would be extremely dangerous to the government.[30] That their pay was reduced eventually indicated the seriousness of the financial situation as well as the precarious position of the army authorities.

The pay of the troops, even in full, was hardly sufficient in times of rising rice prices. The years 1910-11 were rife with natural disasters, floods, locusts and epidemics, which caused immense damage to the crops and untold misery to the people, as the following chapter will show. The soldiers who had families to feed naturally joined the poor masses in expressing their discontent.

Meanwhile, relations between officers and men were bad. Many officers had been appointed through personal connections rather than on their own merits. They had a corrupt and extravagant life-style, and treated the men badly. In August 1911, a dozen soldiers of the transport battalion ransacked the residence of Yu Hualong, commander of the 8th Cavalry Regiment. Not finding him there, they hurt his mother, raped his second wife, and ran away with a large amount of gold. Six of them were apprehended later, all confessing to having the intention of killing Yu because of his ill treatment of them. In September an angry private shot dead an officer who had maltreated him.[31]

As the financial situation deteriorated, corruption increased, particularly in promotion to officer rank and in the purchase of ammunition. There was already much resentment among graduates of the special military primary school against the slim chances of promotion above the level of platoon commander. In fact, most of the soldiers remained privates for life.[32] Financial constraints, coupled with corruption, rendered normal promotion impossible. Besides this, embezzlement of the men's pay was common, and so were deductions of all kinds.

In April 1911 the *Yangzi News* exposed the corruption of Li Xianglin, commander of the 29th Regiment. Li was so furious that he hired a hooligan to murder the correspondent who had investigated his case. But the *Yangzi News* kept attacking him for a few days, and the case alarmed the local community so much that the authorities were obliged to order an inquiry, which resulted in Li's dismissal.[33]

The *Yangzi News* then became extremely popular among the ranks, while corrupt officers 'feared it like a tiger'. On 26 July it carried an inflammatory editorial entitled 'Chaos, the Wonderful Remedy for China', written by He Haiming. On 1 August, the editor-in-chief and publisher, Zhan Dabei, was arrested together with some of his staff, and the newspaper was forced to close. The local press, supported by merchants and public welfare organisations in Hankow, protested against the viceroy's high-handed measure. The provincial assembly was reported to be preparing a petition to the viceroy, threatening to dissolve itself if Zhan was not acquitted.[34] A few days later He Haiming was also arrested. The petition of the provincial assembly, however, was never submitted.

Some weeks later another local newspaper, the *Hankow News (Xiabao)*, which had no association with the revolutionaries, reported in great detail the corruption of Xiao Guobin, commander of the 3rd Battalion of the 31st Regiment. Many letters to the editor from anonymous soldiers who had been illtreated by him were published. Xiao sued the *Hankow News* for defamation, but before the case was dealt with in court, the editor-in-chief, Peng Ximin, was lured to a place where he was beaten up by a group of soldiers, presumably on Xiao's order, and afterwards detained in the criminal court and charged with libel. Xiao's barbaric action evoked so much protest from the local community that Viceroy Ruizheng had to order the department of military administration to have him reprimanded. But no punishment was meted out against him, since he was a protégé of Tiezhong, director of the department concerned.[35]

This situation was complicated by the fact that General Zhang Biao was by no means a 'clean' commander. He was accused of misappropriating a total of a million taels which were earmarked for the soldier's uniforms, clothing, medical services, and so on. Most of the money thus obtained was said to have been invested in real estate, which made Zhang one of the biggest landlords in the Lianghu region.[36]

This state of affairs on the eve of the revolution was summed up by the British acting consul-general in Hankow as follows:

> There are many indications that the 8th Division is in a very un-satisfactory state of discipline, and that serious disaffection exists among the men. The native press has during the past two months continually reported incipient mutinies, acts of insubordination, extensive desertions, harsh treatment and extensive punishment of the privates, as well as cases of peculation of funds by the officers... The authorities did not deny these disquiet conditions, nor do they disguise their anxiety as to the situation and their fear of the presence of revolutionaries among the troops.[37]

Clearly the Hubei revolutionaries would not have acquired the strength they did had it not been for the widespread army discontent which lent itself to revolutionary propaganda. The soldiers did not have to be republican fanatics to join the revolutionary societies. They had many grievances, as well as expectations whose fulfilment the overthrow of the dynasty seemed to promise. Most of them wanted change of some sort. The revolutionaries did not create the disaffection, but identified with it and exploited it to the full. It was, in the final analysis, a combination of revolutionary influence and army grievances that led to the undermining of the military authorities.

SIX

Other armies in the Yangzi region

WHILE HUBEI was atypical because of the unusual strength of the revolutionaries in the local New Army, revolutionary subversion elsewhere was less impressive and less effectual. This is not to say that army disaffection outside Hubei was insignificant, but rather to point out that such discontent was due to a combination of factors other than the result of revolutionary subversion. The outcome was the same: that in the end the troops withdrew their support from the dynasty.

This chapter examines the discontent which existed in the other armies of the Yangzi region, where the revolutionary situation at the turn of the decade was the most volatile and explosive. It first deals with the state of affairs in the region with special reference to the financial conditions, natural disasters and unrest.

The financial crisis

The finances throughout the country before the revolution were in a chaotic state. Neither the imperial treasury nor the provincial coffers had enough money to make both ends meet. The reform scheme was bringing vast expenses in its train, especially in areas of defence and education. Many projects of public utility were shelved owing to lack of funds. The copper currency had depreciated with the result that prices of all commodities had increased and the people became poorer. Everywhere new taxes were levied and old taxes increased. Yet only a small percentage of the taxes levied found its way to the treasuries because of embezzlement by officials and wasteful methods of collection. Indeed, the whole system of internal taxation had to be reorganised before the government could increase its revenues.

Many examples can be cited to illustrate the disorderly condition of the finances. In Shanghai two district magistrates were forced to commit suicide early in 1910 because of official deficits which were due to no fault of their own.[1] In Sichuan the prohibition on cultivation of the opium poppy had disorganised the provincial finances, and in one district taxation was so heavy that even respectable people were said to be prostituting their daughters.[2] In Hubei the native business world was affected by the unusual shipment of sycee silver westward for speculation in opium. Land was practically impossible to sell. The paper money in circulation was worthless; yet the issue of unsecured bank notes continued unchecked, while the treasury refused to redeem them for coin.[3]

In the spring of 1910 there was a phenomenal rubber boom in Shanghai leading to wild speculation by both native banks and foreign companies throughout China. In mid-summer, unfortunately, the boom collapsed, and a few months later a massive financial crisis resulted from the failure of the native banks which were unable to repay the money held by them on government account. A complete breakdown in the native system of banking ensued, and the situation was utterly chaotic until the Peking government, under pressure from the foreign diplomatic corps, rescinded an earlier order to withdraw from the banks in which it had deposited.[4] But the impact of the crisis was felt in every treaty port, especially Shanghai itself, Nanking, Hankow, Swatow, Canton, and Tientsin. In Hankow alone dozens of factories and companies collapsed, resulting in a fall in both external and internal trade.[5]

At the end of 1910 Hubei was faced with an estimated deficit of 3 million taels, and the provincial government was forced to borrow 2 million taels from a number of native banks.[6] Early in the following year, the deficit rose to 2 million in spite of the loan. Even with drastic reductions and rigid economy, it was still impossible to make both ends meet. Additional taxes were levied for both imperial and local purposes. Not only were the common people discontented, but also the merchants protested against the vigorous enforcement of the stamp duty and threatened a general strike as a last resort.[7] The situation was complicated by the fact that the newly formed provincial assembly lacked a proper sense of the need for economy, advocating expensive schemes of education, communications development, and the like without taking into account the resources of the provincial treasury.[8]

In 1911 Hunan had an estimated deficit of over 5 million taels, of which 1-2 million could be attributed to riots, indemnities and famine relief of the previous year.[9] Yet in many government projects little thought was given to financial considerations. There were only about 100,000 taels available for education where between 400,000 and 500,000 taels were required annually. The police expenses amounted to 200,000 taels, of which only one quarter or so was provided for. The New Army alone accounted for 1-2 million taels. Much revenue was lost through the smuggling out of rice without paying dues as a result of a temporary embargo, while returns from the *likin* and other sources either dropped or remained stationary.[10]

In Zhejiang the total deficit by the end of 1910 was well above 700,000 taels,[11] and exceeded the million mark in June 1911, when the provincial treasury was in debt for over half a million taels to the Salt Revenue and Grain Departments and various banks, as well as in arrears with the *likin* revenue due to the Imperial Customs. Another 820,000 taels, which should have been remitted to the central government, was not forthcoming.[12]

Both the Peking and the provincial authorities were compelled to raise foreign loans to enable them to carry on the government of the country. Some were direct loans borrowed openly under Peking's authorisation and guarantee from foreign banks and corporations. Others were indirect loans raised abroad by means of bonds forming part of the so-called domestic, as opposed to foreign, loans. The loans contracted in 1910 amounted to over 10 million taels. China's credit was still good, as she had not failed to meet her foreign obligations. But a continuance of such heavy borrowing, coupled with her inability to reorganise the fiscal system and to increase the national revenue by developing her natural resources, threatened to 'end in a disaster and the establishment of that foreign control over China's finances which her rulers and people have tried so hard to prevent'.[13]

While the impoverished state of the economy was a nationwide phenomenon, the Yangzi provinces on the whole seem to have been more severely affected than north and south China, as far as the New Army was concerned. Not only had the Beiyang Army been fairly well established by 1910, but it had more financial resources than the divisions maintained outside Zhili and Manchuria. The armies in the south, with the exceptions of the Yunnan and Guangdong troops, were much later developments and were never as significant, in terms of size, quality and training, as the divisions in central and north China. Thus the impact of the financial difficulties there did not seem to have been as great as in the Yangzi region, where the New Army was unable to maintain its existing level, not to mention the expansion which some provinces and army officers had expected. The financial cut-backs naturally produced a demoralising effect on the troops who were at the same time suffering from the floods and famines described below.

Flood, famine and unrest

The financial situation in the Yangzi provinces was aggravated by the severe floods which occurred in the two years before the revolution. Since February 1910 there had been continuous rains over the whole of the lower Yangzi. In the middle of the year large parts of northern Jiangsu and Anhui were inundated, the worst disaster area being the Grand Canal on the east, the Huai and the Ge Rivers on the south and west. Over 17,920 square kilometres the autumn crops were a complete failure, and only half of the wheat land could be sown for the spring crops. Multitudes of starving refugees begged their way south to Chinkiang, Kiukiang and Wuhu. Troops were moved to the distressed region to preserve order and suppress brigandage.[14]

In Anhui the floods destroyed 400,000 houses and rendered 2.5 million people homeless. About 500,000 of them had died of cold, starvation, and epidemics; another 200,000 had joined the brigands.[15] In September and October 1910 the low-lying areas of Hubei, from Shashi down to Mianyang and Dangyang, were all under water, and thousands of people were killed.[16]

In early 1911 Nanking and Chinkiang teemed with destitute refugees from the famine-stricken areas. In Nanking alone there were between 50,000 and 100,000 of them who were dependent entirely on charity and government relief. Rice merchants there showed little sympathy for them. Between April and June about 60,000 men had died of typhus and fever, while a particularly virulent epidemic claimed another hundred lives.[17]

The worst was yet to come. In June and July excessive rains caused the Yangzi to rise to an abnormal degree, and at Wuhu the watermark stood, on 12 September, at 9.27 metres, the highest ever recorded. The whole area was turned into a huge inland lake, with thousands of refugees driven to every available piece of rising ground.[18] The scenes of destitution noticeable at almost any point between Shanghai and Hankow were described as extremely pitiable. In Hankow the water had reached a point 'practically unknown in the memory of man'. In the Ichang district travellers portrayed the country as resembling 'a huge inland sea, scores of miles in length'. In Hunan, which was well known for abundant rice production, the district of Changde was covered with water and extensive crop-lands were washed away. Many refugees lived on the leaves and roots of trees, and a few cases of cannibalism were also reported. Thousands of people had perished.[19]

In Anhui the Huai River struck again. Up to August, almost one hundred thousand hectares of rice had been destroyed, leaving absolutely no hope for the autumn crops. Half a million people were homeless, taking shelter in straw huts to await relief. The main streets of Wuhu were flooded to a depth of 0.9 metre. In Jiangxi an extensive area around Nanchang was under water, and 40 per cent of the crops were destroyed, while Kiukiang swarmed with refugees from the nearby areas.[20]

Apart from the immense loss of life and property resulting from these floods, there was a serious shortage of rice and other foodstuffs. In the spring of 1910 the rise in the price of rice led to rioting in various places in Anhui, Jiangsu and Hubei. Some gentry and landowners were notoriously hoarding rice with a view to profiteering. In Changsha the price of rice had been raised by the local gentry who were reported to have kept a large stock at an up-country centre.[21] The rice riots which followed in April and May clearly demonstrated the deplorable conditions of the poor masses. In 1911 the situation in the Yangzi region deteriorated further. In Changsha the price of rice rose from 5000-5200 cash per picul in early July to 6200-6300 later in the month.[22] In Wuhan they rose from 5000 cash per picul in late August to 7000-8000 in September.[23] In Nanking each picul of rice cost 7 yuan in July, it was 9.10 yuan in September. In Shanghai during the same time the highest price on record was 12 yuan per picul.[24] On the eve of the revolution rice was generally more than 50 per cent above its normal value, a situation which was worsened by the 'cornering' of unscrupulous Chinese rice merchants.[25] It was only natural that there should be numerous cases of starving people breaking into public granaries, looting rice shops, and attacking landlords, rich merchants and government officials who were corrupt in the distribution of foodstuffs and relief.[26]

The tragedy of these occurrences was that the floods of the previous years had already produced widespread disaster and famine from which it had been hoped that the year 1911 would afford some relief. Unseasonable weather, continuous rains extending far beyond the normal period, had blighted these hopes. In such circumstances the masses of the population could not help feeling extremely bitter against the government for its neglect of the preventive work which would have minimised the extent of the devastation.

The government troops, or at least some sections of them, sympathised with the poor masses. The shortage of foodstuffs and rise in the price of rice affected them as much as the civil population. Furthermore, most of the soldiers had their families or relatives directly or indirectly hit by the floods and famines. They could not be used indefinitely to suppress civil disorders caused by the extreme misery of the people. There were moral repercussions in the act of the army crushing such disorders, repercussions which increased with the numbers of riots and repression, as the soldiers' suspicions about the mismanagement of the government grew.

There could be little doubt that the financial and social conditions in the Yangzi Valley opened a fertile field for seditious dissemination by political agitators. The greater the area affected at one time, the greater was the danger of local riots gaining the impetus of revolution. We have described the revolutionary activities and disaffection in the Hubei army. Let us now look at the other Yangzi troops.

The Hunan New Army

Hunan was one of the most reformist provinces in the late Qing period. Many changes had taken place there, especially in areas of education, rights recovery and industrialisation, mining, and constitutional reform.[27] Yet in the military field, Hunan lagged far behind Hubei. The 25th Mixed Brigade in Changsha was relatively small, with a strength of 4443 men in 1911. Lack of funds prevented it from expanding to division strength. Demobilisation of the old-style troops was extremely slow, and on the eve of the revolution a large number of them, estimated to be 25,053, were still maintained.[28]

Notwithstanding its size, the Hunan New Army was a competent one. In fact Hunan had long had a reputation for producing good soldiers. In July 1906 a British military officer found that most of the soldiers who came from the northern part of the province were as tall and healthy as the northern Chinese. They were smart-looking, 'very civil and friendly', and the drill was 'very good'.[29] As in other provinces, there were military schools, but they were inferior to those in Hubei. Graduates of the local military primary school usually went to Wuchang for further training, while Hubei officers sometimes served in the Hunan army on secondment.

The Hunan army was also 'notorious' for having many secret society members in the ranks. In December 1906, in the wake of the Ping-Liu-Li uprising, Zhang Zhidong reported that 500 men of the Changsha garrison were members of the Elder Brothers Society, and that there were another 500 in the police force in Yuezhou and 3000 in the provincial forces.[30] Indeed, it was the secret society influence that partly accounted for the extreme inefficiency of the Hunanese troops in dealing with the uprising. Apart from their inadequate training and discipline, a large proportion of them were in sympathy with the rebels. Some of the rebels had rifles, although the majority of them were armed with shot-guns, jingals, swords, lances, bamboo poles and agricultural tools. This led one local magistrate to believe that 'the critical nature of the situation arose less from the preparations of the rebels than from the unreliability and inefficiency of his own troops'.[31] The rebels did not disperse until a regiment of Hubei troops arrived on the scene.

It will be recalled that this relationship between the secret societies and members of the New Army led some leaders of the Society for

Common Advancement to use the secret societies to subvert the army. The man responsible for organising these societies in Hunan was Jiao Dafeng, who was later to become the first military governor of Hunan. Jiao was born into a landlord family in Liuyang. His father was a local militia leader and owner of 500 *mou* of land. He had received some education in Liuyang and Changsha, and was impressed with the revolutionary acts of Tang Caichang and Tan Sitong. In his schooldays he was most interested in martial arts. He seems to have been in conflict with his father, and chose to 'begin a revolution in the family'. Later, he was expelled from home and found himself in good company with the secret societies. He travelled frequently between Hunan and Hubei and, in 1904, met Yu Zhimo, a radical Hunanese student, to whom he owed much of his revolutionary ideas. After Yu was arrested by the Changsha authorities, Jiao fled to Japan and joined the Tongmenghui there. In 1906 he returned to Hunan, and took part in the Ping-Liu-Li uprising. After the uprising was suppressed, he went to Japan again and enrolled in a railway school after being precluded from doing a military course. While in Tokyo he played an active part in the formation of the Society for Common Advancement. In late 1908 he returned to Hunan and set about mobilising the secret societies in co-operation with Sun Wu, who was operating in Hankow.[32]

It was not until 1910 that the Hunanese revolutionaries set their sights on the local New Army (presumably under the influence of their Hubei comrades). At this time there was in the 49th Regiment an artillery platoon chief named Chen Zuoxin, who was keen to advance the revolutionary cause. Chen, also a native of Liuyang, was educated in the Changsha Military Preparatory School and had joined the Tongmenghui before being appointed as a junior officer. In 1909 he held a lecturing position in the regimental and cartography schools. He established a good relationship with the student-soldiers and appeared to have had some influence over them. He was instrumental in distributing anti-imperialist and anti-Manchu tracts to the rank and file clandestinely. In 1910 during the Changsha rice riots, Chen urged the commander of the troops dealing with the rioters to revolt, but succeeded only in getting himself dismissed.[33]

Yet, the Hunanese troops were anything but hostile to the rioters. In April 1910 it was reported that 6000 troops had joined them in looting schools and shops,[34] but this was later found to be untrue.[35] If the troops appeared 'untrustworthy' as the correspondent of *The Times* said, it was because they refrained from firing on the rioters who burned down the yamen. The governor was left unsupported, while the treasurer, other officials, and influential local gentry members, gave the order not to fire on the rioters.[36] One reason for this was their disapproval of the way in which the governor was handling the situation. Another, which was not stated publicly, was their awareness of where the sympathies of the troops lay.

In a dispatch to the Foreign Secretary, Max Müller, the acting British minister in Peking, complained about 'the inactivity of the troops'. There were rumours that two soldiers had been beheaded for firing on the crowd, and the British consul in Changsha believed it to be true.[37] The troops remained 'passive spectators' in Müller's words, but in fact it would be more accurate to describe them as sympathetic.

The situation in Xiangtan was similar. A foreign report from there stated:

> There are several hundred soldiers here now who were in Changsha when the riot occurred. They were fine-looking fellows and very agreeable. I asked some of them today why they allowed the mob to burn and destroy. They said that they could not help themselves as their superiors would not allow them to fire on the mob . . .[38]

The 'mob' referred to above were the poor peasants, craftsmen and others hard hit by the famine. The troops were deliberately inactive, although they had warned the rioters that anyone who ventured to make a disturbance would be shot. Their extraordinarily good behaviour towards the rioters and the civil population can be interpreted as a sign of disapproval of any attempt to suppress the rioting by bloodshed.

In the meantime, the local revolutionaries were becoming increasingly active. Subversion of the troops was now in the charge of a junior cavalry officer named Liu Wenjin. Little is known about Liu's family background. He was a Hunanese and seems to have graduated from the military preparatory school in Changsha and joined the Tongmenghui probably in 1910. His initial tactic was to approach the company officers, but their poor response forced him to concentrate on the common soldiers and the subalterns. In April 1911 a meeting of the revolutionary soldiers was held, with representatives from the 25th Mixed Brigade headquarters, the 49th and 50th Regiments, the artillery, cavalry, engineering, transport, and naval battalions, a total of sixty-eight men, none of whom was a commissioned officer. The feasibility of staging a military coup simultaneously with a projected uprising in Canton was discussed, but no resolution seems to have been made, which suggests that the revolutionaries were not yet prepared for military action. The Changsha authorities got wind of this meeting, but chose to take no punitive action against them for fear of a mutiny in the entire mixed brigade. Liu Wenjin was subsequently asked to go north to buy horses, and there were rumours that he would be killed on his way, which did not happen.[39]

Meanwhile, the railway dispute in Sichuan was creating an impact on Hunan. The protests of the provincial assembly and the nationalist students reacted on the soldiery, giving them an awareness of the government's precarious position. It was in these circumstances that another secret meeting attended by two hundred soldiers was held in August to discuss the revolutionary situation in the country. However, no military action was proposed.[40]

As far as revolutionary subversion was concerned, three points emerge clearly from the account above. The first is the role of the common soldiers and the subalterns, which suggests some parallel between the Hunanese and Hubei patterns of subversion. In Hunan, as in many other cases, the senior commanders were hired from outside provinces. Both Brigadier Xiao Liangchen and regimental commanders Huang Luanming and Yu Qinyi were northerners, and the commissioned officers were either Beiyang or Hubei graduates. Xiao was widely unpopular among his Hunanese subordinates. As regards the rank and file, it was almost impossible for them to be promoted to officer rank, a situation which was fully exploited by the revolutionaries.[41]

Second, the Hunanese revolutionary soldiers lacked the structural strength which distinguished their Hubei counterparts. A compact and systematic organisation comparable to the Literary Society did not exist. Nor was there a system of representatives of the Hubei type. In short the radical soldiers in Hunan were not capable of acting independently of Hubei.

Third, there was a continuous link between the New Army and the secret societies, as exemplified by the relationship between Chen Zuoxin and Liu Wenjin on the one hand and Jiao Dafeng on the other. Jiao had always been closely associated with the secret societies, and seemed most anxious to exert his influence in the local revolutionary movement. But he lacked the ability, charisma or status which were essential to political leadership.

This lack of revolutionary leadership, however, should not obscure the fact that the Hunan New Army was no more politically reliable than the Hubei troops. Here again, the financial stringency of the provincial government contributed to army unrest. In 1911 the New Army expenditure (including contributions to the Beiyang Army) accounted for 34.28 per cent of the total cost of reforms in Hunan.[42] Early in that year the troops' pay had been four months in arrears. With the advent of the Chinese New Year, the soldiers became so angry that they threatened an open mutiny, and this forced Governor

Yu Chengge to order the senior commanders to make every endeavour to raise funds and pay the men before the end of the lunar year.[43]

Yet, in the meantime, Hunan was under severe pressure from Peking to bring the 25th Mixed Brigade up to division strength. This impossible task forced the military authorities to save money by retrenching the coolies, cooks, grooms, and the like, as well as by cutting down on the supply of military uniforms, clothing and fodder.[44] Obviously, the Peking leadership did not understand the mood and the realities prevailing in the province.

In the summer of 1911 graduates of the military primary school also felt the impact of the financial crisis and became discontented. Contrary to earlier expectations, they would not be sent to Wuchang for secondary training. This meant that they would not be commissioned, and would have to content themselves with the junior positions to which they were appointed.[45]

The New Army in Anhui
Anhui was one of the provinces in China that had a great military reputation. Anhui men generally were tall, well built, and well known for their courage and endurance. They had enlisted in the Beiyang Army in large numbers and in other divisions to a lesser extent. Yet in Anhui itself military development was in a most backward state. It was expected to form one division, but it fell far short of that goal. In 1907 there were one infantry brigade of 3000 men, one cavalry squadron of 300, and one artillery battalion of 100, all stationed in Anqing. Added to these were the governor's bodyguard, which had a strength of 130 men, armed with Mausers with magazine (five rounds) made in the Hanyang arsenal. The troops were all Chinese and predominantly Anhui men. There were only a few from Hubei and Hunan. They were young, healthy, and smart looking. Conscription was in force.[46]

Extreme poverty explained why Anhui was militarily more backward than any other province in north and central China. Not only did the 31st Mixed Brigade there fail to expand to division strength, but the new barracks were rickety two-storied buildings, with hollow brick walls and a wooden frame to support the roof, which was covered with thin corrugated iron sheets. Another reason for this state of military affairs was that Governor Enming (1906-7), a Manchu in his sixties, was by no means an ardent reformer. He was assisted by a provincial war board which was managed by three civil officials, two of whom did not appear to possess much military knowledge. He had no desire to increase the strength of the mixed brigade, except for another battalion of transport and engineers.[17]

There was no commandant *(tongling)* in charge of the 31st Mixed Brigade. A local magistrate had management of it in theory, and he was subject to the authority of the provincial war board. There were, however, two middle-aged lieutenant-colonels *(biaotong)* commanding the two infantry regiments. One was Zhang Zhongqi, a native of Anhui, and the other was Peng Yueqi from another province, both graduates of the old local military school. The newly founded Anqing Military Primary School had 220 pupils in 1907, mostly from Anhui. Aged between fifteen and eighteen, they studied six hours a day. The supervisor was a Lieutenant-Colonel Jiang from Anhui, who graduated from the Nanking Military School and had been in Japan for three years.[48]

In November 1908 Anqing was the scene of a mutiny led by an artillery officer named Xiong Chengji. The background against which it took place was the deaths of the Emperor Guangxu and the Empress Dowager, which had caused a general sense of stupefaction and apprehension in Peking, giving rise to considerable speculation on the future of the dynasty. Xiong, a native of Jiangsu, was born into a scholar-gentry family. Both his father and grandfather had been local officials. In his teens Xiong gave little care to his study, leading a dissipated life in Wuhu until the age of nineteen when he felt ashamed of himself and went to Anqing, where he enrolled in the local military school. He later enlisted in the New Army and was recommended to take an intensive artillery course, at the end of which he was appointed lieutenant in the 9th Division in Nanking. Subsequently, he returned to Anqing to take up a post as artillery captain. He joined the Yue Fei Society *(Yuewanghui)*, which consisted of a small number of radical middle-ranking and junior officers who ran an inn to raise money for revolutionary work.[49]

In the fall of 1908 the authorities were preparing for the autumn manoeuvres of the Nanyang Army to be held in Taihu, which would be reviewed by Yinchang and Duanfang, Viceroy of Liangjiang. Xiong and his associates then planned to assassinate Duanfang and start a mutiny at the end of the manoeuvres. The plot did not materialise, however, because Governor Zhu Jiabao (1908-11) kept all the officers whom he suspected of having revolutionary tendencies in Anqing. Xiong then decided to revolt in the provincial capital after a segment of the New Army had been sent to Taihu. His plan was to occupy the city with one squadron of cavalry and one battalion of artillery. The mutinous troops would then march into Nanking in anticipation of support from revolutionaries in other provinces.

The garrison of Anqing consisted of 3854 men. The 1st Battalion of the 2nd Infantry Regiment, 504 strong, were on special deployment in Taihu, while the other two battalions were mostly scattered about in camps to the north of the city. Only two hundred of them were actually inside the city walls. The three battalions of the 1st Infantry Regiment were quartered less than two kilometres to the east of the city, while the cavalry was camped outside the west gate, and the artillery occupied an old fort on the east side of the city on the river bank.

On hearing news of the imperial deaths, Anqing residents circulated rumours of troubles in the city. Governor Zhu hurried back from the manoeuvres, arriving on 18 November. Precautionary measures were taken immediately. On the night of 19 November, Xiong went into action. The artillery major, who had refused to join, was killed. The mutineers then made an attack on the cavalry major, who managed to escape with head wounds. After that the cavalry tried to induce the 2nd Infantry Regiment to join, but the latter refused and remained more or less neutral until the mutiny fizzled out. The cavalry then joined the artillery, which was unable to use the Creuzot guns through lack of ammunition. They tried to force their way into the city, but with no success. Meanwhile, Governor Zhu appeared on the scene, riding a horse in general's uniform, directing the defence of the city, ordering the high officials to come out of their yamens and do their work, keeping the shops open, and calming the fears of the inhabitants. The 1st Regiment remained in the barracks, refusing either to fight or to join the rebels. The old-style provincial troops were then called out, with plenty of ammunition for them. On the following day, the governor was in full control. Owing to his prompt action, the whole affair was confined to just about 800 mutineers (400 infantry, 100 cavalry, 300 artillery) fighting 720 men of the old-style troops. Had the rebels got into the city and captured the armoury, the infantry would probably have joined them.[50]

The mutiny was badly planned and poorly led. The infantry officers who had promised support changed their minds at the last minute. Significantly, most of the officers were still loyal to the government as they were uncertain about the prospects of the revolution, which might be inimical to their career interests. The mutiny was nevertheless serious enough to alarm the authorities. Repressive measures taken by Governor Zhu resulted in the deaths of over three hundred people. Xiong fled to Japan, others to Canton and Hong Kong. The 31st Mixed Brigade was subsequently disbanded and reorganised in order to ensure the loyalty of the troops.[51]

Although the mutiny can be described as a revolutionary attempt, as Xiong seems to have been motivated by revolutionary fervour,

the origin of the trouble must also be traced to the disaffection among
the artillery and cavalry units stationed outside the east gate. As the
North-China Herald reported:

> The officers and non-commissioned officers of these units, it is
> understood, received their training in the same College and on the
> same lines, and influence in high places alone is held to have deter-
> mined the subsequent ranks of the Cadets.[52]

The fact is that the soldiers, deprived of equal opportunities for
self-advancement, were most susceptible to revolutionary influence.

The reconstituted mixed brigade contained about 30 per cent of
the original men. The new lot was exclusively from Anhui itself
(except the officers). Enlistment was popular, and the general commanding officer reported that each vacancy could have been thrice
filled.[53] Many of the officers under suspicion were replaced, and
among the new ones were many officers of the old-style army who
inspired little confidence.[54]

The higher the officers' rank the more incompetent they were. The
brigadier, Yu Dahong from Jiangsu, was educated in the old Nanking
Military School. He went to Japan in 1904 but returned after ten
months' study owing to the outbreak of the Russo-Japanese war. He
squandered considerable funds partly because of his corruption and
partly because of his inefficiency. Other military officials were equally
corrupt, and among them were 'eight venomous snakes' most hated
by the soldiers. In addition to this, the province's financial straits
were creating much unrest. The military school for officers was
closed down, and the salary of the officers was reduced by 20-30 per
cent in July 1911.[55] The men's pay may have been reduced by the
same proportion. In any case this state of affairs sufficed to undermine military morale and facilitated the growth of revolutionary
influence.

The New Army in Jiangxi

The new-style troops in Jiangxi belonged to the 27th Mixed Brigade
(the incomplete 14th Division). One regiment (the 54th), one artillery
battalion, one cavalry squadron, and a transport and engineer corps
were stationed in Nanchang, the provincial capital, and another regiment (the 53rd) of similar strength was maintained in Kiukiang.
Until probably 1909, the regiment in Nanchang was commanded by
a Lieutenant-Colonel Liao, who had studied in Japan for seven years,
had wide experience, and was regarded as a fairly good officer. Four-
fifths of the men in that unit came from Henan, aged between seventeen
and twenty-five, and were active and intelligent looking. They drilled

twice a day and had field exercises twice and target practice once a week. The barracks were in a bad condition and the construction of new ones had been delayed by shortage of funds. There had been considerable desertion for various reasons. The pay of the men was lower than in most other provinces; a first-class soldier only got 4.20 taels a month, and second-class 3.90 taels, and they had to find their own food. Nearly all the officers were graduates of military schools in Wuchang or Nanking, most of them having been to Japan. The 53rd Regiment was in the command of Lieutenant-Colonel Chen Delong from Sichuan, who had studied for two or three years in Japan. Unlike the Nanchang regiment, the officers and men in Kiukiang were mostly natives of the province, although the two battalion commanders were from Hunan and Hubei.[56]

Probably in 1909 Wu Jiezhang, a Jiangsu graduate of the Nanking Military School and former instructor in the Jiangxi Military Preparatory School, was placed in charge of the 27th Mixed Brigade, assisted by two new lieutenant-colonels, Ma Yubao and Qi Baoshan, commanders of the 53rd and 54th Regiments respectively. Many of Wu's former students were appointed as officers, thus replacing those who had come from outside provinces.[57]

The combatant strength of the 27th Mixed Brigade was estimated at 4300 officers and men in 1910, rising to 5324 in 1911. The non-native troops in Nanchang had been substantially replaced by local volunteers. But in physique and general condition the new men were very poor. Those in Kiukiang were much better. Since there were no reserves and the men were not restricted to serving three years, there were many mature men and very few of the young boys so often seen in other armies. They were slovenly and ill turned out, but they were said to be well behaved. The drill in both places was fair, while gymnastics was poor. The men seemed to have firing practice only once a month, and only fifty rounds altogether every year. They did little practical musketry owing to shortage of funds. Brigadier Wu Jiezhang was as inefficient as the regimental commander. On the whole, this Mixed Brigade was one of the worst in the country in terms of quality. Even the few cavalry ponies on parade were in a miserable condition, ill groomed and inadequately fed.[58]

In 1911 the troops further deteriorated both in condition and in numbers as a result of an estimated provincial deficit of 1,780,000 taels. The training of the soldiers was affected and, more importantly, in June of that year the provincial government was compelled to close down some military schools, amalgamate others, and to retrench the men. The extent of retrenchment could not be ascertained, but whatever it was, the situation was bad enough to cause considerable unease among the ranks. At the same time, the salaries of the senior and junior officers were reduced by 30 and 20 per cent respectively, a decrease which coincided with the high rise in the prices of rice and rioting in Nanchang and other parts of the province.[59]

Before 1911 a revolutionary movement was almost non-existent in Jiangxi, and the Tongmenghui activity there was largely limited to the individual efforts of a few activists.[60] Before 1906 there had been several revolutionary societies in the form of study groups, notable among which were the Exchange Knowledge Society *(Yizhihui)* in Nanchang and the Jiangxi Study Society *(Jiangxueshe)* in Kiukiang, but none of these continued after 1906. They were either absorbed into the Tongmenghui, dissolved voluntarily, or banned by the provincial authorities following the Ping-Liu-Li uprising.

There were individual members of the Tongmenghui who attempted to instil revolutionary thought in the local New Army. Prominent among them was Li Liejun, who was later to lead the revolution in Kiukiang in 1911. A native of Jiangxi, Li was educated in the local military preparatory school and later also in the *Shikan gakkō*. Upon his return to Jiangxi in 1909, he served in the 54th Regiment, where the officers were mainly from good family backgrounds, a few being holders of the *lingsheng* and *xiucai* degrees. The regimental commander and the three battalion commanders were Tongmenghui members, and many other officers were Li's former classmates. In 1910 Li was forced to resign following a charge of misappropriation of military funds. He went to Yunnan and obtained a job as instructor in the military officers' school there. In the meantime the 54th Regiment was 'purged' by Governor Feng Rugui (1908-11), resulting in some executions and severe punishments of those who were found to be or suspected of being revolutionaries. Many 'untrustworthy' officers were replaced and the entire regiment was transferred to Pingxiang. A new 55th Regiment was formed by troops of the centre detachment of the Patrol and Defence Force. The troops remaining in Nanchang consisted of only one artillery battalion, one cavalry squadron, the engineers and the transport corps. But they were also unreliable, for there were still a few Tongmenghui members among the officers. In contrast to Nanchang, Kiukiang was relatively free from Tongmenghui influence. None of the officers of the 53rd Regiment seem to have belonged to the Tongmenghui.[61] Yet it was in Kiukiang that the revolution in Jiangxi was first to take place following the Wuchang uprising.

Besides the individual efforts of the officers, there was the activity of the Jiangxi branch of the Society for Common Advancement, formed by Deng Wenhui upon his return from Japan in 1909. Deng made himself the president, assisted by a number of vice-presidents who were teachers of a Nanchang girls' school. About thirty people had joined it by the end of the year. Like other branches elsewhere, it set great store by the secret societies. Propaganda teams were also sent to the countryside during the slack farming seasons, but these piecemeal efforts to enlist peasant support fell far short of a definite program of peasant mobilisation. The attention of the society was quickly focused on the local New Army. Some of its members were sent to infiltrate the troops and the military schools. Direct contact was established with the discontented junior army officers. Unfortunately, there is little further information about the operations of this branch which does not seem to have evolved into an active, cohesive revolutionary organisation like the Society for Common Advancement in the Hubei army. In early 1910, following Deng Wenhui's return to Japan and the subsequent death of one of its more able vice-presidents, the Jiangxi branch became practically defunct.[62]

In Kiukiang's civilian circles there was a reformist society which took the form of a small reading society *(shubaoshe)*. It was founded by Lin Sen, a former revolutionary advocate from Fujian, and Wu Tiecheng, son of the vice-manager of the Kiukiang Chamber of Commerce. It provided newspapers, periodicals and other reading materials from Shanghai and Hong Kong, attracting many interested people from different walks of life, including Qing officials, merchants, educationalists, native bankers, office-workers, and army officers. Reformist ideas were disseminated through the reading materials. The society advocated social reforms such as the abolition of foot-binding and opium-smoking, as well as the improvement of public health and hygiene. In 1910 it supported the petitions organised by the provincial constitutionalists for an early opening of parliament in Peking. Just as the outcome of the petitions had alienated the constitutionalists, so it had convinced Wu Tiecheng and Lin Sen that a more radical attitude towards the dynasty should be taken. Accordingly, the society was changed from reformist to revolutionary. More contacts were developed with the army officers, some of whom were invited to give military instruction to local merchant associations. Lieutenant-Colonel Ma Yubao, who was later to become military governor in Kiukiang, had close connections with Wu, while other members of the New Army also became adherents to the revolutionary cause. In the meantime, liaison was made with revolutionaries in Hubei, particularly Zhan Dabei and He Haiming. To facilitate his work, Wu acted as the Kiukiang correspondent of the *Yangzi News*.[63]

Although there was no plan whatsoever for an uprising, the junior officers in the New Army appeared to be restive, and they later all took part in the revolution in Jiangxi.

The New Army in Jiangsu

Jiangsu was assigned two divisions. The 9th Division began formation in 1904, and was inferior to the Beiyang Army and the 8th Division. The commander, Lieutenant-General Xu Shaozhen, was originally a local expectant *daotai* having little or no military training. He was a drunkard, had tuberculosis, and was notorious for being extremely dishonest. The brigadiers, as well as most other senior officials and staff officers, came from Zhejiang, and had gone through a military course in Japan. The majority of the company officers were natives of Jiangsu who had graduated from the Nanking Military School, while the subalterns were mostly rankers looking old and wizened. Until 1907 the soldiers were predominantly volunteers from Hunan; henceforth they were replaced by conscripts from the southern part of Jiangsu. A substantial number of them were of very poor physique and slovenly. The drill was only moderately good because of insufficient practice.[64] By the end of 1908 the 9th Division was believed to be up to strength, and the whole of it was at Nanking with the exception of the 35th Regiment at Chinkiang and the 36th Regiment at Jiangyin. There was a mixed brigade (designated the 23rd) at Suzhou, which formed the nucleus of the future 12th Division. It had an estimated strength of 2100 men, consisting of the 45th and 46th Regiments (infantry). These troops on the whole were of poor physique, and about half of them looked very young. But at the manoeuvres in Anhui in November 1908, considerable improvement was noticed, and the men looked smarter and better turned out. They were generally well treated and paid regularly, though 'squeezes' were rife regarding fodder and other supplies.[65]

There were four military schools in operation. The Nanking Military School was about to be converted into a military secondary school. The military primary school, which had three hundred indigenous pupils aged from fifteen to twenty, was well established. A third school, the temporary staff training college, was open to officers from Jiangxi, Anhui, and Jiangsu itself, and was attended for three months by all the officers of the 9th Division. Finally, there was a school of military survey which offered a two-year course to twenty students.

In north Jiangsu, which was known administratively as Jiangbei under a special provincial general residing at Qingjiangpu, there was the 13th Mixed Brigade (the nucleus of the future 7th Division),

4500 strong, transferred from Zhengding (in Zhili) in 1906. Most of the officers were from Zhili, Shandong, Anhui, Jiangsu and a few from Henan. The brigadier and the regimental commanders were of 'quite satisfactory bearing, being intelligent in appearance and rather well-informed', while the company officers were inferior material even by Chinese standards. The men were young, healthy and better looking than those in Nanking. However, a section of them had been impertinent on several occasions, and were not as well behaved as soldiers in Hubei and Hunan.[66] The divisional commander was Wang Shizhen, who had succeeded Yinchang in 1907. In 1910 Duan Qirui took over command and became, at the same time, provincial general of Jiangbei. The latter was an important post equivalent to a provincial governorship with both civil and military powers. In that capacity Duan was independent of the Viceroy of Liangjiang and the Governor of Jiangsu, being directly under the Ministry of War as far as his control of the local New Army was concerned. His powers were similar to those of the *dutong*, the Tartar-generals and the military lieutenant-governors at Rehe or Qaha (Kalgan). His appointment was intended to prevent the viceroy from obtaining control over the 13th Mixed Brigade which was originally raised in Zhili. At the time of his appointment, Duan was in command of the 6th Division in Baoding. Under his management, the Jiangbei troops seem to have made substantial progress.[67]

There had always been army disaffection in the lower Yangzi. As early as October 1906 Sir Robert Hart of the Chinese Imperial Customs in Shanghai advised the British legation in Peking of this, adding that Yuan Shikai had anticipated serious trouble in the region and had made some special arrangements for his troops to be sent there at any moment.[68] According to the British consul in Nanking who had spoken to a government official privately on the subject, the whole situation there would depend on how the government might succeed in instilling a spirit of loyalty to the locally levied modern troops who were meant to be a higher class of patriotic soldier. At the time of their recruitment, they were welcomed by 'school processions, waving banners and chanting of patriotic odes'. But they soon found cause for complaint when, contrary to their expectations, they were sent to do the ordinary coolie work of soldiers in peacetime. In July 1906 rioting broke out following a quarrel between soldiers and police, in which the troops disobeyed the orders of their officers.[69] In the summer of 1907 Tieliang informed an American diplomat that while the Beiyang Army was well-disciplined, 'he could not say the same' for the partially disaffected troops of the Yangzi region.[70] In 1908 Captain Leonard reported that there were practically no competent officers with the 9th Division and that the men were 'lawless and entirely undisciplined' and had attempted the lives of two Japanese instructors and threatened those of the Chinese officers sent from the Nanking Military School. Despite the government's efforts to recruit decent youths, many soldiers were still opium smokers. They were by no means modern-drilled and were 'really but *old troops* as yet, except insofar as organization is concerned'. There was also quite an amount of venereal disease and drinking among them, as well as among some officers, including the commanding general himself.[71]

In 1910 the 9th Division became the most notorious of all the New Army divisions in China. On 12 January, serious disaffection in the 36th Regiment stationed in Jiangyin led to the desertion of nearly one hundred men. The cause was reported to have been their dissatisfaction with the restrictions on promotion to non-commissioned rank.[72] Meanwhile, it was also reported that revolutionaries were at work among the Nanking troops, and an anti-dynastic outbreak was expected in June. This prompted the authorities in Nanking to bring in the Patrol and Defence Force from other parts of the province. The conditions became so acute that the viceroy found it necessary to make a speech to the troops and to remove their ammunition and the breech blocks of the guns. It would appear that in the event of an anti-dynastic uprising, the troops were mostly likely to join the revolutionary party.[73]

The army unrest in Nanking was also due, in part, to the differences within the officer corps. There were officers belonging to the *Shikan* clique; others were educated in the local military schools. The latter, who were mainly company officers, resented the fact that all senior positions from battalion commanders upwards were held by young, inexperienced but arrogant cadets returned from Japan. Moreover, the *Shikan* officers had a different life-style from that of the company officers or of the rank and file. For these discontented elements, revolution held out hopes of driving out the returned students and creating new opportunities for their own advancement.[74]

Another cause of discontent was shortage of funds. Early in 1910 in a petition to the viceroy, the army pay department reported a deficit of 690,000 taels for the year.[75] Later in October, there was much agitation among students in the Nanking Military Secondary School when it was announced that all officers who had been granted leave to study in it were to receive only 70 per cent of their normal pay. Previously they had been on full pay, and the change was caused by financial difficulties. The troops were not paid in the following two months, the amount in arrears being in excess of 300,000 taels.

Lieutenant-General Xu Shaozhen was so concerned that he decided to draw on the funds earmarked for 1911, and to withhold the officers' pay, rather than the men's, if necessary.[76]

The troops at Suzhou were also restive. Early in February 1910, a mutiny involving two to three hundred soldiers of the 46th Infantry Regiment broke out there. It stemmed, at first glance, from a trivial matter: that the soldiers were denied admittance to a theatre unless they paid full prices. The soldiers then started wrecking some Japanese shops and attacked four British subjects who were on the scene. Compensation was paid to the foreigners concerned, but the local military authorities failed to deal with the 'unruly soldiery'. On 13 February, a second riot took place, in which a Chinese police officer and several constables were injured. The ultimate cause of the disturbance was, however, not trivial: it was the withholding of the men's pay, which coincided with the fact that there had been a change in the command of the troops and the new general was reputed to be a poor disciplinarian.[77]

Some time later, on 8 March, a mutiny took place in the 13th Mixed Brigade at Qingjiangpu. There had been serious disaffection among the soldiers for a month owing to a reduction of pay and an unduly severe punishment inflicted on a soldier for a minor offence. According to some native newspapers, the mutiny had threatened an entire break-up of the brigade. Asked by foreign diplomats about it, Chinese officials denied that there had been serious mutiny, but admitted that there had been discontent in the regular troops because of their stipends.[78]

This mutiny was premeditated. The sign agreed upon was that the infantrymen were to set fire to their barracks whereupon the men were to rush their officers in charge of the ammunition. Then with machine-guns the mutineers were to sack Qingjiangpu and Huaian and then make for Xuzhou to the north-west. On the evening of 8 March, a lieutenant who was acting sentinel noticed a man pouring kerosene on the roof of the barracks. He shot the man who, when arrested, admitted that a mutiny had been planned. Meanwhile, other mutineers attempted to rush their officers. Some ten ring-leaders were arrested, and officers patrolled the camps throughout the night. The men arrested were released subsequently, for the commanding officer feared that if any of them were punished a general uprising might be precipitated. He also ordered that any men wishing to leave the service be permitted to do so and be given travel allowance to their homes in addition to their pay. Some two hundred men availed themselves of this offer, and no one was punished.[79]

However, the problem of the men's pay was hardly solved. On the contrary, it worsened in the following year as a result of military cut-backs. The 13th Mixed Brigade, which had now expanded into the 7th Division, had its budget reduced by 360,000 taels. By May 1911, the pay had been reduced 20 per cent in the case of officers and 10 per cent in the case of non-commissioned officers and men. The junior officers were further impoverished by the demand of the Ministry of War for a change of uniform to conform with Peking's regulations. After all sorts of deductions, little was left for them to support their families.[80] In Suzhou the military cut-back for the same year was well over 200,000 taels, a situation which was aggravated by the corruption already rampant among the senior officers regarding the troops' pay.[81]

As far as revolutionary activity was concerned, there were a few radical officers in the 9th Division. Before 1907 they had rallied behind Zhao Sheng. A native of Jiangsu and an early graduate of the Nanking Military School, Zhao had been in Japan for a short period of time and met a few Chinese revolutionaries there. After his return to China, he had taught in Shanghai and Changsha until 1905 when he was appointed recruiting officer of the 9th Division and later promoted to company officer. Through his influence a number of educated men had been recruited into the officer corps. Through sheer ability he quickly rose to the command of the 33rd Regiment. At his initiative, a recreational club was formed to serve as a meeting place of soldiers sympathetic to the revolutionary cause. During drill and field practices, he often spoke on the Taiping movement, the national crisis, and topics which lent themselves to anti-dynastic interpretations. It was claimed (certainly with gross exaggeration) that he had a following of 20,000 including soldiers and students, and that he was awaiting an opportune moment to revolt jointly with the armies of Anhui and Jiangxi. In late 1906 or early 1907 he was dismissed by Viceroy Duanfang for promoting revolution among his troops.[82] After his departure for Guangdong in 1907, there was no one in Jiangsu capable of leading and organising the revolutionary elements in the local army. But this did not alter the fact, as the British consul in Nanking observed, that the New Army was 'reputed to be honeycombed with sedition'.[83]

The New Army in Zhejiang
The New Army in this province was designated the 21st Division, which was still incomplete by 1911 although it had been given a divisional staff. It remained a mixed brigade consisting of one infantry brigade, one cavalry squadron, one artillery battalion, and one

company each of engineers and transport, all stationed in Hangchow. As usual the troops were under the governor of the province as nominal commander-in-chief and subject to the authority of the Ministry of War as regards details of organisation. Governor Zhang Zengyi (1905-7) from Zhili was a nephew of Zhang Zhidong and had allegedly shown favouritism by appointing a wholly incompetent relative Li Yizhi as Lieutenant-Colonel of the 1st Regiment. Li was in his thirties, totally ignorant of military affairs and appearing anything but martial as he was always in civilian official robes. He had a great reputation for beating soldiers, which caused many men to desert and join the 2nd Regiment, where the troops were properly treated. The 2nd Regiment was commanded by Lieutenant-Colonel Jiang Zungui, a native of Zhejiang, who had been in Japan for five years and was reputed to be a 'very good man'. There was considerable friction between Jiang and Li, as well as between the men of those regiments themselves.[84]

When Pereira visited the 1st Regiment in June 1907, he learned that the troops drilled twice daily, for an hour each time. The drill was good on the whole, but the gymnastic exercise was not equal to that of the Beiyang divisions. He also observed that: 'In marching the lines were uneven, distances badly kept, the men often looked on the ground and did not keep their arms back when halted. They are supposed to keep a distance of 80 centimetres between front and rear rank, though they were usually closer'.[85] There was no hospital but there were two doctors (it is not clear whether for the whole regiment or for each battalion). One of them, a surgeon-lieutenant, was trained in the local missionary hospital, and the other was a native practitioner. In 1910 Pereira's successor, Lieutenant-Colonel Willoughby, found more doctors there, half foreign trained and half trained in the Chinese style. There was also a fairly well stocked dispensary and store of Chinese drugs.[86]

Between 1906 and 1909 there were some revolutionary efforts to win converts among the troops of the 1st and 2nd Regiments. Lieutenant-Colonel Jiang Zungui was a member of the Restoration Society *(Guangfuhui)* and the Tongmenghui, and had been involved in the Chinese student radicalism of 1903 in Japan. Under his command the 2nd Regiment established a new officer corps composed of educated young men. He helped found the local military schools, and it was due to his influence that some of the students joined the Restoration Society. In 1907 he was implicated in the revolt of Qiu Jin, who had recruited many adherents from the 2nd Regiment and the military schools. Consequently, when the two regiments later combined to form the 41st Mixed Brigade, Jiang, contrary to his expectations, was not appointed to its command. The hostility of the new brigadier, Yang Shande, forced him to resign. After his departure for Guangxi in 1909, revolutionary subversion in the Zhejiang army ceased almost completely.[87]

Another notable military figure in Zhejiang who was considered to be sympathetic to the revolutionary cause was Wu Yuanzhi, director of the military preparatory school. Wu, a native of Jiangsu, held a *jinshi* degree. Although he appeared to be a quiet person, he was believed to have supported revolution indirectly by exhorting his students to become national heroes and to avenge China's national humiliations. Many students appear to have been influenced by him.

One of them was Huang Fu, an outstanding student, who was awarded a scholarship to study in *Shinbu gakkō* even before he had completed his course in the military preparatory school. After finishing a course in *Shinbu gakkō*, Huang enrolled in a special school for military surveying. While in Japan he joined the Tongmenghui and the Iron and Blood Man Corps, which, it will be recalled, was formed by Huang Xing for revolutionary purposes. On his annual home leave, he often spoke to his colleagues on Japanese politics and the international situation. He had translated some Japanese war histories into Chinese and showed them to his colleagues to stimulate their national consciousness. After graduating from Japan, Huang was appointed to the General Staff Council in Peking. But he still regularly kept in touch with radicals in Zhejiang and Jiangsu.[88]

On the whole, revolutionary subversion of the Zhejiang army made little headway. Neither Jiang Zungui, Wu Yuanzhi nor Huang Fu made much impact on the local soldiery. In fact, the revolutionary movement in Zhejiang had already been in eclipse since the abortive uprisings of Xu Xilin and Qiu Jin in 1907.[89] Nevertheless, there were many discontented elements and revolutionary sympathisers among the middle-grade and junior officers, who were divided into two groups, the 'radicals' and the 'moderates' on the eve of the revolution in Zhejiang.[90]

In Zhejiang, as elsewhere, the financial problem produced a demoralising effect on the troops. In late 1910 the provincial government found it impossible to meet its annual military quota of 300,000 taels, and made a plea to Peking for a reduction of 50 per cent, as it was difficult enough to maintain its own army. Severe economy was exercised, which caused desertions to multiply. On every Monday, which was a military holiday, at least one desertion was reported from every platoon. Over one-third of the new recruits were from outside provinces; 20 per cent of them did not have their backgrounds carefully checked by military officials through lack of time. This resulted in many dismissals, but in the next round of recruitment, the same problem arose again.[91] More serious was the fact that there were difficulties in paying the troops. In mid-1911 the stipends of senior officers were reduced by 20 per cent and the company officers by 30 per cent. It is not clear how much the men were affected, but in any case they were the worst of the lot, since they also suffered from the widespread corruption which existed among the senior officers.[92]

Besides this, the rank and file had another cause for complaint. About two-thirds of their officers were from Beiyang divisions and schools, and one-third from Jiangsu, while the men were local conscripts.[93] Not only were the latter unable to establish good relations with the officers owing to their different geographical backgrounds, but they found that their career prospects were affected by the presence of extra-provincials in the entire officer rank.

Summary

In short, the discontent which existed in the Yangzi armies was the outcome of a variety of grievances such as corruption among the officers, maltreatment of the men, diminishing promotion prospects, retrenchment of troops, rising prices of rice and other foodstuffs, reduction in pay, and so on, grievances which were exploited by the revolutionaries and which became increasingly intolerable towards the end of the dynasty. Both officers and men had their own frustrations and grievances, albeit for different reasons. The officers came from the lower gentry class. And so did some sections of the rank and file. The fact that the majority of the common soldiers were of peasant origin and were sympathetic with the rural masses did not necessarily mean that the army disaffection represented 'peasant discontent' as Hatano Yoshihiro has assumed.[94]

Of all the factors contributing to army unrest, the government's inability to pay the troops fully and regularly proved to be the most important. The Ministry of War was acutely aware of the danger of withholding the troops' pay, and had ordered severe penalties for any delinquencies in this respect. However, financial constraints had caused the provincial authorities to ignore the order in many instances.[95]

Low morale bred indiscipline, which in turn contributed to the military riots of 1910. The authorities in Peking and the provinces alike seemed to be afraid of the troops, and were reluctant to punish promptly and severely breaches of discipline, or to uphold the authority of the officers. Consequently, officers feared to take drastic disciplinary actions against the offenders, and the men in many units were beyond control.[96] Furthermore, friction between the 'unruly soldiers' and the police was common. The Ministry of War had hoped to reduce such friction by organising a modern police force on the Japanese model. But up to 1910 this police force was not widely established, and the relations between some sections of the soldiery and the civil constabulary remained strained.[97]

In these circumstances revolutionary seeds found fertile soil in the barracks. The disaffected troops had no affection for the Manchu dynasty and were inclined to blame the government for the social unrest of which they were part. It was not surprising, then, that the Yangzi armies were later to be the first to respond to the Wuchang uprising in collaboration with the provincial assemblies or the revolutionary leaders.

SEVEN

The New Army in south and north China

IN DEALING with south China this chapter confines itself to Guangdong, where Tongmenghui revolutionaries were diligently at work,
and Yunnan, where nationalistic officers did much to spread revolutionary ideas among the troops. As regards north China, the focus
of attention is on the Beiyang Army, which, by 1911, was distributed
in the metropolitan area and the three north-eastern provinces. The
Beiyang Army was supposed to be the bulwark of the imperial
authorities. The extent to which it was subverted by the revolutionaries
was relatively insignificant. However, it was not entirely free from
the discontent and political agitation which undermined the loyalty
of many troops.

The case of Guangdong

According to the imperial plan, Guangdong was to establish two
divisions, one as a beginning and the other depending on future
financial resources. Expansion was extremely slow. In 1906 the
viceroy's bodyguard was transformed into the first two regiments
(3000 strong). There were only infantrymen. Artillery, engineers and
transport units were expected to come into existence in 1907 when
the officers under instruction for these branches in the local military
school had completed their courses. As the province was hilly, cavalry
was considered to be of minor importance. In fact, no cavalry force
was raised for some years. The soldiers were mostly from Anhui and
Sichuan, others from the borders of Guangxi and Yunnan, but few
were natives of Guangdong. They were usually between sixteen and
twenty years of age. There was no age limit on the years of service,
as Acting Viceroy Cen Chunxuan (1903-6) believed that if active men
were discharged without a job to return to, they would become
robbers. There were two or three cases of desertion in 1906. The
fugitives were captured and beheaded, and this seems to have exercised
a deterrent effect on the remaining troops.[1]

Two schools were in operation in 1906. The military officers'
school in Canton had 180 students, 60 for infantry and 40 each for
engineers, artillery and transport, under the instruction of three

captains. Admission was by examination in Chinese literature with an elementary test in mathematics and chemistry. There were two Chinese directors, but the actual instruction was given by Japanese officers who were assisted by Chinese colleagues. The military preparatory school at Huangpu (Whampoa) had 120 students who went through a five-year course, of which two years were in primary instruction. The youngest students were on average fourteen years old, whilst the oldest ones were twenty-six. Between twenty and thirty of them had been expelled for bad conduct.

In late 1906 the military preparatory school was transferred to Canton and merged with the officers' school to form the military intensive school. In 1909 it was converted into a staff training college, which offered a one-year course for the training of senior officers. Earlier, a military primary school had been opened in Huangpu. The plan to establish a military secondary school in Canton was never put into effect.[2]

Early in 1907 Viceroy Zhou Fu (1906-7) started to form a new regiment partly by using some of the troops of the existing two regiments and partly by training raw recruits. This new unit was to be a model for the New Army in Canton. It was required that the new recruits be natives of the province, literate and healthy. Territorial enlistment, which Acting Viceroy Cen Chunxuan had ignored, was to be enforced. Conscription, however, was to be discouraged, as volunteers were considered to be more highly motivated. Recruiting officers were to visit the prefectures and meet local officials who were to afford them such assistance as might be necessary. Before their arrival, local officials were to speak to the youths in their localities on their military obligations to the state. Anyone wishing to enlist was to furnish details of his family background, his personal particulars and the names of his guarantors. Successful candidates were to reside in the recruiting depot and receive a daily allowance, while awaiting transport to Canton.[3]

By then a provincial war board had been set up. Seeing that the troops, particularly the artillery and the engineers, were of an inferior quality, Zhou Fu merged all the infantry troops into two regiments, each of three battalions (plus a student-soldier battalion). Promising privates were selected for training in infantry, engineering and transport duties, so that they could serve as sergeants and corporals. In late 1907 a review of the troops showed that some of them were still not up to the expected standard. The unsatisfactory ones were subsequently dismissed, with the result that each regiment was reduced to two battalions. Some time later, however, a new recruitment campaign was launched to increase the strength of the troops.[4]

Early in 1908 Zhou Fu was succeeded by Zhang Mingqi as Viceroy of Liangguang (1908-11). One of the first things Zhang did upon assumption of office was to effect some significant changes in the provincial war board. In an effort to improve its efficiency, he appointed three able men, Han Guojun and Fu Wentong, both from Henan, and Li Zhexiang from Hubei, as directors of the three departments in the war board. It was Zhang's plan to raise three new infantry battalions so as to bring the New Army in Canton to the strength of a mixed brigade. Afterwards, another four battalions of artillery, engineers and transport were to be formed. The mixed brigade envisaged by the viceroy was estimated to cost 600,000 taels annually. To save money for it, the Green Standard troops were to be substantially retrenched (by at least 70 per cent) in the following years.[5]

The number of new-style troops rose from 2800 men at the end of 1907[6] to 5600 in 1910, compared with (also in 1910) 38,729 men in the Patrol and Defence Force, 7550 Bannermen and 4829 Green Standard troops scattered over the province.[7] A United States military officer put the full strength of the Canton New Army (the incomplete 25th Division consisting of three regiments) at 6400, adding that the actual fighting strength was much less.[8] In 1911, though still a mixed brigade, it was given a divisional staff.[9]

After 1907 enlistment in the New Army was quite popular, and efforts to attract educated youths to the service were fairly successful. By 1910 most of the troops were natives of Guangdong, and many were imbued with a sense of patriotism which they shared with the civil students. Some had enlisted in the knowledge that they would have to fight and probably die for their country, but they did not fear death and pledged to devote themselves to the cause of China.[10]

As Edward Rhoads has documented, many reforms were instituted in Guangdong in the post-Boxer decade. There was, at the same time, a Tongmenghui-led revolutionary movement which was strong and active during 1905-7 and weak and divided in 1911.[11] As far as subversion of the local army was concerned, the Tongmenghui movement was remarkably unsystematic and ineffectual. What little revolutionary activity there was during 1906-8 was concentrated in the rural towns outside Canton and restricted to recruiting a couple of army commanders. No attempt was made to enlist support from the junior officers or to go to the ranks.

During these years Huang Xing had approached detachment commander Guo Renzhang personally on several occasions. Huang met Guo in Shanghai in the autumn of 1904, and since then they had developed a good friendship. In early 1906 Huang went to see Guo in Guilin, where the latter was in command of the Patrol and Defence Force. Guo refused to make any overt move on the grounds that he was not on good terms with his colleague, Cai E, who was then super-intendent of the local military primary school. Huang tried in vain to mediate between them. In May 1907 when another uprising was being plotted at Qinzhou (in south-west Guangdong), Huang again went to see Guo, who had been transferred there. Meanwhile, Hu Yisheng, brother of Hu Hanmin, was instructed to call on Zhao Sheng, then regimental commander of the troops stationed tem-porarily at neighbouring Lianzhou. Zhao had come to Canton after he had been dismissed from the 9th Division. He then joined the Canton New Army as a lieutenant-colonel and also enrolled in the Tongmenghui. Yet, in spite of his revolutionary zeal, Zhao, like Guo, indicated that his troops would support the uprising only if a 'respectable' revolutionary army was formed. This probably meant that unless the commanders of other units had agreed to revolt, they would not be the first to do so. At the time of the uprising in September, Guo was unimpressed by the insurgent forces. Zhao, seeing Guo's reluctance to act, also decided against supporting what appeared to be a poorly organised and militarily weak movement.[12]

In January 1908 Huang and Tan Renfeng appealed to Guo a third time. Guo promised them support, but he changed his mind later when the revolt which occurred in March appeared to have no prospects of success. In the autumn of that year, the Tongmenghui leaders tried to instigate a mutiny in the Canton New Army, but it was later found that Zhao Sheng's 1st Regiment was not quite prepared. This prompted them to turn to the Patrol and Defence Force, which had many secret society elements in the ranks, in an attempt to stage the abortive 'Protect Asia' mutiny.[13] All these events showed that recruiting army support required more than just a few friendly approaches to the commanders, and that sympathetic as they were, no commanders would be inclined to turn against the government until the insurgent forces appeared to have extremely good chances of succeeding.

Apart from these approaches, there were individual efforts by a few frustrated students, who had been expelled from the military preparatory school for bad conduct and poor academic performance, to proselytise the Canton troops. Their revolutionary behaviour was due partly to their failure in school and partly to the influence of the Tongmenghui, in which they had enrolled. They engaged in propa-ganda work among the students in the military schools, as a result of which thirty to forty military students joined the Tongmenghui.[14] However, these individual efforts fell far short of recruiting from within the rank and file of the army, nor did they constitute an organised movement of revolutionary subversion.

Such a movement did not begin until 1909 when the South China Bureau of the Tongmenghui *(Nanfang zhibu)* was set up in Hong Kong. From then on, there was a division of labour between the bureau and the Tongmenghui Hong Kong branch, which had been formed in 1907 with Feng Ziyou as the director. The bureau was now responsible for military subversion and operations in Guangdong, while the branch devoted itself to party affairs and recruitment of new members in Hong Kong.[15]

Hu Hanmin, who was in charge of the bureau, chose Zhao Sheng to be his lieutenant. Although he had lent no material support to the revolts of 1907-8 Zhao had engaged in disseminating revolutionary ideas among the troops, which resulted in his dismissal in early 1909. He then went to Hong Kong and entered Hu's service. Since he was no longer in the army, he had to rely on an old friend, Ni Yingdian. A graduate of the Nanking Military School, Ni once served as a junior artillery officer in the 9th Division. He was later transferred to Anhui, where he was implicated in the Xiong Chengji mutiny. He then fled to Hong Kong and joined the Tongmenghui there. Under an assumed name, he obtained a post in Canton as platoon chief in the 2nd Artillery Regiment.[16]

Ni, then, became the revolutionary organiser within the Canton New Army. His propaganda focused on the racial, anti-Manchu theme, stressing the Manchu ascendancy in the Peking government, and attacking the current constitutional reforms as a fraud. He claimed that the revolutionary cause had gained wide support from students, teachers, scholars, the native press, merchants and government officials. He also planned to organise the revolutionary soldiers along the New Army lines, with brigade, regimental and battalion commanders. He made himself the brigadier of the revolutionary troops. Each revolutionary soldier received a Tongmenghui membership certificate printed in Hong Kong, which recorded his personal particulars and the date of admission and was promised a stipend of 10 *yuan* on enrolment, though the payment was delayed owing to lack of funds. Material incentive was offered. For example, an active and diligent comrade could expect to be rewarded with a watch or some similar gift. Those who had recruited ten comrades were awarded a superior medal *(youdeng xunzhang)*, and those who had canvassed one hundred or more received an extraordinary medal *(youdeng tebie xunzhang)*. Others were promised promotion once the Manchus were overthrown. Anyone who could instigate a certain section of the army to revolt would be appointed to its command.[17] This had a

stimulating effect on the junior officers and privates who had expectations and personal ambitions. On the other hand, the revolutionary zeal of some of them seemed to be conditional upon what
they could get out of it.

On the submission of Ni Yingdian, the South China Bureau adopted
ten rules for military subversion. The avowed objective was to mobilise
'promptly and realistically' all the armed forces in Canton, new and
old troops and the naval forces alike. Three centres were to be set up
which were to be responsible to the bureau. In fact, the bureau
appointed their executives and financed their operations. Recruitment was to begin with those with sergeant *(bianmu)* standing, in the
belief that they would be in a good position to influence the rank
and file. No date was fixed for revolution, but the rule stipulated
that comrades were to be prepared at all times for a general uprising.[18]

The Guangdong subversive pattern differed from the Hubei one in
at least three ways. First, the Cantonese revolutionaries paid as much
attention to the Patrol and Defence Force as to the New Army because
of the great numerical disparity between them. It appeared that even
if the whole of the New Army was won over, the old-style troops, if
they were hostile, would still be strong enough to defend Canton. It
would be useful, therefore, to enlist the support of both kinds of troops.
In Hubei, by contrast, the revolutionaries had reason to concentrate
on the New Army, which had a strength of 16,104 men, compared
with 9539 Bannermen, 7262 Green Standard troops and 7600 in
the Patrol and Defence Force.[19] Once the New Army was won over,
the old-style troops would be easy to deal with.

Second, subversion in Canton was directed and financed by the
South China Bureau, where the prime movers were civilians, even
though some of them had served in the army. The revolutionary
soldiers were thus controlled by a civilian body from which they
were physically separated. Ni Yingdian worked with a few teachers
and students in Canton, and was required to report regularly to
Hong Kong, where Hu Hanmin and Zhao Sheng were the decision-
makers.[20] In Hubei the revolutionary soldiers were not directed by
any organisation *outside* the army, and this prevented a communication gap between leaders and followers from developing. Such a gap
existed in Canton, and it proved to be a serious shortcoming, as will
be shown very shortly.

The third aspect in which Guangdong was different from Hubei
was the role of the subalterns and sergeants who were in the main
graduates from the local military schools. Ni Yingdian took full
advantage of the fact that the commissioned officers were either
appointed from Peking or recruited from among the Japanese-

educated cadets, and that a locally educated soldier could rarely be promoted to the commissioned ranks.[21]

Because Ni Yingdian had to commute regularly between Canton and Hong Kong, his activities attracted the attention of the military authorities. Between June and November 1909 a number of soldiers including Ni himself were dismissed on suspicion of promoting revolution. At this time 3000 soldiers of the New Army were said to have joined the Tongmenghui. The revolutionaries then decided to stage a revolt during the Chinese New Year holiday beginning on 10 February 1910. The New Army was to take the lead, to be supported by the Patrol and Defence Force and an auxiliary commando force composed of natives of the province. The date was set for 24 February. On Chinese New Year's eve some soldiers of the 2nd and 3rd Regiments clashed with the police over a trivial matter, and several of them were detained for some hours. On the following day the soldiers attacked the police. To prevent further trouble, the military authorities cancelled the New Year holiday. After failing to get this order rescinded, the soldiers instigated disturbances.[22]

Worried that the clash with the police might upset his plan, Ni Yingdian, who was able to remain in Canton to carry out his work in spite of his dismissal, left for Hong Kong immediately for consultation with the South China Bureau. He suggested an earlier uprising on the grounds that the soldiers were getting out of control. The bureau then resolved to revolt on 15 February. Ni was sent back to Canton at once, while Huang Xing, Zhao Sheng and Hu Hanmin promised to join him later. However, owing to the suspension of ferry services on 10 February, Ni could not return to Canton until the 12th. By the time he got back, several hundred troops of the 1st Regiment had already mutinied. He had no choice but to go along with them, leading 1000 men to attack the viceroy's yamen. But they were outnumbered by the loyalist troops commanded by General Li Zhun. Ni was killed, and on the following day the city was brought under government control.

The failure of the mutiny reflected the basic shortcomings of a civilian-controlled military movement, especially in a situation where the revolutionary organisation did not exist within the army itself. The Tongmenghui leaders in Hong Kong had failed to achieve sufficient party control over the revolutionary troops in Canton. Consequently, when an abrupt change in the local situation caused a breakdown in communication, the soldiers, unrestrained by party leaders or by an organisation of their own, took matters into their own hands. The gap between Hong Kong and Canton, as well as between civilian leaders and the military rank and file, rendered it difficult for the men in the barracks to effect the decision taken by the bureau chiefs.

The most spectacular episode in the Guangdong revolutionary movement was yet to come: the Canton uprising of April 1911. The story of this uprising has been told and retold.[23] Here it will suffice to make a few interesting points. First, the New Army did not turn against the government as had been expected by the Tongmenghui leaders. Second, the Patrol and Defence Force was quick to defend the city against the civilian assault units. Third, this uprising was the last in a series of military attempts made in south China before the revolution. While it was a great shock to the imperial government, its failure dealt a serious blow to revolutionary morale in Guangdong. Zhao Sheng died in Hong Kong, disappointed. Even stalwarts like Huang Xing and Hu Hanmin despaired of the future of revolution. Huang was so disheartened that for four months he did not care to write to anyone personally. At one time he even contemplated committing suicide on hearing that his friend, Yang Shouren, had killed himself. By its own admission, the Tongmenghui was unable to launch another uprising for five years.

Although the new-style troops did not support the uprising, they were suspected of being in sympathy with the revolutionary movement and were little trusted by the viceroy. Before the uprising, they had been hustled out of the city and sent to guard the crops outside the east gate. Had they gone over to the revolutionaries, their superior equipment would have been of great advantage to them. As the American vice-consul-general in Canton put it: 'They [the New Army] constitute, more probably than not, less a source of safety than of danger to Canton'.[24]

The Patrol and Defence Force commanded by General Li Zhun were the best drilled and best equipped troops that the Canton government could rely on in case of mutiny or revolution. They numbered 4500 men (excluding those stationed outside Canton), divided into fifteen battalions, and their loyalty was well tested during the uprising. Following the trouble, 2700 similar troops had been brought in from Guangxi under their provincial commander-in-chief, Long Jiguang. They were quite as efficient as their Guangdong counterparts and, being from a different province, were thought to be useful in dealing with disturbances in Canton.[25] In mid-August, after the attempted assassination of General Li Zhun by the revolutionaries, the New Army was broken up and dispersed in various parts of the province, thus leaving only a few battalions in Canton.[26]

The case of Yunnan

Under the New Army scheme: Yunnan was to form two divisions. Up to 1907, however, military affairs in the province were in a deplorable state. Viceroy Ding Zhenduo (1904-7) was a corrupt and inefficient administrator who gave little attention to army matters. Nearly all the troops were members of the Green Standard, and it was not until 1905 that half-hearted efforts were made to reform the New Army in Kunming. An infantry regiment of three battalions and one artillery battalion of quarter strength, about 1500 men in all, were organised and put in the charge of a local *daotai*.[27] They were of poor quality, and their strength did not increase noticeably during Ding's remaining years in office.

When Xiliang, a Mongol Bannerman, succeeded Ding as Viceroy of Yungui in May 1907, he found on his arrival in Kunming that the so-called new-style soldiers were the result of a change of name rather than of substance. They were often mixed up with the old troops, and there were few modern weapons ready for their use. As no barracks had been constructed, the troops walked around in the streets at night, and were no better disciplined than the 'old braves'. Furthermore, the military schools had no modern-educated teachers, and everything was in a disorderly state.[28]

Xiliang, who had had some success in reorganising the army of Sichuan, where he was viceroy in 1903-7, was determined to eliminate 'the evils' of the Yunnan military establishment. He subsequently removed much of the corruption by replacing the incompetent officers with able and honest ones who had both civil and military experience. A number of modern-educated instructors and students trained in Sichuan were appointed to responsible positions. Chief among them was Chen Yi, a Hubei graduate of the Wuchang Military Preparatory School, who had studied in Japan and held the position of assistant director of the Sichuan Military Preparatory School before being appointed to the command of the Yunnan New Army.[29]

Xiliang had also brought with him a battalion of well-disciplined new-style troops from Sichuan. Of these, one hundred or so formed the bodyguard. There was, too, a battalion of troops from Canton, sent through Guangxi by Acting Viceroy Cen Chunxuan in anticipation of his transfer to Kunming, which did not come off. There were many deserters from both battalions, because they considered their pay was not enough to compensate for separation from their families.[30]

Under Xiliang's administration, the Yunnan New Army made appreciable progress. He was resolved to organise at least one full-strength division, which was to be financed separately, without having to demobilise all the old-style troops which were still considered to be useful in maintaining local law and order. He established a surveying school and a leather works. He built new barracks, a magnificent training ground, as well as a large fortified camp outside the city of Kunming.[31]

In the space of only six or seven months following his assumption of office, the strength of the New Army in Kunming was increased to 3125 men consisting of four infantry battalions and one artillery battalion. But there were neither cavalry units nor transport corps. Two-fifths of the troops were from other provinces, and were armed with Mauser rifles and supported by forty to fifty mountain guns. Some drilling went on every day, and at least in theory, each soldier attended twice daily. Production in the local arsenal was restored, turning out cartridges of the Mauser pattern. It was expected to resume the manufacture of rifles and mountain guns, which had ceased for some time during the previous administration of Ding Zhenduo.[32]

Military education received considerable attention from Xiliang. Better teachers were appointed. At the end of 1907 the military preparatory school had two hundred cadets, divided into two classes. No tuition fees were paid. However, should any student abscond or retire before completing the course, his parents would be required to reimburse the school. The intensive military school had one hundred students, aged between eighteen and thirty, who received instruction in manoeuvres, army discipline, arithmetic, Chinese ballistics, signalling, and so on. No foreign languages were offered probably because of a dearth of qualified language teachers. In 1908 Xiliang established a military officers' school, which began to train a new generation of Yunnanese army cadets. Considerable energy was being shown in promoting military efficiency, which convinced a senior British diplomat in Kunming that 'more sincere interest is being taken in this than in any other of the reforms on Western lines'.[33]

By 1909 the 19th Division in Kunming had been formed, and was believed to be up to strength. One regiment was stationed at Dachangba outside the north city gate, another at Wujiaba outside the south gate, a third at Li'an (fifty-three kilometres to the north-west of Mengzi), and a fourth at Dali. Each regiment was made up of three battalions of about five hundred men each. There were three battalions of mountain artillery, which were expected to be equipped with fifty-four Krupp mountain guns of the latest 75 mm pattern when the troops had been properly instructed in their use. There were a few engineers, who were of an inferior quality. The transport corps was still not organised owing to difficulties in procuring suitable animals, harnesses and saddles.[34]

The men were paid fully and regularly, looking clean and well-fed. Discipline was good. Probably on Xiliang's insistence, flogging had been abolished, although the officers often complained that the Yunnanese, being, in their opinion, more or less savages, required corporal punishment to enforce discipline.

The vast majority of the officers were from outside provinces and had been trained either in Peking or Tientsin, and a few had been to Japan. Major-General Cui Xiangkui from Anhui had succeeded Chen Yi as the division commander after the latter had followed Xiliang to Manchuria in 1909. Cui had spent fifteen years in military training in north China, and had lived in Japan for two years. He was a strict disciplinarian, able and energetic, and was highly regarded by Xiliang, to whom he owed his appointment in late 1908. The young brigadier, Zhang Yi, was inefficient, and the chief of staff, Colonel Zhang Qingtai, lacked the military spirit of a good officer. The other officers appeared to dislike service in Yunnan and some, including a colonel, had resigned. A couple of them had deliberately committed offences so as to get themselves dismissed. Others had been refused resignation pending the arrival of the new viceroy, Li Jingxi.

Viceroy Li Jingxi (1909-11) shared the reformist zeal of his predecessor. However, owing to financial difficulties, he had no intention of raising a second division. Rather, he insisted that the quality of the 19th Division be improved.[35] His efforts in the following years proved to be fairly successful. Lieutenant (retired) C. Klatt of the German army, who observed the manoeuvres of the Yunnan army in 1909 and again in 1911, was impressed by the remarkable progress made in such a short time, in spite of some tactical errors due to the inexperience of the officers.[36]

Territorial enlistment was in force vigorously. By 1910 all the soldiers were natives of the province. Most of them were conscripts, paid on the same scale as in north China. More significantly, an increasing number of Yunnanese cadets were appointed as officers, to replace those from outside provinces who had no heart in their work. In that year about 50 per cent of the officers were Yunnanese, 25 per cent from Sichuan and the remainder from central and north China. However, it must be pointed out that while the company officers were Yunnanese, the senior ones were still extra-provincials.[37]

Nevertheless, significant changes were taking place in the military personnel. Already in the year before, Li Genyuan, a Japanese-educated Yunnanese cadet, had been appointed director of the military officers' school. Shortly afterwards, Luo Peijin, another Yunnanese military cadet educated in Japan, became principal of the military primary school through Li Genyuan's influence. Both Li and Luo were members of the Tongmenghui, and had been politically active in Japan. Both had been invited to serve in Guangxi, but neither of them found Guangxi an interesting place to work in. Both came from good family backgrounds, both held a *shengyuan* degree, and both appeared to have radical tendencies.[38]

A more prominent figure who appeared on the local scene at the same time was Cai E, the new commander of the 37th Brigade. Cai, a Hunanese with a *shengyuan* degree, studied in a Japanese military preparatory school in 1901, and enlisted in the 2nd Japanese Cavalry Regiment upon graduation. In 1903 he was admitted to the *Shikan gakkō*. During his studies in Japan, he had been actively associated with Chinese reformist and revolutionary groups there. He was, as will be recalled, a firm believer in Chinese militarism, concerning himself seriously with China's national crisis. After graduating from the *Shikan gakkō* in 1904, he had served successively in the Jiangxi, Hunan and Guangxi armies. He had spent five years in Guangxi, where he held concurrently a few important training and commanding posts. It was at the invitation of Viceroy Li Jingxi that he came to Yunnan. Like Li Genyuan and Luo Peijin, he was a member of the Tongmenghui.[39]

Because he enjoyed the confidence of the viceroy, Cai was able to make some new appointments and promotions in 1911 in favour of the Japanese-educated officers. On his recommendation Qu Tongfeng was promoted from the command of the 74th Regiment to that of the 38th Brigade, and the position vacated by him was filled by Luo Peijin. As well as receiving commissions, the returned students had a controlling influence in the military officers' school. Of the twenty-nine instructors and administrators there in 1911, twenty-four were graduates of the *Shikan gakkō*, and three were from the Japanese surveying school. The educational backgrounds of the remaining two are unknown.[40]

Many of these returned students were Yunnanese. Of the eleven regimental and battalion commanders in the 37th Brigade, seven were natives, one was from Sichuan, one from Henan, one from Hunan, and the origin of the other one is unknown.[41] However, it must be noted that no Yunnanese had been appointed to the rank of lieutenant-colonel and above. Major-General Zhong Lintong, who had replaced Cui Xiangkui as the division commander, was from Shandong. Cai E, as we have seen, was a Hunanese. Brigadier Qu Tongfeng was from Henan. Jin Yunpeng, the chief army councillor *(lujun zongcanyi)* was a Shandong man and former subordinate of Duan Qirui. In fact, a good many commissioned officers were from Shandong. As a whole, these northern officers were still an important force to be reckoned with in the politics of the Yunnan army. At the same time, there was ill feeling between the Yunnanese and non-Yunnanese officers, just as there were differences between the *Shikan* group and the Beiyang group.[42]

The Japanese-educated officers and instructors played an important part in the dissemination of revolutionary ideas among the troops in Yunnan. The military officers' school was the centre of revolutionary agitation. William Johnson has listed ten instructors and administrators, of whom seven were active members of the Tongmenghui.[43] There were three classes in the school. Class 'A' consisted of officers from the rank of major to lieutenant who were selected from the 19th Division. The 'B' class was drawn from officers of equivalent rank from the Patrol and Defence Force, and class 'C' offered instruction to graduates of civil, middle and higher schools. In addition to these, there was a special supplementary class composed of graduates of the teachers' college, as well as the best officers of the military schools who were attached to the regular army units. The courses were all for one year, at the end of which graduates of classes A and B returned to their duties with the troops.[44]

Some of the instructors were outspoken revolutionary advocates, and they inculcated a sense of patriotism and nationalism in the students. One of them often talked about Yue Fei, the Song military hero who had fought against the invasion of the *Jin* (Jurchin). Others told stories about late Ming patriots who had died in defence of China against the Manchu Bannermen. Still others were fond of speaking of the revolutionary movement led by Sun Yat-sen. At the same time, propaganda materials, including the *People's Journal (Minbao)*, the Tongmenghui party organ, were read in the school.[45]

The nationalism of the radical officers and instructors was more anti-imperialist than racially anti-Manchu. Yunnan, a border region threatened by the French in Annam and the British in Burma, was fertile soil for the seeds of anti-imperialism. Both the French and the British had obtained railway concessions there, and appeared to be increasing their activities in order to secure more rights and privileges. This spawned a strong spirit of patriotism among the Yunnanese students. Motivated by a desire to defend China against foreign encroachment, a good many of them chose to join the army, and were prepared to sacrifice their lives.[46]

In April 1910, the completion of the French-owned Annam to Yunnan railway intensified Chinese nationalism. When the first train arrived in Kunming, Li Genyuan felt a great sense of shame to see China once again fail to protect her own sovereign rights and railway interests. The students in the military officers' school were allowed one day off to watch the train, and they were asked to write an essay on their impression. One instructor who saw the first train was so grief-stricken that he could not help weeping on the spot. The students who went with him wept too.[47]

At about the same time, the Chinese government was in conflict with Britain over Pianma (Hpimaw), a small village in the disputed border area between Tengyueh (in western Yunnan) and British Burma. In May 1910 Peking formally claimed jurisdiction over Pianma. The British *chargé d'affaires* stated, in reply, that his government considered Pianma part of Burmese territory. Subsequent negotiations merely accentuated the widely divergent views of the Chinese and the British governments. In December the British sent an expedition to Pianma and occupied it in the following month. Peking protested against Britain's violation of the frontier, asserting once again that Pianma was unquestionably under Chinese jurisdiction.[48]

The Yunnan provincial assembly reacted to the British occupation very strongly, demanding that the imperial government take a strong stand, or else further foreign encroachment would ensue.[49] The army officers and military students also got very excited, urging the government not to give in. The feeling of nationalism ran high in the military schools, and hundreds of troops were dispatched to Tengyueh and Pianma. In April 1911 the British became more conciliatory, for they no longer considered the issues involved worth the big expeddition necessary to evict the Chinese from Pianma, and also they had found more evidence of Chinese administration in the disputed district than had been anticipated. Subsequently, the expeditionary force was withdrawn,[50] which, from the Chinese point of view, was a defeat for British imperialism.

In any case, nationalist ideas disseminated and encouraged by the instructors found a responsive audience in the military officers' school, the graduates of which in turn spread them among their troops. It was claimed that in 1910-11, the school had produced eight hundred revolutionary officers who were assigned to active military units and exerted much influence over the rank and file.[51]

Cai E was believed to be a revolutionary leader, and the Guangxi provincial assembly had in fact advised Viceroy Li Jingxi not to put him in charge of army matters.[52] Cai no doubt was party to the revolutionary agitation in the local army. But, as a brigadier, he acted very cautiously, and never appeared to be a radical. In fact, he had spent a few months collecting and annotating the military maxims of Zeng Guofan and Hu Linyi.[53] Whether he did so in order to cover his revolutionary activity, or whether he was in fact a non-revolutionary, is hard to tell. Nevertheless, it seems certain that there were revolutionary elements in the Yunnan officer corps who were working for the demise of the dynasty.

It is not so clear, however, that there was any revolutionary organisation among the officers or the rank and file. The Yunnanese radicals, unlike those in Canton, were not directed by the Tongmenghui. In contrast to revolutionaries in Hubei, they failed to organise themselves or the rank and file cohesively. Nor did they succeed in preventing a rift from developing among themselves over the issue of revolutionary leadership. One group, for example, wanted a Yunnanese to be their leader, another favoured Cai E. This situation was complicated by the fact that the Beiyang officers serving in Yunnan appeared to be unsympathetic, and were thus an obstacle to the revolutionary cause.[54]

Yet the troops did not need a revolutionary movement to be disaffected. In Yunnan, as elsewhere, financial conditions in 1910-11 were disheartening, to say the least. The 19th Division normally cost 1.5 million taels per year, of which 1,100,000 taels were provided for by the provincial government, the rest being met by Peking.[55] In 1910, although the division had been formed, there were difficulties in maintaining it at the existing level. There had been a great loss in government revenue as a result of the abolition of the opium trade, and any further increase in taxes was out of the question because of the general poverty of the population. The division lacked a total of 800,000 taels which was necessary for its own maintenance. Peking's annual aid had been long overdue, while Hubei, which had committed itself to assisting Yunnan with 300,000 taels per annum, had failed to furnish the funds.[56] In August 1910 the British consul-general in Kunming reported that the pay of the officers had been reduced by about 20 per cent by order of the viceroy.[57] In December Pereira also found during his visit to Yunnan that there were great difficulties in finding money to pay the troops.[58]

Owing to inflation and other causes, the budget for the 19th Division for 1911 rose to 2,100,000 taels, or two-thirds of the total provincial expenditure. It was later reduced to 1,900,000 taels, a sum which was still too large for the provincial treasury to meet. Consequently, orders were given that more old-style troops be demobilised quickly. Drastic cuts were applied to the new troops' uniforms, clothing, rations and a variety of supplies, to which they were normally entitled. This brought the budget down to 1,770,000 taels, but at the utmost the provincial treasury could provide only 1,461,000 taels. This meant that further cuts were necessary. Accordingly, the staff of the military schools were retrenched. In July 1911 there was much talk of closing the military officers' school on financial grounds. (Another reason stated by the viceroy was that Yunnan already had enough officers for its troops.)[59]

Yunnan also had its share of natural disasters which exacerbated social unrest. Before 1911 there had been a series of good harvests, accompanied by an appreciable drop in the price of rice. Since the turn of the year, unfortunately, floods had occurred at frequent intervals. In that summer exceptionally heavy rains damaged an estimated 40 per cent of the rice crop and swept away several villagers near Kunming. The scarcity of rice and other foodstuffs generated widespread discontent throughout the province,[60] to which the soldiery was not immune.

There were other causes of army unrest. Strict discipline, for example, was resented by the rank and file. In October 1910, there were military disturbances in north-west Yunnan. One reason for these riots was the advance of deserters from Sichuan, where there had been a mutiny among the troops stationed at Xiangcheng the month before. Another was the execution of two Yunnanese non-commissioned officers for a slight breach of discipline — gambling. The year before, several deserters had been summarily beheaded at Dali, an incident which had almost caused a revolt.[61]

There were desertions in various places. In the summer of 1910 they numbered an average of about 1 per cent, or 120 men, each month. Drastic steps were taken to stop them at Dali. One deserter, on being apprehended, was executed,[62] but the deterrent effect failed to stop desertions altogether.

The discontent and subversion of the troops raised an important question. Would they fight for the government in the event of revolution? A well-informed English journalist and traveller was of the opinion that:

> The rank and file are chosen from the common people, and one would not be surprised to find, should trouble take place fairly soon, while they are still raw to their business, the soldiers turn to those who could give them most. It has been humorously remarked that in case of disturbances the first thing the Chinese Tommy would do would be to shoot the officers for treating him so badly and for drilling him so hard and long.[63]

The Beiyang Army

It has sometimes been assumed that the Beiyang Army was a loyalist army because its officer corps allegedly owed its allegiance to an anti-revolutionary Yuan Shikai. The postulate of this assumption is that Yuan, in spite of his retirement in 1909-11, retained much influence over large parts of the Beiyang Army through his connections with his former associates who were willing to support him, first, in fighting the revolutionary forces and, later, in negotiating a peaceful settlement. This assumption is partly correct and partly false; correct because Yuan did have much influence over the senior commanders who had been politically and professionally associated with him and who had high regard for him as a military reformer; false because the Beiyang Army was not united in its allegiance either to Yuan or to the imperial government. Both Stephen MacKinnon and Ernest Young have expressed serious doubts about the Beiyang officers' personal loyalty to Yuan.[64]

The Beiyang officers had never been a homogeneous group in terms of geographical and educational backgrounds. They came from different provinces in north China, and those who were trained and educated in Peking, Tientsin or Baoding formed the so-called Beiyang clique. But among others were a good many young men who had graduated from the *Shikan gakkō* or other Japanese military schools, especially in the years 1909-11. There were, too, a few officers who were previously commanders of the old-style troops or bandit chiefs. All these officers seemed to have different aspirations and different attitudes towards the ruling dynasty. The young graduates from Japan, for example, tended to resent the authority of the locally trained officers who had been installed in senior positions.

The rank and file appeared to be most concerned with their basic needs and full, regular pay, which were all the more important in 1910-11 because of inflation, food shortages and the deplorable financial conditions throughout the country. As long as they were fully and regularly paid, adequately fed and clothed, they remained contented and obedient, whoever was to lead them. Conversely, if their basic needs were neglected, they would turn against their officers with little hesitation.

Generally speaking, discipline in the Beiyang Army was much better than that in the southern divisions. However, there was no lack of army discontent in the north. A missionary reported in September 1908 that one-third of the troops of the 5th Division stationed in Tsinan were members of the secret societies and that there was 'an appreciable amount of anti-dynastic feeling'.[65] More important was the fact that corporal punishment was still in force with more severity than elsewhere. A senior officer told the British military attaché candidly that:

> . . . on an average about 100 men in the camp are beaten every month, namely 90 per cent with the stick . . . and the rest whipped across the shoulders, a barbarous punishment in the hands of Chinese . . . no antiseptics were applied to the wounds, which were allowed to mortify . . . 1 or 2 men have had their ears pierced with an arrow, whilst in 1907 a soldier had his ear cut off for stealing a revolver.[66]

Added to this was the poor relationship between officers and men. The regimental officers were 'bad and ignorant', having no 'real control over the men'. It was only natural that the rank and file should dislike, even hate, the officers who inspired no confidence. The junior officers in turn resented the authority of their seniors. Few of these senior officers seemed devoted to their work. In the local department of military administration and the staff office, for example, a few officers who had been overseas indulged in drinking and gave little attention to army training.[67]

Conscription also aroused much resentment among those who had no intention of enlisting in the first place, or serving for more than a term of three years. Many wanted to be relieved of service. In Shandong a young man could be relieved on payment of as much as 200 taels. In Baoding, where the 2nd Division was stationed, a man could purchase his discharge for 100 taels. In the 3rd Division, which had been stationed in Manchuria since the summer of 1907, 75 per cent of the troops in 1908 were conscripts. A soldier wishing to be discharged before completing his service had to submit an application to his commanding officer for forwarding to the higher authorities for approval, which would be given only in the most exceptional circumstances.[68] It appeared that conscription could easily lend itself to corruption and extortion.

Desertion was a serious problem in the Beiyang divisions as elsewhere. It was common during the Russo-Japanese War and at the time of the grand manoeuvres in 1905. According to an official of the Commission for Army Reorganisation, there were 15 per cent desertions in 1905 and a little less in 1906.[69] The situation had improved in the following two years. But from 1909 onwards, it became a problem again. Even the Manchu troops were not immune from desertion. Many were reported to have deserted in 1910, especially those of the Imperial Guard Corps and the 1st Division which had a large proportion of Manchus.[70] Generally speaking, desertions were frequent in divisions and brigades where the common soldiers were conscripts. Conversely, 'volunteer' troops who were locally recruited tended to stay on longer.

There were many factors contributing to desertion, e.g. corporal punishment, strict discipline, hard drill, intensive gymnastic training,[71] corruption among the officers, and personal reasons. Drastic actions like the execution of a few arrested deserters failed to eliminate the problem. In Manchuria desertion from the 3rd Division was also caused by the intense cold of the long winter which was unsuitable for drill and intolerable to the conscripts from inner China. Large numbers of them had deserted and joined the local brigands in 1908.[72]

The state of the 3rd Division had deteriorated since its transfer to

Manchuria. In 1908 it was believed to be the worst of the Beiyang divisions. Although the men were well treated and paid regularly, and although the military profession was becoming more popular there as elsewhere, the troops had fallen off partly because of the incompetence of Major-General Cao Kun, who had succeeded the able Duan Qirui as the division commander.[73] In 1909 the division seemed to show some improvement. The training of the troops appeared to be carried out on a uniform system. Musketry drills were assiduously practised, although practice shooting was greatly neglected through lack of funds. The health of the troops was good, and sanitation was well attended to.[74] In the following years, however, there were many complaints about poor food and sanitation and the generally appalling living conditions, which caused widespread discontent in the ranks.[75]

Apart from the 3rd Division, there were also stationed in Manchuria the 1st and 2nd Mixed Brigade, which, when up to full strength, would be 5179 and 5185 strong, respectively. The 1st Mixed Brigade in Xinminfu, commanded by Wang Zhenji from Tientsin, was formed by troops from the 5th and 6th Divisions. The men were quite well turned out. The drill was splendid, and all in all it was an impressive force. [76] The 2nd Mixed Brigade in Mukden was in the charge of Wang Ruxian from Peking until late in 1910 when he was replaced by Lan Tianwei. It was considered by the British military attaché to be 'the smartest body of troops' he had ever seen in Manchuria, owing to the fact that the troops were originally from the fine 4th and 2nd Divisions.[77]

In addition to the troops which had been transferred from within the Great Wall, local New Army had been raised in Mukden (with one infantry regiment and one battalion of mountain artillery), and Jilin (with one infantry brigade), but none in Qiqihaer until 1910. It was Peking's plan to raise eventually four divisions in Manchuria, two in Fengtian, and one each in Jilin and Heilongjiang.[78]

In 1909 the 1st Mixed Brigade merged with other troops in Fengtian to form the 20th Division under the command of Chen Yi, who had come to Manchuria with Xiliang, the new viceroy. In 1910 the 23rd Division was established in Jilin in the charge of Meng Enyuan. In the following year the 24th Division assigned to Heilongjiang also began formation.[79] At the same time a new mixed brigade for Zhili, stationed at Langfang mid-way between Peking and Tientsin, had been started by the formation of two infantry battalions from the reservists of the Beiyang divisions. This latter unit was estimated at an annual cost of 490,000 taels, of which sum about 220,000 taels were to come from the fund destined for the pay of the reservists, and the balance to be met by taxes on tobacco and wines in Zhili. The raising of this mixed brigade had aroused some criticism from foreign observers. The British military attaché, for example, felt that it was inconsistent to form a new mixed brigade while so many existing divisions were still under strength. The fact that it was under the control of the Viceroy of Zhili also contradicted the policy of centralisation whereby the same viceroy had been stripped of his management of the 2nd and 4th Divisions only the year before.[80]

The formation of these new units suggested one important point: that the finances of the New Army in north China had not been as seriously affected as in central and south China. The already completed divisions appear to have been able to maintain themselves at the existing level, while there were still funds to organise new ones. Of course, there had been reductions in military expenditure, which affected the men's drill, training, and equipment, and which made it impossible for the officers' school in Peking to open in 1911. But on the whole there had been no serious retrenchment of troops or reduction in their pay. As has been pointed out previously, paying the troops fully and regularly was the key to maintaining military morale and loyalty. Any commander who ignored this rule did so at his own peril. In the summer of 1906, for example, Yuan Shikai was hard up for funds, with 4 million taels in arrears of pay, and this almost caused a mutiny in his divisions.[81] Later in the year when Yuan lost his control of the 1st, 3rd, 5th and 6th Divisions, there were rumours that the troops' pay would be interfered with,[82] which again did much to undermine military morale. Henceforth, however, Peking was determined not to allow the troops' pay to be in arrears, and this largely accounted for the absence of mutinies in the Beiyang Army in spite of the discontent described earlier on.

Furthermore, in contrast to the severe economy of the provincial military administrations, officials of the Ministry of War and the General Staff Council received a substantial pay rise in the summer of 1911, which aroused much criticism from the native press. There were also reports of senior military officials squandering government funds while making preparations for the autumn manoeuvres of the New Army for that year.[83] In short, although the Peking government was dependent upon foreign loans to deal with its financial problems, and although there had been reductions in military expenditure following the budget debate in the National Assembly, the Beiyang divisions were financially far better off than the southern armies.

There were no major floods, droughts or famines in Zhili and Manchuria, although in the latter region a bubonic plague epidemic broke out in late 1910, threatening to spread to parts of north China.

Regular troops who were employed on plague preventive duty conducted themselves extremely well. The 3rd Division on duty in Haerbin (Harbin) had lost three hundred men, but the troops appeared to have done their work willingly and cheerfully.[84] No serious problems or unrest resulted from the plague. Nor were there serious food shortages throughout north China, except in Shandong, where the wheat crop had been spoilt by drought in the spring of 1910 and by rain at harvest time, and where the Yellow River burst its banks in the Lijing district later in the year and caused more damage than had occurred there for the previous six years.[85]

There was no revolutionary movement in the Beiyang Army, in spite of a few junior officers who had expressed much dissatisfaction with the state of military affairs. For example, in the 20th Division there was a small body known as the Society for Military Studies *(Wuxue yanjiuhui)*, which was formed to bring together from time to time discontented elements who wanted to air their grievances. It was not a revolutionary organisation, however. By the admission of its president, Feng Yuxiang, it lacked a clear, specific political platform. Although its members were concerned about foreign encroachments upon Manchuria, the corruption and incompetence of the Qing government, and regarded the overthrow of the dynasty as a precondition for building up a strong China, their political thinking and activities were 'very childish'. There was, as Feng pointed out, no theoretical study of revolution, nor did the members devise means of organising themselves systematically or of enlisting wide support. The little that they did was restricted to promoting good relations among discontented fellow soldiers.[86]

It was certainly more difficult to promote revolution in the Beiyang Army than elsewhere. Financed and managed by the Peking government, this army had always been under fairly effective imperial control; any subversive movement there would have been crushed promptly and with relative ease. Moreover, the nationalistic Japanese-educated officers who could have been agents of revolution had been comfortably installed in commanding or staff positions. Their political attitudes towards the dynasty seemed very ambivalent, wavering between revolution and constitutional monarchy, and probably more inclined towards the latter.

A few of these commanders are worthy of note. The first was Wu Luzhen, commander of the 6th Division stationed in Baoding. It will be recalled that Wu had worked in Hubei briefly upon his graduation from the *Shikan gakkō*, and that he was later transferred to Peking, where he served on the Commission for Army Reorganisation as a cavalry superintendent. There he incurred the animosity of

Tieliang, as a result of which he did not have much opportunity to prove his usefulness. In 1907 Wu was invited by Xu Shichang, the first Viceroy of Manchuria, to work for him as a military councillor. Later, the Japanese encroachment upon Yanji on the Heilongjiang border afforded Wu an opportunity to demonstrate his exceptional ability. He mobilised the local powerful bandits against the Japanese and drove the intruders out of Manchuria. Consequently, he was promoted to the rank of colonel *(zheng cailing)* in charge of border affairs in Yanji, and rose to brigadier-general in 1909. A year later he was awarded the prestigious title of deputy lieutenant-general *(fu dutong)*, of which there were forty-eight in all, two to each national division of the Banners. Afterwards, he was sent to observe army manoeuvres in France and Germany, returning to China in December 1910 to assume command of the 6th Division.[87]

This division, it will be recalled, was originally formed out of the troops brought to Peking by Yuan Shikai in 1900 and contained many men who had been recruited under the old regulations. A lot of the officers were of an inferior order. Naturally Wu had very low regard for them, a fact which did not endear him to the troops. In his opinion only half of the four hundred officers there were well qualified, and the other half should be dismissed. His threat to dismiss them created disturbances among those concerned, and aroused strong opposition from Shouxun, the Deputy Minister of War, who had some of his protégés among them. Wu then wrote angrily to Yinchang, but succeeded only in incurring the latter's enmity. He complained to the Minister of the Interior, Prince Su, describing the unsatisfactory state of the 6th Division and expressing his anxiety to improve it. Wu also proposed to the Throne that changes be made in the military establishment. But none of these efforts was successful. During the early months of 1911 Wu had spent much of his time in Peking rather than with his troops, partly because he found the 6th Division unmanageable, and partly because he wanted to recruit support from some Manchu princes for his reform scheme.[88]

Whether or not Wu's frustration turned him into a revolutionary is not clear. What seems certain is that during the last few years of the dynasty, he had been in correspondence with Liang Qichao on various matters, one of which had been to work for the political demise of Yuan Shikai in late 1908. They may have talked about the possibility of staging a *coup d'etat*, which had been on Liang's mind since the spring of 1911.[9] In the meantime, Wu also seems to have maintained contacts with some members of the Literary Society in Wuchang, giving the revolutionaries there the impression, rightly or wrongly, that he would return to Hubei to become the military governor in the event of revolution.[90] As Ernest Young has pointed out, there was no sharp distinction between 'reformer' and 'revolutionary'.[91] It was possible for Wu to be 'reformist' and 'revolutionary' at the same time, depending on the political and military realities existing in the country.

There were two other commanders who were alleged to have spread revolutionary ideas among their troops, namely, Zhang Shaozeng and Lan Tianwei. Zhang, a native of Zhili, was sent to Japan in 1899 under the auspices of the Viceroy of Zhili, and graduated from the *Shikan gakkō* in 1902 in the same class with Wu Luzhen. He returned to Zhili, filling various posts in the army until he was promoted to assistant commander. When the 5th Division was formed, he became its chief councillor. In 1904 he became director of the Beiyang Training Bureau and director of the General Staff. In 1909 he was appointed president of the Noble's College, and became commander of the 20th Division in December 1910, when Chen Yi was sent overseas for training.[92]

Lan Tianwei from Hubei was among those who graduated from the *Shikan gakkō* in 1904, (the second class). Upon his return to China, he had served in Wuchang for a short while as an instructor in the school for commissioned officers. In the autumn of 1904 he was transferred to north China (it is not clear where exactly) and subsequently to Manchuria. In 1909 he was placed in charge of the 2nd Mixed Brigade in Mukden.[93] As the following chapter will show, Wu, Zhang and Lan jointly made twelve demands to the court on 19 October 1911, for constitutional government. There is no evidence that any one of them was committed to the overthrow of the dynasty. On the other hand, it is fair to say that their loyalty was somewhat dubious.

According to a former official of the Ministry of War and member of the Tongmenghui, Jiang Zuobin, revolutionary influence in the Beiyang Army was very weak. Jiang, a Hubei graduate of the *Shikan gakkō* in 1908 (the fourth class), claimed to have helped promote revolution in the army. Upon his return to China, he was appointed as instructor in the intensive military school in Baoding, where he took advantage of his position to disseminate revolutionary ideas and organise subversive activities. In October 1909 he attended a military examination set by the Ministry of War, and came out second on the list. In recognition of his excellent performance, he was recruited into the War Ministry's department of selection *(junhengsi)*, which supervised the appointment and transfer of military officials, and the granting of hereditary titles. He then recommended to Yinchang that the old, incompetent officers of the New Army throughout the country, including the Beiyang divisions, be replaced by modern-educated officers, especially graduates of foreign military academies. Jiang believed that within five years, the Beiyang Army would have been controlled by a new generation of nationalistic officers, many of whom were considered to be revolutionary sympathisers. The recommendation struck a responsive chord in the Ministry of War, as Yinchang himself was anxious to achieve military efficiency by appointing more returned students. This resulted in some significant changes in the military command. Apart from Wu Luzhen, Zhang Shaozeng and Lan Tianwei, there were many other nationalistic, Japanese-educated officers appointed to various officer ranks. In Jiang's opinion, the Wuchang uprising was premature; given another two or three years, he believed, the revolutionaries would have gained control of the Beiyang Army and accomplished the revolution without Yuan Shikai becoming its chief beneficiary.[94]

Conclusion

It has been shown in the last three chapters that army disaffection was widespread in the Yangzi region and to a lesser extent in south China, and that there was an organised revolutionary movement within the Hubei army but not in those of other provinces. The disaffection was caused by a combination of traditional grievances, nationalism and revolutionary propaganda, which varied in degree from place to place. The Beiyang Army, too, had its share of discontent, but as a whole it was less a threat to the dynasty than were the divisions outside north China.

The pattern of revolutionary activity also varied from one place to another. In Hubei the common soldiers were both the focus of subversion and the source of revolutionary leadership. In Hunan the pattern was similar, but there was no cohesive structural framework like the Literary Society, and the secret society elements there seem to have played a more active part. In Guangdong the Tongmenghui influence was at its strongest, but that did not make the subversive movement more successful because of its organisational weaknesses. In Yunnan the military instructors and officers were the moving spirit, but the subversion there lacked a unity of purpose as well as organisational strength. Elsewhere revolutionary activity was restricted to the individual efforts of middle-grade and junior officers.

As far as the loyalty of the officers was concerned, the senior ones, in the north and the south alike, tended to be more reliable, as they were loath to jeopardise their career interests unless they were guaranteed a better future, and any such guarantee was impossible. By contrast, the allegiance of the middle-grade and junior officers was far from certain. They tended to be more idealistic as well as more ambitious, with less substantial stakes in preserving the dynasty, and were more impatient for command and rewards. They were also closer to the rank and file and were more likely to have their support in the event of revolution.

Indeed, the junior officers constituted a danger to the Qing government. In a dispatch to the Secretary of State, the American minister to China, W.J. Calhoun, summed up the situation in July 1910:

> While it is impossible to obtain reliable information with regard to the 'morale' of the army or the degree of its discipline, it would not be surprising if the example of Turkey were one day to be repeated here and the real revolution start with junior officers.[95]

EIGHT

The revolution, 1911-12

THE ARMY disaffection discussed previously was part of the social unrest which took on dangerous proportions in the last two years of Manchu rule. From 1910 the dynasty was in an increasingly precarious position owing to a combination of factors. We have dealt with some of them such as the weakness of the central government, the impoverished state of the economy, natural disasters, the failure of the crops, popular discontent caused by new taxes, inflation and food shortages. Others included the widespread anti-imperialist sentiment among students and the people, the liberty of the native press, the railway dispute, and above all the alienation of the provincial assemblies.

The ingredients for revolution were all there. The stage was set by the railway disturbances, followed by the revolt of the troops in Wuchang. The New Army played the leading role in the south and eastern provinces at the beginning of the revolution, which was later accomplished by the joint efforts of the provincial assemblies and rich merchants, as well as Tongmenghui leaders. In the north the Beiyang Army also displayed divided loyalties, and some sections of it took advantage of the turmoil to demand a constitutional monarchy. In the end, even the imperial troops realised that the monarchical cause could no longer be sustained, and this compelled the monarchy to negotiate for a peaceful abdication.

The partition rumours and the native press

In 1910-11 there were widespread rumours that China was about to be carved up like a melon and divided among the foreign powers. The anti-imperialist feeling was not a new phenomenon, but it became more pronounced in early 1910 when a 'carved melon' document appeared in the native press and similar circulars were posted on many city walls. The students became violently excited, expressing a strong desire to enrol themselves as volunteer soldiers to repel foreign aggression. In many schools, including several missionary ones, students demanded arms and permission to drill. In Hunan, where the anti-foreign feeling had always been especially strong, students were severely reprimanded for asking the governor to issue arms to them. At a public meeting of the law students in Changsha, it was resolved that any foreigners who made the first aggressive move against Hunan were to be massacred.[1] In Nanking students held aloof from their foreign teachers. The government did not issue any arms to them, but there was much latent hostility towards foreigners there.[2]

The anti-imperialist sentiment was fanned by a voluntary subscription movement to pay off foreign loans and indemnities and to build China's railways with her own funds. Boxes to receive subscriptions were placed in some of the streets and all the schools in Nanking. In Chengtu meetings were held to discuss the repayment of the national debt, and regulations were drawn up.[3] The native newspapers, which had increased both in number and in circulation, teemed with references to foreign designs on China, impending troubles in Manchuria, and the need for universal military training. Violent statements appeared, attacking the central government and officials for their venality and inability to resist foreign encroachments. As the British consul in Nanking reported:

> The native press . . . is actively engaged in stirring up anti-foreign feeling, and the Shanghai papers frequently publish sensational telegrams, said to have addressed to the Central Government by Chinese Ministers abroad, attributing to the European Powers insidious designs on China's territory and rights. The servile condition of the Chinese *vis-a-vis* foreigners is a constant theme in leading articles, and the fate of India, Egypt, Poland, and Corea is continually held up as a warning to China.[4]

Although the foreign powers repeatedly denied such designs, the partition rumours did not die out easily. During the first quarter of 1911, the native press, especially in Hankow, devoted considerable space to the inequities and aggressive behaviour of the British, Russian, and Japanese governments. Various schemes were suggested for the salvation of the country, including a proposal for organising a 'people's army'. Early in March a telegram from Chinese students in Japan was published in Shanghai and Hankow, stating that Yili and Pianma had been occupied by the Russians and the British, respectively, and that the French were pressing for mining concessions in Yunnan. It added that 20,000 taels had been raised and a movement initiated to save China from danger, and it urged the provincial assemblies to organise a 'people's army'. Reacting to this promptly, Peking ordered the Wuchang authorities to suppress the student movement there and to prohibit the press from publishing such telegrams from abroad. Furthermore, all letters addressed to students from their associates in Japan were to be submitted to the education department for inspection before delivery. [5]

These rumours and student telegrams also created considerable excitement in Fujian. Placards were posted in the city walls of Amoy, Foochow, and Quanzhou, calling upon the people to levy and train bands so as to increase China's military strength. The visit of some Japanese gun-boats and a Japanese admiral to Foochow early in 1911 added to the excitement and gave rise to suspicions of their motives. [6]

In the following months the rumours spread far and wide in Changsha, Chengtu, Chungking, Ichang, Kunming, Guilin, Wuzhou, and Amoy. In Ichang a volunteer corps, four to five hundred strong, was formed, but elsewhere, the volunteer movement seemed to have little success because of government suppression. In Sichuan, although the general attitude of the people towards foreigners was not hostile, the work of foreign missionaries was looked upon with less friendliness. Early in June there were some small disturbances outside Chengtu involving two American missionaries. [7]

The persistence of the partition rumours led the United States minister in Peking to suspect 'some organized activity with the intention of stirring up the people against the foreigners and against their own Government'. [8] This anti-imperialist feeling, however, was different from the blind hatred of the foreigner that had led to the Boxer uprising of 1900. It was more civilised and had more purpose, directed not so much against the foreigner as such, as against his assumed superiority, privileges, and direct threat to China's existence as a nation. It reflected a curious admixture of an admission on the part of Chinese students of China's own weaknesses and confidence in their ability to follow in the footsteps of the imperialists. Reform in China was aimed at strengthening her position in dealing with the foreigner, and if the imperial government failed to achieve this, it would have to go.

Significantly, the anti-imperialist sentiment was not the monopoly of the student class. Government officials in some places were 'unfriendly' to foreigners for precisely the same reason. In Nanking, for example, officials frequently disregarded the rights and privileges accorded to foreigners both by treaty and agreement, and made it almost impossible for any foreign merchant to purchase land outside the settlement. [9] In Shandong an anti-imperialist spirit had evolved among government officials who strove to regain complete sovereignty over the areas of the province controlled by Germany after 1898.

These officials, resolute and resourceful, contained German authority in the leased territory and frustrated German ambitions to spread its influence throughout the province.[10]

The constitutionalists and the provincial assemblies

The precarious position of the Qing government in 1911 was due not only to popular discontent but, more importantly, to the alienation of the reformist elite associated with the constitutional movement. This elite, a mixture of new and traditional scholars, furnished the membership of the provincial assemblies. Had it not been for their desertion in 1911, the Qing dynasty would probably have been given another reprieve. Their political attitudes, their social backgrounds and composition, and their involvement in the constitutional movement, have been treated elsewhere.[11] Here it is necessary only to summarise the main developments.

The cause of their alienation was the imperial government's refusal to comply with their demand for the immediate opening of parliament. When their petitions for an early parliament brought no results, the constitutionalists who had spent some time in Peking in 1910 returned to their provinces at the end of the year, feeling so estranged from the government that they resolved to support the cause of revolution. The formation on 8 May, 1911 of a Manchu-dominated royal cabinet added to their frustrations. As a result, forty representatives from sixteen provinces met in Peking in June to establish the Friends of the Constitution Association *(Xianyouhui)* and the 1911 Club *(Xinhai julebu)*. The formation of these parties was evidence of the constitutionalists' desire to expand their power as an effective opposition force.[12] Should there be an opportunity for them to gain power as a 'ruling party', they would certainly seize it. The government's reluctance to broaden political participation in the interests of the ardent reformists proved to be fatal to itself. The days were gone when the Manchu dynasty could count on the allegiance of the reformists in its cause against revolution.

The relationships between the provincial assemblies and the government revolved around three major issues: constitutionalism versus autocracy; provincial concerns versus imperial interests; and anti-imperialism versus foreign encroachment. The question of representative and local self-government was fundamental to the theory and practice of constitutionalism. The provincial assemblies saw themselves as new mechanisms for the representation of 'public opinion', which was to be the future basis of government. As representatives of the people, the assemblymen felt that the right of deliberation which they were granted was insufficient, and they demanded a more direct and more significant voice in the provincial administration and the power to carry out their resolutions. They tended to reject the Qing authority (both central and provincial), which was autocratic and was therefore an obstacle to constitutionalism.

Seeing the provincial administration as an agency of the imperial government, the provincial assembly was anxious to assume for itself the right of financial control. An example of this was the difficulty Chen Kuilong, Viceroy of Zhili (1909-11), found in raising a new industrial loan of 3,200,000 taels in the autumn of 1910. Although the loan had received imperial sanction, it was opposed by the provincial assembly until the viceroy agreed to hand over one million taels to it for improving the cotton cultivation and other important industries.[13]

Indeed, the most important issue on which the assembly and the government was likely to clash was the provincial budget, which was subject to criticism by the former. A similar case to Zhili's was the resignation *en bloc* of the delegates of the Jiangsu provincial assembly in May 1911 in consequence of the viceroy's refusal to effect the reductions suggested by them in the provincial estimates. In August the viceroy, although his action had been approved by the central government, gave way on every point to the assembly, and the delegates then withdrew their resignation.[14]

The assemblymen, being overwhelmingly natives of the province (while the viceroy and the governor were not because of the rule of avoidance), were concerned about defending and promoting provincial interests. When these interests clashed with those of the central government, there was confrontation between the provincial elite and the Qing bureaucracy. The promotion of provincial interests was part of the rationale for the setting up of various provincial institutions during the years 1909-11. This expressed a form of provincialism. But as John Fincher has pointed out, it was oriented to the national polity both through and outside the bureaucracy and [was] therefore transitional to rather than an obstacle to nationalism'.[15]

The issues affecting the relationships between the assemblies and the government were brought into focus in the summer of 1910 as a result of Peking's policy of nationalising the country's trunk railways. It was in Sichuan that the provincial assembly was in the forefront of the struggle against the central government.

The Sichuan railway disturbances

On 9 May, 1911 an imperial decree ordered that China's trunk lines be placed directly under the control of the central government.[16] It stated that the merchant-managed enterprises in various provinces had not accomplished as much as was expected of them, and that nationalisation was intended to achieve rapid completion of the lines. Branch lines within the prefectures were, however, to remain under private control. On 20 May 1911 Sheng Xuanhuai, the Minister of Posts and Communications, contracted a loan of 6 million taels with the four-power consortium (Britain, the United States, France and Germany) for the completion of the Peking-Hankow and Canton-Hankow lines. This aroused a storm of protest in Hubei, Hunan, Guangdong and Sichuan, where the gentry shareholders and provincial assemblymen were convinced that the imperial government was selling out the country to foreign interests.

As far as these provinces were concerned, nationalisation of the trunk lines meant that the central government would exercise further control over them, both politically and financially. From the assemblymen's point of view, such control was detrimental to the development of provincial autonomy, local self-government, and above all constitutional rule. The railway loan had been negotiated without consultation with the provinces, and the assemblies had reason to fear that their power, far from expanding as they wished, would be further restricted. They were anxious to defend their political and financial interests and they also resented the intrusion of Western capital into an enterprise which should have been purely Chinese.

A railway protection movement was launched, and support was sought from people from all walks of life. The poor peasants and the urban workers responded very strongly, for they realised that they would have to pay heavier tax for the repayment of the railway loan. The students, who were always sensitive to foreign encroachment, became extremely excited and angry with the imperial government's policy.

In Hubei, Hunan and Guangdong the disturbances did not assume serious proportions because the shareholders were quickly appeased by capital repayment partly in cash and partly in interest-bearing bonds. In Sichuan, however, the capital involved was so large that the imperial government was unable to repay the shareholders on the same basis. A Railway League was formed, led by the local gentry, including some of the most enlightened men of the province, who demanded that the railway loan agreement be submitted to the national and provincial assemblies and that the railways concerned be handed back to the province and to private management.[17]

The Sichuanese shareholders met a few times to discuss the situation. On 25 August, they resolved that no 'benevolences' or 'voluntary levies' *(juanshu)* be paid, that the land and poll taxes be appropriated for payment of interest on the 'rent' shares, that there be no dealings in real property (so as to avoid paying transfer fees), and that Sichuan admit no liability for any government loan thereafter contracted. It was also decided that shops and schools in Chengtu be closed and local militia be organised to resist official suppression. Subsequently, tablets were affixed to the doors of shops bearing the name of the late Emperor Guangxu, who had once granted the right of commercial construction of railways to the Sichuanese. In many streets platforms were erected, surmounted by mat-sheds, under which were placed portraits of the late Emperor, with vases, incense pots, and the other paraphernalia of a commemorative altar. Demonstrators shouted the slogan 'Sichuan for the Sichuanese', which reflected the interests of the provincial assembly in local self-government and provincial autonomy, as well as a profoundly nationalistic stand against imperialist encroachment.

On 7 September the government intervened with troops and arrested the 'ringleaders' of the Railway League. Prominent among those arrested were the president, vice-president and another member of the provincial assembly, the vice-chairman of the shareholder's extraordinary general meeting, the director of telegraphs, and a member of the local education department. When the public demanded the release of these notable 'rebels', the troops of the Patrol and Defence Force fired on the rioters, killing a number of them. In the following weeks there occurred a series of skirmishes between government troops and the insurgents who were made up of local militia and trained bands. Foreign residents were beginning to evacuate Chengtu.[18] Before long the violence spread to other parts of the province, and the insurgents were joined by Tongmenghui revolutionaries and members of the Elder Brothers Society and other secret societies.[19] Viceroy Zhao Erfeng (1908-11) was obliged to ask for assistance from the imperial government. In late September contingents of the Hubei New Army arrived in Sichuan,[20] which was practically in a state of rebellion.

The reason why the Hubei troops were sent was that the New Army in Sichuan itself was extremely unreliable. In fact, the new-style troops in Chengtu were 'inactive' towards the rioters and insurgents. In September Lieutenant-General Zhu Qinglan, commander of the incomplete 17th Division, held a review of the troops. When he asked that all those who were members of the Railway League should stand up, as he wished to expel them from the ranks, all stood up! Zhu was forced to withdraw, and the men subsequently refused to drill. 'The police and territorial army troops were mainly educated Szechwanese in sympathy with the league', reported the acting British consul in Chengtu, 'and they had proclaimed their intention of refusing to fire on their fellow provincials'.[21]

There can be little doubt that the agitation and opposition excited by the railway question fomented a spirit which tended towards revolution. But it must be pointed out that the immediate cause of the revolutionary outbreak which followed very shortly in Wuchang was not the railway problem but a military mutiny on the night of 10 October. Until then, none of the provincial assemblies outside Sichuan had any plan to revolt or to challenge directly the authority of the imperial government, however frustrated they were. For one thing, they were not sure that they would win the support of the New Army. Unless such support was forthcoming, the reformist elite would rather wait and see.

The Wuchang uprising

With the exception of a few writers in the People's Republic of China, historians have given little serious treatment to the Wuchang uprising.[22] Orthodox Guomindang writers have regarded it as the last of a series of uprisings instigated by the Tongmenghui. Western scholarship on the Revolution of 1911, while it has shown the fragmentary nature of the revolutionary movement, does not attach much importance to the uprising. Most writers, Chinese and Western alike, believe that the event of 10 October was a mere accident. Sun Yat-sen himself attributed its success to the flight of Viceroy Ruizheng and General Zhang Biao.[23] Powell agrees that 'since the original mutiny was begun by two battalions, had the governor-general and Chang Piao [Zhang Biao] acted with firmness and courage, they could probably have retained the loyalty of the majority of the troops'.[24] V.P. Dutt also takes the view that 'had it not been for the lack of nerve shown by Jui-cheng [Ruizheng] and, to a lesser extent by Chang Piao, the victory of the revolutionaries would have been by no means certain'.[25] Other authors, who have pointed out that the Revolution of 1911 owed its success not so much to the revolutionary movement as to the alienation of the reformist elite (principally the constitutionalists), have tended to belittle the contributions of the soldiers who fired the first salvo of revolution.

To see the success of the Wuchang uprising as fortuitous is to ignore the strength of the Hubei revolutionaries and the extent of subversion already achieved in the Hubei New Army. Although it had no on-the-spot top revolutionary leadership and began suddenly and somewhat prematurely, thus bearing all the portents of certain failure, it proved to be a triumphant and immediate success, and became the beacon for all southern and western provinces to rise in rebellion. Had it not been able to maintain itself against the efforts of the government to crush it, it would have been just another fiasco like the Canton uprising of April 1911 or the Xiong Chengji mutiny of November 1908, the alienated reformist elite would have continued to wait and see, and the provincial assemblies would not have declared for the revolution as promptly as they did. The Wuchang uprising was a military coup, while the ensuing revolution was much larger than that. We can explain the success of the uprising in military terms, but not the revolution itself. The final outcome of the revolution may have had little to do with the mutinous troops of Hubei, but had the latter not turned against the government at a time when the constitutionalists were frustrated and estranged, there probably would not have been a revolution in 1911.

The provincial assemblies seemed to realise that from a military point of view the Wuchang uprising was different from the Sichuan disturbances, the April Canton uprising and all the earlier revolts. Neither April nor September of 1911 had been the right moment for the assemblymen to revolt. After 10 October, however, the situation was altered by the fact that significant sections of the New Army had unmistakably deserted the Throne. It was only then that the alienated assemblymen dared to act decisively. And only then was the overthrow of the Qing authority inevitable.

The outbreak of the Wuchang uprising was an interesting episode in itself. Following the amalgamation of the Literary Society and the Society for Common Advancement (see chapter 5), a meeting of the revolutionary leaders was held on 24 September 1911, at which a revolt was tentatively set for 6 October, the Chinese mid-autumn festival. This plan was communicated to Jiao Dafeng in the hope of instigating a simultaneous uprising in Hunan. Jiang Yiwu and Sun Wu were appointed provisional commander-in-chief and provisional chief of staff of the revolutionary forces, respectively. The mutineers were organised in different units, each of ten, thirty or ninety men, all of whom were to be led by representatives elected from the regular troops. A plot was carefully worked out. The transport and supply corps, as well as the engineer battalion, both stationed outside the Wuchang city wall, were to give the signal for action by setting their camps on fire. Then the artillery battalion was to seize the forts, while the engineer battalion was to force its way to the ammunition depot. The infantry units were to join the others for an attack on the viceroy's yamen. The cavalry was assigned patrol duties outside the city wall, while another artillery unit stationed in the southern suburbs was to enter the city. In Hankow, according to the plan, one section of the 42nd Regiment was to occupy the strategic pass of Wushengguan, and another to seize the Hanyang arsenal and the forts nearby. In any case, the revolutionary troops were to be commanded by their chief representatives.[26]

This conspiracy owed little to the work of the Tongmenghui. The Tongmenghui Central China Bureau, which was formed in Shanghai in July 1911, did not significantly influence the developments leading to the revolutionary outbreak in Wuchang. The Hubei men, in fact, failed to secure the leadership of Huang Xing and Song Jiaoren on the eve of the revolution.[27]

On 29 September Viceroy Ruizheng warned the diplomatic corps in Hankow that he had received a telegram from Canton stating that one thousand revolutionaries had left Wuchang and that trouble might arise.[28] The following day the American mission was warned by a Chinese student of an impending army mutiny and attack on the viceroy's office. The Hubei authorities admitted having heard such rumours and expressed much anxiety about the situation. Indeed, the situation was so serious that the British acting consul-general in Hankow found it desirable to maintain the presence of a British man-of-war in port for some time to come.[29]

Meanwhile, the native press in Hankow gave wide publicity to rumours that an uprising had been set for 6 October. The revolutionary leaders, therefore, were forced to postpone the revolt. No final date was fixed.[30] On 9 October Sun Wu and a few other revolutionaries were injured in an accidental explosion while manufacturing bombs in the revolutionary headquarters in Hankow's Russian Concession. Sun Wu was rushed to a private hospital. The authorities acted promptly, raided the headquarters, seized the membership register and other documents and made some arrests. Three revolutionaries were executed immediately. The revolutionaries now had no alternative but to rise in revolt according to the plan of 24 September, even though their leaders were either injured or still hiding somewhere.

There were revolutionaries in every unit except in the division and brigade headquarters, the military instructor corps and the 8th Transport and Supply Battalion. But they were not predominant either inside or outside the city wall of Wuchang, and only about one-third of the soldiers were definitely on their side (see Tables 5 and 6). However, substantial numbers of the remaining troops were either neutral or vacillating, and were likely to join the revolution when it got under way. Less than 10 per cent of the soldiers were Manchus.

Led by its chief representative, Xiong Bingkun, the 8th Engineer Battalion was the first to revolt.[31] The revolutionaries encountered little resistance and quickly occupied the ammunition depot. The

Table 5. Troops inside Wuchang city on 10 October 1911

Units	Attitudes of commanders	Revolutionary representatives	Remarks
8th Division Headquarters	Anti-revolutionary	—	No revolutionaries
21st Mixed Brigade Headquarters	Anti-revolutionary	—	No revolutionaries
29th Regiment (Infantry)* 1st & 2nd Battalions	Anti-revolutionary	5	One in three was a revolutionary
30th Regiment (Infantry)* 1st & 3rd Battalions	Commander of the 3rd Battalion was educated in Japan; attitude not clear. Other commanders were anti-revolutionary.	4	1st Battalion predominantly Manchus; 3rd Battalion half Manchu and half Chinese; one in three was a revolutionary
8th Battalion (Engineers)*	Anti-revolutionary	12	One in three was a revolutionary
41st Regiment (Infantry)#	Commander was educated in Japan; attitude not clear.	1	One in three was a revolutionary
80 students of the school of cartography#	No commander	1	One in ten was a revolutionary
Military police	?	1	Mostly Manchus, very few revolutionaries
Military instructors#	?	—	No revolutionaries
Three battalions of Patrol and Defence troops	?	—	Called into city to guard the viceroy's yamen on 9 October; no revolutionaries.
One unit of machine-gunners	?	—	Stationed in the viceroy's yamen; no revolutionaries.
One detachment of cavalry	?	—	
The fire brigade	?	—	

Miscellaneous: The 3rd Battalion of the 29th Regiment and the 1st and 2nd Battalions of the 41st Regiment had each a small number of troops

Table 5 (continued)

remaining behind in the city. Residing with the 3rd Battalion of the
41st Regiment were 100 troops transferred from the 42nd Regiment
for training.

Source: XHSYHYL, I, pp. 23-4; Li Lianfang, pp. 77a-80a;
          KGWX, *bian* 2, *ce* 1, *Wuchang shouyi*, pp. 268-9.
*   Units belonging to the 8th Division.
#   Units belonging to the 21st Mixed Brigade.

transport and supply corps, the engineers and the artillery units outside Wuchang city, responded quickly. After forcing their way into the
city, they occupied the forts, while a detachment was sent to join
those already in the ammunition depot. Meanwhile, the mutineers
inside the city moved swiftly. The 29th, 41st and 31st Regiments
revolted one after the other. The Manchus who formed a majority in
the 30th Regiment were helpless; most of them fled the city as soon
as they could.

The mutineers had the advantage of artillery support. Under
artillery pressure, the cavalry was forced to revolt, followed by the
32nd Regiment, 400 strong (the other battalions of this regiment
had been sent to Sichuan to deal with the railway disturbances).
Viceroy Ruizheng was not exaggerating when he subsequently reported
to the imperial government that the revolutionaries had emerged
from various quarters in large numbers. The revolutionary representatives had successfully carried out their task, while the commanders
and officers were unable to control the men. The neutral soldiers
had either run away or joined the revolutionaries in the end.

General Zhang Biao was forced onto the defensive. He moved
promptly after the revolt of the 8th Engineer Battalion, and set
up two lines of defence around the viceroy's yamen. His main support
was the 8th Transport and Supply Battalion, which had some days
before been brought into Wuchang. There were also the Patrol and
Defence Force, the viceroy's bodyguard, and other loyal troops from
the military headquarters. Zhang Biao commanded these troops in
person, trying in vain to persuade the mutineers to return to their
barracks. The revolutionaries, backed by the artillery, were able
eventually to break through the blockades set up by the loyal troops.
Viceroy Ruizheng then fled from Wuchang, after ordering Zhang
Biao to remain behind and await reinforcements. But, before long,
Zhang Biao was also forced to retreat to Hankow. Had it not been
for the strength of the revolutionaries, a competent official like
Ruizheng[32] and an able commander like Zhang Biao would not have
fled.

According to Hu Zushun, there were about four thousand new-

Table 6. Troops outside Wuchang city on 10 October 1911

Units	Attitudes of commanders	Revolutionary representatives	Remarks
32nd Regiment (Infantry)* Part of 2nd Battalion	Anti-revolutionary	3	Only the Left and Right Companies remained behind; others had been transferred; only a small number of revolutionaries.
8th Regiment (Artillery)* 1st, 2nd & 3rd Battalions	Regiment commander was educated in Japan; attitude not clear. Commander of 2nd Battalion was also educated in Japan, and was known to be sympathetic to revolution. Commanders of the 1st and 2nd Battalions were anti-revolutionary.	7	Two out of three were revolutionaries
8th Regiment (Cavalry)* 1st & 3rd Battalions	Anti-revolutionary	5	A small number of revolutionaries
8th Battalion (Transport & Supply)*	Anti-revolutionary	—	No revolutionaries
21st Battalion (Cavalry)#	Anti-revolutionary	?	A few revolutionaries
21st Battalion (Artillery)#	Anti-revolutionary	2	A few revolutionaries
21st Company (Transport & Supply)#	Anti-revolutionary	3	One in three was a revolutionary
21st Company (Engineers)#	Anti-revolutionary	2	One in three was a revolutionary

Source: As for Table 5.
*, # As for Table 5.

style troops in Wuchang, half of whom deserted during the uprising. The revolutionaries had mustered some two thousand men, including students from the school of cartography.[33] Hu did not know the strength of Zhang Biao's loyalist troops, but his estimate of the size of Wuchang's New Army is wrong. Qing official sources reported a total of 16,104 men in Hubei in 1910.[34] There was no substantial change before the revolution. On the eve of the uprising, almost half of them had been transferred to Sichuan or other parts of Hubei, thus reducing the number of troops remaining in Wuchang to about eight thousand, which was twice as large as Hu estimated.

A Japanese officer in Wuchang, Lieutenant-General Teranishi, reported that at the time of the outbreak, there was a total of about six thousand combatants, composed of five infantry battalions, three artillery battalions and one battalion each of engineers and transport. He said all of them had revolted, which, as we have seen, is not true. Besides, he made no mention of the cavalry, of which there were four squadrons in Wuchang.[35]

Another writer, Shao Baichang, who personally experienced the Wuchang uprising, estimated a total of 8517 troops in Wuchang on 10 October. The rest of them, 7587 strong, had been transferred to Sichuan (among them were a good many revolutionaries). Five hundred men were on sick leave or leave of other sorts. The revolutionary troops, including those who joined on the spur of the moment, numbered 3959. On the other hand, the loyalist forces, including the police, were 5049 strong. However, five hundred military constables and 1500 civilian policemen fled Wuchang shortly after encountering the mutineers, thus reducing the number engaged in actual fighting to 3049, that is, five hundred fewer men than the revolutionaries.[36]

Although Shao's figures cannot be verified, his estimate, which is based on his own personal experience, as well as on semi-official and various private sources, is probably correct. Certainly, it had been the strength of the mutineers which made the efforts to suppress them difficult. The transfer of allegiance of the soldiery had taken place before the flight of Ruizheng and Zhang Biao, neither of whom was to blame for the fall of Wuchang.

The Hubei military government

On the night of 11 October, Hanyang rose in revolt under the leadership of the Yangxia branch of the Literary Society. After forcing Song Xiquan, commander of the 1st Battalion of the 42nd Regiment, to side with them, the revolutionaries took possession of the arsenal and the ironworks, and secured a large quantity of ammunition. The 2nd Battalion stationed in Hankow mutinied the following moring. Before noon the revolutionaries gathered at the Hanyang arsenal, and elected Song Xiquan provisional commander of the revolutionary troops.[37] Zhang Biao's forces were driven to Kilometre 10 near the railway station, where they awaited reinforcements from the imperial government.

With the capture of Wuhan, the opening phase of the revolution was well begun. It was now imperative that a military government in Hubei be established immediately to restore law and order. Tang Hualong, president of the provincial assembly, was considered to be a suitable candidate for the military governorship *(dudu)*. A *jinshi* degree holder who had petitioned for the early opening of parliament, Tang had become very disappointed with the imperial government's constitutional reforms and had attacked the royal cabinet and its railway policy. He had expressed sympathy for the revolutionary cause by contributing twenty yuan to the Literary Society some months before the uprising. Tang's asset was, of course, his position in the Hubei provincial assembly and his influence among the local elite. But, when approached by the revolutionaries, Tang hesitated to be the military governor. His assembly colleague, Hu Ruilin, strongly advised him not to accept the offer, pointing out that they had no close relations with the revolutionary group, and that the prospects of the revolution were extremely uncertain. Tang appeared equally worried about the strength of the revolutionary forces, and that was why he declined the offer on the grounds that he had no knowledge of military affairs and was willing to serve in civil matters only.[38]

In the end Li Yuanhong, a non-revolutionary, was forced at gunpoint to be the military governor of Hubei, a choice which was dictated by a number of factors. The status of the revolutionary soldiers was too low to lend respectability to their movement, and leaders of the Literary Society had some time before considered appointing Li to the military governorship.[39] Li had a reputation for treating his troops well, and thus was acceptable to the military. As he was a man of note in Wuchang, it was expected that with him in the revolutionary camp the provincial assembly would be sympathetic and contribute towards establishing a new regime. The chaos resulting from the uprising called for immediate efforts to maintain law and order. The respective leaders of the Literary Society and the Society for Common Advancement were not on the scene, but even if they had been at hand, their mutual jealousies would have made it difficult to choose someone among them to be the military governor. After all, the overriding concern of the revolutionaries was the overthrow of the dynasty. They had no objections to a non-party military governor, as long as he suited their purposes and was willing to co-operate.[40]

Historians in the People's Republic of China have deplored Li's appointment as a political compromise between the revolutionary and non-revolutionary forces, a compromise which, they maintain, reflected the political weaknesses of the revolutionary party and which marked the beginning of the failure of the revolution.[41] But, from the point of view of the mutinous troops of Hubei, they had now secured the service of a man who commanded respect from the local army, who enjoyed the support of the provincial assembly and the local population, and who seemed capable of influencing the attitudes of other disaffected provinces. Not least important, he was to lead a movement which appeared to the foreign community in Hankow to be in possession of 'the foresight and powers of organisation'.[42] Li's personality attracted foreign sympathy, for he looked capable and well-intentioned, and his ability to communicate in English gained him the respect of foreigners in Hankow.[43]

Li was significant as a symbol of law and order around which the provincial assembly, the local elite and the local populace could rally, thus giving the Hubei military government a firm local base.[44] Tang Hualong and his colleagues in the provincial assembly supported Li and served in civil administration. The prestige of Li and Tang attracted the constitutionalists and former bureaucrats, many of whom were installed in important positions in the military government. The revolutionaries turned to them in the hope of gaining respectability for their movement and organising a new regime quickly and effectively. A compromise with the provincial assembly and Qing officials was seen as the shortest way to the establishment of a new order with a minimum of bloodshed. This compromise began with Li Yuanhong, not with Yuan Shikai. Indeed, this pattern of collaboration between the New Army and the provincial assembly was soon to be followed in many other provinces which declared their independence.

Revolution in the provinces

On 22 October revolution broke out in Hunan, an event which significantly strengthened the revolutionary cause. Reinforcements from Changsha were sent to Wuchang to fight the loyalist troops arriving from north China. Before the end of October, six provinces including Hubei had declared for the revolution, followed by another ten provinces before the end of the year.

Table 7 sets out the dates and the circumstances in which the revolution occurred in the provinces in October–December 1911. An analysis of the events shows a number of interesting points. First, all the uprisings which occurred in October (in Hubei, Hunan, Jiangxi (Kiukiang), Shaanxi, Shanxi, and Yunnan) were led by the New Army, though in the case of Hunan gentry leaders soon asserted themselves because of the weakness of the secret society and New Army leadership. The fall of Qingjiangpu, Chinkiang and Nanking (all in Jiangsu) was also the work of the new-style troops.

Second, in nine provinces, Guizhou, Zhejiang, Guangxi, Anhui, Fujian, Guangdong, Sichuan (Chengtu), Jiangxi (Nanchang), Jiangsu (Suzhou), the revolution was initiated by the provincial assemblies acting in conjunction with the gentry, merchants, and chambers of commerce They were supported by the New Army, which would probably have revolted on its own had the assemblies not acted first. With the exception of the revolution in Nanchang, these provinces had watched the course of developments and carefully assessed the political and military realities existing in the country before taking the grave step of rising against the established authority. Much had depended on opportunities to secure the sympathy and support of the army. The opportunities presented themselves eventually, since there was a substantial number of revolutionary adherents among the officers and men of all ranks. Thus, in many instances, the assemblies collaborated with the military commanders in running the new military governments.

Third, of the twenty-five successive military governors (excluding Sun Baoqi of Shandong who shortly withdrew the independence of his province) belonging to sixteen provinces, fourteen were connected with the New Army, two were presidents of provincial assemblies, three were provincial governors, four were Tongmenghui leaders, one was a Qing official (but not governor), and one was a revolutionary and secret society leader. Of the fourteen military governors who had been members of the New Army, six were graduates from Japanese military schools, and twelve were major-generals, brigadiers or lieutenants, most of whom had been prompted into revolting by the junior officers.

Fourth, with the exception of Wuchang, Nanking, Xi'an, Taiyuan, Foochow and Kunming, the political takeover in the provinces was a peaceful process. In some instances the Patrol and Defence Force offered some resistance, but on the whole the old-style troops realised that it was futile to resist a movement led by the New Army or the provincial assemblies.

It is evident then that the New Army contributed significantly to the revolution either independently or in conjunction with the assembly-men, local gentry, rich merchants and chambers of commerce. The collaboration between the New Army and the assemblies ensured a

Table 7. Revolution in the provinces, October-December 1911

Provinces	Date	Military governors	Circumstances
Hubei	10 October	Li Yuanhong*	As already described.
Hunan	22 October	Jiao Dafeng[S] (first) Tan Yankai[P] (later)	Started by junior officers of the New Army; the commander of the Patrol and Defence Force was killed; revolution supported by the provincial assembly. On 31 October, a party of mutinous troops assassinated Jiao Dafeng and Chen Zuoxin, the deputy military governor. Tan Yankai, president of the provincial assembly, became the new military governor.
Shaanxi (Xi'an)	22 October	Zhang Fenghui*•	The New Army led by battalion officer Zhang Fenghui revolted; some resistance from the Patrol and Defence Force; fighting in the province for three days. The provincial assembly supported revolution and held the reins of civil administration.
Jiangxi (Kiukiang)	23 October	Ma Yubao*	The 53rd Regiment under the command of Ma Yubao revolted; joined by other troops of the New Army. All the senior Qing officials fled Kiukiang.
Shanxi (Taiyuan)	29 October	Yan Xishan*•	Junior officers of the New Army revolted; resistance from the Patrol and Defence Force. The governor and his sons were killed; the provincial assembly supported revolution.
Yunnan (Kunming)	30 October	Cai E*•	Initiative taken by instructors of the military officers' school and officers of the 73rd and 74th Regiments of the New Army; some resistance from loyalist troops led by the commander of the 19th Division and the military police.

Provinces	Date	Military governors	Circumstances
Jiangxi (Nanchang)	31 October	Wu Jiezhang* (first) Peng Chengwan* (later) Li Liejun• (finally)	Kiukiang having revolted, the governor of Jiangxi was helpless; the provincial assembly, supported by merchant organisations, school teachers, scholars and students, resolved to declare for the revolution. They co-operated with the New Army and elected Brigadier-General Wu Jiezhang as military governor.
Guizhou (Guiyang)	3 November	Yang Jincheng*•	Resolution of various circles, students, merchants, journalists, who rallied behind the provincial assembly. The governor was asked to declare for the revolution. When he refused to do so, the provincial assembly turned to Yang Jincheng and made him military governor. The New Army supported revolution; little violence.
Jiangsu (Shanghai)	3 November	Chen Qimei[R]	'People's army' organised by Tongmenghui leaders took the lead; supported by merchant organisations and the police; resistance from loyalist troops in the arsenal. Shanghai fell into revolutionary hands fairly quickly, followed by Wusong.
Zhejiang	4 November	Tang Shouqian[O]	When the governor refused to declare for the revolution as requested by the provincial assembly, the New Army revolted. The local Manchu garrison, under strong artillery pressure, surrendered. The new military governor was formerly manager of the railway bureau.

Table 7 (continued)

Provinces	Date	Military governors	Circumstances
Jiangsu (Suzhou)	5 November	Cheng Dequan[G]	A party of revolutionaries from Shanghai consulted with officers of the New Army in Suzhou, sought the support of the local gentry and merchants, and resolved to ask the governor to declare for the revolution, which he agreed to do.
(Qingjiangpu)	7 November	Jiang Yanheng*•	The New Army revolted and established a branch military government.
(Chinkiang)	7 November	Lin Shuqing*	The 36th Regiment revolted. The naval ships anchored in the port, twelve in all, sided with the revolutionaries. Little violence. A branch military government was set up.
Guangxi (Guilin)	7 November	Shen Bingkun[G] (first) Lu Rongting* (late)	Resolution of the provincial assembly, supported by the New Army. Little violence. The governor became the new military governor.
Anhui (Anqing)	8 November	Zhu Jiabao[G]	Resolution of the provincial assembly, supported by merchant organisations.
Fujian (Foochow)	9 November	Sun Daoren*	Resolution of the provincial assembly, supported by the New Army. Some resistance from Manchu troops. The commander of the 10th Division became military governor.
Shandong (Tsinan)	12 November (independence withdrawn on 24 November)	Sun Baoqi[G]	The provincial assembly, local gentry and merchants, the New Army and the police, jointly submitted eight demands to the Manchu court. When these demands were rejected, they organised a 'protect peace association', which elected Governor Sun Baoqi as military governor. This declaration of independence was later with-

Provinces	Date	Military governors	Circumstances
			drawn owing to internal strife between Sun Baoqi and officers of the 5th Division.
Guangdong	13 November	Hu Hanmin[R]	Resolution by merchant organisations and the provincial assembly. Supported by the New Army. Acting Viceroy Zhang Mingqi refused to be the military governor and fled Canton. Hu Hanmin was elected. Pending his arrival in Canton, Jiang Zungui, an army officer, was acting military governor.
Sichuan (Chongqing)	22 November	Zhang Peijue[R]	Tongmenghui revolutionaries took the initiative, backed by the New Army.
(Chengtu)	27 November	Pu Dianjun[P]	Pu Tianjun, president of the provincial assembly who had been arrested in connection with the railway disturbances, was released by Viceroy Zhao Erfeng. He was elected by the provincial assembly to be the military governor. Later Zhao Erfeng was killed by the troops of the New Army.
Jiangsu (Nanking)	2 December	Xu Shaozhen*	The New Army revolted, supported by troops from Zhejiang. Fierce battle with the loyalist forces commanded by Zhang Xun.
Shandong (Chefoo)	12 December	Hu Ying[R]	Tongmenghui revolutionaries induced the navy in Chefoo to support revolution and set up a military governor there.

Source: Compiled by the author from a variety of sources.
*   associated with the New Army
•   Japanese-educated officers
R   Tongmenghui revolutionary leaders
G   provincial governors
P   presidents of provincial assemblies
O   Qing official, but not governor
S   revolutionary and secret society leader

relatively non-violent revolution accomplished in the space of a few months. After the Wuchang uprising, law and order became a serious problem in many provinces, with considerable social and political unrest, coupled with fears, anxiety and uncertainty on the part of the populace.[45] The army and the assemblies quickly moved into this situation, both seeing the overthrow of the imperial authority as a political necessity and a means of restoring law and order. In provinces where independence was declared with their provincial administrations intact, disturbance of the peace was prevented. In others the overthrow of the established order led to lawlessness and crime.[46] Thus the new revolutionary authorities made every effort to preserve order with the co-operation of the army and the assemblies.

For its part the New Army needed the civil elite to further its republican cause. The latter, too, was anxious to establish a new order partly to avert the danger of foreign intervention which might result from a protracted civil war, and partly to install themselves in positions of power. The military leaders were, however, not an appendage of the civil elite. Rather, they were mutually dependent, as evidenced by the fact that only two military governors were former presidents of provincial assemblies, and that most of the assembly-men served as civil administrators in the military governments. Indeed, these new provincial regimes were military-gentry coalitions.

The ability of the new regime to maintain peace and stability through civil-military co-operation was conditioned by the potential for disaffection and internal dissension in either the civil or the military ranks, or both. As far as the soldiers were concerned, their actions and behaviour would depend on the extent to which their old grievances were redressed, and whether or not new grievances would emerge. Unfortunately, new problems were quick to arise, causing considerable army unrest throughout the country as soon as the old regime was overthrown (see chapter 9).

The military situation in north China

The Wuchang uprising took the imperial government by surprise. Only a week or two before, the General Staff and the Ministry of War had been preparing for the autumn manoeuvres, and troops of the 2nd, 4th, 6th and 20th Divisions, and the Imperial Guard Corps, had been assembled in the vicinity of Kaiping and Luanzhou along the Peking-Mukden line. On the night of 13 October, it was officially announced that the manoeuvres were cancelled. Yinchang, the Minister of War, was commanded to lead a southern expeditionary force to suppress the revolution in Hubei. On the following day Yuan

Shikai was appointed Viceroy of Huguang, with command of the provincial troops and the forces under Yinchang. As the loyalty of the northern troops was doubtful, it was hoped that Yuan's appointment would strengthen the hands of the government in dealing with the crisis.[47]

When the first batch of imperial troops was sent to the south, Sheng Xuanhuai, the Minister of Posts and Communications, told G.E. Morrison in Peking that these troops were 'thoroughly untrustworthy'. The 6th Division was 'in the highest degree dangerous'. It was disaffected, and contained large numbers of Hubei troops who appeared to be sympathetic towards the mutinous troops of Wuchang. Sheng was worried that this division, which was about to be sent to the front, would join the rebels. He also suspected the loyalty of the 4th Division in Tientsin.[48]

On 14 October, it was reported that sections of the 6th Division in Baoding had mutinied and that Tientsin was also in trouble. Little was known about the real situations there, but on 15 October the Peking government admitted that the New Army in Baoding, Tientsin and parts of the metropolitan area had 'revolutionary intentions'.[49]

The Beiyang troops were divided into three armies. The 1st Army which formed the southern expeditionary force consisted of two battalions of the 1st Division (mostly Manchu troops), almost the entire 2nd, 4th and 6th Divisions, and the Henan 29th Mixed Brigade. The 2nd Army, commanded by Feng Guozhang, was made up of the 20th Division in Luanzhou, the 3rd Division in Changchun, and the 2nd Mixed Brigade in Mukden. The 3rd Army, commanded by Zaitao, was composed of the Imperial Guard Corps and the bulk of the 1st Division, sections of the 4th Division and the 5th Division in Tsinan.[50]

As soon as the 1st Army had left for Hankow, the government feared that the troops in the rear, especially in Henan Province, might revolt, a possibility which was increased by the shortage of ammunition and military funds.[51] These fears proved to be well founded. On 22 October, shortly after the revolution in Hunan, the troops in Xi'an, the provincial capital of Shaanxi, mutinied, and declared their adherence to the republican cause. Commenting on the revolutionary situation in north China, G.E. Morrison reported from Peking on 26 October:

> There is wide-spread disaffection in the Army. The revolutionary movement is extending so rapidly and so peacefully. It has been so well organised, and is so well directed that the possibility is now being discussed here of the revolutionaries gaining all they need without bloodshed, bringing the Government to terms . . .

There seems little doubt that Tung Kuan [Tongguan in Shaanxi] has joined the rebels. If Kaifeng [in Henan] should do so, there will be a belt across the course of the railway of disaffected country, which would prevent the return of the troops. Such an act might also lead to an early settlement of the trouble.[52]

On 29 October the Shanxi army in Taiyuan revolted. Led by young officers, these troops killed the governor and his two sons, and then moved down the railway to its junction with the Peking-Hankow line, with the intention of cutting the communications of the imperial troops under Yinchang with Peking. This disheartened Yinchang's men who were reported to have shown no disposition to fight.[53]

Meanwhile, 5000 troops of the 20th Division stationed at Luanzhou refused to entrain for the south, and their commander, Zhang Shaozeng telegraphed Peking, demanding twelve conditions as the price for the advance to the front. The telegram was signed also by Lu Yongxiang, commander of 5th Brigade, Lan Tianwei, commander of the 2nd Mixed Brigade, Wu Xiangzhen, commander of the 39th Brigade and Pan Juying, commander of the 40th Brigade. The twelve demands were as follows:

1. The emperors of the Da Qing Dynasty shall transmit the succession to ten thousand generations.
2. Parliament shall be established this year.
3. The constitution shall be drawn up by parliament and endorsed and promulgated by the Throne.
4. All proposals regarding constitutional changes must originate in parliament.
5. The armed forces of the empire, though subject to the control of the emperor, shall not be used in domestic troubles except under special regulations to be drawn up by parliament.
6. Sentence of 'death on sight' or 'summary execution' may not be pronounced by the Throne. Arrest and imprisonment of the people shall not take place except by due process of law.
7. A general amnesty shall be proclaimed for all political offenders.
8. The premier shall be elected by parliament and appointed by the emperor. The ministers of state shall be appointed by the premier. Members of the imperial clan shall be forever ineligible to serve as members of the cabinet or as ministers of state.
9. All treaties which add to the burdens of the people or concern the general interests of the nation shall be approved by parliament before final signature by the emperor.
10. The budget for any year shall be first approved by parliament before it can be used for the payment of the national expenses of the succeeding year.

11. The election of members of parliament shall be in accordance with the special requirements fixing the qualifications of electors.

12. The above methods specified for the calling of parliament and the establishment of constitutional government, as well as for the settlement of all important questions of state, shall be subject to discussion by the army.[54]

A week or so before, some revolutionaries had tried in vain to induce Zhang Shaozeng to declare for the republican cause. In his preference for a constitutional monarchy, Zhang had the support of Wu Luzhen, who had been sent to 'reason' with him. But Wu's attitude was in fact ambivalent. Before he left Peking, he was said to have confided to some friends that he had two alternatives: either to join forces with the 20th Division to overthrow the dynasty, or to join forces with it to demand a constitutional monarchy. The first option was difficult because the other divisons of the Beiyang Army were strong enough to defend Peking. The second was preferable since it would gain the support of some Manchu princes with whom Wu was on good terms. It could also result in the political demise of Yuan Shikai, whom Wu hated. When Yuan was 'settled', Wu would watch the course of future developments before attempting to accomplish the 'ultimate goal'. Wu, however, did not say what the 'ultimate goal' was.[55]

Wu had discussed with Zaitao and Liang Qichao the desirability of staging a *coup d'état* in Peking. At the same time, he seems to have communicated with Yan Xishan, commander of the Shanxi revolutionary forces, about the possibility of a joint advance on Peking. These commanders may have assumed that the imperial government would reject their demands, thus providing a legitimate cause for attacking Peking. But, as Ernest Young has pointed out, they were not necessarily revolutionary; Wu for one 'was neither fixed in his aims nor certain of the proper means to effect them'.[56]

The 'twelve demands' remains an intriguing incident. The American military attaché doubted that Zhang Shaozeng and Wu Luzhen were the authors of the memorial, and claimed that the author was Chen Jintao, a member of the National Assembly.[57] According to Sir John Jordan, the aim of the mutinous troops at Luanzhou was 'to extort guarantees for constitutional reform from the Throne', and they were understood 'to be acting with the approval, if not at the instigation of Yuan Shi-k'ai, who has been in close communication with them'.[58] There can be no doubt that Yuan wanted a constitutional monarchy. But the question of his relationships with Zhang Shaozeng, Lan Tianwei, Wu Luzhen and others who had signed the memorial still awaits answers which more intensive research might provide.

In any case, the strong position held by the mutinous troops at Luanzhou had an important bearing on the political situation. On 30 October a penitential edict was issued in which the imperial house stood self-condemned for the trouble brought upon the country. Another edict excluded the 'princes of the blood' from holding offices of state. Two other edicts respectively ordered the National Assembly to frame a constitution and granted a general amnesty to all political offenders.[59]

The mutinous troops were, however, dissatisfied with these edicts. The Shandong army, 15,000 strong, and the 6th Division in Baoding joined in urging the Throne to comply with all the other demands.[60] On 1 November Zhang Shaozeng sent a small detachment to Peking with an ultimatum. On the following day his troops seized two train-loads of ammunition going south. This immediately forced the Throne to order the National Assembly to draw up the constitution. The assembly, then, lost no time in passing nineteen articles embodying the principles of the constitution. At the same time, Yuan Shikai was summoned to Peking to form a new cabinet. Two days later, an edict approved the nineteen articles and authorised, as a temporary measure, the discussion by the army of matters pertaining to constitutional reform.[61]

From a military point of view, the position of the imperial government was precarious. The 1st Army was fully occupied in Hankow, and its communications with Peking were cut by the Shanxi rebels, who were holding the rail junction of Jingxing. The 2nd Army at Luanzhou, Mukden and Changchun was in a state of partial mutiny. The troops likely to remain loyal (including the provincial troops) were kept in Peking.[62]

Another danger was the condition of the 6th Division, part of which had been dispatched to the railway junction of Shijiazhuang under the command of Wu Luzhen, who had been designated Governor of Shanxi with a mission to pacify the rebels there. On 7 November Wu was murdered by a party of Manchu soldiers of the 1st Division probably on the orders of some faction of the Peking court.[63] Only two days before, he had impeached Yinchang for the imperial troops' excesses in Hankow. His assassination further complicated the situation and intensified the antagonism between Manchus and Chinese.[64]

The state of affairs at Luanzhou, too, remained unsettled. Although most of its demands had been complied with by the imperial government, the 20th Division was still untrustworthy from the government's point of view. Zhang Shaozeng, shortly after the penitential edict of 30 October, was ordered to go to the front and pacify the rebels in the Yangzi area. He refused, and instead asked for cars to rail his troops to Peking, which the General Staff rejected on the grounds of shortage of railway stock.[65] On 8 or 9 November, probably the latter, Zhang resigned as commander of the 20th Division. Rumours were then rife that Zhang, infuriated by Wu Luzhen's assassination, wanted to march on Peking with his troops. On 11 November, Zhang declared himself a military governor, and advised the Tientsin diplomatic corps of his intention to seize Tientsin. The attack on Tientsin was, however, not carried out. Three days later, Zhang was ordered to come to Peking, an order which he disobeyed. But shortly afterwards, he went to the capital, accompanied by seven staff officers and a bodyguard of thirty-seven men. After some discussion with Yuan Shikai (the subject of the discussion is unknown), Zhang went to Tientsin, where he was to 'convalesce from his illness', and where he said in public that he supported neither the Manchus nor the Chinese.[66]

By the end of November, Zhili was practically the only province which had not been outwardly affected by the revolutionary movement. It would appear that the north could not possibly hope to bring the remaining provinces again into line, even if the Beiyang Army remained loyal. The arrival in Peking of Yuan Shikai on 13 November could not save the dynasty, although it would save Zhili from civil strife. Yuan had more effective control of the imperial troops than anyone else in Peking, but that did not alter the fact that these troops were 'entirely defensive', as Yuan frankly told Sir John Jordan.[67] They were concentrated on three areas: Peking, Shijiazhuang and Baoding. To protect these places, Yuan even took troops from the lines of communication of the 1st Army.[68]

Yuan's task was a stupendous one. Apart from the uncertainty of the Beiyang troops, he was faced with serious financial problems. The dire financial straits were evident from the fact that the palace treasure hoarded by the late Empress Dowager had been used for defraying the current expenses of the government. Nearly a third of the total amount of money derived from the sale of the treasure had been remitted to the Ministry of War for the purchase of ammunition and the payment of the troops.[69] But this money would not last very long. Supplies from the provinces had been practically cut off. Should the shortage of funds affect their pay and food, the loyalty of the remaining imperial troops would be severely strained.[70]

It was in these circumstances that Yuan Shikai, acting through the intermediary of the British acting consul-general in Hankow, proposed a three-day armistice between the revolutionary forces and the 1st Army operating in Hubei. Already on 2 November and 27

November loyalist troops had reoccupied Hankow and Hanyang respectively. But the imperial victory was more than offset by the loss of Nanking to the revolutionary forces on 2 December, the day before the truce officially began. The subsequent peace negotiations will be omitted here. The fall of Nanking, however, deserves some attention.

The fall of Nanking

Following the outbreak in Wuchang, there was much talk of revolution in Nanking. As a matter of precaution, Viceroy Zhang Renjun stripped the disaffected modern troops of ammunition and the bolts of their rifles. The troops demanded the return of their ammunition for fear that in the event of trouble they would be massacred by their rivals, the old-style troops who were reputed to be fiercely hostile. The viceroy conceded to the demand, but Tieliang, the Tartar-general, backed by the provincial treasurer, objected so strongly that in the end no ammunition was handed out. Consequently, a mutiny nearly broke out among the men, who were finally pacified by a compromise, whereby they were to move out of the city and to receive the ammunition at Molingguan, a camp about twenty-five kilometres south-west of Nanking. Subsequently, the 9th Division, already depleted by desertion, marched out of the city.[71]

On 6 November an imperial edict ordered Viceroy Zhang to offer no opposition to the revolutionaries should they attack Nanking. Tieliang, however, refused to credit the edict, and announced his intention of holding out against the revolutionaries to the bitter end. He entrenched himself with 2000 Manchu troops in the Tartar city, and mined the approaches to it. He had the support of General Zhang Xun, commander of the old-style troops, of whom there were fourteen battalions inside the city. When the local gentry and merchants urged the viceroy to declare for the revolution, he refused. But in fact the viceroy and practically all the other officials in Nanking favoured surrender, for the revolutionaries in the city were just awaiting reinforcements from Zhejiang, Shanghai, Suzhou and Chinkiang. Tieliang's bluster was not taken seriously. General Zhang Xun, it was believed, could be bought off.[72]

On 8 November the advance-guard of the revolutionary army, composed of the 34th Regiment of the 9th Division, marched to Nanking from Molingguan. The following morning an attack was made on the Yuhuatai fort, less than a kilometre outside the south city gate. The revolutionaries were repulsed by Zhang Xun's forces and sustained heavy losses because of misplaced confidence in the disloyalty of the garrison of the fort.[73]

In the following weeks there was renewed fighting outside Nanking city. The loyalist troops who had many reverses were forced to abandon almost every vantage point held by them. Towards the end of the month, Nanking was practically besieged. The revolutionaries were now joined by reinforcements from Zhejiang and other parts of Jiangsu. On 28 November Nanking was bombarded. Two days later, there was heavy firing from Pukou, which was attacked by the revolutionaries from Yangzhou and Qingjiangpu with a view to cutting off the only means of escape for General Zhang Xun and his troops.

On 2 December Nanking surrendered. Zhang Xun, who was believed to have been bought off, crossed the river to Pukou, accompanied by the viceroy and the Tartar-general. He then retired up the Tientsin-Pukou railway to Xuzhou.[74]

With the capture of Nanking, the major operations between the revolutionary and the imperial forces were concluded, despite some minor fighting which took place on the Shanxi border later in December.[75] Politically, the revolutionary leaders found themselves in a stronger position at the peace conference, and persisted in their uncompromising opposition to the retention of the monarchy. Finally, they could now set about establishing a provisional government in a venue acceptable to most of the provinces which had declared for the new order.

Abdication of the Monarchy

On 6 December an imperial decree announced the abdication of the Regent and appointed two high officials, one Manchu (Prince Chun, the ex-Regent) and one Chinese (Xu Shichang), to be guardians of the Emperor. The conduct of the government was to be carried on by Premier Yuan Shikai and his cabinet ministers, while Empress Dowager Longyu and the Emperor would preside at audiences and ceremonial functions.[76] This announcement was, however, not taken by public opinion in Peking at its face value as a further step towards constitutional government. Rather, it gave rise to considerable suspicion that the Empress Dowager's party had gained ascendancy over that of the Regent, and that the former was trying to return to the previous system under which the late Empress Dowager Cixi had controlled the imperial government.[77]

In spite of the peace negotiations throughout December and the early months of 1912, there was a general feeling among military leaders of the revolutionary party that the Beiyang Army was still a force to be reckoned with and could not be won over to the republican cause without further fighting.[78] In Hunan, for example, the distrust of Yuan Shikai was 'bitter and deep-seated', and the general opinion of the revolutionary leaders there was that fighting would eventually be resumed.[79] Preparations were made for a simultaneous advance on Peking from Hankow and Nanking. A Cantonese revolutionary contingent arrived in Shanghai on 4 December, and threatened to land at Qinhuangdao at the Gulf of Zhili.[80]

Before the end of 1911, over ten thousand troops had been sent north from Nanking, and were concentrated at Linhuaiguan and Bangbu on the Peking-Pukou line. The Nanking army was expanding rapidly, numbering 55,000 men at the beginning of 1912, composed of new levies as well as regular troops from Jiangsu, Zhejiang, Fujian, Canton and Guangxi. Reinforcements were sent to Wuchang, where the revolutionary forces had been brought up to a strength of 45,000 men, consisting of the local New Army, raw recruits and contingents from Anhui, Jiangxi, Hunan and Guangxi.[81] On 16 January 1912 the 'northern punitive army', composed of troops from Shanghai and the southern provinces, landed at Chefoo, and secured a footing in Shandong by seizing the port of Dengzhou. These troops formed the advance-guard of an expeditionary force against Peking, which was to be under the command of Lan Tianwei, who had failed to start a revolution in Fengtian two months before.[82]

These military movements, coupled with the revolutionaries' uncompromising attitude towards the dynasty, forced Yuan Shikai to accept the inevitable. He had been advised by Tang Shaoyi, the imperial peace envoy, that the feeling in the southern and eastern provinces was entirely in favour of a republic, and that the only way to meet the popular demand was to convoke a National Assembly to deliberate upon the future form of government.[83] Furthermore, Yuan realised that there were increasing difficulties in paying the imperial troops and in purchasing military equipment. Earlier, the government had issued 'patriotic bonds', a compulsory levy upon government officials. Another 2,000,000 taels had been obtained from members of the imperial family, and more treasure stored in the Imperial Palace had been converted for the use of the government.[84] Finally, the declaration of independence in Luanzhou on 3 January, although it was crushed a few days later,[85] had increased Yuan's sense of uncertainty regarding the loyalty of the northern troops.

Yuan's position was becoming extremely precarious. He was hated by the Manchus as pro-revolutionary and distrusted by the republicans as a stubborn loyalist. On 16 January an unsuccessful attempt was made on his life. The assassins were allegedly associated with some members of the imperial house who opposed peace with the revolutionaries.[86]

On 17 and 22 January, the Manchu and Mongol princes met for consultation. Zaize, Zaitao, Zaixun and Natong advocated war, while the ex-Regent, Prince Qing and Pulun favoured abdication of the monarchy. Zaize was the most aggressive of all, and he found an ally in Tieliang, the ex-Tartar-general of Nanking who had lately arrived in Peking. A scheme was on foot to place Tieliang in command of the imperial forces to resist the revolutionaries. It was also common talk in Peking that Tieliang wanted to kill Yuan and make Zhao Erxun, Viceroy of Manchuria, the new premier. (Zhao Erxun had hardened his attitude towards the republicans because they had recently executed his brother, Zhao Erfeng, the late Viceroy of Sichuan.) Afterwards, the rumours went, a Boxer-type movement would be launched to defend the dynasty.[87]

Another Manchu who strongly opposed any idea of abdication of the monarchy was Liangbi, deputy chief of the General Staff. A *Shikan* graduate (the third class), Liangbi was an able official who had done much to increase Manchu influence in the Imperial Guard Corps.[88] Together with Zaixun, he formed a royalist party called *Zongshedang*. He worked closely with Tieliang, and they had some discussion with the Japanese minister in Peking, Ijuin, who was in favour of a monarchy in China and seems to have encouraged them to sustain the imperial cause.[89]

The other officials in Peking were non-commital, shirking as much responsibility as they could. Nearly every cabinet minister and vice-minister was either on sick leave or was begging for leave on some excuse.[90] The delay in reaching a peaceful settlement gave the opportunity for court intrigue. There was increasing pressure from the 'war party' to get Yuan Shikai out of Peking, and at one time arrangements were said to have been made for a train to take Yuan to Tientsin.[91]

On 27 January Liangbi was seriously wounded by a bomb thrown by a fanatic who was himself killed by the explosion. Liangbi died a few days later. On 29 January an unsuccessful attempt was made to assassinate Zhang Huaizhi, the imperial general commanding at Tientsin, who had recently displayed unusual vigour in opposing the republicans.[92] These outrages had a powerful effect on the Manchu princes who opposed abdication. There was an aura of terror in Peking. As Sir John Jordan observed,

The machinery of government is entirely disorganised, and the legation quarter and the concessions at Tien-tsin are full of refugees like Na T'ung and others who in the days of their power were never tired of abusing these privileged resorts of foreigners.[93]

At this juncture the condition of the imperial forces pointed to the probability of an imminent peaceful settlement. As of 2 February, there were in Peking a total of approximately 33,400 troops, of whom 14,400 belonged to the provincial troops called *Wuwei zuojun*. Significantly, the Manchu troops, 14,000 men in all, were outnumbered by Chinese troops who were 19,000 strong. Moreover, the Imperial Guard Corps had recently indicated, in a leaflet distributed in the streets, that it had no hostility towards Chinese soldiers, and that in view of the trouble and miseries that had been brought upon the central provinces, it was determined to ensure that there would be no disturbance of the peace in the capital.[94]

Meanwhile, the southern expeditionary force had become very disaffected. The troops had been influenced by revolutionary litera- ture and notices from Wuchang urging them not to fight against their fellow countrymen and offering rewards for desertion.[95] Those who had fought hard for the imperial cause were infuriated by Yuan's orders that they were to retire from positions won by them while the revolutionaries were advancing along the Peking-Hankow line.[96]

On 28 January a telegraphic memorial, signed by Duan Qirui and forty-three other generals and commanders of the Beiyang Army, was presented through the cabinet, the General Staff and the Ministry of War, urging the immediate formation of a republican government. The signatories included the names of such stout adherents of the old regime as Jiang Guiti, commander of the *Wuwei zuojun*, He Zonglian, commander of the 1st Division and Acting Military Lieutenant- Governor of Qaha, and Zhang Xun, who commanded the imperial forces at Xuzhou. It would be interesting to know the inner history of this memorial. It was obvious that the document did not represent a spontaneous wish on the part of all the commanders concerned for a cessation of hostilities. Indeed, several of them would have welcomed an opportunity of trying conclusions with the revolutionary troops. The memorial was most probably intended to be an answer favoured by Yuan Shikai to the machinations of Tieliang and the younger Manchu princes who objected to abdication but could not provide the means to continue hostilities. Yuan was known to have expressed extreme reluctance to allow another appeal to arms. He had declined, however, to attend any meeting of the imperial clan at which abdica- tion had been discussed. In the meantime, he and his adherents seem to have tried to convince the Throne that it had little to lose that was not already lost and much to gain by abdication.[97]

With the desertion of the army, the cause of the Manchu dynasty was lost. Zaize and his reactionary associates subsequently left for Mukden to see if there was any chance of resuscitating the fallen fortunes of the dynasty in their homeland.[98] What remained to be done was to negotiate the terms on which the Emperor was to retire with honour.

On 12 February an imperial edict invested Yuan Shikai with full powers to organise a provisional republican government and to negotiate with the leaders of the republican party for the unification of the north and the south. Another edict enumerated the terms of treatment acceptable to the imperial family. A third edict exhorted the officials and people to do their duties under the new government and to take every measure to preserve the peace.[99]

Thus ended the Manchu dynasty. The subsequent events leading to the establishment of the Republic and Yuan's assumption of the presidency have been documented elsewhere.[1] It is of interest to add that once the republicans had resolved to accept Yuan as the president, most military leaders throughout the country pledged their support for him. Their attitude was summed up in a letter from V.K. Ting (Ding Wenjiang, a notable geographer educated in England) to G.E. Morrison in May 1912:

A good deal of nonsense has been inculcated about the differences between the North and the South, especially the distrust the Southern Army has for Yuan. This is quite groundless, I think. The Southern troops are quite enthusiastic about Yuan's personality. I have numerous friends occupying important military posts here [Shanghai], and I find them one and all supporters of Yuan's policy. I shall not be surprised if someday the country may find the army (northern or southern) too enthusiastic about the President whose title may be changed into another. I heard at least one high military official expressing his belief that if we want the country to be united, we shall make him emperor.[2]

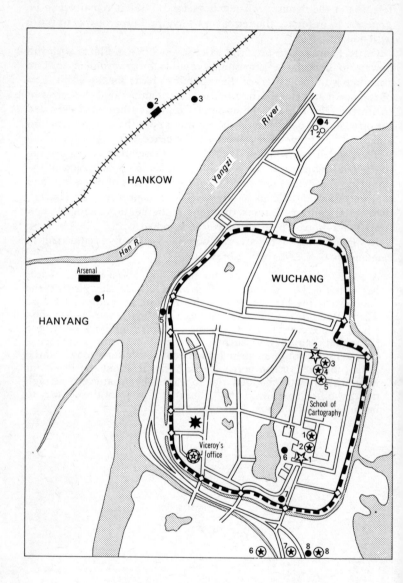

2. Troops in Wuhan, 10 October 1911

Key to map 2

✸	Headquarters of the 8th Division
☆ 1	Headquarters of the 15th Infantry Brigade
☆ 2	Headquarters of the 21st Mixed Brigade and the 16th Infantry Brigade
✪ 1	29th Infantry Regiment
✪ 2	30th Infantry Regiment
✪ 3	31st Infantry Regiment
✪ 4	41st Infantry Regiment (a small number of troops only)
✪ 5	42nd Infantry Regiment (a small number of troops only)
✪ 6	32nd Infantry Regiment (a small number of troops only)
✪ 7	8th Cavalry Regiment
✪ 8	8th Artillery Regiment
● 1	1st Battalion of the 42nd Infantry Regiment
● 2	2nd Battalion of the 42nd Infantry Regiment
● 3	3rd Battalion of the 42nd Infantry Regiment
● 4	21st Artillery Battalion
● 5	8th Transport and Supply Battalion
● 6	8th Engineer Battalion
● 7	Military Police Battalion
● 8	21st Cavalry Battalion
○ 1	21st Transport and Supply Company
○ 2	21st Engineer Company
✪	Forces stationed in the viceroy's office:

           Three battalions of the Patrol and Defence Force
           One battalion of military instructors
           One unit of military police
           One unit of machine-gunners
           One detachment of cavalry
           The fire brigade

┼■┼┼┼	Railway station
◇	City gates

NINE

The state of the army in 1912-13

FOLLOWING THE demise of the Qing dynasty, the Chinese authorities were faced with the problem of law and order. The presence of a large number of superfluous troops, the growing influence and power of the military leaders, the rivalries between different political groups, financial difficulties, and above all the inability of the civil administration to establish itself in most parts of the country, all contributed to instability of the early Republic. The use of violence in 1911 produced both desirable and undesirable effects. It destroyed Manchu authority; it raised the level of military spirit; and it gave the soldier a sense of pride and importance. On the other hand, the revolution brought the military into the forefront of national politics, thereby creating considerable disorder after the fall of the old regime. The troops in the south had increased more than necessary, and those returning from the front caused a great deal of trouble to the new order which was yet to be firmly established. As a result of their role in the revolution, these troops became arrogant and too unruly to subordinate themselves to the civil authorities. Indeed, with the collapse of the imperial institutions and centuries-old ideologies and the inability of new ones to emerge quickly enough to hold state and society together, the traditional concept of civil supremacy was seriously challenged.

During the revolution, there were encouraging signs of a burgeoning martial spirit among the troops and evidence of improved efficiency from a professional point of view. Unfortunately, the New Army, for the most part, was soon disorganised by the revolution, as a result of which much of the work of the Qing reformers was undone.

There was a wide range of problems arising from the destruction of the imperial system. This chapter confines itself to an examination of the state of the military in 1912-13 and of the issues which directly affected it. The chapter begins by assessing the efficiency of the New Army in actual service, followed by an analysis of the revolutionary impact on the army and a brief account of the Republic's efforts to reorganise it. Finally, the chapter describes the performance of the

Troops marching towards Hankow

In camp

Artillery in position

Hospital corps of the Chinese army

Captured rebels

Reconstructing a destroyed railway near Hankow

government troops during the 'second revolution' of 1913 and the state which they were in by the end of the year.

The combat effectiveness of the New Army

The New Army had not been tested in any foreign war, and without such a test, it would be difficult to assess it as a military institution. The Revolution of 1911 provides probably the only basis on which the discipline and efficiency of the Chinese troops during a period of actual service can be judged. Thus, a look at the operation of the 1st Army, the expeditionary force in the recapture of Hankow in November 1911, is instructive.

According to eyewitness accounts by foreign military experts, the imperial army was very 'business-like' in conducting itself on the battlefield. It was led by officers who had good control over their men. The soldiers were on the whole well disciplined, although they paid little outward deference to their company officers. They looked sturdy, healthy, cheerful and contented, even during the worst weather and hardest fighting, and showed great strength of character, pluck and endurance under frequently depressing circumstances. More significantly, there was a good *esprit de corps*. Professional pride was noticeable in every branch, especially after each success. Indeed, they impressed all foreign observers with a 'decided air of independence' which marked the advent of a new China.[1]

The actual fighting reflected both the strengths and weaknesses of the imperial troops. Their Maxim guns worked well and the engineer corps was well equipped. Their artillery dispositions seemed good. Earth-works were well done; ammunition and guns' crew shelter pits were 'very snug and well concealed'. Their war equipment was satisfactory; both the time and percussion fuses were good, and there were very few blind shells. On the other hand, their shooting left much room for improvement. The time-shrapnel frequently burst too high to produce any real effect. They were also somewhat slow in their tactical and strategic movements, and were particularly weak in holding positions.

Another major criticism of the imperial troops related to the medical department which had always been of a low standard. Although the sanitation corps and the stretcher bearers carried out their work well and the rearward transport of the wounded soldiers was efficiently done, the personnel of the field hospitals was insufficient to cope with the numerous cases, and they would have fared badly but for the ready assistance of foreign, missionary doctors.[2]

Foreign observers generally agreed that the revolutionary troops were markedly inferior to the imperial army. This was true not only of the revolutionary soldiers in Hubei but also of those elsewhere. A study conducted by an officer of the 6th Australian Light Horse in February 1912 of the troops in Canton, Shanghai, Suzhou, Wuchang and Nanking showed that with a very few exceptions the revolutionary troops were 'an undisciplined rabble' who would have been no match for the Beiyang Army if it had fully supported the dynasty, a fact which was emphasised in accounts from many other quarters.[3] Thus, in military terms, it was more the desertion of the Beiyang Army than the fighting efficiency of the southern revolutionary troops that proved to be the instrument for the eventual undoing of the imperial government.

Yet, the revolution revealed Chinese soldiers in an entirely new light. The fighting in Hankow belied the traditional assumption that Chinese soldiers had no stomach for war. The combatants on both sides displayed a remarkable military spirit. The revolutionaries, though badly officered and badly armed, fought with a courage and enthusiasm which commanded general admiration. According to an eyewitness,

> There was not the least sign of malingering; the one anxiety of the wounded in the hospitals was to get back into the fighting line at the earliest possible moment. It is impossible to ignore the fact that these men were animated by zeal for a cause in which they thoroughly believed, and that they felt themselves to be fighting to free their country from a foreign yoke which had become intolerable. This new spirit will have to be reckoned with in all future dealings with the Chinese.[4]

The growth of the military spirit was also noticeable elsewhere. In Ichang, for example, children between eight and fourteen years of age were drilled every day, armed with various weapons, some of which were made of wood, and calling themselves 'dare-to-dies'. In the graveyards outside the British consulate, as well as in the neighbouring hills, they were taught various tactics in attack and defence. Drilling continued to be practised intensively throughout 1912. 'If the Revolution had no other result', said a British diplomat, 'the awakening of the military ardour is sufficient to make it a note-worthy movement'.[5] It was evident that Chinese troops had become more soldierly and that they were capable of fighting hard for a cause if they considered it to be fair, just and important for their self-preservation.

Disorganisation of the New Army

One of the immediate results of the revolution was the disorganisation of the New Army in south, west and central China. Partly because of their zeal for change and partly because of a need to increase the strength of their fighting force during the civil war, the revolutionary authorities had deliberately broken up or altered the existing military organisations. New formations of all sorts had sprung into existence, and were in such a constant state of change that it was impossible to obtain accurate details regarding their numbers and groupings. The composition was of an extremely varied nature. In most cases the nucleus was composed of the regular and provincial troops of the regions concerned. The majority of the soldiers, however, were newly raised levies, including large numbers of discharged soldiers, rickshaw men, bandits, loafers, coolies, and (especially in Canton and Guangxi) criminal elements. In Nanking the newly raised levies included even corps of 'Amazons' whose existence was a source of embarrassment to the military authorities.[6]

That these new forces were largely inefficient should have occasioned no surprise, since they were hastily raised heterogeneous elements without any military training whatsoever. Actually, not all of them were soldiers in the sense the term would have been used in the New Army. Large numbers of them had no uniforms, no drill or discipline. Many were without weapons of any description; they had been enlisted or enrolled voluntarily as soldiers of the revolution.[7]

Furthermore, the officers of these armies were far inferior to those of the northern divisions. Some of them, probably the better ones, had previously been regular officers and non-commissioned officers of the New Army. Others, notably the company officers, were either promoted from the ranks or young lads fresh from the military primary schools. The field and staff officers consisted of young men who had been educated in a foreign military college or in a Chinese military secondary school. Brigadier-generals were as far as possible returned military students from Japan. Division and army commanders, however, were for the most part political appointments of old men who had held high command in one of the armed forces existing at the time of the revolutionary outbreak. Many of them, especially battalion and company officers, had been elected by the men themselves, and most were incompetent and immature.[8] The non-commissioned officers in Shanghai, for example, still lacked the dignity to resist chewing sugar cane in uniform in the street.[9] In short, only a small proportion of these revolutionary troops, notably those who were drawn wholly from contingents of the New Army, were good in a professional sense.

These new formations were given numbers and a divisional organisation similar to those of the New Army. In practice, however, such divisions were only skeleton ones, consisting chiefly of infantry and staff. They were, as a rule, numbered independently by provinces. The divisions based on Nanking were, however, numbered, with some omissions, from 1 to 26 because of the presence of several contingents which had come from a number of provinces during the capture of the city the previous December.[10]

It is of interest to note that the Republican Army of the central and southern provinces adopted a new organisation for its troops and used new terms in designating the various units and officers, as shown in Tables 8 and 9.

In the north, however, the framework of the original New Army organisation remained intact, though many divisions had been greatly reduced by war losses and subsequent desertions. During the revolution, the composition of the military forces of Manchuria, Zhili, Henan and Shandong had not been altered to a very great extent. After Yuan Shikai's return to power as President of the Republic, the Right Division of the Military Defence Army, Yuan's original force before the Boxer uprising, was revived. It was now called the Republican Guards *(Gongweijun)*, organised on the model of the old Military Defence Army. Another change during 1912 was the addition to the force in Shandong of the Front Division of the Military Defence Army under General Zhang Xun, a similar force to the Republican Guards. The nucleus of this formation was the original force of the Righteous Army *(Yijun)* quartered at Pukou at the outbreak of the revolution.

Other changes, though not extensive, were effected in the Beiyang Army. Early in 1912 Yuan Shikai, in an effort to make up for the troops lost during the revolution, ordered the immediate formation of a supplementary force known as the *Beibujun*, which was to be divided into five districts *(lu)*.[11] Despite objections from the revolutionary authorities in Nanking to any attempts by the President to increase troops in the north, there was a restrengthening of the Beiyang Army. In Shandong, the 5th Division had recruited a new regiment of infantry, designated the 18th, to replace the troops who had been sent to Manchuria in 1907 to form the 1st Mukden Mixed Brigade. In Manchuria, although it had been less affected than other provinces by the revolution as regards disorganisation of the army, the unsettled conditions in 1912 caused a number of military changes there. The provincial troops had been considerably augmented, and were moved about frequently from one place to another to prevent disturbances. Regarding the New Army, the 2nd Mixed Brigade in Mukden was being expanded to division strength (the future 29th Division), while two new regular divisions, designated the 27th and 28th, had begun formation by the end of the year.

Table 8. Organisation of the Chinese Republican Army showing
the new and old terms for the various units

Units	Old terms	New terms
Corps or army	*jun*	*jun*
Division	*zhen*	*shi*
Brigade	*xie*	*lü*
Regiment	*biao*	*tuan*
Battalion	*ying*	*ying*
Company	*dui*	*lian*
Section	*pai*	*pai*
Squad	*peng*	*ban*

Source: WDGS, No. 6562-9, Organisation of the Chinese army of the south. Major
Bowley to War Department, 24 May, 1912.

Table 9. Organisation of the Chinese Republican Army
showing the new and old terms for the military ranks

Military ranks	Old names	New names
Field Marshal	*da jiangjun*	*da jiangjun*
General Commanding an Army Corps	*zheng dutong*	*da jiangjun (?)*
Lieutenant-General (or Major-General)	*fu dutong*	*zuo jiangjun*
Brigadier-General	*xietong*	*you jiangjun*
Colonel	*zheng canling*	*da duyu*
Lieutenant-Colonel	*fu canling*	*zuo duyu*
Major	*xie canling*	*you duyu*
Captain	*zheng junxiao*	*da junxiao*
Lieutenant	*fu junxiao*	*zuo junxiao*
Second Lieutenant	*xie junxiao*	*you junxiao*
Sergeant	*zhengmu*	*shangshi*
Corporal	*fumu*	*zhongshi*
Second Corporal	nil	*xiashi*
1st Class Soldier	*zhenbing*	*shangdengbing*
2nd Class Soldier	*fubing*	*yidengbing*
3rd Class Soldier	nil	*erdengbing*

Source: As for Table 8 [Old names added]

There were also plans to augment the troops in Jilin and Heilongjiang. Elsewhere in the north, the losses of the Beiyang divisions caused by desertions or otherwise during the revolution were being gradually made up in 1912. The 1st (Manchu) Division was drafted during the course of the year to Qaha (Kalgan) and the Mongolian frontier, where it was scattered in small detachments over a wide area. In its stead the Republican Guards were placed as the central force in Peking, with detachments posted around the residence of the President and in various parts of the city. The Imperial Guard Corps was still, for the most part, quartered in the vicinity of the Summer and Winter Palaces. The 3rd Division, part of which had mutinied in Peking at the end of February 1912, had mostly been brought back to the Nanyuan barracks near Peking.[12]

Disbandment of troops and army unrest

The army, which had been instrumental in maintaining law and order in the early months of the revolution, became a source of trouble as soon as the dynasty collapsed. Throughout 1912 and in most parts of 1913 there were numerous cases of army mutiny, disturbance and unrest in the country. The principal cause of trouble was the excessively large size of the army as a result of the revolution. In a speech before the Nanking Assembly on 29 March, 1912, Premier Tang Shaoyi estimated the strength of the Republican forces at eighty divisions. What the Premier meant probably was, as War Minister Duan Qirui believed, that there were eighty different commands or organisations and not divisions as the term was used in the New Army. The important point was that the total strength of men who had been enlisted by the revolutionary leaders numbered approximately one million.[13] This estimate might have been exaggerated, but even conservative estimates would have put the figure in the order of between forty-five and fifty thousand men whose existence prevented an early resumption of authority.[14] In Hubei there were about one hundred thousand troops quartered mainly in Wuchang.[15] In Changsha there were over fifty thousand men, most of whom had returned from the front.[16] In Nanking the troops numbered twenty thousand including contingents from Canton, Zhejiang, Jiangxi, and Hunan, as well as local levies.[17]

It was generally agreed among senior government officials that many of these troops should be disbanded as speedily as possible, especially in view of the increasing difficulties in paying them. Tang Shaoyi recommended the immediate disbandment of twenty divisions (each varying in strength from a few companies to twelve thousand men) of the southern army. He had the blessing of Yuan Shikai, who announced in his inaugural presidential speech in the Senate on 29 April that the Ministries of War and Finance had been ordered to reduce the army significantly.[18] Likewise, Vice-President Li Yuanhong expressed grave concern over the danger to the country of the presence of so many men under arms with their pay in arrears. Indeed, Li deplored the chaotic state of affairs in a telegram to Yuan Shikai:

When the civil war began, troops were enlisted throughout last autumn and winter; they were without discipline and regarded crime as a title to merit, and anarchy as duty. To them mob law spelled equality and browbeating coercion was freedom; their general's prestige afforded them a talisman on which to trade, and honourable names became material for party catchwords. The example spread from above, and if one went under, another took his place. Rewards and punishments were not distributed with impartiality, commands ceased to carry weight: each province assumed independence of action, and each army acted like masters in their own house . . .[19]

The interrelated problems of finance and troop disbandment taxed the skill and ingenuity of every responsible government official. Even Yuan Shikai had experienced trouble with his troops in late February and early March 1912 in consequence of, among other things, the order of the Ministry of War to discontinue the special 'active service rate', and the rumour that wholesale disbandment of troops was contemplated.[20] It was quite common for the pay of the troops to be a few months in arrears, a situation which was as bad as before the revolution. Thus, to disband a large proportion of the troops would require, first of all, paying them all that was due to them. Second, it would be necessary to give them gratuities and provide them with transport to their original place of abode. Lastly, but not least important, they must be found alternative jobs.

For their part, the soldiers who did not receive their pay became extremely unruly, and were given to mutinies, looting, extorting money from the local gentry and merchants, and molesting the civil population. Those awaiting disbandment often found the terms on which they were to be sent away unacceptable, and that they did not have a job to return to. After being disbanded or dispersed in the country, many took to brigandage and other criminal activities.

Disbandment affected the officers as well, and herein lay another source of trouble. The military authorities found it impossible in the case of the disbanded regiments to pay off the officers as well as the men. In Nanking the viceroy was forced to appease the officers concerned by giving them temporary commissions as military aides-de-camp on his staff.[21] Elsewhere retrenched officers proved to be as much a problem to the authorities as disbanded soldiers.

This situation was aggravated by the shortage of funds. From the very beginning the Republic was beset by a practically empty treasury and was therefore unable to provide funds to the provinces for sending their superfluous troops home. To meet the financial exigencies, the government was obliged to resort to foreign loans. Even before the Manchus had abdicated, Yuan Shikai had begun negotiations with the six-power banking consortium (now including Japan and Russia). In April 1912 Tang Shaoyi was trying to borrow money from a Belgian bank, and this annoyed the consortium so much that it protested to the President and made a number of demands as conditions for future loans. These conditions included, among other things, the setting up of an army association in Peking to which foreign military attachés were to be appointed as supervisors to disband troops in Nanking, Wuchang and elsewhere. Tang Shaoyi opposed this demand very strongly for it was an infringement upon China's sovereign rights in the management of military affairs. Yuan disavowed his intention to borrow from the Belgian bank, but Tang was supported by Li Yuanhong and other leaders in the south, where a strong anti-foreign feeling was aroused. The consortium refused to recede from its position of foreign supervision, and this brought the loan question to a standstill.[22]

In June Tang resigned as Premier because of his political differences with Yuan. Xiong Xiling, the Minister of Finance, then renewed negotiations with the consortium, and the demand for foreign supervision was eventually dropped. Subsequently, the consortium advanced an initial 12,000,000 taels to the Chinese government.[23]

The receipt of the proceeds of the foreign loan helped to ease the problem of the soldiers' pay. Disbandment was being gradually effected. Abundant harvests were anticipated, and this relieved the situation and assisted in sending the troops back to their homes.[24] During the months of July and August, a total of 83,583 troops was disbanded in various provinces.[25]

The state of affairs early in 1913 was more peaceful than the previous months. Brigandage was still rife throughout the country; army disturbances were still frequently reported, but the authorities were active in repressing disorders. In some places village volunteer corps had been formed to preserve law and order. Disbandment of troops seems to have made appreciable headway, although no official figures had been issued by the Chinese government. Nevertheless, the presence of the superfluous troops and of a substantial number of ex-soldiers who had no means of making a decent living constituted the most dangerous factor in the country.[26]

There were, of course, other factors contributing to the unsettled state of affairs after 1911. One of them was the bearing of those who had played an active part in the overthrow of the established authority. A case in point was Changsha, where the behaviour of the troops who had returned from the front was 'exceptionally arrogant and lawless'. They went about pilfering and looting, intimidating and maltreating the people. The gendarmeries, too, were in a state of revolt because an officer unacceptable to them had been placed in command of their corps; their agitation did not subside until the officer in question was replaced.[27]

Another cause of unrest was the internal dissension among various political factions and revolutionary groups. Among those who had participated in the civil war were many who had expected to profit substantially from the political change and were disappointed that they did not receive, in their view, a fair share of the spoils. In Jiangxi, for example, there were five military governors in five different places before the province was united under Ma Yubao in Nanchang. In March 1912 internal strife led to Ma's replacement by Li Liejun, after the cold-blooded killing of Ma's protégé, Zhu Hantao, the security chief.[28] In Changsha a plot was made by an army faction sympathetic towards Jiao Dafeng, the first military governor of Hunan, and his deputy, Chen Zuoxin, both of whom had been killed on 31 October 1911, to murder the new military governor Tan Yankai. In August another similar plot almost succeeded. The ringleaders were executed, but the disorders among the soldiery continued for some time. Many outbreaks were subsequently engineered by Jiao's adherents who had formed a secret society known as the *Hong-jianghui* (great River Society) to avenge his death.[29]

In Wuchang, Sun Wu, head of the general staff, quarrelled with some of his revolutionary colleagues who accused him of placing his friends in positions they were incompetent to fill. Towards the end of February 1912, he was deposed from office after the return to Wuchang of the 31st Regiment which had been sent to Sichuan the previous September.[30] Li Yuanhong, in his capacity both as military governor of Hubei and as Vice-President of the Republic, endeavoured to keep the peace between rival political groups. Yet, in spite of his personal popularity, he did not enjoy the confidence of the local revolutionaries, and was always in danger of falling victim to assassination. His political rivals wanted to remove him, but he was quick enough to remove some of them from important positions and had a couple of hostile commanders executed.[31]

Military intervention in politics was not confined to the provinces. In Peking army commanders had also taken to politics and supported one party against the other. Early in June 1912, five districts of the Zhili army (from Tientsin and the metropolitan area) expressed strong opposition to the intended appointment of Wang Zhixiang, a pro-Tongmenghui element, as military governor of Zhili. The appointment had been made officially by the Zhili provincial assembly and endorsed by Premier Tang Shaoyi. But Yuan Shikai regarded Wang as an undesirable person for the post; so, with the support of the Beiyang Army, he announced on 15 June the appointment of Wang as Pacification Commissioner of the Southern Army *(Nanfangjun xuanfushi)*.[32] This appointment was not countersigned by the premier as required by the constitution.

Attempts at reorganisation

From the beginning, the Republic attached considerable importance to military affairs, and Yuan Shikai himself took a particular interest in them. Scarcely had he been installed in power when he ordered the formation of a military secretariat in the presidential palace *(Zongtongfu junshichu)* headed by Feng Guozhang, commander of the Imperial Guard Corps. In the meantime, the Ministry of War was reorganised into five bureaux. However, relatively little work was done there, since important matters were dealt with in the military secretariat, which became a small but influential advisory body to the President.[33]

The government's military policies were stated at a session of the Senate on 13 May 1912, by Duan Qirui, the Minister of War. The main tasks the government set itself were as follows:

    a. reorganisation of the army and disbandment of supernumerary and ineffective troops;

    b. adoption by officers of military service as a definite and lifelong profession;

    c. improvement of military education;

    d. conscription;

    e. establishment of factories for the manufacture of arms, accoutrements, and uniforms;

    f. improvement of horse-breeding.[34]

Meanwhile, Li Yuanhong also issued a similar policy statement from Wuchang emphasising the following points:

    a. unification of the nation's armed forces;

    b. compilation of a military atlas of China;

    c. further implementation of military education;

    d. adoption by officers of military service as a permanent profession;

    e. disbandment of troops and increases in pay for the military profession.[35]

Central to the reorganisation scheme was the unification of military administration and command. The assumption underlying this was that unless such unification was achieved, the central government would have little effective control over the provinces which were largely dominated by army commanders. The disorders and assertiveness of the military after 1911 warranted renewed efforts to bring the nation's armed forces under one system. In June 1912, Duan

Qirui proposed that the Ministry of War review the appointment of all middle-ranking officers and above with a view to dismissing the inefficient ones; investigate and manage all the provincial arsenals and arms depots; audit the financial accounts of the provincial military establishments; and assess the impact of the revolution on the state of military education in the provinces.[36]

To standardise the armies throughout the country, the Peking government revived the late Qing system whereby they were designated regular armies, first reserves, and second reserves. A total of forty divisions of regular troops was envisaged. Conscription was to be the rule, applied without discrimination to the five races which made up China's population.[37] For Peking, conscription was more than a military issue: it had a political dimension which could prevent the provinces from recruiting as freely as had been the case during the revolution. But conscription was predicated on a nationwide census, which would take a long time to complete.

Centralisation raised the question of the power relationship between the civil and military officials in the provinces. This meant a review of the functions of the military governor, a new title created by the revolutionaries to denote the official who exercised both civil and military powers in a province or district. He had access to the troops in his province or territory and rode roughshod over the civil administrators. His rule not only ran counter to the celebrated tradition of civil supremacy but also threatened the central government with military separatism.

To prevent the military leaders from establishing themselves as regional satraps, the Peking leadership found it necessary to separate civil and military powers. In other words, the responsibilities of the military governor should be confined to the military realm, while the powers of the chief civil executive officer (governor, *minzhengzhang*) should be increased to a comparable level in terms of administrative control. This would still fall short of subordinating the military governor to civil control, but at least his powers would be curtailed and a semblance of civil rule would be maintained.

Li Yuanhong, whose power base was in Hubei, supported Peking's policy. On 10 April 1912, he sent a telegram to Peking, listing ten disadvantages of the military in politics which would beset China if the military governor's role was not redefined. A week later, he appointed Fan Zengxiang as the chief civil executive officer to pave the way for the restoration of civil authority in Hubei.[38] In June, he set an example by giving up voluntarily his military rule of Hubei and turning over the government to the civil authorities. He retained his position as Vice-President of the Republic and his influence as the strong man of the south. Though a soldier himself, Li abhored military participation in politics and appeared sincere and honest in supporting the separation of civil and military powers.[39]

However, the reactions of the other provinces were far from favourable. It was generally felt that given the existing state of law and order throughout the country, the time was not yet appropriate for such division of power. The strongest opposition came from the south, particularly from Fujian, Jiangxi and Guangdong, where the military governors feared that they would have too much to lose.[40] Such fears were not completely unwarranted, since the Peking government was unable to define clearly the respective duties of the military governor and his civilian counterpart. Apparently, the government was extremely wary about the whole matter, trying to avoid as far as possible any direct confrontation with the provincial leaders at a time when the Republic was still so insecure. It had to temporise and to move slowly. In August 1912 an association for the discussion of civil-military separation was formed in Peking by order of Yuan Shikai. Provinces were asked to send delegates to the capital to discuss means of achieving such separation. But once again, this yielded no results. Most provinces were still opposed to it, Shanxi and Sichuan being the only ones, apart from Hubei, which expressed support for it.[41] Thus, by the end of the year, only a few provinces, including Zhili and Jiangsu, had established separate civil authorities.[42] But even so, there could be no doubt that the military governors there, as elsewhere, still retained their influence and were actually the real power holders.

An attempt to define the military governorship was made in January 1913 when a presidential order was promulgated to the effect that China was to be divided, for purposes of military administration, into several regions, two or three of which were to be placed under one military governor. It did not state when such division was to take place, but it added that until then each province was to remain under the administration of a military governor who was to have control over all the troops within his territory. He was to be under the direct authority of the President as well as the General Staff and the Ministry of War in all military affairs. In case of local disturbances, he might dispatch troops to the aid of the civil governor or other officials upon request. But in the process, he was required to report to the President as well as to the Chief of Staff and the Minister of War.[43]

Apparently, the Peking leadership was anxious to subordinate the provincial military leaders to central control. Only two months before, Yuan Shikai had resolved at a high-level meeting with senior government officials that all senior army commanders throughout the country be appointed by the President.[44] Indeed, Yuan and now gathered into his hands the power to appoint, transfer and dismiss military governors as well as army commanders. In July 1913, Yuan ordered military governors Li Liejun of Jiangxi and Hu Hanmin of Guangdong to vacate their offices because of their open defiance of the central government. Li Liejun gave up his office quietly and went to Shanghai to launch a movement against the President. Hu Hanmin accepted philosophically his transfer to Tibet as Commissioner of Tibetan Affairs and left for Hong Kong, later joining the anti-Yuan forces in Shanghai.[45]

Another important question the Republic had to resolve was the number of military districts and the desired strength of the Chinese army. Yuan Shikai's wish was to divide the country into eight military districts, each with five divisions of regular troops managed by a military governor who was responsible to the central government.[46] The strength of a division (now called *shi*) was a few thousand men less than a Qing division. Under a lieutenant-general, it consisted, at full strength in times of peace, of 12,368 to 12,512 officers, men and non-combatants. It contained one cavalry regiment, one artillery regiment, one engineer battalion, one battalion army service corps, one band and one sanitary detachment. In theory the war footing of a division was about 20,900 officers, men and non-combatants.[47]

At the beginning of 1913, one native newspaper reported that the strength of the Chinese army (both the regular and provincial troops) was estimated at one million men, which was about the same as in March the previous year.[48] This figure seems to have been highly exaggerated; one suspects that there were padded rolls and that the provincial authorities tended to inflate the figures in order to ask for more money on the grounds that they wanted to disband the superfluous troops. A more reasonable estimate would be 529,000 men, as reported by the British military attaché.[49]

On 11 February 1913 a high-level meeting was held in the Ministry of War, with representatives from the provinces. It resolved to maintain the Chinese army at a strength of fifty divisions, not forty as previously suggested by the government, to be distributed among the provinces depending on their size, resources and strategic importance. It also noted that Guangdong had the largest number of divisions (eight), followed by Hubei (four), while other provinces ranged between two and three. It further resolved that when the distribution of divisions and the problem of funding were settled, the Ministry of War should prepare a more detailed scheme of reorganisation for submission to the National Assembly.[50]

In August the estimated total strength of the Chinese army was

500,000 men.[51] It rose slightly towards the end of 1913 to 588,000 because of the increase in strength of the northern units and the re-enlistment of troops during the 'second revolution'.[52] The government's policy to maintain a national army of fifty divisions was upheld, even though this would appear to be an impossible task for some years to come because of financial difficulties. In December, a scheme for the division of the country into nine military districts was considered. It involved the abolition of the post of the military governor, as well as a complete reorganisation of the provincial administration. The military districts were planned as shown in Table 10.

Table 10. Proposed military districts, December 1913

District	Provinces included	Strength
A	Fengtian	4 divisions
	Jilin	2 divisions
	Heilongjiang	2 divisions
	Rehe	1 (?) division
	Suiyuan	1 (?) division
B	Zhili	6 divisions
	Henan	2 divisions
	Shandong	2 divisions
	Shanxi	2 divisions
C	Hubei	3 divisions
	Hunan	1 division, 1 brigade
D	Jiangsu	3 divisions
	Anhui	1 division
	Jiangxi	1 division
E	Zhejiang	1 division, 1 brigade
	Fujian	1 division, 1 brigade
F	Guangdong	3 divisions, 1 brigade
	Guangxi	2 divisions, 1 brigade
G	Yunnan	2 divisions
	Sichuan	2 divisions
	Guizhou	2 divisions
H	Gansu	2 divisions
	Shaanxi	2 divisions, 1 brigade
I	Yili	1 (?) division
	Qinghai	1 (?) division

Source: *The China Year Book, 1914*, p. 321.

However, this scheme was not carried out. The plan for fifty divisions proved to be too ambitious and unrealistic. In 1915, the Ministry of War reverted to the earlier suggestion for forty divisions to be distributed between five military districts as shown in Table 11.

Table 11. Proposed military districts, 1915

District	Provinces included	Divisions
I	Zhili, Shandong, Henen, Shanxi, Shaanxi	11
II	Jiangsu, Jiangxi, Anhui, Zhejiang, Fujian, Hunan, Hubei	8
III	Sichuan, Yunnan, Guizhou, Guangxi, Guangdong	6
IV	Manchuria, Inner Mongolia	6
V	Gansu, Xinjiang, Qinghai, Alashan	4

Source: *The China Year Book, 1916,* p. 229.

Table 11 shows only a total of thirty-five divisions. But each district was also to have two mixed brigades, which probably were regarded as equivalent to five divisions. Owing to a combination of internal and external factors, this scheme, like the previous one, was never implemented.

At this juncture one might wonder what role foreign experts played in this reorganisation scheme. After the revolution, the number of foreign instructors remained small. An American source states that up to the end of 1913 there was one German officer, one French officer and several Japanese officers acting as instructors in the military schools.[53] The Republic had no intention of dispensing with them or of making more appointments. However, in the autumn of 1913 there were rumours that China had called upon Germany to assist her in training Chinese troops. Duan Qirui quickly denied that, assuring the American military attaché, Major A.J. Bowley, that the rumours were totally without foundation. Yet, some time later, Duan stated to Major Bowley privately that he hoped some day to have American officers on duty as instructors in the Chinese army. The Washington government reacted to this with great enthusiasm.[54]

Duan's attitude conflicted with the government's existing policy, which was not to engage foreign officers in the training of the Chinese army. Whether it was his personal preference or whether it represented a desire of the government to change its policy, is difficult to ascertain. Whatever may have been the case, the Acting Minister

of War, Jiang Zuobin, later told Major Bowley in a personal interview that while the Chinese government greatly appreciated the
willingness of the US government to detail officers for duty with the
Chinese army, existing political conditions in China did not permit
this to be done. Jiang further explained that Japan was extremely
envious of every move made by the United States, and that if China
accepted an American military officer she would be forced to accept
many times more from Japan. The Chinese government, Jiang
stressed, was not prepared to take Japanese officers as instructors
with the troops.[55]

Yet, to reject foreign officers as such was one thing, to appoint
them as advisers to the government was quite another. There were,
in fact, foreign advisers in nearly every branch of the central government. In the Ministry of War there were Lieutenant-Colonel Brissaud-
Desmaillet, Major von Dinkelmann, and Colonel Banzai Rihachirō.
Lieutenant-Colonel Brissaud-Desmaillet of the French infantry was
formerly military attaché of the French legation in Peking. A
graduate of the École de Guerre, he was a respected officer in the
corps of foreign military attachés.[56] Major von Dinkelmann was
previously employed as an instructor in a Chinese military school.
He had retired from the German army and his appointment was
made at the request of the German government.[57] Colonel Banzai
from the Japanese army had been an adviser to Yuan Shikai and the
chief umpire in the grand manoeuvres of the Chinese army in 1906.[58]
The different nationalities of these advisers showed that the Chinese
government did not wish any particular country to exert a dominant
influence in the administration of Chinese military affairs. It was
not until 1917 when Major-General Aoki Norizumi, formerly military
attaché of the Japanese legation in Peking, was appointed special
adviser to Duan Qirui, the Premier and Minister of War (in the new
cabinet appointed by President Li Yuanhong following Yuan Shikai's
death), that Japanese influence in the Chinese army became apparent.[59]

It is difficult to say how much these advisers did to improve the
Chinese army. So far there is no evidence to show that they played an
active part in reorganising it, at least not in the years 1912-14.[60] The
little that they did during this period was relatively unimportant and
somewhat unrealistic. To illustrate this point, we need only look at
the contribution of Lieutenant-Colonel Brissaud-Desmaillet. He spent
much of his time devising a scheme for the creation of a mobile national
gendarmerie in China. Under this scheme, the gendarmerie was to
have a strength of 5500 officers and 125,000 men, in addition to the
ordinary police and the active army. The main objects of this force
were, first, to reinforce the police in the maintenance of law and

order and, second, to suppress brigandage. The scheme also appeared to aim at the conversion of the semi-regular troops throughout the country into a more homogeneous force under the control of the central government. They were to be supplied with modern weapons, gunboats and river launches, and trained by a cadre of Norwegian officers. It was argued that the regular army, freed from the duties of suppressing brigandage, would be able to devote itself to training for national defence.[61]

This scheme was an extremely expensive one. Lieutenant-Colonel Brissaud-Desmaillet hoped that it would be financed by a foreign loan. However, there was no reason to believe that the powers would authorise the associated banks to advance the necessary funds on the plausible plea that the scheme would help solve the problem of troop disbandment. Furthermore, it was doubtful whether China would need such a large police force. Rather, it could be argued that a relatively small corps of gendarmerie, well trained and well equipped, would be more desirable and effective in maintaining law and order and suppressing brigandage. In any case, the scheme never materialised.

The army in the 'second revolution'

One of the political problems facing the infant Republic was the antagonism between the north and the south, which had been developing rapidly since the assassination of Song Jiaren on 20 March 1913, culminating in the so-called 'second revolution' in the summer of that year. Unlike the Revolution of 1911, the 'second revolution' was a purely military rising. It did not have the support or sympathy of the people at large who felt that they had little to gain from another civil war. There was a general desire for a return to peace and order. The merchants, in particular, almost unanimously opposed further disturbances to trade and fully supported Yuan Shikai, who represented the cause of law and order. Most thoughtful Chinese believed that the 'second revolution' was a personal struggle between rival candidates for office.[62]

On the other hand, a number of discontented army officers were sympathetic to the movement. These were the young generals of 1911 who had expected rapid mobility and found that high posts were not sufficiently numerous for them all. Consequently, many had to content themselves with the empty title of general and the somewhat unsatisfactory post of adviser. During 1912, the new formations in the south were maintained for some time in a skeleton form to provide employment for some of these officers. But as they were gradually reduced, the number of unemployed officers increased. Their frustrations and discontent led the rebel leaders into believing that sedition could be spread among the troops.[63]

Contrary to the expectations of the rebel leaders, little support came from the government troops. Yuan Shikai fortunately had the loyalty of the Beiyang Army. He was probably the only man for whom the bulk of the northern troops retained something of traditional respect. Moreover, he was the only person who could obtain a foreign loan to get the country out of difficulties, at least temporarily. For this reason many army commanders in both north and south, with their prospects of regular pay rendered uncertain by the impoverished state of the economy, seemed inclined to support him.[64]

There was obviously an important money factor in Chinese politics. With relative ease Yuan crushed the 'second revolution'. He had ready cash to pay his troops under the new Reorganisation Loan Agreement (signed on 26 April 1913), and thus appeared to be 'the wielder of the long purse and dispenser of benefits'. The revolutionary party of the south had no funds, but only promises of plunder to offer in a land where there was little left to loot.[65] In any case, it was common knowledge that the troops were loyal to whoever paid them adequately. It had been like that before the Revolution of 1911. It was the same in 1913. With few exceptions, the high provincial authorities were also steadfast in their loyalty to the Peking government.

However, from a professional point of view, the performance of the government troops during the 'second revolution' left much to be desired. Though faced with relatively weak opposition, they showed a total lack of some of the primary essentials of a military power. They adopted the practice of breaking up existing formations and creating new ones haphazardly. The units which existed in peace time as more or less complete ones in themselves were seldom used as such, but were broken up into mixed forces which were then re-grouped. For example, instead of leaving a complete unit in Hubei, portions of the 2nd, 3rd, and 20th Divisions were used, while other sections of the 20th Division were sent to Shanghai and Nanking. Likewise, in Jiangxi, instead of alloting separate tasks to the 2nd and 6th Divisions under their own commanders, mixed columns were formed from them.[66]

Furthermore, the loyalist troops followed the custom of not giving a definite task to any one complete unit or a definite responsibility to any one officer. This inhibited co-operation between the different parts of any military formation. There were at the attack on Nanking three absolutely independent commanders, Feng Guozhang, Zhang Xun and Lei Zhenchun, none of whom was assigned any special task. There was no supreme commander and no concept of co-ordination.[67] Mutual distrust probably accounted for this system of check and balance, since the Chinese were accustomed to playing off one official against another.

The quality of the officer corps remained the principal weakness of the Chinese army. Most of the educated officers were very young and inexperienced. Over seven hundred general officers had been gazetted since the Revolution of 1911, many being about thirty years of age. Colonels of twenty-five were quite common, and their positions were hardly justifiable by their knowledge, training, service or experience. Staff appointments were in nearly all cases held by the modern-educated officers, especially by those who had been educated overseas. Unfortunately, staff officers who combined practical experience with theoretical knowledge were few. They were quite out of touch with both the regimental officers and the troops, and displayed no *esprit de corps* among themselves. During the 'second revolution', they appeared to rely for victory entirely on prestige, noise or display of force without showing any real desire to come to grips with the enemy. When these methods failed, bribery was freely resorted to with a good measure of success.[68] This was in marked contrast to the Beiyang Army which had exhibited a distinct military spirit and much professionalism in the recapture of Hankow in November 1911.

The rank and file varied greatly in quality. Those of the New Army who had joined before the Revolution of 1911 were first-class material physically. But the new recruits were of a much lower standard both in terms of physique and in terms of training. Unfortunately, both showed unsatisfactory discipline, and both were reluctant to take the offensive. The old-style troops, such as Zhang Xun's, were physically as good as soldiers of the New Army. But they also varied in quality, the rule being that new recruits were far inferior to those kept permanently under arms.

The operations in 1913 demonstrated two other weaknesses of the government troops employed in the attack on Nanking. First, there was no organised system of command in the general military control of the railways. The Peking-Hankow and Tientsin-Pukou lines were used by the 1st Army and 2nd Army respectively. But they were not taken over by the military authorities which interfered very little, if at all, with the ordinary service of trains, and this caused considerable delay in transporting troops from north to south. Commandants were appointed at the larger stations to take charge of the posts on the line of communication, but since troops only obeyed their own officers, these commandants had very little authority.[69] Second, there was a total lack of arrangements for supplies. Small towns through which the troops passed were forced to produce the necessary rice, pork, bread and other foodstuffs. It was only after they had reached Pukou that rice and flour were shipped to them from Shanghai by boat and rail.[70]

During the 'second revolution', a new 7th Division was raised by General Lei Zhenchun and sent to Yangzi and afterwards to Shandong.[71] A new 8th Division was also organised, after the disbandment of the old one in Nanking, from part of the Republican Guards and part of the supplementary troops, as well as new recruits. After the 'second revolution', practically all the troops of Jiangsu, Anhui, Jiangxi, Hunan and Fujian were dispersed or disbanded.[72] New organisations were formed from northern men and in many cases given no names so as not to excite the southerners. Some were called 'reserve troops' of a certain division, although in fact they were not so. Their strength varied greatly from one another, while their nomenclature and organisation still suffered from constant change.[73]

This state of affairs reflected the government's failure to uplift the army from the state of disruption caused by the Revolution of 1911. Although the troops had been retrenched and reduced to a more manageable level there was, for instance, little progress in military education. Few schools in the provinces which had been interrupted by the revolution had been reopened and many were abandoned through lack of funds.[74] In July 1912 the officers' school was opened in Peking, to replace the temporary officers' school in Baoding. The students were mainly trainee officers who had graduated from the four secondary schools which were now known as military preparatory schools. Others were cadets from the Naking Military School, which had been suspended for financial reasons.[75] Before long, however, the Peking school was abandoned (the reasons for this are obscure), and in October the government announced the opening of the new Baoding Officers' School *(Baoding junguan xuexiao)*, which had its premises in a former quick-course school. It intended to enrol 1500 students for a two-year course, but the first enrolment was reported to be 1700. Unfortunately, despite the official enthusiasm which accompanied its opening, its progress in the first couple of years was handicapped by the inferior quality of the instructors, many of whom were graduates of local intensive officers' classes who were not qualified to be appointed officers themselves. Added to this were considerable political intrigues between the Ministry of War and the school authorities, which caused its frustrated principal, Jiang Fangzhen, to attempt suicide unsuccessfully on 17 June 1913.[76]

In a few other areas the government's performance was equally unimpressive. No attempt was made towards conscription. Although a census was taken in various places over very limited areas, generally by direction of the provincial authorities, no nationwide one was organised. Li Yuanhong attempted with little success to institute compulsory service, and later gave up.[77] Soldiers were now secured by promises of pay and prospects of loot and an easy life. Officers on the whole were inclined to stay with the army for as long as they could, since it had become a more secure and more profitable profession than many others.

The efforts to enlarge the arsenals and to increase arms production were not very successful. Work was progressing towards the expansion of the Hanyang arsenal, but the Shanghai arsenal was being practically abandoned and all its spare material shipped north. The one in Canton was greatly delayed because of problems of management. Consequently, the Chinese government was obliged to purchase a fair amount of small arms, machine guns and field artillery from overseas.[78]

The government recognised the need for more military railways to connect important strategic points. However, lack of funds prevented any such plan from being implemented. During the latter half of 1913, the government granted further railway concessions to various foreign financial organisations, but in very few cases had a time limit been imposed on their construction, and few railways had been completed by the end of the year.

It can thus be concluded that the Chinese army had deteriorated from its state of efficiency achieved before the revolution. The rank and file had been demoralised by the relaxation of discipline consequent on the demise of the dynasty. The troops had become a medley of different elements. The cohesion of the regular units, some of which had reached a good level of competence before 1911, had broken down. Many of the well-trained soldiers had disappeared, while the new recruits were inferior in quality. Finally, many officers had taken to politics and associated themselves with political parties, an action which undermined the discipline and cohesion of the army.

TEN

Implications beyond the revolution

THE NEW Army is of great significance not only because it proved to be the instrument for the partial undoing of the dynasty but because it was an important product of an era of reform. As an integral part of the late Qing reform program, its development was facilitated by a number of factors. First and foremost, the central government took the initiative from the provincial leaders and played an active role. The reforms after 1900 were not confined to a handful of provinces under the direction of a handful of officials. Rather, they assumed a national dimension which could best be seen in Peking's endeavours, albeit not always successful, to bring all the new-style troops under one system. It was this central role which created a social and political climate conducive to military change.

Added to this was the fact that there was little deeply entrenched professional conservatism during the post-Boxer period. No government officials were prepared to argue that the old-style troops were adequate from a professional point of view. On the contrary, they generally supported the new military program in so far as funds were available for that purpose. The training of new officers, for example, encountered little resistance either from conservative scholar-officials or from old commanders whose position might have been threatened. In fact, the old-style troops also underwent a similar process of reorganisation and modern training, and some of their officers were recruited into the New Army. This is not to say that all the old-style soldiers were well disposed towards change. Zhang Xun, for one, still clung to ancient customs and was devoid of any modern ideas; his 'pigtailed' troops proved to be some of the most terrifying in the country. There were also rivalries between the new and the old. But, on the whole, there was a more progressive professional attitude towards change than at any previous period in the military history of China.

The post-Boxer decade was not one of 'restoration' like the Tongzhi reign. No efforts were made to reinforce Confucian institutions on which the imperial system was based. On the contrary, much was done to render these institutions more flexible so as to effect the desired changes necessary for the defence of China as well as of the dynasty. The erosion of Confucianism after the turn of the century, particularly following the abolition of the examination system, made it possible for those of the educated class and members of the gentry to make useful contributions to the military profession.

Compared with the period of the self-strengthening movement in the nineteenth century, the last decade of Manchu rule witnessed a marked growth in Chinese student nationalism as a result of the intensifying foreign threat and the inability of the Qing government to deal with it. Nationalism was conceived in terms of wealth and power, as well as of China's struggle for survival. Many educated men regarded a military career as an honourable thing partly because of considerations of national security and partly because it opened a new avenue of upward mobility. At the same time, many new values associated with nationalism were beginning to assert themselves, which caused a gradual psychological reorientation of the young students. This in turn exercised a salutary effect on army reform.

Of course, the social stigma attached to soldiering had not been completely eradicated, and it might still be difficult to find very able men to run China's military establishments. But by the end of the dynasty, many educated men had shown themselves willing to undergo some sort of military training and willing to stay in it once trained and put in a responsible position. There is no evidence of a high drop-out rate in the new military schools. Nor were there cases of modern-educated officers resigning because of disillusionment with their profession.

The imperial government, though constantly under attack from a significant section of the educated class, made its own contributions to Chinese nationalism. It had become increasingly aware of the foreign threat. Late Qing officials were no longer as submissive to foreign demands as they had been before. Chinese sovereignty over the border regions was reasserted. Patriotism was fostered in some sections of the New Army. All in all, there was a more positive response to the foreign challenge.

Unfortunately, the development of the New Army was also hampered by a host of problems. First, the weak leadership in Peking after 1909 affected decision-making and morale at every point. The deaths of the Empress Dowager Cixi, Emperor Guangxu, and the eminent reformer, Zhang Zhidong, lost to China the strong leadership that any far-reaching reforms required. The disgrace of Yuan Shikai that followed did little to improve the situation. In fact, the New Army during the period 1910-11 showed little progress, despite a small increase in the number of divisions and mixed brigades.

A second problem was, to borrow John Rawlinson's term, 'the established provincial compartmentalization of China's military forces'.[1] Despite central direction, many of the reforms in the provinces were made within a decentralised political framework which prevented unified command. Provincial authorities often found it necessary to depart from Peking's regulations and guidelines for a variety of reasons, political, financial and strategic. They retained much control over the troops which they managed and financed, and thus thwarted Peking's plans to achieve a truly national army.

There was also the financial problem. China was poor, but perhaps not too poor to afford a modern army on a modest scale. The trouble was that considerable money was embezzled or expended improperly by corrupt and incompetent officials. Moreover, the haphazard manner in which the army was financed was aggravated by the lack of a national budget until late in 1910. The new budget, however, was no solution to the problem, since the Chinese fiscal system remained as chaotic and antiquated as before. Until this system was thoroughly reformed, there was no way in which adequate funds could be made available for such an expensive project as army development.

One should also mention China's failure or inability to create an industrial base on which to establish a modern army which almost by definition is an industrial enterprise. The Chinese economic structure was not sophisticated enough to produce the quality and quantity of modern weaponry. Nor did it suffice to develop the transport infrastructure which was necessary for troop movement and reinforcement in a country as large as China.

Nevertheless, the New Army marked a significant stage in the development of Chinese military power. It occupies a place in history as the first modernising army China ever had, and serves as a historical link between the piecemeal military reforms of the nineteenth century and the reorganisation of the Guomindang army along German lines in the Nanking decade.[2] Despite its shortcomings, it was a great improvement on the old troops of imperial China. There had emerged a whole new class of scholar-officers whose main weakness was their inexperience. The soldiers were recruited from a better class than in the old days; they possessed in a marked degree many soldierly qualities. Given good leadership and good organisation, the material was there for a fine fighting force.

Like many other late Qing reforms, the New Army produced a boomerang effect on the government which had spent so much money on it. Just as the establishment of the provincial assemblies led to the alienation of the constitutionalists, so the development of the New Army nurtured many discontented soldiers. Why and how did the army ultimately turn against the dynasty? Some Chinese communist writers have argued that this was largely the outcome of the basic contradiction of a 'feudal regime' seeking to defend itself with a 'bourgeois-type army'.[3] Whether the Qing dynasty could be labelled a 'feudal regime' need not be debated here. On the other hand, the claim that the New Army was a bourgeois-type cannot be accepted without reservation. The reason for this claim is the fact that educated men made significant inroads into the military profession, thus changing its social composition.[4] However, it must be pointed out that such inroads did not alter the fact that the overwhelming majority of the soldiers were still of peasant origin. Moreover, the educated men who had enlisted had by no means developed a distinct 'bourgeois' character or a distinct 'bourgeois' ideology. As we have noted before, Hatano Yoshihiro tends to see the New Army as a peasant army, and he is right up to a point. Without attempting to give it a label or to coin a new sociological term for it, one can argue that the New Army was neither 'bourgeois' nor 'peasant'. It was in fact a fusion of peasants, the urban poor, young students and members of the lower gentry, with the peasants being predominant in the ranks.

Other Chinese historians have suggested that the desertion of the army in 1911 had little to do with its organisation, equipment and training, and that the real causes were the impact of a general revolutionary situation in the country and the efforts of the revolutionaries operating within the army.[5] Certainly, there was revolutionary influence at work, particularly in Hubei, where the radical soldiers were quite successful in organising themselves into a conspiratorial body. Elsewhere, revolutionary efforts were also made by civilians or members of the New Army, or both, to undermine the loyalty of the troops with varying degrees of success.

However, revolutionary subversion was only one of the factors contributing to the unreliability of the army. Military reform by its very nature was a politicising experience. The whole range of changes made in the military profession, in terms of organisation, technology, education, and training, all contributed to a modernising outlook of the soldier who developed an awareness of the shortcomings of Chinese society and the problems facing the nation. This furnished an impetus to the growth of national consciousness in the army which the government was at pains to foster itself. But nationalism was double-edged. It cut the Manchu rulers while it was used to fight foreign incursion.

The process of change was not a smooth one. For all the government's efforts to improve the military profession, the New Army was bedevilled by a host of problems, particularly in the two or three years before the revolution. These included corruption, embezzlement, arrears of pay, diminishing prospects of promotion, and conflicts between officers and men. The soldiers' grievances appeared to be of a traditional nature, compounded by natural disasters and rising prices of rice and other foodstuffs. Army disaffection thus became part of the popular discontent which was growing apace in the country.

This situation played into the hands of the revolutionaries. By October 1911 the men of the Hubei army were quite prepared to take the initiative, in the hope that they would have the support of other provinces. Outside support was imperative for any province which made the first move. Such support, however, would depend as much on the local military situation as on the conditions of the disaffected provinces. When the provincial government was able to deal with a local uprising, it became an isolated incident. But when the Hubei revolutionary soldiers showed that they could engage in a sustained struggle, the Wuchang uprising became a successful signal for revolution. What distinguished the Wuchang uprising from any other previous revolt was the fact that the provincial government was unable to suppress it. Nor did the loyalist troops, promptly reinforced from the north, succeed in restoring imperial authority. The military success of Wuchang was awe-inspiring, forcing the other disaffected provinces into a situation where they had to decide quickly whether or not to throw in their lot with the republican cause. The New Army in the south declared its adherence to it, while the northern troops generally favoured a constitutional monarchy. But the loyalist forces were not without discontent, nor were they committed to the old regime. When it became obvious that the monarchy could no longer be supported without a protracted and undesirable civil war, Yuan Shikai and his Beiyang commanders entered into negotiations with the south for the abdication of the emperor.

The New Army played a crucial role in the Revolution of 1911 both directly and indirectly. Directly because it took the lead in the military struggle, and indirectly because it exerted pressure on the already disaffected provincial assemblies and local gentry. No sooner had the revolution begun than the army commanders emerged as leaders of their own provinces in collaboration with the provincial assemblies. It was this collaboration which accounted for the immediate success of the revolution. The assemblymen allowed themselves to be prompted into action, partly because they had been alienated from the government owing to its procrastination on constitutional reform, and partly because they wanted to influence the course of development, thereby hoping to increase their political power in the new regime. In any case, it was not the New Army alone which brought about the ultimate fall of the dynasty. Nor was it simply the alienated constitutionalists who probably would not have acted decisively but for the support of the army. One thing is certain: when the dynasty had lost the allegiance of both the army and the civil elite, its fate was sealed.

For the most part the New Army was disorganised by the revolution, and as soon as the dynasty was destroyed it became a source of trouble. Its size had grown so large during the civil war that it constituted a serious threat to the new order which was yet to be fully established. In many parts of the country, particularly in the south, the army had become a motley of diverse elements, many of which would have been refused enlistment a year or two before. The new recruits were no longer carefully selected as regards character, social and family background; so inferior were they that their recruitment amounted to a negation of the reforms which had sought to recruit sons of decent families. The Republic under the presidency of Yuan Shikai had little success in resolving this problem. Up to Yuan's death in 1916, the Chinese army still contained a lot of undesirable elements from the lower classes.

This phenomenon continued well into the so-called 'warlord' period, during which the personal armies of the regional militarists were mostly made up of heterogeneous elements. As James Sheridan has observed, 'a large number of jobless and hungry men in the cities and countryside were willing to join an army in order to be clothed and fed, and perhaps paid. *At the very least they expected an occasional opportunity to loot, . . .*'[6] [Emphasis added.] It is indeed deplorable that the Chinese army after 1911 should deteriorate so rapidly to the position where regional militarists took practically anybody they could get into their personal armies. In some 'warlord' armies, like those of Feng Yuxiang and Yan Xishan, the troops were regularly and rigorously trained, and discipline was enforced. But in most other units, 'discipline was lax, training was careless or nonexistent, and life was irregular and disorderly'.[7] It was quite common for peasants to be pitilessly squeezed and the civil population molested and abused. The public image of the soldier which the late Qing reformers had taken so much care to improve was greatly tarnished.

As well as undoing much of the work of the earlier reformers, the Revolution of 1911 brought about a significant change in the traditional civil-military relationship. In imperial China the army, though a significant political force, 'did not constitute a permanent, semilegitimate (or at least accepted) factor in the political process'.[8] The Chinese had always preferred civilian rule by moral sanctions based on the Confucian system. As Joseph Needham puts it, imperial China was ruled 'basically by the prestige of literary culture, enormously important in Chinese traditional society and not by open dominance and force'.[9] Despite the usually long periods of military domination between the fall of a dynasty and the rise of another, each new dynasty, once established, was normally followed by a weakening of the soldier's position in relation to the civil administrator.[10] The Revolution of 1911 almost irrevocably altered the traditional relationship between the army and the state bureaucracy, the result of which was the ascendancy of the military as illustrated in the period of 'warlordism'. The nominal reunification of the country by the National Revolutionary Army in 1928 stopped short of tipping the scales in favour of the civil administrator. The Guomindang government maintained itself on its armed forces, just as the Chinese communists later rose to power by way of military strength.

The ascendancy of the military has been attributed to the existence of an ideological vacuum after the abolition of the imperial system and the concept of the Son of Heaven. The new Republic lacked the traditional sanctions for the exercise of supreme power. Neither the President nor the provincial authorities could rely on Western-style democratic institutions which were yet to be established; they invariably relied increasingly on the support, or at least goodwill, of the army commanders.[11] The revolution had destroyed the traditional patterns of government and disrupted Chinese society to the extent that the Chinese people had lost their political and psychological orientations. During the period of political instability in the early Republic, the military was naturally inclined and better equipped than the civil organisations to compete for political power. Certainly, in the absence of a new satisfying ideology, any successors to the Son of Heaven were bound to have serious problems in government. Yuan Shikai was no exception, nor were the rulers of Peking after 1916.

Thus, the emergence of the military in positions of power and their broadening participation in the political process distinguished the role of the New Army in 1911 from the revolts of the generals in the downfall of any previous Chinese dynasty. Every government after 1911 sought, with varying degrees of success, to maintain civil supremacy. Mao Zedong, for one, believed that the Party should command the gun and the gun should never command the Party. But the fact that Mao had to issue that directive and to stress its importance repeatedly was excellent testimony to the expansion of military influence. Even in China today the traditional civil-military relationship does not seem to have been fully restored.

However, the increasing importance of the military in the post-1911 era can also be seen in a different perspective as representing a step forward in the evolution of a new military tradition in a society in which the pacifist elements had often been dominant. The efforts of the late Qing reformers in promoting Chinese militarism as we have defined it had been successful. The Chinese people after 1911 did become more militant in the sense of being more appreciative of the role and functions of a modern army, especially during periods of foreign invasion. Military national education was advocated. Jiang Jieshi called for the militarisation of life in the New Life Movement. Mao Zedong asked the communist troops to serve the people and the people to learn from them. The important question, of course, has been how to keep the army under civil control while maintaining its militancy towards foreign aggression.

Appendix 1

Distribution of the thirty-six divisions projected
by the Qing government in 1906

Province	Number of divisions
The metropolitan area *(jinji)*	4*
Jiangsu	2
Anhui	1
Henan	1
Hubei	2
Fujian	1
Guangxi	1
Guizhou	1
Shanxi	1
Gansu	2
Rehe	1
Jilin	1
Zhili	2
Shandong	1
Jiangbei**	1
Jiangxi	1
Hunan	1
Zhejiang	1
Guangdong	2
Yunnan	2
Sichuan	3
Shaanxi	1

Appendix 1 (continued)

Province	Number of divisions
Xinjiang	1
Fengtian	1
Heilongjiang	1

* The Imperial Guard Corps was not contemplated at the time.

** Jiangbei (northern Jiangsu) was to be under a special provincial general residing at Qingjiangpu.

Appendix 2

Distribution of the Chinese army at the outbreak of the revolution

Denomination	Station headquarters	Commander
Imperial Guards	Nanyuan, Peking	Liangbi
1st Division	Beiyuan, Peking	He Zonglian
2nd Division	Baoding, Zhili	Ma Longbiao
3rd Division	Changchun, Jilin	Cao Kun
4th Division	Machang, Zhili	Wu Fengling
5th Division	Tsinan, Shandong	Zhang Yongcheng
6th Division	Baoding, Zhili	Wu Luzhen
7th Division	Qingjiangpu, Jiangbei	Duan Qirui
8th Division	Wuchang, Hubei	Zhang Biao
9th Division	Nanking, Jiangsu	Xu Shaozhen
10th Division	Foochow, Fujian	Sun Daoren
19th Division	Kunming, Yunnan	Zhong Lintong
20th Division	Mukden, Fengtian	Zhang Shaozeng
23rd Division	Changchun, Jilin	Meng Enyuan
24th Division	Haerbin, Heilongjiang	?

TOTAL: 14 Divisions (excluding the Imperial Guard Corps)

17th Division	Chengtu, Sichuan	Zhu Qinglan
21st Division	Hangchow, Zhejiang	Xiao Xingyuan
25th Division	Canton, Guangdong	Long Jiguang

The above three incomplete divisions were given a divisional staff in 1911.

Mixed Brigade*	Langfang, Zhili	?
2nd MB	Mukden, Fengtian	Lan Tianwei
21st MB	Wuchang, Hubei	Li Yuanhong
23rd MB	Suzhou, Jiangsu	Ai Zhongqi
25th MB	Changsha, Hunan	Xiao Liangchen
27th MB	Nanchang, Jiangxi	Wu Jiezhang
29th MB	Kaifeng, Henan	Ying Longxiang
31st MB	Anqing, Anhui	Zhao Litai
33rd MB	Chengtu, Sichuan	Shi Chengxian
35th MB	Ürümqi, Xinjiang	Ma Shengfu

Appendix 2 (continued)

Denomination	Station headquarters	Commander
41st MB	Hangchow, Zhejiang	Xiao Xingyuan
43rd MB	Taiyuan, Shanxi	Yao Hongfa
49th MB	Canton, Guangdong	Long Jiguang
Mixed Brigade*	Xi'an, Shaanxi	Wang Yujiang
Mixed Brigade*	Lanzhou, Gansu	Zhao Ti
Mixed Brigade*	Guiyang, Guizhou	Yuan Baoyi
Mixed Brigade*	Tibet	Zhong Ying
Mixed Brigade*	Guangxi	Hu Jingyi

TOTAL: 18 Mixed Brigades (including the one in Guizhou which was in fact less than a regiment and the one in Tibet probably with similar strength).

   *   The denominations of these units are not clear.

N.B.   The 1st Mixed Brigade garrisoned in Xinminfu had merged with other troops in Fengtian to form the 20th Division and so is not included in the above table.

39th Brigade	?	Wu Xiangzhen
40th Brigade	Luanzhou, Zhili?	Pan Juying
Total: 2 Brigades		

Notes

Abbreviations used in notes

BPP	Great Britain, Parliamentary Papers (Blue Books).
DFZZ	*Dongfang zazhi* [The Eastern miscellany].
FO	Great Britain, Foreign Office Archives, Public Record Office.
GMWX	Luo Jialun ed. and the Guomindang Historical Commission comp., *Geming wenxian* [Documents on the revolution], vols 1-4, Taipei, 1953.
KGWX	Editorial Committee on Documentary Collections for the 50th Anniversary of the Founding of the Chinese Republic comp., *Zhonghua minguo kaiguo wushinian wenxian* [Documents on the 50th anniversary of the founding of the Chinese Republic], 2 *bian* (series), Taipei, 1964.
MP	The Papers of George Ernest Morrison, 1850-1932, Mitchell Library, New South Wales Library, Sydney.
USDS	United States Department of State, Decimal File, China, Internal Affairs, 1910-29, National Archives Microfilm Publications, Washington, DC.
XHGM	Chinese Historical Association comp., *Xinhai geming* [The Revolution of 1911], 8 vols, Shanghai, 1957.
XHGMHYL	Committee on Written Historical Materials of the National Committee of the Chinese People's Political Consultative Conference ed., *Xinhai geming huiyilu* [Recollections of the 1911 Revolution], 6 vols, Peking, 1961.
XHSYHYL	Hubei Committee of the Chinese People's Political Consultative Conference ed., *Xinhai shouyi huiyilu* [Recollections of the first (Wuchang) uprising in 1911], 3 vols, Wuhan, 1957.
WDGS	United States War Department, General Staff, National Archives Microfilm Publications, Washington, DC.
WGZ	Wen Gongzhi, *Zuijin sanshinian Zhongguo junshishi* [History of Chinese military affairs in the last thirty years], 2 vols, reprint, Taipei, 1962.
WO	Great Britain, War Office Archives, Public Record Office.
ZWXG	Zhang Zhidong, *Zhang Wenxianggong quanji* [The complete works of Zhang Zhidong], eds Wang Jingqing *et al.*, reprint, Taipei, 1963.

NOTES

INTRODUCTION

1. See Esherick's review of the Sun Yat-sen-centred orthodoxy, in '1911: A Review'.
2. This term is borrowed from Esherick, who describes the progressive gentry of Hunan, and for that matter the progressive gentry of other major provincial capitals, as 'the urban reformist elite'. This was a new elite which pressed for educational reforms and rights recovery, and which dominated the provincial assemblies established in 1909 as part of the imperial government's preparations for constitutional rule. See Esherick, *Reform and Revolution*, pp. 43-4, 66-9.
3. See, for example, Esherick, *Reform and Revolution*; Rhoads, *China's Republican Revolution;* Chang P'eng-yüan, 'The Constitutionalists', pp. 143-83; Fincher, 'Political Provincialism and the National Revolution', pp. 185-226.
4. For earlier studies of the revolutionary movement in Hubei in English, see Fass, 'Revolutionary Activity in the Province Hu-pei and the Wu-ch'ang Uprising of 1911';

Vidya Prakash Dutt, 'The First Week of the Revolution: The Wuchang Uprising', pp. 383-416. Liew has also dealt with it in his book, *Struggle for Democracy*, pp. 105-15, in which he points out that the success of the Wuchang uprising was 'a natural outcome of Hupeh's peculiar development in the preceding decade or even decades,...' A recent account of the Hubei revolutionary movement is, of course, Esherick, *Reform and Revolution* (chapter 5), in which he contends that the revolutionary activity in Hubei was not 'markedly different' from the activities in other parts of China.
5. Josef Fass has suggested that the growing number of 'members of the petty and middle bourgeoisie in the new-style army' was the major factor in the spread of revolutionary ideas among the troops. Fass does not define 'the petty and middle bourgeoisie', but uses the term to denote the educated and literate soldiers of the Hubei army, and by extension, of other modern divisions. See 'The Role of

the New Style Army in the 1911 Revolution in China', pp. 185-6; also Fass, 'Revolutionary Activity in the Province of Hu-pei and the Wu-ch'ang Uprising of 1911', p. 147.

6. Hatano Yoshihiro has asserted that peasant discontent was siphoned into 'organised, revolutionary form' through the New Army. In other words, the revolutionary movement in the New Army represented peasant discontent. See 'The New Armies', p. 382. This book will show, however, that army disaffection was not confined to the soldiers of peasant origin, and that it was shared by both officers and men of different social backgrounds.

7. Hobsbawn, pp. 24-5. Sharman, p. 109.

8. GMWX, III, p. 401.

9. XHGMHYL, I, pp. 183-4; Yan Xishan, p. 8.

0. For the revolutionary 'preparatory stage', the Tongmenghui's operational program enumerated eleven principal tasks: to recruit comrades; to raise funds; to investigate the conditions of the populace; to explore available resources; to observe changes in the revolutionary situation; to spy on the Qing troops; to reorientate government officers; to sow discord in the Qing court; to harass the palace; to expose administrative corruption; and finally to act according to the general conditions outside the Tongmenghui. See GMWX, II pp. 101-2. It is noteworthy that infiltration of the New Army was not on the list, and that the task of spying on Qing troops ranked sixth in priority.

11. Esherick has warned us that 'there are literally hundreds of accounts of the revolutionary parties' activities in Hubei, but they all give the impression that revolutionary plotting occurred in a vacuum'. See *Reform and Revolution*, p. 158.

1. FORMATION OF THE NEW ARMY

1. For a study of the military reforms introduced in the latter half of the nineteenth century, see Teng and Fairbank, pp. 46-131; Wright, *The Last Stand of Chinese Conservatism*, pp. 196-221. For an analysis of the *ti-yong* dichotomy, see Levenson, I, pp. 59-78.

2. See Rawlinson, *China's Struggle for Naval Development*.

3. For a detailed account of this army, see Liu Fenghan, *Xinjian lujun*.

4. Liu Fenghan, pp. 93-5.

5. Powell, pp. 60-2; WGZ, I, pp. 38-9.
6. Powell, pp. 69-70.
7. Hu Poyu, I, pp. 17-18, also table 4 facing p. 34.
8. Liu Fenghan, pp. 318-20, 327-8.
9. Powell, pp. 133-5; *DaQing Guangxu xinfaling*, I, pp. 3b-4a.
10. For different reasons, conservative elements in the government also favoured a modern system of national defence which they saw as a means of protection against Westernisation of other sorts. See Gascoyne-Cecil, p. 14; Cameron, p. 96.
11. Quoted in Liu Fenghan, p. 192.
12. ZWXG, *zouyi*, 40, pp. 1b-2a, 65, pp. 3b-4b.
13. Leonard, p. 13.
14. FO 17/1655, Notes by Lieutenant-Colonel Ducat on the situation in China, encl. in Intelligence Division to Foreign Office, 5 July, 1904.
15. 'The Chinese Army', *The Far Eastern Review*, October 1909, p. 171.
16. Gascoyne-Cecil, pp. 12, 15.
17. 'The Chinese Army', *The Far Eastern Review*, October 1909, pp. 180-82.
18. 'China's Army and Navy', *The Far Eastern Review*, August 1910, p. 93.
19. 'The Chinese Army', *The Far Eastern Review*, October 1909, p. 179.
20. FO 228/1733, Report on the Yunnan Army, encl. in Acting Consul-General Wilton to Sir John Jordan, No. 41, 21 September 1909.
21. Dingle, *Across China on Foot*, p. 215.
22. Dingle, *Across China on Foot*, p. 427.
23. FO 371/1063, Report on the Burma-China frontier for the open season 1910-11, encl. in Acting Consul Rose to Sir Edward Grey, No. 1, 25 February 1911.
24. Ross, pp. 113-14.
25. Cohen, pp. 29-32.
26. Huntington, p. 155.
27. Jerome Ch'en, *Yuan Shih-k'ai*, p. 34.
28. FO 17/1522, Notes on the strength of the Chinese forces in north China, by military attaché Colonel Browne, 24 April 1902, encl. in Sir Ernest Satow to the Marquess of Lansdowne, No. 111, 24 April 1902.
29. ZWXG, *zouyi*, 57, pp. 22b-27a. According to Powell (p. 148) Zhang Zhidong's figures were somewhat underestimated. Powell also cites a French military officer, Captain Gadoffre, to show that the nucleus of Zhang's troops was German-trained; but this is highly suspect, as Zhang seems already to have given up the practice of using foreign officers to train Chinese troops.
30. FO 17/1523, Report by Colonel Browne, 2 June 1902,

encl. in Satow to Secretary of State, No. 149, 2 June 1902; ZWXG, *gongdu*, 19, pp. 21b-22b.

31. Powell, p. 151, citing Captain Gadoffre.

32. See Powell, pp. 157-9.

33. FO 17/1523, Browne in Satow to Secretary of State, 149.

34. *DaQing Guangxu xinfaling*, I, 8a.

35. *DaQing Guangxu xinfaling*, XIV, military administration. The commission's regulations had been translated into English by Leonard, United States military attaché, as part of his report on 'The Chinese Army', *c.* 1908.

36. For a brief account of the formation and development of the first six divisions, see Jerome Ch'en, 'A Footnote on the Chinese Army in 1911-12', pp. 426-433. Ch'en points out that the denominations of these divisions were sometimes confusing because Yuan Shikai tended to change them, as well as the commanders, from time to time.

37. *The China Year Book, 1912*, pp. 244-6; WGZ, I, pp. 53-7.

38. My estimate of the divisions agrees with Powell's (p. 288), but unlike him, I have found only eighteen mixed brigades. (Powell says twenty brigades had been formed.) I also differ from Jerome Ch'en ('The Chinese Army', p. 436) who asserts that there was a total of sixteen divisions. My estimate is smaller because the 17th, 21st and 25th Divisions were in fact incomplete although they had been given a divisional staff in 1911. See FO 405/229, Annual report on China, 1911, pp. 55-6; FO 371/1347, Changes report for the Chinese army, 1911, p. 2.

39. FO 405/229, Annual report on China, 1910, p. 70.

40. U.S. Navy Department, Office of Naval Intelligence, No. A-4-a, reg. no 159, Report on the Chinese army, by 2nd Lt N.A. Eastman, USMC, 25 January 1910.

41. Wright, *The Last Stand of Chinese Conservatism*, p. 201.

42. Leonard, pp. 33-4.

43. Leonard, pp. 35-9.

44. ZWXG, *zouyi*, 57, p. 32b.

45. ZWXG, *zouyi*, 57, p. 34b.

46. For detailed information on the pay scale from senior officers to privates, see Leonard, pp. 87-95. There were exceptional circumstances where the men's pay was lower than was normally the case. In poor provinces like Jiangxi and Guizhou, a first-class private received only 4.20 taels and a second-class private got 3.90 taels a month. See FO 371/214, Lieutenant-Colonel Pereira's report on troops at Kiukiang, encl. in Jordan to Grey, No. 321, 7 July 1907; FO 371/1085, Pereira's report on the troops

of Guizhou, encl. in Jordan to Grey, No. 18, 12 January 1911.

47. Leonard, pp. 93, 170.
48. Leonard, pp. 39-40. All the new recruits entering the ranks after the first enlistment of one-fifth were registered as second-class privates. At the end of five months' drill, they might be selected for promotion to first-class privates.
49. ZWXG, *zouyi*, 57, p. 28a. One revolutionary soldier recalled writing an essay entitled 'To enlighten virtues and to reform the people', when he enlisted. See XHSYHYL, I, p. 8.
50. FO 405/195, Annual report on China, 1909, p. 38.
51. ZWXG, *zouyi*, 65, p. 10b.
52. See Pereira's reports: FO 371/39, On the 6th Division, encl. in Carnegie to Grey, No. 332, 6 August 1906; FO 371/41, On the 1st Division, encl. in Jordan to Grey, No. 420, 15 October 1906; On the 3rd Division, encl. in same; On the 5th Division, encl. in same; FO 371/214, On the 2nd Division, encl. in Jordan to Grey, No. 488, 23 November 1906; FO 371/415, On the 4th Division, encl. in Jordan to Grey, No. 548, No. 25, 1907.
53. FO 371/620, Changes report for the Chinese army, 1908, p. 11.
54. FO 371/33, Pereira's report on troops in Canton, encl. in Satow to Grey, No. 82, 24 February 1906; FO 371/34, Some notes on the province of Guangxi, by Pereira, encl. in Carnegie to Grey, No. 296, 9 July 1906; FO 371/214, Pereira's report on the army at Hangchow, encl. in Carnegie to Grey, No. 319, 5 July 1907.
55. FO 371/214, Pereira's report on the army at Baoding, encl. in Jordan to Grey, No. 504, 29 October 1907. See also WDGS, No. 6562-1, Report of changes in the Chinese army in 1910, p. 26.
56. WO 33/454, 'Handbook of the Military Forces of China', comp. General Staff, War Office, London, 1908, pp. 8, 63.
57. FO 371/214, Pereira's report on the 8th and 11th Divisions, encl. in Jordan to Grey, No. 221, 13 May 1907.
58. Thomson, p. 32.
59. Leonard, p. 182.
60. FO 371/642, Lieutenant-Colonel Willoughby's report on troops in Manchuria, encl. in Jordan to Grey, No. 421, 16 November 1909.
61. Leonard, pp. 209-11.
62. Leonard, pp. 171, 174, 180, 187, 190, 195, 208. FO 371/859, Changes report for the Chinese army, 1909, p. 15.
63. FO 405/195, Annual report on China, 1909, p. 46.
64. Leonard, pp. 166-7.
65. FO 405/195, Annual report

on China, 1910, p. 72.

66. *The Times* (London), 21 October 1911, p. 6.

67. FO 371/859, Changes report for the Chinese army, 1909, p. 13.

68. On the whole Chinese horses were relatively small, and this greatly hampered the efficiency of the cavalry and artillery.

69. Leonard, pp. 26-8.

70. FO 405/171, Annual report on China, 1908, p. 34; FO 405/195, Annual report on China, 1910, p. 74; FO 371/859, Changes report for the Chinese army, 1909, p. 41; FO 228/1748, Changes report for the Chinese army, 1910, pp. 1, 39.

71. WDGS, No. 6562-1, Report of changes in the Chinese army in 1910, p. 13.

72. *Qingchao xuwenxian tongkao, juan* 220, *bing* 19, pp. 9670-1.

73. FO 371/435, Pereira's report on the 22nd Division, encl. in Jordan to Grey, No. 505, 2 November 1908.

74. WDGS, No. 6562-1, Report of changes in the Chinese army in 1910, p. 14.

75. FO 405/171, Annual report on China, 1908, p. 34.

76. *The China Year Book, 1912*, p. 247; FO 405/195, Annual report on China, 1910, p. 74; FO 371/859, Changes report for the Chinese army, 1909, p. 41.

77. See *Qingchao xuwenxian*

tongkao, juan 222, *bing* 21, pp. 9685, 9687.

78. WDGS, No. 6562-1, Report of changes in the Chinese army in 1910, pp. 59-60; FO 371/859, Changes report for the Chinese army, 1909, p. 46.

79. Brunnert and Hagelstrom, pp. 309-10; FO 405/195, Annual report on China, 1909, p. 45.

80. FO 371/620, Changes report for the Chinese army, 1908, p. 3. However, the French military attaché in Peking, Major Brissaud-Desmaillet, found that the best of the Patrol and Defence troops were those raised in Zhili and Manchuria. See his 'Situation de l'armee chinoise au 1er Mars 1910', pp. 412-33.

81. FO 371/415, Changes report for the Chinese army, 1907, p. 5. In January 1911 Pereira's successor, Lieutenant-Colonel Willoughby, also found the average soldier of the Patrol and Defence Force as good as his New Army *confrere*, and that individually the former was a better fighting man in spite of the latter's superior organisation, better equipment and more modern training. See FO 371/1085, Notes on the Chinese Army, encl. in Jordan to Grey, No. 18, 12 January 1911.

82. FO 371/859, Changes report for the Chinese army, 1909, p. 46.

83. FO 371/229, Pereira's report on his journey from Canton to Nanchang and from Nanchang to Foochow, 31 December 1906 to 4 February 1907, encl. in Jordan to Grey, No. 181, 15 April 1907.

84. Kent, p. 127.

85. FO 371/859, Changes report for the Chinese army, 1909, p. 57.

86. WDGS, No. 6562-1, Report of changes in the Chinese army in 1910, p. 59.

87. WDGS, No. 6283-4, Summary of military news for November 1910, p. 6.

88. On Banner privileges, see Hsieh Pao-chao, pp. 58-62.

89. FO 371/41, Pereira's report on the 1st Division, encl. in Jordan to Grey, No. 420, 15 October 1906.

90. FO 371/435, Pereira's report on the 2nd Division, encl. in Jordan to Grey, No. 505, 2 November 1908.

91. *Qingshilu* (Xuantong), 4, p. 3a.

92. 'The Chinese Army', *The Far Eastern Review*, October 1909, p. 178.

93. *The China Year Book*, 1912, p. 248; FO 371/875, Müller to Grey, No. 488, 11 November 1910.

94. FO 371/214, Pereira's report on troops in Hubei, encl. in Jordan to Grey, No. 289, 13 June 1907.

95. *Qingshilu* (Dezong), 578, pp. 7b-8a. Earlier in August 1907, Duanfang, Viceroy of Liangjiang, had proposed to the Throne that the Manchu Bannermen be placed under the same local control as the Chinese, that they be disbanded year by year and be given a pension equivalent to ten years' stipend which would enable them to start a new life, and that those stationed in Peking be sent to Manchuria to help develop the virgin land there *(Qingshilu* (Dezong), 576, p. 15b). Meanwhile, a senior official of the Ministry of the Interior, Zhao Bingjun, also pointed out in a memorial that the disbandment of the Bannermen would contribute towards achieving racial equality between Manchus and Chinese. See *Qingshilu* (Dezong), 57b, p. 21.

96. *Qingshilu* (Xuantong), 4, p. 7a-b.

97. Brissaud-Desmaillet, p. 1191.

2. ADMINISTRATIVE REFORMS AND MILITARY FINANCES

1. Pye, p. 76.

2. Claude E. Welch, Jr, 'Political Modernization and the African Military', in Welch, *Political Modernization*, p. 358.

3. *Qingshilu* (Guangxu), 522, p. 10a.

4. DFZZ, I, 1 (1904), *junshi*, pp. 1-2; also 4 (1904), *junshi*, pp. 197-200.

5. DFZZ, I, 1 (1904), *zazu*, p. 5.

6. Boorman, III, pp. 330-1.

7. Boorman, III, pp. 393-4.

8. *Qingshi liezhuan*, 3, pp. 17a-b.

9. Shen Zuxian and Wu Kaisheng, 3, p. 15; Powell, p. 167.

10. FO 17/1655, Intelligence diary for the period ending 1 March 1904, encl. in Director of Military Operations to Under Secretary of State for Foreign Affairs, 15 April 1904.

11. DFZZ, I, 7 (1904), *shiping*, p. 42.

12. FO 371/31, Pereira's report on the New Army, encl. in Satow to the Marquess of Lansdowne, No. 28, 17 January 1906.

13. Brunnert and Hagelstrom, pp. 303-4. Powell (p. 203) points out that the Tientsin war board was 'largely a redesignation of the department which had been organized in 1902' for the training of the troops there.

14. Zhu Wu, pp. 65-66. Brunnert and Hagelstrom, p. 202; WO 33/454, 'Handbook of the Military Forces of China', p. 36.

15. FO 371/229, Pereira's report on a journey overland from Canton to Nanchang in Jiangxi, encl. in Jordan to Grey, No. 181, 15 April 1907.

16. FO 371/214, Pereira's report on the troops at Hangchow, encl. in Jordan to Grey, No. 319, 5 July 1907; DFZZ, II, 12 (1905), *junshi*, pp. 379-81.

17. FO 371/435, Pereira's report on the troops in Manchuria, encl. in Jordan to Grey, No. 425, 21 September 1908.

18. FO 371/642, Pereira's report on the troops in Manchuria, encl. in Jordan to Grey, No. 8, 16 November 1909.

19. FO 371/642, Pereira's report on the 5th Division in Shandong, encl. in Jordan to Grey, No. 420, 16 October 1906; FO 371/434, Pereira's report on the 5th Division, encl. in Jordan to Grey, No. 407, 12 September 1908.

20. Brunnert and Hagelstrom, pp. 337-9; FO 371/34, Some notes on Hunan, by Pereira, encl. in Carnegie to Grey, No. 296, 9 July 1906.

21. FO 371/34, Some notes on Hunan, by Pereira, encl. in Carnegie to Grey, No. 296, 9 July 1906.

22. FO 371/214, Pereira's report on the New Army at Suzhou, encl. in Jordan to Grey, No. 319, 5 July 1907; FO 371/229, Pereira's report on a journey from Canton to Nanchang, encl. in Jordan to Grey, No. 181, 15 April 1907.

23. FO 371/214, Pereira's report on the 9th Division in Nanking, encl. in Jordan to

Grey, No. 321, 7 July 1907.

24. Cameron, pp. 105-7.

25. Brunnert and Hagelstrom, pp. 139-45.

26. FO 405/171, Annual report on China, 1906, p. 14.

27. FO 371/214, Pereira's report on the organisation of the War Ministry, encl. in Jordan to Grey, No. 395, 20 August 1907.

28. FO 371/226, Jordan to Grey, Telegram No. 71, 5 May 1907.

29. Cameron (p. 92) wrote: 'It may have been that she [the Empress Dowager] both feared and distrusted Yuan as her accomplice in 1898 and was alarmed at his growing power . . . There was talk that he [Yuan] was using the power which he possessed . . . to strengthen himself against the day of Tzu Hsi's death, when Kuang Hsu would resume the imperial power and have the opportunity to vent his long-accumulating hatred of the man whom he considered responsible for his downfall'.

30. Guo Tingi, II, p. 1260. The issues over which Tieliang quarrelled with Yuan are not clear. Guo Tingyi, however, noted that Tieliang was opposed to a series of institutional changes in the metropolitan administration presumably proposed by Yuan. Cameron (p. 92) stated that the rift between them came during a series of military conferences held in the latter half of 1906, after the second grand manoeuvres. Stephen MacKinnon suggests that the issues may have been the Manchus' pursuit of centralisation and control of Chinese officials, as well as Tieliang's proposal for the abolition of provincial governors and viceroys. See 'Yuan Shih-k'ai in Tientsin and Peking', p. 151.

31. FO 371/226, Jordan to Grey, No. 99, 21 February 1907. Duan Qirui and Zhang Huaizhi, commanders of the 3rd and 5th Divisions, respectively, resigned in disgust rather than serve under Fengshan. See FO 371/434, Pereira's report on the 5th Division, encl. in Jordan to Grey, No. 407, 12 September 1908; Powell, p. 218.

32. FO 371/217, Memo by Pereira on the new War Ministry, encl. in Jordan to Grey, No. 504, 20 November 1906. See also FO 405/171, Annual report on China, 1906, p. 14.

33. FO 371/226 Jordan to Grey, No. 99, 21 February 1907.

34. FO 371/226, Jordan to Grey, No. 99, remark in minutes.

35. FO 228/1664 encl. in Consul-General Fraser (Hankow) to Jordan, No. 14, 23 February 1907.

36. FO 405/171, Annual report on China, 1907, pp. 5-6.

37. *Qingshilu* (Guangxu), 576,

p. 1b. FO 371/220, Imperial decree, encl. in Jordan to Grey, No. 406, 21 August 1907.

38. This is my own calculation based on information from DFZZ, V, Nos 7-12 (1908), *gebiao*, pp. 1, 7, 13, 19, 31, 31, respectively.

39. FO 405/195, Annual report on China, 1909, p. 2.

40. *North-China Herald* (Decrees), 9 January 1909, p. 79; Ch'en, *Yuan Shih-k'ai*, p. 75.

41. DFZZ, V, 10 (1908), *gebiao*, p. 19.

42. *Qingshilu* (Xuantong), 14, pp. 20a-21a.

43. FO 371/633, Jordan to Grey, No. 259, 20 July 1909.

44. *The Times*, 11 October 1909, p. 4; DFZZ, VI 9 (1908), *gebiao*, p. 43.

45. Brissaud-Desmaillet, p. 1182; Brunnert and Hagelstrom, pp. 61-4; WDGS, No. 6562-1, Report of changes in the Chinese army in 1910, pp. 4-6.

46. FO 405/195, Annual report on China, 1909, p. 38.

47. WDGS, No. 6283-1, Summary of military events for August 1910, pp. 1-2; No. 6283-3, Summary of military events for October 1910, p. 1.

48. These sections were (1) the adjutant-general's under Feng Guozhang and Ha Hanzhang; (2) personnel of officers and assignments under Lu Zhongyuan; (3) military information

under Feng Guanguang; (4) operations and communications under Jian Zhicai; (5) topographical section under a colonel Zhang; and (6) translation bureau under a colonel Cai. See WDGS, No. 6283-4, Summary of military news for November 1910, p. 3. Although Feng Guozhang was not Japanese-educated, he had been in Japan a couple of times. The first occasion was in 1895 when he served as military attaché in the Chinese legation in Tokyo, and became acquainted with several Japanese officers. Again, in the autumn of 1905 he was in Japan, to observe Japanese army manoeuvres. See Boorman, I, p. 25.

49. WDGS, NJ. 6562-1, Report of changes in the Chinese army in 1910, pp. 4-5.

50. *North-China Herald* (Decrees), 25 February 1909, p. 433. It had been known for some time that the Throne was not satisfied with the conduct of affairs in the Ministry of War owing to the friction between Tieliang and Prince Zaitao. See *Peking Daily News*, encl. in FO 371/870, Müller to Grey, No. 123, 25 April 1910. There were other reasons for Tieliang's resignation. One was that the Prince Regent had refused to recognise a loan of 800,000 taels which Tieliang had

contracted on behalf of the War Ministry. Other authorities accredited his fall to his recognition of his waning influence since the organisation of the Imperial Guard Corps, the independence of the General Staff and the establishment of the Naval Council. Others claimed that he was untrue to his old ally Yuan Shikai, and that influences friendly to Yuan had forced him out in the cold. See 'China's Army and Navy', *The Far Eastern Review*, August 1910, pp. 90-1. In any case Tieliang had never succeeded in gaining control of the Beiyang Army or in stripping Yuan of his influence. Yuan's old associates had in fact increased their power after 1907. Feng Guozhang, as we have seen, held a senior position in the General Staff Council. Xu Shichang was appointed Viceroy of Manchuria, and the 3rd Division and two mixed brigades, which were to be composed of units from Yuan's 2nd and 4th Divisions and Fengshan's 5th and 6th Divisions, were transferred there. Tang Shaoyi, a supporter of Yuan's, was made Governor of Fengtian, while Wang Yingkai, who was formerly in command of the 2nd Division, was appointed temporary Vice-President of the War Ministry and chief

deputy to Fengshan. Wang Shizhen was appointed commander-in-chief of the Jiangbei area in Jiangsu, which gave him command of the 7th Division. Furthermore, not all the Manchu dignitaries were opposed to Yuan. Prince Qing, for one, was Yuan's friend and patron. See Powell, pp. 251-2; MacKinnon, 'Yuan Shih-k'ai in Tientsin and Peking', pp. 152-3. For the relations between Prince Qing and Yuan and their alliance against their political opponents, see Liu Housheng, pp. 115-56.

51. Powell, pp. 272-3; WDGS, No. 6562-1, Report of changes in the Chinese army in 1910, pp. 6-7; Reid, p. 150; 'China's Army and Navy', *The Far Eastern Review*, August 1910, p. 91.

52. WDGS, No. 6283-3, Summary of military events for October 1910, pp. 2-3; No. 6562-1, Report of changes in the Chinese army in 1910, pp. 7-8; No. 6562-4, Reorganisation of the War Ministry, pp. 1-18. The eight sections of the reorganised ministry were the adjutant-general, military regulations, military examination, military equipment, military law, military accounting, military pasturage and military education.

53. WDGS, No. 6283-1, Summary of military events for

August 1910, p. 3.

54. WDGS, No. 6283-3, Summary of military events for October 1910, p. 2.

55. WDGS, No. 6283-5, Summary of military events for December 1910, p. 4.

56. WDGS, No. 6283-3, Summary of military events for October 1910, p. 3; No. 6283-4, Summary of military events for November 1910, p. 6. The new code was reported to be working with success. See No. 6283-5, Summary of military events for December 1910, pp. 5-6.

57. WDGS, No. 6283-2, Summary of military events for September 1910, pp. 1-2; No. 6562-1, Report of changes in the Chinese army in 1910, pp. 7, 9.

58. WDGS, No. 6283-2, Summary of military events for September 1910, pp. 2-3.

59. WDGS, No. 6283-5, Summary of military events for December 1910, p. 14.

60. WDGS, No. 6283-4, Summary of military events for November 1910, p. 1.

61. WDGS, No. 6283-6, Summary of military events for January 1911, pp. 1-2.

62. WDGS, No. 6283-5, Summary of military events for December 1910, pp. 4, 7.

63. WDGS, No. 6562-5, Provincial military war boards, pp. 1-3; *The· China Year Book, 1912*, pp. 247-9.

64. In February 1911 the commanding officers of the 10th, 5th and 6th Divisions were in Peking for such consultations. See WDGS, No. 6283-7, Summary of military events for February 1911, p. 2-3.

65. An example can be cited. In September 1910 the Viceroy of Liangjiang removed some military officers of the 9th Division in Nanking from their positions. On Lieutenant-General Xu Shaozhen's objection that such matters should be dealt with by him alone, the viceroy reported him to the Ministry of War. The ministry supported Xu, and the viceroy thereupon sent a memorial to the Throne. The memorial was simply handed to the Ministry of War, and the viceroy was again informed that military matters were under the sole direction of the military authorities and that the ministry had every confidence in Xu. See FO 228/1762, Intelligence report for the September quarter, 1910, encl. in Consul Goffe's 'Separate' of 30 September 1910.

66. Before he took up the appointment to the War Ministry, Yinchang was well aware of his new post being a difficult one. When the Berlin correspondent of the *North China Daily* asked him on the eve of his return to China whether he was glad to be going home, he replied: 'No,

I am not glad to be going back. I would rather have remained and worked here. I do not think that our country is yet sufficiently far advanced for a man to be able to achieve great results in a short space of time. I do not look upon my appointment either as an enviable one or one in which I am likely to be able to achieve any very striking results'. See 'China's Army and Navy', *The Far Eastern Review*, August 1910, p. 91.

67. WDGS, No. 6283-8, Summary of military events 1 March-20 April, 1911, p. 4.

68. WDGS, No. 6283-5, Summary of military events for December 1910, p. 3.

69. WDGS, No. 6283-3, Summary of military events for October 1910, p. 2; No. 6283-7, Summary of military events for February 1910, p. 3.

70. FO 405/195, Annual report on China, 1909, p. 2.

71. FO 371/641, Memo by Little on political and commercial conditions in China, encl. in Messrs Brunner, Mond, and Co. to Grey, 31 August 1909.

72. WDGS, No. 6283-6, Summary of military events of January 1911, p. 14.

73. WDGS, No. 6283-6, pp. 6-7; Powell, p. 278.

74. Gittings, p. 187.

75. Shen Jian, pp. 392-3.

76. 'The Peiyang Army', pp. 405-22.

77. FO 17/1654, Intelligence diary for the period ending 2 February 1904, encl. in Director of Military Operations to Under Secretary of State for Foreign Affairs, 28 March 1904.

78. MP 312/119 Army; *Qingshilu* (Guangxu), 524, pp. 10a-1a.

79. FO 17/1655 Intelligence diary for the period ending 26 April 1904, encl. in Director of Military Operations to Under Secretary of State for Foreign Affairs, 7 June 1904.

80. FO 17/1657, Intelligence diary for the period ending 16 August 1904, encl. in Director of Military Operations to Under Secretary of State for Foreign Affairs, 25 September 1904. For the financial state in Guangdong and Guangxi, see DFZZ, I, 10 (1904), *caizheng*, pp. 260-3.

81. FO 17/1655, Intelligence diary for the period ending 16 February 1904, encl. in Director of Military Operations to Under Secretary of State for Foreign Affairs, 14 April 1904.

82. DFZZ, I, 10 (1904), *caizheng*, pp. 257-60.

83. DFZZ, I, 5 (1904), *junshi*, pp. 218-21.

84. DFZZ, I, 10 (1904), *caizheng*, pp. 253-4.

85. FO 17/1655, Intelligence diary for the period ending 1 March 1904, encl. in Director of Military Operations to Under Secretary of State for Foreign

Affairs, 15 April 1904.

86. FO 17/1655, Intelligence diary for the period ending 10 May 1904, encl. in Director of Military Operations to Under Secretary of State for Foreign Affairs, 21 June 1904; DFZZ, I, 10 (1904), *caizheng*, pp. 271-5.

87. FO 17/1657, Intelligence diary for the period ending 30 August 1904, encl. in Director of Military Operations to Under Secretary of State for Foreign Affairs, 14 October 1904.

88. DFZZ, I, 8 (1904), *sheshuo*, pp. 181-5; 9 (1904), *sheshuo*, pp. 210-12; Powell, pp. 187-8.

89. FO 17/1639, Satow to the Marquess of Lansdowne, No. 421, 7 December 1904.

90. DFZZ, II, 7 (1905), *caizheng*, pp. 125-7; Ch'en, *Yuan Shih-k'ai*, pp. 62-3.

91. FO 371/217, Memo by Pereira on the new War Ministry, encl. in Jordan to Grey, No. 504, 29 November 1906; MacKinnon, 'The Peiyang Army', p. 407.

92. During the winter of 1906-7, there were rumours that Yuan's system of paying the troops regularly would be disrupted under Tieliang's management

of the army. See *The Times*, 7 February 1907, p. 7, 9 February p. 7; Cameron, p. 93; *North-China Herald*, 4 January 1907, p. 30.

93. FO 317/852, Willoughby's report on the war budget, encl. in Jordan to Grey, No. 470, 18 December 1909.

94. WDGS, No. 6562-1, Report of changes in the Chinese army in 1910, p. 37.

95. Shen Jian, pp. 396-7, using Chinese War Ministry and Finance Ministry sources.

96. Shen Jian, pp. 398-403.

97. WDGS, No. 6560-1, Chinese budget for 1911, pp. 7, 10.

98. WDGS, No. 6562-1, Report of changes in the Chinese army in 1910, pp. 20, 24. The War Ministry had ordered that any province in need of supplies from arsenals should make requisitions to the Ministry, and if approved, they would be referred to the provincial authorities concerned before being transmitted to the arsenal for issue. But this order seems to have been virtually ignored. See also No. 6283-7, Summary of military events for February 1911, p. 8.

3. MILITARY EDUCATION AND NATIONALISM

1. Leonard, pp. 160-1.

2. DFZZ, I, 12 (1904), *jiaoyu*, pp. 275-9.

3. DFZZ, 4 (1905), *jiaoyu*, p. 60; 6 (1905), *jiaoyu*, pp. 109-16.

4. Yoshihiro Hatano, 'The New Armies', p. 373.
5. DFZZ, II, 6 (1905), *jiaoyu*, pp. 122-6; Leonard, pp. 255-6.
6. ZWXG, *gongdu*, 15, pp. 27a-28b, 17, pp. 23a-24a, 19, pp. 21b-22b.
7. For a list of these schools and their distribution, see DFZZ, IV, 9 (1907), *jiaoyu*, pp. 204-7.
8. FO 228/1748, Changes report for the Chinese army, 1910, p. 21.
9. ZWXG, *zouyi*, 70, pp. 2a-b; Leonard, p. 267.
10. XHSYHYL, I, pp. 110-1.
11. FO 371/435, Pereira's report on military schools in China, encl. in Jordan to Grey, No. 506, 8 November 1908.
12. Leonard, p. 269.
13. FO 371/435, Pereira's report on Chinese troops in Manchuria, encl. in Jordan to Grey, No 424, 21 September 1908.
14. DFZZ, I, 12 (1904), *jiaoyu*, pp. 276-7.
15. FO 371/435, Pereira's report on military schools in China.
16. DFZZ, II, 12 (1905), *jiaoyu*, pp. 332-3; FO 405/195, Annual report on China, 1909, p. 46; WDGS, No. 6562-1, Report of changes in the Chinese army in 1910, pp. 16-17.
17. DFZZ, I, 12 (1904) *jiaoyu*, p. 277.
18. FO 371/435, Pereira's report on military schools in China; Brunnert and Hagelstrom, p. 315; Brissaud-Desmaillet, p. 1184; WDGS, No. 6562-1, Report of changes in the Chinese army in 1910, p. 17.
19. FO 405/171, Annual report on China, 1908, p. 35.
20. FO 371/435, Pereira's report on military schools in China; see also FO 371/214, Pereira's report on the New Army at Baoding, encl. in Jordan to Grey, No. 504, 29 October 1907. According to Brissaud-Desmaillet (p. 1184), there were only 120 students in early 1909.
21. WDGS, No. 6562-1, Report of changes in the Chinese army in 1910, p. 17.
22. Leonard, pp. 261-2. As a rule, each college was supervised by the viceroy, governor, or provincial general, and was divided into two classes for different grades of officers who attended them in alternate batches.
23. FO 371/435, Pereira's report on military schools in China; Leonard, pp. 261-2.
24. WDGS, No. 6562-1, Report of changes in the Chinese army in 1910, p. 17. *The China Year Book, 1912*, p. 247; FO 371/1092, Willoughby's report on the engagement of German military instructors for Peking's Officers' School, encl. in Jordan to Grey, No. 294, 20 July 1911; FO 405/229 Annual report on China, 1911, p. 57.

25. FO 228/1748, Changes report for the Chinese army, 1910, pp. 13, 20-1.

26. Swift, p. 182.

27. WDGS, No. 6562-1, Report of changes in the Chinese army in 1910, p. 16. The American military attaché corrected his French counterpart's claim (Brissaud-Desmaillet p. 1184) that there were twenty-nine primary schools.

28. Powell, p. 299; *The China Year Book, 1912*, p. 247.

29. DFZZ, II, 12 (1905), *jiaoyu*, pp. 321-2; FO 371/214, Pereira's report on the Nobles' College, encl. in Jordan to Grey, No. 395, 20 August 1907.

30. FO 371/435, Pereira's report on military schools in China; WO 33/454, 'Handbook of the Military Forces of China', p. 90. Because of the poor quality of teaching in the college, the Peking government was anxious to send some of the good students to study in England, Germany and Japan. See DFZZ, V, 1 (1908), *jiaoyu*, pp. 12-13.

31. Hackett, p. 139.

32. Qu Lihe, pp. 39-40; Nagai Michio, p. 77.

33. Fang Zhaoying, pp. 1-45, provides a list of the Chinese students in Japan during 1903.

34. KGWX, *bian* 1, *ce* 8, *Lieqiang qinlue*, I, p. 284.

35. KGWX, *bian* 1, *ce* 8, *Lieqiang qinlue*, I, pp. 267-71, 284-5.

36. Fang Dongying, p. 15; Tao Juyin, pp. 22-3.

37. Fang Dongying, p. 14.

38. Shi Jin, p. 164.

39. FO 371/415, Changes report for the Chinese army, 1907, Appendix IV.

40. Brissaud-Desmaillet, p. 1185.

41. Swift, p. 182.

42. WDGS, No. 6790-42, Notes on the Chinese Revolution of 1911-12, p. 9; Pekin Shina Kenkyūkai, II, pp. 392-5; Young, *The Presidency of Yuan Shih-k'ai*, p. 60.

43. ZWXG, *zouyi*, 37, p. 29a; Qu Lihe, p. 401.

44. FO 17/1654, Intelligence diary for the period ending 2 February 1904, encl. in Director of Military Operations to Under Secretary of State for Foreign Affairs, 28 March 1904; FO 17/1655, Intelligence diary for the period ending 16 February 1904, encl. in same to same, 7 April, 1904.

45. DFZZ, II, 9 (1905), *jiaoyu*, pp. 209-10, 223.

46. DFZZ, III, 2 (1906), *jiaoyu*, pp. 296-8.

47. DFZZ, V, 6 (1908), *jiaoyu*, pp. 106-7.

48. Jiang Zuobin, p. 7. Yinchang was anxious to improve the troops which had been in a state of lethargy in the two years before he became Minister of War. In October 1910 one hundred military students, mainly returning from Japan, sat for a five-day examina-

tion held by a board composed of Yinchang himself, Prince Zaito and General Duan Qirui. In the meantime, preparations were made to hold a similar examination for all the officers of the 8th Division in the following month. See WDGS, No. 6283-2, Summary of military events for September 1910, pp. 2-3; No. 6283-3, Summary of military events for October 1910, pp. 4-5.

49. WDGS, No. 6283-2, Summary of military events for September 1910, p. 5; No. 6283-3, Summary of military events for October 1910, p. 5. The graduates from the West Point Military Academy, New York, had at first refused to take the examination, but were later advised by the US military attaché to do so.

50. FO 405/171, Annual report on China, 1908, p. 35.

51. Leonard, pp. 162-3.

52. FO 405/195, Annual report on China, 1909, p. 46.

53. Brissaud-Desmaillet, p. 1184.

54. WDGS, No. 6562-1, Report of changes in the Chinese army in 1910, p. 16.

55. Brissaud-Desmaillet, p. 1184.

56. WDGS, No. 6790-42, Notes on the Chinese Revolution of 1911-12, p. 9. A British diplomat in Peking also wrote: 'Military education continues to extend, but the quality of the instruction in the schools suffers from the lack of adequate teachers and the widespread desire to be free from foreign tutelage'. See FO 405/195, Annual report on China, 1910, p. 72.

57. *The China Year Book, 1912*, p. 247; Leonard, p. 263.

58. McKenzie, *The Unveiled East*, p. 222.

59. Swift, p. 182.

60. See, for example, Zhang Nanxian, pp. 176, 204 ff. The formation of student-soldier battalions was actually ordered by Peking as part of the educational system for the men in the ranks.

61. Hatano has argued that these troops 'responded readily to revolutionary propaganda and sympathized with the developing nationalism of the enlightened literati, rich merchants, and modern intellectuals'. See 'The New Armies', p. 382.

62. Young describes these new officers as 'an appendage of the gentry class'. See *The Presidency of Yuan Shih-k'ai*, p. 2. I have used a different expression to avoid the pejorative connotation which Young's description seems to have.

63. See, for example, Pye, pp. 77-9, 82-3; Janowitz, pp. 80-1.

64. Dingle, *Across China on Foot*, p. 417.

65. Henry B. Graybill, *The Educational Reform in China*, Hong Kong, 1911, pp. 63-4, cited in Peake, p. 68.

66. FO 371/863, Willoughby's memo on the indiscipline in the Chinese army, encl. in Müller to Grey, No. 134, 30 April 1910.
67. Swift, p. 182.
68. FO 371/214, Pereira's report on the 8th Division, encl. in Jordan to Grey, No. 221, 13 May 1907; Leonard, p. 211.
69. FO 228/1082, Acting Consul-General Goffe (Hankow) to Jordan, No. 53, 31 May 1911, enclosing an extract from the native press.
70. WDGS, No. 6283-3, Summary of military events for October 1910, p. 5.
71. FO 471/863, Memo by Little on the political situation in China, encl. in Messrs Brunner, Mond, and Co. to Foreign Office, 2 March 1910; Consul-General Fraser to Müller, No. 38, encl. in Müller to Grey, No. 200, 17 June 1910.
72. *Minlibao* (Shanghai), 31 March 1911, p. 4.
73. XHGMHYL, II, pp. 80-1. Li was later considered to be unsuitable because of his position as commander of the 21st Mixed Brigade.
74. FO 371/864, Fraser to Müller, No. 38, encl. in Müller to Grey, No. 200, 17 June 1910.
75. FO 371/214, Pereira's report on the army at Hangchow, encl. in Jordan to Grey, No. 319, 5 July 1907; FO 371/214, Pereira's report on the troops at Anqing, encl. in Jordan to Grey, No. 321, 7

July 1907; Leonard, p. 277.
76. In fact there were senior officers who encouraged the cutting of the queue in one way or another. Li Yuan-hong, for example, not only condoned it but was pleased to find some of his men already had their queues discarded. On at least one occasion he spoke to the soldiers that he supported their action and that he would have been the first to cut off his had it not been for the fact that the government's policy on the matter was still unclear. See *Minlibao*, 3 January 1911, p. 2.
77. WDGS, No. 6562-1, Report of changes in the Chinese army in 1910, p. 11.
78. FO 371/214, Pereira's report on the 9th Division, encl. in Jordan to Grey, No. 321, 7 July 1907.
79. FO 371/875, Willoughby to Müller, encl. in Müller to Grey, No. 425, 23 November 1910.
80. FO 371/875, Willoughby to Müller.
81. FO 371/875, Willoughby to Müller.
82. Dingle, *Across China on Foot*, pp. 213-14.
83. For the role of foreign military officers in the Chinese army during the Tongzhi period, see Wright, *The Last Stand of Chinese Conservatism*, pp. 214-7.
84. FO 17/1655, Intelligence diary

for the period ending 10 May 1904, encl. in Director of Military Operations to Under Secretary of State for Foreign Affairs, 21 June 1904.

85. FO 371/214, Pereira's report on the 9th Division, encl. in Jordan to Grey, No. 321, 7 July 1907.

86. FO 228/1624, Report on the troops in Canton, encl. in Pereira to Satow, 7 February 1906; FO 228/1653, Report on the troops in Canton, encl. in Broadwood to Jordan, 25 January 1907.

87. FO 371/34, Some notes on Hunan by Pereira, encl. in Carnegie to Grey, No. 296, 9 July 1906.

88. FO 371/39, Memo by A.G. Major on a visit to the Hanyang arsenal, encl. in Carnegie to Grey, No. 326, 4 August 1906.

89. FO 405/171, Annual report on China, 1908, p. 35.

90. FO 371/26, Pereira's report on the Chinese manoeuvres, encl. in Satow to the Marquess of Lansdowne, No. 408, 27 November 1905; MP 312/119 Army.

91. FO 371/41, Brigadier-General W.H.H. Walters to Secretary of War, encl. in Jordan to Grey, No. 462, 8 November 1906.

92. Three British military officers who observed the manoeuvres of 1908 commented very unfavourably: 'Manoeuvres were, as usual, a set piece . . . The commanders therefore were hampered about taking the initiative, tied down to direct frontal attacks, and unable, if they were capable of doing so, of seizing opportunities for flanking movements. Attacks were carried out with very little intelligence, there were the usual wild advances across open valleys without any cover or any attempt to obtain it by entrenching, and each day the troops were pushed up to close quarters. The absence of umpiring enabled troops to move exposed across the front with calm indifference . . . Little attention was paid to scouting or to advanced guards, and that little was poorly done. The ground was practically never searched. Tactical advantages of ground were often neglected and there was much unreality'. See FO 371/629, Report on the manoeuvres, encl. in Jordan to Grey, No. ?, 10 December 1908.

93. McKenzie, *The Unveiled East*, p. 229; Leonard, p. 160.

94. FO 371/875, Willoughby to Müller, encl. in Müller to Grey, No. 425, 23 November 1910.

95. FO 371/871, Memo by Willoughby, encl. in Müller to Grey, No. 290, 25 August 1910.

96. FO 405/195, Annual report on China, 1910, p. 17; WDGS,

No. 6283-4, Summary of military events for November 1910, p. 3.

97. The British Foreign Office made the following comment: 'It is perhaps natural that the Chinese should turn to Germany in this case — firstly German military methods are admittedly excellent; secondly, the present Minister of War at Peking is ex-minister at Berlin. It is equally natural that Japan should dislike seeing instructors of Japanese nationality replaced by Germans'. FO 371/1092, Willoughby's report on the engagement of German military instructors, encl. in Jordan to Grey, No. 294, 20 July 1911.

98. *The Times*, 21 October 1911, p. 5.

99. WDGS, No. 6562-1, Report of changes in the Chinese army in 1910, p. 27; FO 405/195, Annual report on China, 1910, p. 72.

4. SOCIAL ATTITUDES

1. FO 371/435, Pereira's report on Chinese troops in Manchuria, encl. in Jordan to Grey, No. 425, 21 September 1908.

2. WDGS, No. 6562-1, Report of changes in the Chinese army in 1910, pp. 25-6.

3. FO 371/875, Willoughby to Müller, covering a report by Lieutenant-Commander Mulock on the Chengtu arsenal, encl. in Müller to Grey, No. 425, 23 November 1910.

4. *The Times*, 8 March 1910, p. 5.

5. Quoted in McKenzie, 'Four Hundred Million Chinamen Awaken' pp. 702-3.

6. An English translation of this edict, which is used here with some slight stylistic changes, can be found in WDGS, No. 6562-3, Edict on military reform, 10 April 1911. For the Chinese text, see *Qingshilu* (Xuantong), 50, pp. 6b-9b.

7. Dreyer, p. 18.

8. Translated in Thomson, pp. 323-4.

9. Thomson, p. 324.

10. Philip C. Huang, pp. 56-61.

11. Jerome Ch'en has argued that Chinese nationalism in the 1895-1919 period was theoretically and historically inspired and rationalised by social Darwinism. 'It was introspective', he adds, 'blaming China's weaknesses on China's ills; it was incapable of being outward-looking in this sense and anti-imperialistic'. See Ch'en, *Yuan Shikai*, pp. 201-3.

12. Lan Tianwei, 'Junjie', pp. 57-61.

13. Feisheng, p. 65.
14. Lan Tianwei, 'Junshi yu guojia zhi guanxi', pp. 49-50.
15. Lan Tianwei, 'Junshi yu guojia zhi guanxi', p. 51.
16. Anon., 'Junren zhi jiaoju', p. 38.
17. Lan Tianwei, 'Junshi yu guojia zhi guanxi', pp. 51-2.
18. Lan Tianwei, 'Junguomin sixiang pujilun', pp. 41-2.
19. Liang Qichao, 'Lun shangwu', in *Yinbingshi quanji*, 3, pp. 10b-11a.
20. Fen Gesheng, I, pp. 79-87.
21. Fen Gesheng, II, pp. 65-8; Liang Qichao, 'Lun shangwu', *Yinbingshi quanji*, 3, pp. 13a-b; Chang Hao, p. 278.
22. Fen Gesheng, II, pp. 48-51.
23. Liang Qichao, 'Lun shangwu', *Yinbingshi quanji*, 3, pp. 4b-6b; Chang Hao, pp. 277-8.
24. DFZZ, II, 5 (1905), *sheshuo*, pp. 98-9.
25. Baili, pp. 42-8. Similar views were expressed by another group of students. See Min-youshe (ed.), 'Wubei jiaoyu', *Youxue yibian*, 1 (November 1902), *junshi*, pp. 1-7; 2 (December 1902), *junshi*, pp. 13-16; 4 (February 1903), *junshi*, pp. 17-20.
26. Baili, pp. 37-8; Feisheng, pp. 65-8.
27. Feisheng, 'Zhen junren', pp. 70-2. Similar ideas were entertained by nearly every student whose writings have been examined here.
28. *International Encyclopedia of the Social Sciences*, X, pp. 300-1.
29. Andreski, pp. 184-6.
30. See, for example, Anon., 'Lishishang youmin zhi shangwuguo', pp. 196-8. In 1904 Liang Qichao published a popular book entitled *Zhongguo zhi wushidao* [Chinese Bushidō]. The theme of the book was a didactic one: that although the Chinese had been a physically weak and spiritually pacifist people in a historical sense, originally they did not lack a martial spirit. It was therefore possible for the Chinese people to activate that spirit which was rooted in the Chinese cultural tradition. See Chang Hao, p. 278.
31. Lary, p. 11.
32. It is interesting to point out that in February 1934 when Jiang Jieshi launched the New Life Movement in China, he exhorted the Chinese people to make their life 'militarised, productive, and aesthetic'. What did the militarisation of life mean? Jiang's answer was that: 'It does not mean that all of us should join the armed forces and march into the battlefield; it merely means that we should emphasise organisation, unity, order, enthusiasm, and seriousness in the conduct of our daily lives, discarding once and for all such bad habits as disor-

ganisation and disorientation, lack of discipline and purpose, drift and shiftlessness, and complacency and inertia'. See Dun J. Li, pp. 130-1.

33. Chiu-san Tsang, p. 76; Powell, p. 156.

34. Peake, pp. 180-1, 190-1. The *New National Reader* was published by the Commercial Press in 1904.

35. Cited in Tsang, pp. 40-1.

36. Cited in Peake, p. 69.

37. Cited in Peake, p. 69.

38. The History of the Chinese Republic Chronology Editorial Committee, pp. 142, 201; FO 371/1090, Willoughby's report on military drill and musketry in the civil schools of Manchuria, encl. in Jordan to Grey, No. 161, 19 April 1911.

39. The History of the Chinese Republic Chronology Editorial Committee, pp. 408, 465.

40. Chen Qitian, p. 109.

41. See Chang Chung-li *The Chinese Gentry*.

42. See Ho Ping-ti, pp. 34-5, 37-8, 40.

43. Kuhn, pp. 3-4.

44. Hsiao Kung-ch'üan, pp. 447-52, 472, 478-81.

45. Hedtke, pp. 170-1.

46. Buck, pp. 427-8.

47. Chang Chung-li, pp. 51-2.

48. Rhoads, 'Merchant Associations', p. 108.

49. Elvin, pp. 43-4.

50. Rhoads, 'Merchant Associations', p. 101.

51. Of some members of the gentry who became merchants, the most notable was Zhang Jian of Jiangsu, who chose a career in business rather than in government service. See Samuel C. Chu, *Reformer in Modern China*.

52. See Rosenbaum, pp. 689-90.

53. In making this point, I was inspired by Hedtke, p. 300.

54. Chang P'eng-yüan, 'The Constitutionalist', pp. 149-50.

55. Ichiko Chūzō, 'The Role of the Gentry', pp. 301-2.

56. XHSYHYL, I, p. 68.

57. The Joint Hubei Philosophy and Social Science Association, I, pp. 158-9.

58. This claim is based on a study of various biographical sketches of the revolutionary soldiers on record. See, for example, such sketches in XHSYHYL.

59. XHSYHYL, III, pp. 142-3; KGWX, *bian* 2, *ce* 1, *Wuchang shouyi*, pp. 272-3; Esherick, *Reform and Revolution*, p. 148.

60. I was inspired by Janowitz, pp. 58-61.

61. *Qingchao xuwenxian tongkao, juan* 221, *bing* 20, pp. 9679.

62. For detailed treatment of this incident, see Hatano, pp. 375-8; Rhoads, *China's Republican Revolution*, p. 180-97.

63. *The Times*, 3 June 1911, p. 5. Meanwhile, merchant militia units had been formed

in various parts of China. Their purpose was partly nationalistic and partly to protect the merchant community interests in times of disturbances or revolution. See Marie-Claire Bergère, pp. 245-6.

64. Fincher, 'Elite Militarism', pp. 224-30. See also The History of the Chinese Republic Chronology Editorial Committee, pp. 246, 265, 280.

65. XHSYHYL, I, p. 3. Powell (p. 291) also notes that poor illiterate peasants formed the bulk of the soldiery, although some enlisted personnel consisted of literate men from the lower middle class.

66. See, for example, Sheridan, pp. 6-7.

67. Liu Fenghan, p. 192. Other 'commandments' forbade looting, raping, wandering in the street in the night, trespassing on the rice fields, and so on. There was a military song exhorting every soldier to be loyal, to help the people, to discipline himself, and in short to be a respected member of the community of which the army was an important part. Liu Fenghan, pp. 142-4, 194.

68. FO 371/26, Report on manoeuvres of Chinese troops by Colonel H. Bower, commandant of the legation guard, encl. in Satow to Marquess of Lansdowne, No. 408, 27 November 1905.

69. FO 371/415, Pereira's report

on the Zhuozhou manoeuvres, encl. in Jordan to Grey, No. 548, 25 November 1907.

70. FO 371/629, Report on manoeuvres of Chinese troops by Pereira and two other British military officers, encl. in Jordan to Grey, No. ?, 10 December 1908.

71. FO 371/859, Changes report for the Chinese army, 1909, p. 30. See also FO 371/1089, Annual report on China, 1910, p. 73.

72. *Minlibao*, 5 December 1910, p. 4.

73. FO 371/214, Pereira's report on the 7th Division, encl. in Jordan to Grey, No. 321, 7 July 1907.

74. FO 228/1733, Report on the New Army of Yunnan, encl. in Acting Consul-General Wilton to Jordan, No. 41, 21 September 1909.

75. See, for example, *Minlibao*, 12 December 1910, p. 4; 8 December, p. 4; 12 December, p. 4.

76. XHGM, III, pp. 469-71; DFZZ, VII, 7 (1910), *jizai*, pp. 92-3.

77. *Minlibao*, 29 March 1911. Young notes that 'before the revolution it [the New Army] actually fired its weapons only in the suppression of unrest among the rural and urban poor'. See *The Presidency of Yuan Shih-k'ai*, p. 4.

78. XHGM, III, p. 509; Esherick, *Reform and Revolution*, p. 133.

79. XHGM, III, pp. 528-9.

5. REVOLUTIONARY MOVEMENT IN THE HUBEI ARMY

1. Esherick, *Reform and Revolution*, pp. 157-8. However, I do not share Esherick's view that the subversive activity in the Hubei army was not 'markedly different from accounts of revolutionary activity at other times and in other provinces of China'.

2. WGZ, I, pp. 280-1.

3. *Qingshigao, bingshi*, 3, p. 9b.

4. See below, chapter 9, p. 204.

5. Quoted in Leonard, p. 104.

6. Quoted in Leonard, pp. 152-6.

7. FO 371/214, Pereira's report on the 8th and 11th Divisions, encl. in Jordan to Grey, No. 221, 13 May 1907.

8. Leonard, pp. 208-9, 268.

9. FO 371/635, Some notes on the troops of the 8th Division, by Captain Collins, encl. in Jordan to Grey, No. 106, 9 March 1909.

10. Wang Jingyu, I, pp. 424-5.

11. FO 371/39, Memo on the Hanyang arsenal, by A.G. Major, encl. in Carnegie to Grey, No. 326, 4 August 1906.

12. Chen Kuilong, 9, p. 18b.

13. FO 405/195, Annual report on China, 1910, p. 72.

14. Esherick, *Reform and Revolution*, p. 146.

15. Esherick, *Reform and Revolution*, p. 43.

16. Powell, p. 256.

17. WGZ, I, p. 281.

18. See, for example, WGZ, I, p. 281; *Minlibao*, 2 September 1911, p. 4.

19. Leonard wrote of Zhang Biao in 1908: '. . . a man who will play a very important part in Chinese military affairs if war or disturbance comes during his time. He impresses one as a man of about 52, having a very Japanese face, and being rather lean instead of rotund as is too frequently the result of much good living on the part of higher officers. He has been in Japan quite a little and is quiet and dignified in demeanor'. Leonard, pp. 206-7.

20. See below.

21. Chen Kuilong, 9, pp. 24a-b.

22. For a complete list of the officers of the 8th Division and the 21st Mixed Brigade, see Hu Poyu, I, tables 10 and 11, facing p. 22.

23. ZWXG, *zouyi*, 70, p. 4b.

24. ZWXG, *zouyi*, 65, pp. 11a-12b.

25. ZWXG, *diandu*, 68, pp. 11a-b; 68, p. 15b.

26. For different interpretations of this uprising, see Smythe, 'The Tzu-li Hui: Some Chinese and their Rebellion'; Fung, 'The T'ang Ts'ai-ch'ang Revolt'; Esherick, *Reform and Revolution*, pp. 28-33; Li Shoukong, 'Tang Caichang yu zilijun'. In a recent work, Charlton M. Lewis has ably delineated a pattern by which conservative literati, radical literati reformers and the secret societies merged in the

interest of reform but broke into separate camps that set revolution in motion. See *Prologue to the Chinese Revolution*, pp. 83-109. See also Bays, pp. 78-91.

27. See Schiffrin, ch. IX; Liew, ch. 3.

28. *Subao*, 28 February, 11 April 1903; *Zhejiangchao*, 6 (July, 1903), *sheshui*, p. 3.

29. Ju Zheng, II, pp. 476-7.

30. Schiffrin, pp. 260-2; Liew, pp. 26-7.

31. *Subao*, 21 and 31 May 1903; GMWX, II, p. 113; Zhang Nanxian, pp. 58, 106-7.

32. GMWX, II, pp. 113-4; Zhu Yanjia, pp. 166-7.

33. Bays, pp. 147-8; Young, 'The Reformer as a Conspirator', pp. 251-4.

34. XHGMHYL, I, p. 181; Li Lianfang, pp. 3b-4a; Yang Yuru, pp. 10-11.

35. GMWX, II, p. 113; Li Lianfang, pp. 2b, 4a.

36. Li Lianfang, pp. 4a-4b; Yang Yuru, p. 11; Zhang Yukun, p. 2.

37. Zhang Nanxian, p. 62.

38. For Song, see Liew, pp. 8-9. For Lü, Cao and Zhu, see Zhang Nanxian, pp. 58, 64-5.

39. Zhang Nanxian, pp. 55-7, provides a list of the members.

40. XHGM, I, pp. 553-4. Song Jiaoren, for example, was one of them.

41. Cao Yabo, I, Introduction, pp. 3-4.

42. Zhang Nanxian, pp. 55, 65.

43. Zhang Nanxian, pp. 55-6;

Li Lianfang, pp. 5a-5b; Yang Yuru, pp. 11-12; Hsüeh, pp. 20-1.

44. While in Europe, the Hubei students were also politically active, and contributed significantly to the founding of the European branch of the Tongmenghui in 1905. See GMWX, II, pp. 115-20.

45. ZWXG, *gongdu*, 21, pp. 1a-13a.

46. FO 405/157, Consul-General Hopkins to Satow, encl. in Satow to Grey, No. 452, 26 December 1905.

47. GMWX, II, p. 34. Since Liu had never been to Japan, it seems certain that he joined in Wuchang and sent his sworn statement to Tokyo.

48. Zhang Nanxian, pp. 73-7; XHSYHYL, III, pp. 64-5; Feng Ziyou, II, pp. 62-6.

49. Yang Duo, pp. 5-6.

50. Cao Yabo, I, pp. 13-14.

51. XHSYHYL, I, pp. 76-7. According to Cao Yabo (I, p. 10), there were five assessors. But it is not clear what their duties were.

52. For a list of the members, see Zhang Nanxian, pp. 89-92.

53. XHSYHYL, I, p. 77. It is not true, as has been alleged by two writers, that the Society for Daily Increase in Knowledge, in subverting the army, gave greater weight to the officers than the common soldiers. See Li Chunxuan, 'Xinhai shouyi jishi benmo',

in XHSYHYL, II, p. 112; Xiong Bingkun, 'Xinhai Hubei Wuchang shouyi shiqian yundong zhi jingguo ji linshi fanan zhi jushu', in KGWX, *bian* 2, *ce* 1, *Wuchang shouyi*, p. 263. Neither Li Chunxuan nor Xiong Bingkun was a member of the society, and their accounts are both questionable. Gathering from all available sources, I cannot find more than six officers who were known to have been members of the society. Moreover, none of these officers was an office-bearer in the society.

54. XHSYHYL, I, p. 78; Li Lianfang, p. 6a; Yang Yuru, p. 12.
55. XHSYHYL, II, pp. 75-8; Feng Ziyou, *Geming yishi*, IV, pp. 195-6.
56. Cao Yabo, I, p. 130.
57. Cao Yabo, I, pp. 135-6.
58. XHGM, I, pp. 11-12; Munholland, pp. 77-95, particularly p. 86; Zhang Nanxian, p. 82.
59. XHGMHYL, III, p. 11.
60. For an account of the uprising, see XHGM, II, pp. 461-536; Esherick, *Reform and Revolution*, pp. 58-65.
61. The others arrested were Ji Yulin, Li Yadong, Wu Gongsan and Yin Ziheng.
62. Cao Yabo, I, pp. 147-8; XHSYHYL, III, pp. 17-27.
63. FO 371/223 Consul-General Warren to Jordan, encl. in Jordan to Grey, No. 9, 7 January 1907.
64. Cao Yabo, I, p. 130.
65. XHSYHYL, I, p. 77.
66. FO 371/220, Newspaper extract, encl. in letters from Messrs Brunner, Mond, and Co., Shanghai, to Grey, 29 April 1907.
67. FO 371/220, Pereira's memo on unrest in China, encl. in Jordan to Grey, No. 211, 2 May 1907.
68. FO 371/220, Extract from the Wuhu intelligence report, encl. in Jordan to Grey, No. 343, 22 July 1907.
69. For a detailed account of these uprisings, see Cheng, pp. 220-39.
70. Zhang Nanxian, p. 142.
71. XHSYHYL, III, p. 23; Li Lianfang, pp. 8b-9a; Zhang Nanxian, pp. 63, 100.
72. Xu Tongxin, pp. 205-6, 209; Chen Kuilong, 9, pp. 7a-8a.
73. Zhang Nanxian, p. 145-6; Zhang Yukun, pp. 4-5; Li Lianfang, pp. 9a-9b.
74. Li Liuru, I, pp. 143-6.
75. Zhang Nanxian, pp. 147-9; Zhang Yukun, pp. 7-8; Li Lianfang, p. 10a.
76. My interview with Wan Yaohuang in his Taipei home in January 1970. Wan, a native of Hubei, was one of the organisers of the Society for the Study of Popular Government. He was known as Wan Qi when he enlisted in the Wuchang army in 1908. During the Republican period, Wan held several senior mili-

tary positions. After the war with Japan, he was appointed chairman of the Hubei provincial government. In 1949 he went to Taiwan with the Guomindang government and served as adviser on party affairs and director of the Research Institute for Revolutionary Practice.

77. XHSYHYL, I, p. 118.
78. XHSYHYL, III, pp. 35-6; Zhang Nanxian, p. 147; Zhang Yukun, pp. 9-10; Li Lianfang, p. 10b.
79. XHGMHYL, I, p. 308; Li Liuru, I, pp. 158-9.
80. Zhang Nanxian, pp. 168-9; XHGMHYL, II, pp. 47-9.
81. Zhang Yukun, pp. 17-18.
82. Zhang Nanxian, pp. 166-7.
83. Zhang Nanxian, pp. 262-3; Zhang Yukun, p. 10.
84. Yang Du (1875-1931) was an enigmatic figure liked by neither the revolutionaries nor the constitutionalists. In the early 1900s he appeared to be in favour of revolution. In 1905, however, he declared his preference for a constitutional monarchy. Yet he never became very close to the constitutionalists who suspected him. In 1908 he became a fourth-ranking official charged with the responsibility of preparing a constitution. In 1911 he was director of the bureau of statistics attached to the royal cabinet. Se Wu Xiangxiang, I, pp. 69-85.

85. Zhang Yukun, p. 12; Li Liuru, I, pp. 163-71.
86. Zhang Yukun, pp. 12-5; Zhang Nanxian, pp. 152-3.
87. Zeng Shengsan, 'Wuchang shouyi zhi yuanqi'; Ju Zheng, II, p. 483; KGWX, *bian* 2, *ce* 1, *Wuchang shouyi*, p. 266.
88. Li Liuru, I, p. 155.
89. Zhang Yukun, p. 16; XHGMHYL, I, p. 308.
90. Zhang Yukun, p. 17.
91. Zhang Yukun, pp. 18-21.
92. Li Liuru, I, p. 235.
93. XHSYHYL, I, p. 51.
94. Zhang Yukun, pp. 22-3.
95. Zhang Yukun, pp. 23-4.
96. XHGMHYL, II, pp. 17-21; GMWX, IV, pp. 62-3.
97. Zhang Yukun, p. 26.
98. XHGM, V, p. 4; *Minlibao*, 7 October 1912, p. 3; 8 October 1912, p. 3.
99. According to the above source, the figure rose to 3000 in August-September. Zhang Yukun (p. 7) put the peak at 5000 in August. It is difficult to say how reliable these figures are, since they cannot be verified by official documents of the Literary Society, most of which were burnt shortly before the Wuchang uprising. However, considering the intensive operation of the society, a membership of three thousand is not incredible. On the other hand, Zhang's figure may have been somewhat exaggerated.

1. Li Lianfang, p. 14b.
2. Fung, 'The Kung-chin-hui:

A Late Ch'ing Revolutionary Society'; also see Liew, pp. 74-6. A more recent account is Esherick, *Reform and Revolution*, pp. 153-8.

3. Deng Wenhui, pp. 16-17.
4. Sun Wu, a native of Hubei, was a graduate of Wuchang's military preparatory school. In 1900, after serving a short period as a junior officer, he was transferred to Hunan as a military instructor. He was soon promoted to be a battalion commander at Yuezhou, where he took part in the Tang Caichang uprising. After the revolt, he fled to Guangdong and then to Guangxi under an assumed name. He returned to Hubei in 1904, and subsequently went to Japan to pursue a course in naval affairs. He returned to Wuchang in 1906, and before he left for Japan a second time in the following year, he went to Manchuria and Hong Kong to study the revolutionary situation there. See Zhang Nanxian, pp. 189-90.
5. XHGMHYL, I, pp. 503-5; GMWX, IV, pp. 13-14.
6. These regulations are recorded in Lin Yue *et al.* (eds), *Qian sanshierbiao geming shilu*, Xiayuan, 1913, which is available in the Guomindang Archives. They have been reproduced in KGWX, *bian* 2, *ce* 1, *Wuchang shouyi*, pp. 125-6. They were signed

by the regiment representative, Li Chengmu, and dated late 1908. This date is an error, because it was not until 1909 that Sun Wu began to subvert the New Army systematically. It is of interest to note, too, that Sun Wu, though not a member of the New Army, was designated as director *(zongjian)* of the Society for Common Advancement within the 32nd regiment.

7. XHSYHYL, I, pp. 3, 15.
8. XHSYHYL, I, pp. 93, 121. Here again, all these figures are open to doubt. However, since it seems true that the Literary Society had recruited three thousand or more members, it is reasonable to assume that the Society for Common Advancement had about two thousand members.
9. Yang Yuru, pp. 34-7. Three other resolutions were adopted: in view of the government vigilance in Wuchang, all Sunday meetings were to be cancelled and all the secret cells in Wuhan to cease activity temporarily; Hubei and Hunan were to take the lead in the revolution with each supporting the other on the day of uprising; and the New Army in Wuchang was to be the major force to bring about the revolution.
10. XHSYHYL, I, p. 71; Cai Jiou, p. 56.
11. XHSYHYL, I, p. 93.

12. According to *Qingshigao, bingshi* 3, p. 9b, there was a total of 16,104 officers and men in the Hubei army in 1910. Most of the secondary sources I have consulted put the figure for 1911 at approximately 15,000.

13. This claim is based on various sources, particularly Li Lianfang, pp. 77a-80b; KGWX, *bian* 2, *ce* 1, *Wuchang shouyi*, pp. 268-9.

14. Zhang Yukun, pp. 28-9.

15. Fass, 'Revolutionary Activity in the Province Hu-pei and the Wu-chang Uprising of 1911', p. 138.

16. See Fung, 'The Kung-chin-hui', pp. 200-1; also Fung, 'The T'ungmeng-hui Central China Bureau and the Wuchang Uprising', pp. 487-93. Esherick shares this view. See *Reform and Revolution*, p. 143.

17. Liu Yusheng, pp. 56-9.

18. *Minlibao*, 19 October 1910, p. 3; 20 October 1910, p. 2; 25 October 1910, p. 3; 22 November 1910, p. 4.

19. *Minlibao*, 24 March 1911, p. 4; 25 June 1911, p. 4.

20. *Minlibao*, 29 March 1911, p. 4; FO 288/1801, Intelligence report for the March quarter, 1911, encl. in Goffe's 'Separate' of 14 April 1911.

21. *Minlibao*, 26 March 1911, p. 4. Another source puts the desertion figure at 261; see FO 228/1801, Goffe to Jordan, No. 46, 4 May 1911.

22. FO 228/1802, Goffe to Jordan, No. 94, 9 October 1911.

23. *Minlibao*, 3 October 1911, p. 4.

24. Esherick, *Reform and Revolution*, p. 113.

25. FO 371/863, Memo on the political situation in China by E.S. Little, encl. in Messrs Brunner, Mond, and Co. to Foreign Office, 2 March 1910; FO 228-1761, Intelligence report for December quarter, 1909, encl. in Fraser's 'Separate' of 14 January 1910; also Fraser to Jordan, No. 73, 5 July 1910.

26. *Minlibao* 24 December 1910, p. 4.

27. FO 371/867, Summary of consular intelligence reports for third quarter of 1910, encl. in Müller to Grey, No. 428, No. 24, 1910; FO 228/1801, Goffe to Jordan, No. 22, 6 March 1911.

28. *Minlibao*, 9 May 1911, p. 4.

29. Esherick, *Reform and Revolution*, p. 163.

30. *Minlibao*, 9 May 1911, p. 4; 10 July 1911, p. 4.

31. *Minlibao*, 31 August 1911, p. 4; 7 September 1911, p. 4; 10 October 1911, p. 4.

32. XHGMHYL, I, p. 506.

33. *Minlibao*, 25 April 1911, p. 4; 31 May 1911, p. 4; 6 June 1911; p. 4.

34. Zhang Yukun, pp. 27-8; *Minlibao*, 6 August 1911, p. 3; 9 August 1911, p. 4; 11 August 1911, p. 4; 18 August 1911, p. 4; 23 August 1911,

p. 4; 24 August 1911, p. 4.

35. *Minlibao*, 8 August 1911, p. 4; 18 August 1911, p. 4; 27 August 1911, p. 4; 28 August 1911, p. 4.

36. *Minlibao*, 2 September 1911,

p. 4.

37. FO 228/1802, Intelligence report for the two months ended 30 September 1911, encl. in Goffe's 'Separate' of 5 October 1911.

6. OTHER ARMIES IN THE YANGZI REGION

1. FO 371/864, Consul-General Warren to Müller, encl. 2 in Müller to Grey, No 200, 17 July 1910.

2. FO 371/864, Consul-General Wilkinson to Müller, encl. 6 in Müller to Grey, No. 200, 17 June 1910. See also FO 371/867, Summary of intelligence reports for 1st quarter of 1910, encl. in Müller to Grey, No. 194, 10 June 1910.

3. FO 371/864, Consul-General Fraser to Müller, encl. 1 in Müller to Grey, No. 200, 17 June 1910.

4. FO 405/195, Annual report on China, 1910, pp. 64-6. See also *Minlibao*, 13 October 1910, p. 5; 14 October 1910, p. 3.

5. Zhang Shoubo, *supplement*, chapter 3.

6. *Minlibao*, 19 December 1910, p. 4.

7. FO 371/1090, Summary of intelligence reports for 2nd quarter, 1911, encl. in Jordan to Grey, No. 363, 16 September 1911.

8. FO 371/1090, Report by Ramsay for the quarter ending December 1910, encl. in

Jordan to Grey, No. 176, 25 April 1911.

9. FO 371/1090, Summary of intelligence report for 2nd quarter, 1911, encl. in Jordan to Grey, No. 363, 16 September 1911. According to Esherick, the provincial budget showed an income of 6,745,000 taels and expenses of 8,317,000 taels. See *Reform and Revolution*, p. 115. Esherick's source is the memorial of Governor Yang Wending, whose deficit figure may have been an underestimation.

10. FO 371/1090, Summary of intelligence reports for 2nd quarter, 1911, encl. in Jordan to Grey, No. 363, 16 September 1911.

11. *Minlibao*, 24 December 1910, p. 3.

12. FO 371/1090, Summary of intelligence reports for 2nd quarter, 1911, encl. in Jordan to Grey, No. 363, 16 September 1911.

13. FO 405/195, Annual report on China, 1910, p. 68.

14. FO 371/867, Summary of intelligence reports for 1st

quarter of 1910, encl. in Müller to Grey, No. 194, 10 June 1910. FO 371/1090, Report by Ramsay for the quarter ending December 1910, encl. in Jordan to Grey, No. 176, 25 April 1911.

15. *Minlibao*, 14 October 1910, p. 4.

16. *Minlibao*, 11 October 1910, p. 3; 14 October 1910, p. 3; 28 October 1910, p. 3.

17. FO 371/1090, Intelligence reports for the 1st quarter, 1911, encl. in Jordan to Grey, No. 200, 22 June 1911.

18. FO 405/229, Annual report on China, 1911, p. 53.

19. *Minlibao*, 8 July, 1911, p. 2; 17 July 1911, p. 3; 19 July 1911, p. 2; 29 August 1911, p. 4; *The Times*, 15 August 1911, p. 3.

20. *Minlibao*, 21 July 1911, p. 4; MP 312/305, unidentified newspaper cutting dated 16 August 1911.

21. FO 371/1090, Intelligence reports for the 1st quarter, 1911, encl. in Jordan to Grey, No. 200, 22 June 1911.

22. *Minlibao*, 17 July 1911, p. 4.

23. Esherick, *Reform and Revolution*, p. 163.

24. *Minlibao*, 6 September 1911, p. 5; 9 September 1911, p. 4.

25. FO 405/229, Annual report on China, 1911, p. 53.

26. XHGM, III, section on peasant uprisings, particularly pp. 413-23, 497-525. See also Li Shiyue, pp. 39-41.

27. On the reform movement in Hunan during the late Qing period, see Esherick, *Reform and Revolution*; Lewis, *Prologue to the Chinese Revolution*; also Lewis, 'The Hunanese Elite and the Reform Movement, 1895-1898'.

28. Shen Jian, pp. 374-5; WGZ, I, pp. 296-300.

29. FO 371/34, Pereira's report on the New Army in Hunan, encl. in Carnegie to Grey, No. 296, 9 July 1906.

30. FO 371/223, Confidential instructions from the Huguang Viceroy, encl. 2 in Jordan to Grey, No. 9, 7 January 1907.

31. FO 371/220 Extract from Changsha intelligence report for quarter ended 31 December 1906, encl. in Jordan to Grey, No. 98, 21 February 1907.

32. XHGM, VI, p. 164; Yang Shiji, pp. 166-7; Li Shiyue, pp. 97-8; Cao Yabo, II, pp. 137-8; XHGMHYL, II, pp. 130-1.

33. XHGMHYL, II, p. 160; Yang Shiji, pp. 170-1.

34. *The Times*, 18 April 1910, p. 7.

35. FO 371/864, Consul-General Warren to Müller, enc. 2 in Müller to Grey, No. 200, 17 June 1910.

36. XHGM, III, pp. 497-8; *North-China Herald*, 27 May 1910, pp. 512-13.

37. FO 371/867, Müller to Grey, No. 142, 5 May 1910.

38. *North-China Herald*, 6 May

1910, p. 310.

39. Yang Shiji, p. 179; KGWX, *bian* 2, *ce* 3, *Gesheng guangfu*, I, pp. 9-10.

40. *Gesheng guangfu*, I, p. 11.

41. XHGM, VI, p. 147; XHGMHYL, II, p. 159.

42. Esherick, *Reform and Revolution*, p. 114, table 4.

43. *Minlibao*, 2 January 1911, p. 2.

44. *Minlibao*, 18 July 1911, p. 4; 27 July 1911, p. 4.

45. *Minlibao*, 7 September 1911, p. 4.

46. FO 371/214, Pereira's report on the troops in Anqing, encl. in Jordan to Grey, No. 321, 7 July 1907; WGZ, I, p. 255.

47. FO 371/214, Pereira's report on the troops in Anqing.

48. Leonard, p. 232.

49. Feng Ziyou, *Zhonghua minguo kaiguoqian gemingshi*, II, pp. 221-9; Zou Lu, pp. 766-70; Rankin, p. 180.

50. FO 371/435, Report of a mutiny at Anqing, encl. 2 in Jordan to Grey, No. 543, 4 December 1908.

51. USDS 893.20/18, Consul in Nanking to Secretary of State, No. 92, 14 April 1911; *North-China Herald*, 28 November 1908, pp. 527-8.

52. *North-China Herald*, 28 November 1908, p. 528.

53. FO 371/871, Military report by Willoughby, encl. in Müller to Grey, No. 195, 14 June 1910.

54. WGZ, I, p. 256.

55. *Minlibao*, 19 November, 1910, p. 4; 23 May 1911, p. 3; 13 July 1911, p. 4; 23 July 1911, p. 4; 25 August 1911, p. 4.

56. Leonard, pp. 229-31; FO 372/214 Pereira's report on the New Army in Kiukiang, encl. in Jordan to Grey, No. 321, 7 July 1907.

57. XHGMHYL, IV, p. 304.

58. *The China Year Book, 1912*, p. 255. FO 371/871, Military report by Willoughby, encl. in Müller to Grey, No. 195, 14 June 1910.

59. *Minlibao*, 8 July 1911, p. 3; 5 July 1911, p. 4; 13 July 1911, p. 4.

60. For a detailed study of the revolutionary movement in Jiangxi, see Kupper, 'Revolution in China'. I have relied largely on it in the writing of this section on Jiangxi.

61. Kupper, pp. 112-13, citing Li Liejun, p. 7.

62. XHGMHYL, IV, pp. 345-9. Apart from the source cited here, I have been unable to find any other information about the Jiangxi branch of the Society for Common Advancement.

63. Wu Tiecheng, pp. 16-21; Kupper, pp. 103-6.

64. Leonard, p. 218; FO 371/214, Pereira's report on the 9th Division, encl. in Jordan to Grey, No. 321, 7 July 1907.

65. XHGMHYL, IV, p. 234; FO 371/432, Report on the 9th Division, encl. in Jordan to Grey, No. 497, 3 November

1908; WO 33/549, Military report on the province of Jiangsu, prepared by the General Staff, War Office, London, December 1908, pp. 59-63.

66. XHGMHYL, IV, pp. 233-4; Leonard, p. 199; FO 371/214, Pereira's report on the 7th Division and other troops at Qingjiangpu, encl. in Jordan to Grey, No. 321, 7 July 1907.

67. WGZ, I, p. 208; WDGS, No. 6562-1, Report of changes in the Chinese army, 1910, p. 9; WO 33/552, Military report on the province of Jiangsu (north of the Yangzi), prepared by the General Staff, War Office, London, August 1910, pp. 51-2.

68. FO 371/223, Jordan to Grey, No. 9, 7 January 1907.

69. FO 371/223, Consul Ker to Jordan, encl. in Jordan to Grey, No. 9, 7 January 1907.

70. Powell, p. 245.

71. Leonard, p. 219.

72. FO 371/863, Memo by Willoughby on the indiscipline in the Chinese army, encl. in Müller to Grey, No. 134, 30 April 1910.

73. USDS 893.20/14 Consul in Nanking to Calhoun, No. 76, 20 February 1911; WDGS, No. 6562-1, Report of changes in the Chinese army, 1910, pp. 26-7.

74. XHGMHYL, IV, pp. 235-6.

75. FO 228/1762, Intelligence report for the March quarter,

1910, encl. in Goffe's 'Separate' of 13 April 1910.

76. *Minlibao*, 19 October 1910, p. 3; 25 January 1911, p. 3.

77. FO 371/863, Memo by Willoughby on the indiscipline in the Chinese army; *North-China Herald*, 18 February 1910, p. 356.

78. FO 371/863, Memo by Willoughby on the indiscipline in the Chinese army. See also FO 371/863, Müller to Grey, No. 108, 4 April 1910.

79. USDS 1518/374, Vice-Consul in Nanking to Fletcher, encl. in Fletcher to Assistant Secretary of State, No. 160, 1 April 1910.

80. *Minlibao*, 20 June 1911, p. 4; 15 August 1911, p. 4; FO 228/1799, Intelligence report for the September quarter, 1911. encl. in Consul Pitzipios to Jordan, No. 26, 3 October 1911.

81. *Minlibao*, 11 April 1911, p. 4; 1 July 1911, p. 4.

82. XHGMHYL, IV, pp. 298-302; KGWX, *bian* 1, *ce* 14, *Geming zhi changdao yu fazhan*, VI, pp. 415-20.

83. FO 228/1804, Intelligence report for the June quarter, 1911, encl. in Consul Wilkinson to Jordan, No. 21, 13 July 1911.

84. FO 371/214, Pereira's report on the troops in Hangchow, encl. in Jordan to Grey, No. 319, 5 July 1907; FO 228/1663, Intelligence report for the September quarter, 1907,

encl. in Acting Consul Smith's 'Separate' of 1 October 1907.

85. FO 371/214, Pereira's report on the troops in Hangchow.

86. FO 371/871, Military report by Willoughby, encl. in Müller to Grey, No. 195, 14 June 1910.

87. XHGMHYL, IV, pp. 93-6; Rankin, pp. 194-7.

88. XHGMHYL, IV, pp. 91-3, 96-7.

89. Rankin, p. 190.

90. KGWX, *bian* 2, *ce* 4, *Gesheng guangfu*, II, p. 147.

91. *Minlibao*, 15 October 1911, p. 3; 12 November 1910, p. 3.

92. *Minlibao*, 25 August 1911, p. 3; FO 228/1801, Intelligence report for six months ended 30 June 1911, encl. in consul Savage to Jordan No. 7, 16 July 1911.

93. FO 371/871, Military report by Willoughby, encl. in Müller to Grey, No. 195, 14 June 1910.

94. Hatano, 'The New Armies', p. 382.

95. FO 371/863, Memo by Willoughby on the indiscipline in the Chinese army.

96. Commenting on the military riots in Canton and Suzhou in 1910, the *North-China Herald* correspondent called on the Chinese government to 'fix the responsibility upon those commanders who have allowed their men to get out of hand . . .' *North-China Herald*, 18 February 1910, p. 354.

97. FO 371/863, Memo by Willoughby on the indiscipline in the Chinese army.

7. THE NEW ARMY IN SOUTH AND NORTH CHINA

1. FO 228/1624, Report on troops in Canton, encl. in Pereira to Satow, No. ?, 7 February 1906.

2. WGZ, I, p. 347; XHGM, III, p. 337; XHGMHYL, II, pp. 287-8; Zou Lu, p. 778.

3. DFZZ, IV, 5 (1907), *junshi*, pp. 49-54.

4. DFZZ, V, 4 (1908), *junshi*, pp. 49-50.

5. DFZZ, V, 4 (1908), *junshi*, pp. 50-2.

6. FO 371/415, Chinese changes report, 15 November 1907, encl. in Jordan to Grey, No. 548, 25 November 1907, Appendix 1.

7. Shen Jian, pp. 375-6.

8. WDGS, No. 6562-1, Report of changes in the Chinese army in 1910, p. 47.

9. FO 405/229, Annual report on China, 1911, p. 56.

10. Rhoads, *China's Republican Revolution*, p. 82.

11. Rhoads, *China's Republican Revolution*, p. 82.

12. Rhoads, *China's Republican Revolution*, pp. 110-1, 115, 119; Hsüeh, *Huang Hsing*, pp. 57-8, 65-9.

13. For a brief account of the 'Protect Asia' mutiny, see Rhoads, *China's Republican Revolution*, pp. 187-9; Zou Lu, pp. 772-4; Feng Ziyou, *Geming yishi*, III, pp. 290-313.

14. Zou Lu, p. 778; XHGMHYL, II, pp. 281-2.

15. Hu Hanmin, pp. 35-6.

16. Hu Hanmin, pp. 35-6; Feng Ziyou, *Geming yishi*, I, pp. 201-2; XHGM, III, p. 359.

17. KGWX, *bian*1, *ce* 13, *Geming zhi changdao yu fazhan*, VI, pp. 521, 524-6, 521, 528, 530; XHGMHYL, II, p. 289.

18. KGWX, *Geming zhi changdao yu fazhan*, VI, pp. 517-18.

19. Shen Jian, pp. 374-5.

20. See Deng Muhan.

21. XHGMHYL, II, p. 283.

22. KGWX, *Geming zhi changdao yu fazhan*, VI, pp. 505, 511-16; Zou Lu, pp. 778-82; XHGM, III, pp. 349-54; XHGMHYL, II, pp. 285-6.

23. For an account of this uprising in English, see Hsüeh, *Huang Hsing*, ch. 6; Rhoads, *China's Republican Revolution*, pp. 197-203.

24. USDS 893.00/530, Report on the Canton uprising, by Hamilton Butler, encl. in Calhoun to Secretary of State, No. 253, 5 June 1911.

25. USDS 893.00/530, Hamilton Butler.

26. Rhoads, *China's Republican Revolution*, p. 212.

27. FO 371/420, Some notes on the military forces in Yunnan, trans. from the *Courrier d'Haiphong* of 26 October 1907, encl. in Consul-General Wilkinson to Pereira, 10 December 1907.

28. Des Forges, pp. 88-9.

29. Des Forges, pp. 92-3. On Chen Yi's activities in Sichuan, see XHGMHYL, III, pp. 347-8.

30. FO 371/420, Notes on the Yunnan army, encl. in Wilkinson to Pereira, 10 December 1907.

31. Sutton, p. 39; Institute of Historical Research, Chinese Academy of Science, *Xiliang yigao zougao*, p. 705.

32. FO 371/420, Notes on the Yunnan army, encl. in Wilkinson to Pereira, 10 December 1907.

33. Institute of Historical Research, Chinese Academy of Science, *Xiliang yigao zougao*, p. 705. FO 228/1733, Intelligence report for the June quarter, 1907, encl. in Acting Consul-General Wilton to Jordan, 8 January 1909.

34. FO 228/1733, Report on the Yunnan army, encl. in Wilton to Jordan, No. 41, 21 September 1909.

35. FO 228/1765, Notes on the modern army in Yunnan, encl. in Consul-General O'Brien-Butler to Jordan, No. 28, 13 August 1910.

36. Wright, *China in Revolution*, Introduction, p. 27; FO 228/1809, Klatt's report on the army manoeuvres, encl. in O'Brien-Butler to Jordan, No. 14, 21 February 1911.

37. FO 371/1085, Pereira's report on the 19th Division in Yunnan, encl. in Jordan to Grey, No. 18, 12 January 1911.

38. XHGMHYL, III, p. 390; Johnson, pp. 27-31.

39. For a scholarly account of Cai E during the 1911 period, see Johnson, ch. 2.

40. XHGMHYL, III, p. 366; Sutton, p. 55.

41. Johnson, p. 32, Table 1.

42. XHGMHYL, III, pp. 365-6, 409, 427; XHGM, VI, p. 267; Su An and Shi Sheng, p. 15.

43. Johnson, p. 32, Table 2.

44. Su An and Shi Sheng, p. 15; XHGMHYL, III, p. 392.

45. Sutton, p. 69; XHGMHYL, III, p. 391; Su An and Shi Sheng, p. 16.

46. *North-China Herald*, 12 January 1909, cited in Sutton, p. 48.

47. Su An and Shi Sheng, p. 16; Smedley, p. 90.

48. FO 405/195, Annual report on China, 1910, pp. 14-15; FO 405/229, Annual report on China, 1911, p. 12.

49. *Minlibao*, 28 February 1911, p. 4.

50. FO 405/229, Annual report on China, 1911, pp. 12-13.

51. XHGMHYL, III, p. 392.

52. XHGMHYL, III, p. 367.

53. Sutton, p. 73.

54. Johnson, pp. 69-71.

55. FO 228/1733, Report on the army in Yunnan, encl. in Wilton to Jordan No. 41, 21 September 1909.

56. *Minlibao*, 15 November 1910, p. 4.

57. FO 228/1765, Notes on the modern army in Yunnan, encl. in O'Brien-Butler to Jordan, No. 28, 13 August 1910.

58. FO 371/1085, Pereira's report on the 19th Division in Yunnan, encl. in Jordan to Grey, No. 18, 12 January 1911.

59. *Minlibao*, 4 May 1911, p. 3; 5 May 1911 p. 3; 10 July 1911, p. 3; 18 August 1911, p. 4.

60. *Minlibao*, 15 August 1911, p. 3.

61. FO 371/873, Acting Consul Rose (in Tengyueh) to Grey, encl. in Jordan to Grey, No. 17, 19 October 1910.

62. FO 228/1765, Notes on the modern army in Yunnan, encl. in O'Brien-Butler to Jordan, No. 28, 13 August 1910.

63. Dingle, *Across China on Foot*, pp. 215-16.

64. See MacKinnon, 'The Peiyang Army'; Young, 'Yuan Shih-k'ai's Rise to the Presidency', pp. 419-42.

65. FO 371/434, Pereira's report on the 5th Division, encl. in Jordan to Grey, No. 407, 12 September 1908.

66. FO 371/434, Pereira's report on the 5th Division.

67. FO 371/434, Pereira's report on the 5th Division. See also Feng Yuxiang, p. 113.

68. FO 371/859, Changes report for the Chinese army, 1909, p. 31; FO 371/435, Pereira's report on the 2nd Division, encl. in Jordan to Grey, No. 505, 2 November 1908; FO 371/435, Pereira's report on Chinese troops in Manchuria, encl. in Jordan to Grey, No. 425, 21 September 1908.

69. FO 371/31, Pereira's report on the Chinese army, encl. in Satow to Grey, No. 28, 17 January 1906; FO 371/214, Pereira's report on the 2nd Division, encl. in Jordan to Grey, No. 488, 23 November 1906; FO 371/41, Value of the Chinese army, by Pereira, encl. in Jordan to Grey, No. 420, 15 October 1906; FO 405/171, Annual report on China, 1906, p. 14; Mac-Kinnon, 'The Peiyang Army', p. 419.

70. FO 405/195, Annual report on China, 1910, p. 73.

71. The intensive gymnastic training was often very dangerous and unnecessarily tough. There were many cases of soldiers being injured during training. Foreign observers, as well as Chinese doctors, generally disapproved of many of the dangerous exercises. See, for example, McKenzie, *The Unveiled East*, pp. 221-2.

72. FO 371/435, Pereira's report on Chinese troops in Manchuria, encl. in Jordan to Grey, No. 425, 21 September 1908.

73. For a biography of Cao Kun, see Boorman, III, pp. 302-5.

74. FO 371/642, Troops in Manchuria, encl. in Jordan to Grey, No. 421, 16 November 1909.

75. Feng Yuxiang, pp. 98-9.

76. FO 371/435, Pereira's report on Chinese troops in Manchuria, encl. in Jordan to Grey, No. 425, 21 September 1908.

77. FO 371/642, Troops in Manchuria, encl. in Jordan to Grey, No. 421, 16 November 1909.

78. FO 371/435, Pereira's report on Chinese troops in Manchuria, encl. in Jordan to Grey, No. 425, 21 September 1908; FO 405/195, Annual report on China, 1910, p. 71.

79. Feng Yuxiang, p. 126; Jerome Ch'en, 'The Chinese Army', p. 436; FO 405/229, Annual report on China, 1911, p. 56.

80. FO 371/1088, New Mixed Brigade for Zhili Province, encl. in Jordan to Grey, No. 100, 3 March 1911.

81. FO 371/217, Pereira's memo on the new Chinese Ministry of War, encl. in Jordan to Grey, No. 504, 29 November 1906.

82. *North-China Herald*, 4 January 1907, p. 30; *The Times*, 7 February 1909, p. 7; Came-

ron, p. 93.

83. *Minlibao*, 2 August 1911, p. 3; 17 August 1911, p. 3.

84. WDGS, No. 6283-7, Summary of military news for February 1911, p. 10; FO 405/229, Annual report on China, 1911, p. 60.

85. FO 371/867, Summary of intelligence reports for the 2nd quarter of 1910, encl. in Müller to Grey, No. 302, 8 September 1910; FO 371/1090, Report by Ramsay for the quarter ending December 1910, encl. in Jordan to Grey, No. 176, 25 April 1911.

86. Feng Yuxiang, pp. 120-4.

87. Zhu Yanjia, pp. 168-80; Chen Xizhang, II, p. 379.

88. XHGMHYL, V, pp. 452-3; *Minlibao*, 4 April 1911, p. 2.

89. Young, 'The Reformer as a Conspirator', p. 253.

90. See Wan Dixiu.

91. Young, 'The Reformer as a Conspirator', p. 252.

92. Chen Xizhang, II, p. 376. WDGS, No. 6790-42, Notes on the Chinese Revolution of 1911-12, by Captain Reeves, Appendix F, pp. 2-3.

93. Chen Xizhang, II, pp. 380-1.

94. Jiang Zuobin, pp. 6-8.

95. USDS 1518/422, Calhoun to Secretary of State, No. 46, 5 July 1910.

8. THE REVOLUTION, 1911-12

1. FO 371/863, Memo by Little on the political situation in China, encl. in Messrs Brunner, Mond, and Co. to Foreign Office, 2 March 1910; FO 371/863, Müller to Grey, No. 108, 14 April 1910.

2. FO 371/864, Consul Goffe to Müller, encl. 3 in Müller to Grey, No. 200, 17 June 1910.

3. FO 371/864, Consul-General Wilkinson to Müller, encl. 6 in Müller to Grey, No. 200, 17 June 1910.

4. FO 371/864, Goffe to Müller, encl. 3 in Müller to Grey, No. 200, 17 June 1910. Similarly, Consul-General Fraser (in Hankow) reported that 'The native newspapers have certainly fomented the antiforeign agitations . . .' See encl. 1 in Müller to Grey, No. 200.

5. FO 371/1090, Intelligence reports for the 1st quarter, 1911, encl. in Jordan to Grey, No. 200, 22 June 1911.

6. FO 228/1800, Intelligence report for the March quarter, 1911, encl. in consul Werner's 'Separate' of 23 April 1911.

7. FO 371/1090, Summary of intelligence reports for the 2nd quarter, 1911, encl. in Jordan to Grey, No. 363, 16 September 1911.

8. USDS 893.00/530, Calhoun to Secretary of State, No.

253, 5 June 1911.

9. FO 371/863, Memo by Little on the political situation in China, encl. in Messrs Brunner, Mond, and Co. to Foreign Office, 2 March 1910; FO 371/864, Goffe to Müller, encl. 3 in Müller to Grey, No. 200, 17 June 1910.

10. See Schrecker, *Imperialism and Chinese Nationalism*.

11. See, for example, Zhang Peng-yuan, *Lixianpai yu xinhai geming;* Chang P'eng-yüan, 'The Constitutionalists', pp. 143-83; Ichiko Chūzō, 'The Role of the Gentry; pp. 297-317; Rhoads, *China's Republican Revolution*, pp. 153-75; Esherick, *Reform and Revolution*, pp. 91-8.

12. Esherick, *Reform and Revolution*, p. 97.

13. FO 371/1090, Report by Ramsay for the quarter ending December 1910, encl. in Jordan to Grey, No. 176, 25 April 1911.

14. FO 371/1090, Summary of intelligence reports for the 2nd quarter, 1911, encl. in Jordan to Grey, No. 363, 16 September 1911. FO 405/229, Annual report on China, 1911, pp. 41-2. Not all the provincial assemblies acted responsibly in financial matters, however. Many, in fact, showed little understanding of the difficulties which the authorities had in meeting current requirements. As Sir John Jordan pointed out, this was due to the fact the assemblies were 'under no obligation to provide the necessary funds for carrying out the measures which they advocate, or to create new sources of revenue in place of the taxes they propose to abolish'. See FO 405/195, Annual report on China, 1910, p. 53.

15. Fincher, 'Political Provincialism and the National Revolution', p. 220.

16. This brief account is based on the following sources: Quan Hansheng, 'Tielu guo-you wenti yu xinhai geming', Ichiko Chūzō, 'The Railway Protection Movement in Szechwan in 1911'; Hedtke, ch. 4. A useful documentary study of the subject is Zhou Kaiqing (ed.), *Sichuan yu xinhai geming*, A contemporary account by a Qing official sympathetic with the Sichuanese agitators is Zhou Shanpei, *Xinhai Sichuan zheng-lu qinliji.*

17. Moreover, the provincial assembly and the gentry resented the corrupt and conservative nature of the royal cabinet, and they were particularly indignant with Prince Qing and wished to curtail his 'evil influence'. See BPP *China No. 1 (1912)* Acting Consul Brown to Jordan, encl. 1 in No. 22, Jordan to Grey, 13 October 1911.

18. BPP *China No. 1 (1912)*, Wilkinson to Jordan, encl. 2

in No. 22, Jordan to Grey, 13 October 1911.

19. KGWX, *bian* 2, *ce* 5, *Gesheng guangfu* III, pp. 9-14; XHGMHYL, III, pp. 107, 132, 175-6.

20. *Minlibao*, 18 September 1911, p. 3; 24 September 1911, p. 3; Li Lianfang, 72b-73a; Yang Yuru, p. 48.

21. BPP *China No. 1 (1912)*, Brown to Jordan, encl. 1 in No. 22, Jordan to Grey 13 October 1911. The American *chargé d'affaires* in Peking also reported that the Sichuanese troops 'are suspected of sympathy with malcontents [the rioters]'. See USDS 893.00/541, Williams to Secretary of State, 7 September 1911.

22. For a review of Chinese communist works on the subject, see Fung, 'Post-1949 Chinese Historiography on the 1911 Revolution'.

23. XHGM, I, p. 18.

24. Powell, p. 307.

25. Dutt, ' The First Week of the Revolution', p. 402.

26. GMWX, IV, pp. 21-2; Zhang Nanxian, pp. 247-8; Li Lianfang, pp. 75a-76a.

27. For a reinterpretation of the role of the Central China Bureau in the revolutionary outbreak, see Fung, 'The T'ung-meng-hui Central China Bureau and the Wuchang Uprising'.

28. FO 228/1802, Intelligence report for the two months ended 30 September 1911,

encl. in Goffe's 'Separate' by 5 October 1911.

29. FO 228/1802, Goffe to Jordan, Telegram 58, 30 September 1911; Goffe to Jordan, No. 92, 2 October 1911.

30. Li Lianfang (p. 74b) claimed that the revolt was postponed to October 11. This date, however, was only a suggestion made by some revolutionaries, and it had not been unanimously agreed upon or finalised.

31. The following account is based on KGWX, *bian* 2, *ce* 1, *Wuchang shouyi*, pp. 279-92; Li Lianfang, pp. 86b-100a; Zhang Yukun, pp. 40-1.

32. A contemporary writer wrote of Ruizheng: 'In the course of his career, he had shown himself not lacking in many of the qualities that go to the making of men. Amongst many he had earned the reputation of being one of the most competent of provincial officials. Nor was he without experience. He had an intimate knowledge of the Yangtze Valley and of the fierce anti-dynastic sentiment which prevailed. A Manchu himself, doubtless he could scarcely have failed to realise all that the loss of Wuchang must mean to the ruling House, and it is but reasonable to suppose that he would have resisted further had he not imagined that resistance would be in vain'. See Kent,

p. 72.

33. KGWX, *bian* 2, *ce* 1, *Wu-chang shouyi*, pp. 355-6.

34. *Qingshigao, bingshi* 3, p. 9b.

35. WO 106/26, Willoughby to Assistant Director of Military Operations, No. 210, 16 October 1911.

36. Shao Baichang, pp. 13-15.

37. For the role of the Yangxia branch of the Literary Society in the capture of Hankow and Hanyang, see GMWX, IV, pp. 62-6; XHGMHYL, II, pp. 17-48.

38. Li Lianfang, pp. 15a, 103b; Cao Yabo, II, p. 36.

39. Wan Dixiu, 'Wan Dixiu yu Zeng Shengsan lun xinhai shouyi jieyao shu'. See also Zhang Guogan, pp. 86-7; XHSYHYL, I, pp. 122-3.

40. XHSYHYL, II, pp. 159-60; Yang Yuru, p. 72.

41. See Fung 'Post-1949 Chinese Historiography on the 1911 Revolution', pp. 193-6.

42. *The Times*, 14 October 1911, p. 7. Foreigners in China were generally impressed by the way in which the Hubei military government showed that the revolutionary movement was anti-dynastic and not anti-foreign. See BPP *China No. 1 (1912)*, No. 47, Jordan to Grey, 23 October 1911.

43. Dingle, who interviewed Li in October (or November) 1911, spoke very highly of Li: 'General Li Yuan Hung seemed to be a great national carpenter, taking now the rough trees, shaping them into purpose and real use. This was my first impression of the man, for by his extreme calmness, his practical insight into things — it was almost impossible to conceive a mere military man capable of such patience in the midst of extreme mental and physical strain — he was showing the world that he was a leader born'. See Dingle, *China's Revolution*, p. 35.

44. This point is fully developed in Fung, 'Li Yüan-hung and the Revolution of 1911', pp. 151-71.

45. An instance of this was the revolution in Jiangsu. See Young-tsu Wong, "Popular Unrest and the 1911 Revolution in Jiangsu'.

46. USDS 893.00/826, Calhoun to Secretary of State, No. 362, 21 November 1911.

47. WDGS, No. 6790-42, Notes on the Chinese Revolution of 1911-1912, by Captain Reeves, p. 31. Qingshilu (Xuantong), 61, pp. 28b-29a. BPP *China No. 1 (1912)*, No. 8, Jordan to Grey, 14 October 1911. *Qingshilu* (Xuantong), 61, pp. 34a-b.

48. MP 312/193, Memorandum, 13 October 1911.

49. *Minlibao*, 14 October 1911, p. 3; 15 October 1911, pp. 2-3.

50. *Qingshilu* (Xuantong), 61, pp. 34b-35a; MP 312/193

Notes, 22 October 1911; BPP *China No. 1 (1912)*, Report by Captain Otter-Barry on the rising in Hubei, encl. 2 in No. 79, Jordan to Grey, 5 November 1911.

51. MP 312/193 Notes, 22 October 1911.

52. MP 312/61, Morrison to E.T. Nystrom, 26 October 1911.

53. Zhang Guogan, pp. 215-16; XHGM, VI, pp. 174-75; Yan Xishan, pp. 14-22; Gillin, pp. 14-16; MP 312/193, Memorandum, 25 October 1911; BPP *China No. 1 (1912)*, No. 47, Jordan to Grey, 23 October 1911; *Minlibao*, 27 October 1911, p. 2.

54. Zhang Guogan, pp. 198-9. An English translation of this document can be found in WDGS, No. 6790-42, Notes on the Chinese Revolution of 1911-12, Appendix F. I have used this translation with some stylistic changes.

55. Zhang Guogan, pp. 195-6.

56. Young, 'The Reformer as a Conspirator', pp. 253-4; Yan Xishan, pp. 25-6.

57. WDGS, No. 6790-42, Notes on the Chinese Revolution of 1911-1912, by Captain Reeves, Appendix F, p. 3.

58. BPP *China No. 1 (1912)*, No. 79, Jordan to Grey, 5 November 1911.

59. *Qingshilu* (Xuantong), 62, pp. 49a-53b.

60. USDS 893.00/620, *Chargé d'affaires* Williams to Secretary of State, 31 October 1911; *Minlibao*, 2 November 1911, pp. 2-3.

61. *Qingshilu* (Xuantong), 63, pp. 5b-6b, 10b. USDS 893.00/632, Telegram (unsigned) to Secretary of State, 3 November 1911; BPP *China No. 1 (1912)*, No. 80, Jordan to Grey, 6 November 1911.

62. BPP *China No. 1 (1912)*, Report by Captain Otter-Barry on the rising in Hubei, encl. 2 in No. 79, Jordan to Grey, 5 November 1911.

63. There are two versions of Wu's assassination. One is that Wu's murder was ordered by the court. The other is that Yuan Shikai was behind it because he was allegedly apprehensive of Wu's growing influence. The first version, according to Young, is more reliable. See Young, 'The Reformer as a Conspirator', p. 257, n. 42.

64. *The Times*, 8 November 1911, p. 5; Zhang Guogan, p. 204. On 11 November 1911, *Minlibao* (p. 2) reported that a number of Chinese had clashed with the Manchu soldiers in Shijiajuang resulting in the defeat of the latter.

65. FO 371/1096, Report by Captain Otter-Barry on the Chinese revolution, encl. in Jordan to Grey, No. 430, 10 November 1911.

66. *Minlibao*, 11 November 1911, pp. 2-3; 14 November 1911, p. 3; 21 November 1911, pp. 2-3.

67. BPP *China No. 1 (1912)*, No. 78, Jordan to Grey, 26 November 1911.

68. FO 371/1096, Report on the revolution, by Otter-Barry, encl. in Jordan to Grey, No. 453, 20 November 1911.

69. *Qingshilu* (Xuantong), 62, pp. 27a-b, 9a-10b. BPP *China No. 1 (1912)*, No. 101, Jordan to Grey 16 November 1911.

70. FO 371/1096, Report on the revolution, by Otter-Barry, encl. in Jordan to Grey, No. 453, 20 November 1911.

71. BPP *China No. 1 (1912)*, Consul Wilkinson to Jordan, encl. 1 in No. 79, Jordan to Grey, 5 November 1911; Wilkinson to Grey, encl. 1 in No. 120, Jordan to Grey 23 November 1911; Zhang Guogan, p. 232.

72. Zhang Guogan, p. 232; XHGM, VII, p. 77; BPP *China No. 1 (1912)*, encls. 2 and 3, in No. 120, Jordan to Grey, 23 November 1911. Zhang Xun was said to have asked for 800,000 taels as a price for the withdrawal of his troops from the city, and the viceroy, on behalf of the local gentry, would only give him half that amount.

73. XHGM, VII, p. 78; KGWX, *bian* 2, *ce* 4, *Gesheng guangfu*, II, pp. 26-7.

74. XHGM, VII, pp. 78-9, 163-5; *Gesheng guangfu*, II, pp. 28-34, 51-69; BPP *China No. 1 (1912)*, Wilkinson to Grey,

encl. 4 in No. 120, Jordan to Grey, 23 November 1911.

75. See Gillin, pp. 17-18. FO 405/229, Annual report on China, 1911, p. 59.

76. *Qingshilu* (Xuantong), 66, pp. 1a-2b.

77. BPP *China No. 3 (1912)*, No. 28, Jordan to Grey, 20 December 1911.

78. USDS 893.00/1093, Consul Fraser in Nanking to Calhoun, No. 175, 20 January 1912.

79. BPP *China No. 3 (1912)*, Consul Giles in Changsha to Jordan, encl. 5 in No. 112, Jordan to Grey, 29 January 1912.

80. FO 371/1310, Report by Willoughby, encl. in Jordan to Grey, No. 521, 30 December 1911.

81. USDS 893.00/1093, Consul Fraser to Calhoun, No. 175, 20 January 1912; WDGS, No. 6790-42, Notes on the Chinese Revolution, p. 92; FO 405/229, Annual Report on China, 1911, p. 57; *The Times*, 12 February 1912, p. 5.

82. WDGS, No. 6790-42, Notes on the Chinese Revolution, p. 90; FO 371/1312, Addendum in Willoughby's report, encl. in Jordan to Grey, No. 33, 17 January 1912. For Lan Tianwei's unsuccessful attempt to start a revolution in Fengtian, see Institute of Historical Research, Jilin Branch, Chinese Academy

of Science, and the History Department of the Jilin Normal University, pp. 207-34; Zhang Guogan, pp. 263-5.

83. BPP *China No. 3 (1912)*, No. 62, Jordan to Grey, 2 January 1912.

84. *Qingshilu* (Xuantong), 66, pp. 18a-b; 67, pp. 22a-b; 68; pp. 1a-2b. *BPP China No. 3 (1912)*, No. 65, Jordan to Grey, 6 January 1912. It should also be mentioned that Yuan had tried in vain to raise foreign loans because of the neutrality of the Western powers. See Chan Lau Kit-ching, 'British Policy of Neutrality during the 1911 Revolution in China', pp. 361-70.

85. Zhang Guogan, pp. 257-9; XHGM, VI, pp. 268-70, 349-52.

86. MP 312/63, T.S. Wei to Morrison, 29 January 1912; MP 312/241, Morrison to Rockhill, 24 January 1912. According to Morrison, the bombs were thrown from two corner houses which belonged to Zaize, and this gave rise to an erroneous report that Zaize was behind the assassination attempt.

87. MP 312/63, Morrison to T.S. Wei, 24 January 1912; MP 213/141, Cai Tinggan (Yuan Shikai's secretary) to Morrison, 18 January 1912; MP 312/194, Memorandum, 21 January 1912. *Minlibao*, 23 January 1912, p. 2; 25 January 1912, pp. 2-3; 27 January

1912, p. 2; FO 371/1312, Report by Willoughby, encl. in Jordan to Grey, No. 45, 27 January 1912.

88. Tao Juyin, I, p. 24.

89. MP 312/194, Memorandum, 21 January 1912. On 23 January, Morrison wrote that there was no direct communication whatsoever between Ijūin and Tieliang, but he added that 'it cannot be denied that General Aoki [the Japanese military attaché] is in communication with Liang Pi [Liangbi]'. See MP 312/141, Morrison to Cai Tinggan.

90. MP 312/214, Morrison to Rockhill, 24 January 1911.

91. Morrison strongly urged Yuan not to leave Peking. He felt that if Yuan found his position untenable, he should rather resign. It would not be 'dignified' for Yuan to go to Tientsin, Morrison added, for Yuan was 'the restraining force now who has prevented hostilities and has prevented the northern provinces from declaring themselves republican'. See MP 312/141, Morrison to Cai Tinggan, 23 January 1912.

92. *Minlibao*, 28 January 1912, p. 2; 1 February 1912, p. 3.

93. BPP *China No. 3 (1912)*, No. 99, Jordan to Grey, 27 January 1912. Morrison also reported that 'terrorisation is extending, and the fear of death has been put into the

Manchu princes'. He expected to hear that 'even a more serious misadventure has befalled that fat-headed fanatic Tieh Liang [Tieliang]'. See MP 312/263, Morrison to Colonel A.W. Wingate, 29 January 1912.

94. FO 371/1313, Report by Willoughby, encl. in Jordan to Grey, No. 64, 5 February 1912.

95. Fifty dollars were promised to any soldier who would desert with his arms to the revolutionary side, and the facilities for doing so were explained by the Hubei military government in detail. See FO 371/1098, Report by Willoughby, encl. in Jordan to Grey, No. 492, 4 December 1911.

96. FO 371/1313, Report by Willoughby, encl. in Jordan to Grey, No. 64, 5 February 1912; WDGS, No. 6790-42, Notes on the Chinese Revolution, p. 90.

97. *Qingshilu* (Xuantong), 70, p. 1a; WO 106/26, Willoughby to Assistant Director of Military Operations, No. 29, 29 January 1912. The memorial was believed to have been drafted by Xu Shuzheng, Duan's secretary and protégé, who was later to have great influence over him. See Xu Daolin, p. 153.

98. BPP *China No. 3 (1912)*, No. 127, Jordan to Grey, 10 February 1912.

99. *Qingshilu* (Xuantong), 70, pp. 13b-15b.

1. See, in particular, Young, 'Yuan Shih-k'ai's Rise to the Presidency', pp. 433-42; also Liew, ch. 10.

2. MP 312/65, V.K. Ting to Morrison, 5 May 1912.

9. THE STATE OF THE ARMY IN 1912-13

1. FO 371/1311, Remarks on the Chinese army during the revolution, by S.W. Whitehall, encl. in Admiralty to Under Secretary of State, 3 January 1912; FO 371/1347, Military operations of revolutionary war in China, report by Willoughby, encl. in Jordan to Grey, No. 280, 3 July 1912; Changes report for the Chinese army, 1911, p. 12.

2. The American military attaché, Captain Reeves, also found the medical organisation of the 1st Army 'particularly defective'. See WDGS, No. 6790-42, Notes on the Chinese Revolution, p. 39.

3. WO 106/26, Lieutenant-Colonel W.F. Everett's remarks on the condition of the imperial troops, encl. in Willoughby to Assistant Director of Military Operations, No.

37, 2 February 1912.

4. FO 228/1841 Goffe to Jordan, No. 17, 20 February 1912.

5. WO 106/26, Willoughby to Assistant Director of Military Operations, No. 53, 13 February 1912; FO 228/1843, Intelligence reports for the December quarter 1911, June and September quarters 1912, encls. in Consul Hewlett's 'Separate' of 18 January, 10 July, and 15 October 1912.

6. FO 405/229, Annual report on China, 1912, p. 42; FO 371/1347, Changes report for the Chinese army, 1911, p. 2; WO 106/26, Willoughby to Assistant Director of Military Operations, No. 51, 12 February 1912.

7. WDGS, No. 6283-10, Current military notes, by Captain Reeves, 18 April 1912, p. 2.

8. WDGS, No. 6283-10, Chinese Republican Forces, Reeves to War Department, 30 June 1912; FO 405/229 Annual report on China, 1911, p. 56.

9. WO 106/26, Willoughby to Assistant Director of Military Operations, No. 51, 12 February 1912.

10. FO 371/1602, Changes report for the Chinese army, 1912, pp. 2-5; FO 405/229, Annual report on China, 1912, pp. 41-2.

11. Feng Yuxiang, p. 167.

12. FO 371/1602, Changes report for the Chinese army, 1912, pp. 2-4; FO 405/229, Annual report on China, 1912, pp. 41-2.

13. WDGS, No. 6283-10, Current military notes, by Reeves, 18 April 1912, pp. 1-2.

14. MP 312/64, Morrison to Molyneux, 14 March 1912.

15. Li Yuanhong, 8; p. 15a, Li to President Yuan, 19 March 1912.

16. FO 228/1837, Intelligence report for the March quarter, 1911, encl. in Giles to Jordan, No. 18, 26 April 1912.

17. FO 228/1836 Wilkinson to Jordan, No. 19, 19 March 1912.

18. *The China Year Book, 1913*, pp. 306, 502; Lu Chun, p. 11.

19. Li Yuanhong, 8, pp. 16a-b, Li to President Yuan, 22 March 1912.

20. FO 371/1316, Pereira's report on mutiny in Peking, encl. in Jordan to Grey, No. 133, 21 March 1912. See also Young, 'Yuan Shih-k'ai's Rise to the Presidency', pp. 438-40.

21. *Minlibao*, 5 May 1912, p. 7; FO 228/1836, Wilkinson to Jordan, No. 48, 15 August 1912.

22. *Shuntian Shibao*, 18 May 1912; Huang Yuanyong, II, pp. 1-3; WDGS, No. 6283-12, Current military notes, by Reeves, pp. 5, 7-8; No. 6283-13, Current military notes, pp. 5-7.

23. Jia Shiyi, pp. 12-13.

24. See the various monthly summaries of events in FO 371/

1347 and FO 371/1620.

25. *The China Year Book, 1913*, p. 285.

26. FO 228/1873, Intelligence report for the March quarter, 1913, encl. in Wilkinson's 'Separate' of 11 April 1913; FO 371/1620, Summary of events for the 1st quarter, 1913, encl. in Jordan to Grey, No. 183, 3 May 1913.

27. FO 228/1837, Giles to Jordan, No. 9, 28 February 1912.

28. XHGMHYL, IV, pp. 332-3.

29. FO 228/1837, Intelligence reports for the March and September quarters 1912, encls. in Giles to Jordan, Nos. 18 & 40, 26 April & 25 October 1912, respectively.

30. Cai Jiou, pp. 195-7; FO 228/1873, Intelligence report for the December quarter 1912, encl. in Wilkinson's 'Separate' of 14 January 1913.

31. Cai Jiou, pp. 205-7; Shen Yunlong, pp. 39-46; FO 228/1841, Goffe to Jordan, No. 25, 29 February 1913.

32. Li Jiannong, pp. 266-7.

33. WDGS, No. 6283-11, Casual military notes, by Reeves, 4 May 1912, p. 3.

34. *The China Year Book, 1913*, p. 507; Ding Zhongjiang, I, p. 328.

35. *Minlibao*, 17 May 1912, p. 3. I cannot locate this document in Li Yuanhong.

36. *Minlibao*, 10 June 1912, p. 5.

37. *Minlibao*, 23 June 1912, p. 3.

38. Li Yuanhong, 9, pp. 11a-14a, Li to President Yuan, 10 April 1912; 9, p. 22b, Li to President Yuan, 17 April 1912.

39. *Minlibao*, 1 July 1912, p. 12; WDGS, No. 6283-12, Current military notes, by Reeves, 3 June 1912, p. 2.

40. *Minlibao*, 1 July 1912, p. 2; WDGS, No. 6283-20, Current events, by Bowley, 11 April 1913, p. 2.

41. *Shuntian Shibao*, 6, 7 and 29 August 1912; *Minlibao*, 9 October 1912, p. 3.

42. *Minlibao*, 24 November 1912, p. 8.

43. DFZZ, IX, 8 (February 1913), *Zhongguo dashiji*, p. 19.

44. *Minlibao*, 18 November 1912, p. 6.

45. Hu Hanmin, p. 88; WDGS, 6283-22, Current events, by Bowley, 3 July 1913, p. 1.

46. *Shuntian Shibao*, 13 June 1912; *Minlibao*, 24 June 1912, p. 5.

47. *The China Year Book, 1913*, p. 281.

48. *Minlibao*, 1 January 1913, p. 11; 4 January 1913, p. 6.

49. FO 371/1602, Changes report for the Chinese army, 1912, p. 48.

50. *Minlibao*, 20 February 1913, p. 8.

51. *The China Year Book, 1914*, pp. 327-9, shows a table of the approximate strength and distribution of the army.

52. FO 371/1934, Changes report for the Chinese army,

1913, Appendix A, p. 7, encl. in Jordan to Grey, No. 202, 21 May 1914.

53. WDGS, No. 6562-26, Military attaché to Chief of War College Division, 13 January 1914.

54. WDGS, No. 6562-26, Military attaché to Chief of War College Division. See also 6562-24, War College Division to Secretary of War, 21 October 1913; No. 6562-25, Secretary of War to War Department, 25 November 1913, and State Department to Secretary of War, 4 December 1913.

55. WDGS, No. 6562-26, Military attaché to Chief of War College Division, 13 January 1914.

56. For a list of the foreign advisers to the Peking government, see WDGS, No. 7829-8, Foreign advisers, by Bowley, 16 September 1913.

57. WDGS, No. 6283-20, Current events, by Bowley, 11 April 1913, p. 2.

58. See above, ch. 3, p. 83.

59. Major-General Aoki's appointment was made in September 1916, but he did not arrive in China until early 1917. See WDGS, No. 7829-32, Current news, by Bowley, 26 February 1917, pp. 2-3. On 5 May 1917 Bowley reported that while the military of China was 'not friendly towards Japan, 'the Premier has undoubtedly been con-verted to the friendship of Japan'. He added, however, that General Aoki had not made himself felt in China as a military adviser to the President, but the Japanese Vice-Chief of Staff, General Tanaka, was on his way to China for a tour of inspection. See WDGS, No. 7829-36, Current News.

60. The American military attaché remarked in February 1914: 'Although Colonel Brissaud . . . and Major Dinkler . . . have devoted their time to the re-organization of the General Staff, nothing worth mentioning has been accomplished'. See WDGS, No. 6562-29, Changes in the Chinese army, 1913, p. 4.

61. FO 371/1934, Lieutenant-Colonel Brissaud-Desmaillet's scheme, encl. in Jordan to Grey, No. 40, 31 January 1914. Jordan could not help commenting: 'China at the present moment, like Corea in its moribund days, is afflicted with a multitude of counsellors who seek to justify their existence by putting forward all sorts of grandiose schemes'.

62. FO 405/229, Annual report on China, 1913, p. 46.

63. FO 405/229, Annual report on China, 1913, p. 46.

64. *The Times*, 1 August 1912, p. 5.

65. *The Times*, 15 August 1913, p. 5.

66. FO 371/1934, Major Robertson's report on the Chinese army in the rebellion of 1913, encl. in Jordan's No. 58, 9 February 1914.
67. FO 371/1934, Robertson's report on the Chinese army in the rebellion of 1913.
68. FO 371/1934, Robertson's report on the Chinese army in the rebellion of 1913.
69. FO 371/1934, Robertson's report on the Chinese army in the rebellion of 1913.
70. WDGS, No. 7829-9, China's second revolution, by Bowley, 3 October 1913, p. 10.
71. WGZ, II, p. 6.
72. FO 371/1934, Changes report for the Chinese army, 1913, pp. 1-11.
73. WDGS, No. 6562-29, Changes in the Chinese army, 1913, by Bowley, 26 February 1914, p. 2.
74. WDGS, No. 6562-29, Changes in the Chinese army, 1913, p. 4.
75. *Minlibao*, 2 July 1912, p. 10; 13 July 1912, p. 12.
76. *Zhengfu gongbao*, No. 147, September 1912; Wang Ranzhi, pp. 31-3; Sheling Waishi, pp. 2-3.
77. WDGS, No. 6562-29, Changes in the Chinese army, 1913, p. 2.
78. WDGS, No. 6562-29, Changes in the Chinese army, 1913, p. 2.

10. IMPLICATIONS BEYOND THE REVOLUTION

1. Rawlinson, p. 201.
2. For the reorganisation of the Guomindang army, see F.F. Liu, *A Military History of Modern China.*
3. Joint Hubei Philosophy and Social Science Association, I, p. 158.
4. Josef Fass takes a similar view. See Fass, 'The Role of the New Style Army', pp. 185-6.
5. Joint Hubei Philosophy and Social Science Association, II, pp. 456-63.
6. Sheridan, *Chinese Warlord*, pp. 17-18.
7. Sheridan, *China in Disintegration*, p. 82.
8. Eisenstadt, p. 172.
9. Needham, p. 154.
10. Fairbank, *The United States and China*, pp. 50-1.
11. Fairbank, Reischauer and Craig, p. 642. See also Jerome Ch'en, 'Defining Chinese Warlords and Their Factions', p. 567; Kapp, p. 1.

Glossary

To help readers who may not be familiar with the *pinyin* system, this glossary provides parenthetical Wade-Giles spellings for personal names and terms used in the book. It excludes the names of provinces and cities, as well as people who appear as authors in the bibliography. Those marked with an asterisk are Japanese names and terms.

Ai Zhongqi (Ai Chung-ch'i) 艾忠琦
*Aoki Norizumi 青木宣純

ban (pan) 班
*Banzai Rihachirō 坂西利八郎
Baoding junguan xuetang (Pao-t'ing chun-kuan hsüeh-t'ang) 保定軍官學校
Beibujun (Pei-pu-chün) 備補軍
Beiyang (Pei-yang) 北洋
Beiyang wubei xuetang (Pei-yang wu-pei hsüeh-t'ang) 北洋武備學堂
bianmu (pien-mu) 弁目
biao (piao) 標
biaojiangtang (piao-chiang-t'ang) 標講堂
Bingguan xuetang (Ping-kuan hsüeh-t'ang) 兵官學堂
bu (pu) 部
*bushidō 武士道

Cai E (Ts'ai O) 蔡鍔
canmou (ts'an-mou) 參謀
Canmou daxuetang (Ts'an-mou ta-hsüeh-t'ang) 參謀大學堂
canmouchu (ts'an-mou-chu'u) 參謀處
canyi (ts'an-i) 參議
Cao Kun (Ts'ao K'un) 曹錕

Cen Chunxuan (Ts'en Ch'un-hsüan) 岑春煊
changbeijun (ch'ang-pei-chün) 常備軍
Chen Delong (Ch'en Te-lung) 陳得龍
Chen Jintao (Ch'en Chin-t'ao) 陳錦濤
Chen Tianhua (Ch'en T'ien-hua) 陳天華
Chen Qimei (Ch'en Ch'i-mei) 陳其美
Chen Yi (Ch'en I) 陳宧
Chen Zuoxin (Ch'en Tso-hsin) 陳作新
Cheng Dequan (Ch'eng Te-ch'üan) 程德全
Chun, Prince (Ch'un) 醇親王
Cixi, Empress Dowager (Tz'u-hsi) 慈禧太后
Cui Xiangkui (Ts'ui Hsiang-k'uei) 崔祥奎

da duyu (ta tu-yü) 大都尉
Dai Hongci (Tai Hung-tz'u) 戴鴻慈
da jiangjun (ta chiang-chün) 大將軍
dajiang shengwei (ta-chiang sheng-wei) 大將聲威

da junxiao (ta chün-hsiao) 大軍校
daotai (tao-t'ai) 道臺
Ding Wenjiang (Ting Wen-chiang)
　丁文江
Dingwujun   (Ting-wu-chün)
　定武軍
Ding Zhenduo   (Ting Chen-to)
　丁振鐸
Duanfang (Tuan-fang) 瑞方
Duan Qirui   (Tuan Ch'i-jui)
　段祺瑞
Duan Zhigui   (Tuan Chih-kuei)
　段芝貴
duban (tu-pan) 督辦
duban dachen (tu-pan da-ch'en)
　督辦大臣
Duban junwuchu (Du-pan chün-
　wu-ch'u) 督辦軍務處
dudu (tu-tu) 都督
dui (tui) 隊
dulianchu (tu-lien-ch'u) 督練處
dulian gongsuo (tu-lien kung-so)
　督練公所

Enming (En-ming) 恩銘
erdengbing (erh-teng-ping) 二等
　兵

Fan Zengxiang (Fan Tseng-hsiang)
　樊增祥
Feng Guozhang (Feng Kuo-chang)
　馮國璋
Feng Rugui (Feng Ju-kuei)　馮汝
　騤
Fengshan (Feng-shan) 鳳山
fubing (fu-ping) 副兵
fu canling (fu ts'an-ling) 副參領
fu dutong (fu tu-t'ung) 副都統
fu junxiao (fu chün-hsiao) 副軍校
fumu (fu-mu) 副目
fuqiang (fu-ch'iang) 富強
Fu Wentong (Fu Wen-t'ung) 傅文
　通

Gangyi (Kang-i)　剛毅
Ge Baohua (Ko Pao-hua) 葛寶華
Gelaohui (Ko-lao-hui) 哥老會
Gemingjun (Ko-ming-chün) 革命
　軍
Gong, Prince (Kung) 恭親王
gongde (kung-te) 公德
Gongjinhui   (Kung-chin-hui)
　共進會
gongsheng (kung-sheng) 貢生
Gongweijun   (Kung-wei-chün)
　拱衛軍
Guangfuhui   (Kuang-fu-hui)
　光復會
Guangxu, Emperor (Kuang-hsü)
　光緒皇
Guizhou   xuetang   (Kuei-chou
　hsüeh-t'ang) 貴冑學堂
Guo Renzhang (Kuo Jen-chang)
　郭人漳
Guomindang   (Kuo-min-tang)
　國民黨
guomin jiaoyu (kuo-min chiao-
　yü) 國民教育

Ha Hanzhang   (Ha Han-chang)
　哈漢章
Haijunchu (Hai-chün-ch'u) 海軍
　處
Han Guojun   (Han Kuo-chün)
　韓國鈞
He Haiming (Ho Hai-ming) 何海
　鳴
He Zonglian   (Ho Tsung-lien)
　何宗蓮
Hongjianghui (Hung-chiang-hui)
　洪江會
Huang Fu (Huang Fu) 黃郛
Huanggang junxuejie jiangxisuo
　(Huang-kang chün-hsüeh-chieh
　chiang-hsi-so)   黃岡軍學界講
　習所
Huang Luanming (Huang Luan-
　ming) 黃鸞鳴

Huang Xing (Huang Hsing) 黃興
huantie baiba (huan-t'ieh pai-pa)
換貼拜把
Huaxinghui (Hua-hsing-hui)
華興會
Hubei jundui tongmenghui (Hupei chün-tui t'ung-meng-hui)
湖北軍隊同盟會
Hubei xueshengjie (Hu-pei hsüehsheng-chieh) 湖北學生界
huiban (hui-pan) 會辦
Hu Jingyi (Hu Ching-i) 胡景伊
Hu Lanting (Hu Lan-t'ing)胡蘭亭
Hu Linyi (Hu Lin-i) 胡林翼
hunchengxie (hun-ch'eng-hsieh)
混成協
Hu Ruilin (Hu Jui-lin) 胡瑞霖
Hu Ying (Hu Ying) 胡瑛
Hu Yisheng (Hu I-sheng) 胡毅生
Hu Yufen (Hu Yü-fen) 胡燏棻
Hu Yuzhen (Hu Yü-chen) 胡玉珍
Hu Zushun (Hu Tsu-shun)胡祖舜

jiangbian xuetang (chiang-pien hsüeh-t'ang) 將弁學堂
Jiang Guiti (Chiang Kuei-t'i) 姜桂題
Jiang Jieshi (Chiang Chieh-shih, Chiang Kai-shek) 蔣介石
jiangmeng youhou (chiang-meng yu-hou) 將門有後
jiangshi wanqi (chiang-shih wanch'i) 將十萬騎
jiangwutang (chiang-wu-t'ang) 講武堂
jiangxiao jiangxisuo (chiang-hsiao chiang-hsi-so) 將校講習所
jiangxueshe (chiang-hsüeh-she) 講學社
Jiang Yanheng (Chiang Yen-heng) 蔣雁行
Jiang Yiwu (Chiang I-wu) 蔣翊武

Jiang Zungui (Chiang Tsun-kuei) 蔣尊簋
Jiao Dafeng (Chiao Ta-feng) 焦達峯
jiaolianchu (chiao-lien-ch'u) 教練處
jiexiang (chieh-hsiang) 解餉
Jin (Chin) 金
jinji (chin-chi) 近畿
jinshi (chin-shih) 進士
Jingshizhong (Ching-shih-chung) 警世鐘
Jin Yunpeng (Chin Yün-p'eng) 靳雲鵬
Ji Yulin (Chi Yü-lin) 季雨霖
juanshu (chüan-shu) 捐輸
JuE yiyongdui (Chü-O i-yung-tui) 拒俄義勇隊
Junguan xuetang (Chün-kuan hsüeh-t'ang) 軍官學堂
junguomin (chün-kuo-min) 軍國民
junguomin jiaoyu (chün-kuo-min chiao-yü) 軍國民教育
*junhengsi (chün-heng-ssu)*軍衡司
junlingsi (chün-ling-ssu) 軍令司
junshi choubeichu (chün-shih ch'ou-pei-ch'u) 軍事籌備處
junxuesi (chün-hsüeh-ssu) 軍學司
junzhengsi (chün-cheng-ssu) 軍政司
Junzichu (Chün-tzu-ch'u) 軍諮處
Junzifu (Chün-tzu-fu) 軍諮府
juren (chün-jen) 舉人

Kang Jiantong (K'ang Chientang) 康建唐
*Katō Hiroyuki 加藤弘之
ke (k'o) 科
Kexue buxisuo (K'o-hsüeh pu-hsi so) 科學補習所
Kong Geng (K'ung Keng) 孔庚
*kyoken 富强

Lei Zhenchun   (Lei Chen-ch'un) 雷震春

lian (lien) 連

Lianbingchu   (*Lien-ping-ch'u*) 練兵處

lianjun (lien-chün) 練軍

Liang Dunyan (Liang Tun-yen) 梁敦彥

Liang Zhonghan (Liang Chung-han) 梁鍾漢

Liangbi (Liang-pi) 良弼

liangjia zidi (liang-chia tzu-ti) 良家子弟

lianxi guanbian (lien-hsi kuan-pien) 練習官弁

Li Changling   (Li Ch'ang-ling) 李長齡

Li Genyuan (Li Ken-yüan) 李根源

Li Hongzhang (Li Hung-chang) 李鴻章

Li Jingxi (Li Ching-hsi) 李經義

Li Minchen (Li Min-ch'en) 李岷琛

Lin Sen (Lin Sen) 林森

Lin Shuqing   (Lin Shu-ch'ing) 林述慶

lingsheng (ling-sheng) 廩生

Liu Daxiong (Liu Ta-hsiung) 劉大雄

Liu Fuji (Liu Fu-chi) 劉復基

Liu Jiayun (Liu Chia-yün) 劉家運

Liu Jing'an (Liu Ching-an) 劉敬安

Liu Wenjin (Liu Wen-chin) 劉文錦

Liu Yongqing (Liu Yung-ch'ing) 劉永慶

Liu Zhenyi (Liu Chen-i) 劉貞一

Li Xianglin (Li Hsiang-lin) 李襄麟

Li Yadong (Li Ya-tung) 李亞東

Li Zhexiang (Li Che-hsiang) 李哲湘

Li Zhun (Li Chun) 李準

Long Jiguang (Lung Chi-kuang) 龍濟光

Longyu, Empress Dowager (Lung-yü) 隆裕太后

lu (lu) 路

Lu Chuanlin (Lu Ch'uan-lin) 鹿傳霖

lü (lü) 旅

Lü Dasen (Lü Ta-sen) 呂大森

Lujun (Lu-chün) 陸軍

Lujunbu (Lu-chün-pu) 陸軍部

Lujun daxuetang (Lu-chün ta-hsüeh-t'ang) 陸軍大學堂

lujun ruwusheng (lu-chün ju-wu-sheng) 陸軍入伍生

lujun sucheng xuetang (lu-chün su-ch'eng hsüeh-t'ang) 陸軍速成學堂

lujun zhongxuetang (lu-chün chung-hsüeh-t'ang) 陸軍中學堂

lujun zongcanyi (lu-chün tsung-ts'an-i) 陸軍總參議

lunjun xiaoxuetang (lu-chün hsiao-hsüeh-t'ang) 陸軍小學堂

Luo Peijin (Lo P'ei-chin) 羅佩金

Lu Rongting (Lu Jung-t'ing) 陸榮廷

lüying (lü-ying) 綠營

Lu Yongxiang (Lu Yung-hsiang) 盧永祥

Ma Longbiao (Ma Lung-piao) 馬龍標

Mao Zedong (Mao Tse-tung) 毛澤東

Ma Shengfu (Ma Sheng-fu) 馬盛富

Ma Yubao (Ma Yü-pao) 馬毓寶

Meng Enyuan (Meng En-yüan) 孟恩遠

Menghuitou (Meng-hui-t'ou) 猛回頭

Minbao (Min-pao) 民報

minzhengzhang (min-cheng-chang) 民政長

mou (mou) 畝

mubing (mu-ping) 募兵

Nanfangbao (Nan-fang-pao) 南方報

Nanfangjun xuanfushi (Nanfang-chün hsüan-fu-shih) 南方軍宣撫使

Nanfang zhibu (Nan-fang chih-pu) 南方支部

Ni Yingdian (Ni Ying-tien) 倪映典

nonghui (nung-hui) 農會

pai (p'ai) 排

Pan Juying (P'an Chü-ying) 潘榘楹

Pan Kangshi (P'an K'ang-shih) 潘康時

peng (p'eng) 柵

Peng Chengwan (P'eng Ch'eng-wan) 彭程萬

Peng Ximin (P'eng Hsi-min) 彭希民

Pu Dianjun (P'u Tien-chün) 蒲殿俊

Puliang (P'u-liang) 溥良

Puting (P'u-t'ing) 溥廷

qiangquan (ch'iang-ch'üan) 強權

Qi Baoshan (Ch'i Pao-shan) 齊寶善

qibing (ch'i-ping) 旗兵

qinbing (ch'in-ping) 欽兵

Qing, Prince (Ch'ing) 慶親王

Qiu Jin (Ch'iu Chin) 秋瑾

Qu Hongji (Ch'ü Hung-chi) 瞿鴻禨

Qunzhi xueshe (Ch'ün-chih hsüeh-she) 群治學社

Qu Tongfeng (Ch'ü T'ung-feng) 曲同豐

Ren Zhongyuan (Jen Chung-yüan) 任重遠

*Rikugun seijo gakkō 陸軍成城學校

*Rikugun shikan gakkō 陸軍士官學校

Rizhihui (Jih-chih-hui) 日知會

Ronglu (Jung-lu) 榮祿

Rongqing (Jung-ch'ing) 榮慶

Ruizheng (Jui-cheng) 瑞澂

Sanguo (San-kuo) 三國

Sa Zhenbing (Sa Chen-ping) 薩鎮冰

shangdengbing (shang-teng-ping) 上等兵

shanghui (shang-hui) 商會

shangshi (shang-shih) 上士

shangwu (shang-wu) 尚武

Shangwubao (Shang-wu-pao) 商務報

shangwu zhuyi (shang-wu chu-i) 尚武主義

shao (shao) 哨

Shen Bingkun (Shen Ping-k'un) 沈秉堃

Sheng Xuanhuai (Sheng Hsüan-huai) 盛宣懷

shengyuan (sheng-yüan) 生員

shenshang (shen-shang) 紳商

shi (shih) 士，師

Shi Chengxian (Shih Ch'eng-hsien) 施承先

Shi Gongbi (Shih Kung-pi) 時功璧

*Shikan 士官

*Shinbu gakkō 神武學校

shiwei (shih-wei) 侍衞

Shizihao (Shih-tzu-hao) 獅子吼

Shoushan (Shou-shan) 壽山

Shouxun (Shou-hsün) 壽勳

shubaoshe (shu-pao-she) 書報社

Shuihuzhuan (Shui-hu-chuan) 水滸傳

Song Jiaoren   (Sung Chiao-jen)
宋教仁

Songshou (Sung-shou) 松壽

Song Xiquan   (Sung Hsi-ch'üan)
宋錫全

Sucheng shifan xuetang (Su-ch'eng shih-fan hsüeh-t'ang) 速成師範學堂

suiying xuetang (sui-ying hsüeh-t'ang) 隨營學堂

Sun Baoqi (Sun Pao-ch'i) 孫寶琦

Sun Daoren (Sun (Tao-jen) 孫道仁

Sun Wu (Sun Wu) 孫武

Sun Yat-sen 孫逸仙

Sunzi bingfa   (Sun-tzu ping-fa) 孫子兵法

Taipusi (T'ai-p'u-ssu) 太僕寺

Tang Caichang (T'ang Ts'ai-ch'ang) 唐才常

Tang Hualong (T'ang Hua-lung) 湯化龍

Tang Shaoyi (T'ang Shao-i) 唐紹儀

Tang Shouqian (T'ang Shou-ch'ien) 湯壽潛

Tan Renfeng (T'an Jen-feng) 譚人鳳

Tan Sitong (T'an Ssu-t'ung) 譚嗣同

Tan Yankai (T'an Yen-k'ai) 譚延闓

tenpu jinken 天賦人權

tianfu renquan (t'ien-fu jen-ch'üan) 天賦人權

tidiao (t'i-tiao) 提調

tidu (t'ti-tu) 提督

Tieliang (T'ieh-liang) 鐵良

Tiexue zhangfutuan (T'ieh-hsüeh chang-fu-t'uan) 鐵血丈夫團

Tiezhong (T'ieh-chung) 鐵忠

ting (t'ing) 廳

Tingjie (T'ing-chieh) 廷杰

titai (t'i-t'ai) 提臺

ti-yong (t'i-yung) 體 — 用

tongling (t'ung-ling) 統領

Tongmenghui   (T'ung-meng-hui) 同盟會

tuanlian (t'uan-lien) 團練

Wang Shizhen (Wang Shih-chen) 王士珍

Wang Wenshao (Wang Wen-shao) 王文韶

Wang Yingkai (Wang Ying-k'ai) 王英楷

Wang Yujiang (Wang Yü-chiang) 王毓江

Wang Zhenji (Wang Chen-chi) 王振畿

Wang Zhixiang (Wang Chih-hsiang) 王芝祥

Wei Guangtao (Wei Kuang-t'ao) 魏光燾

weiliangmin (wei-liang-min) 衛良民

wenjing wuwei (wen-ching wu-wei) 文經武緯

wenwu quancai (wen-wu ch'üan-ts'ai) 文武全才

Wenxueshe (Wen-hsüeh-she) 文學社

wenzhi wugong (wen-chih wu-kung) 文治武功

wubei xuetang (wu-pei hsüeh-t'ang) 武備學堂

Wu Fengling (Wu Feng-ling) 吳鳳嶺

Wu Gongsan (Wu Kung-san) 吳貢三

Wu Jiezhang (Wu Chieh-chang) 吳介璋

Wu Luzhen (Wu Lu-chen) 吳祿貞

wuku (wuku) 武庫

Wuputong zhongxuetang (Wu-p'u-t'ung chung-hsüeh-t'ang) 武普通中學堂

Wuwei youjun (Wu-wei yu-chün) 武衞右軍

Wu Xiangzhen (Wu Hsiang-chen) 伍祥楨

Wuxue yanjiuhui (Wu-hsüeh yen-chiu-hui) 武學研究會

Wuwei youjun xianfengdui (Wu-wei yu-chün hsien-fang-tui) 武衞右軍先鋒隊

Wuwei zuojun (Wu-wei tso-chün) 武衞左軍

Wu Yuanzhi (Wu Yüan-chih) 伍元芝

Wuyijun (Wu-i-chün) 武毅軍

Xiabao (Hsia-pao) 夏報

Xianyouhui (Hsien-yu-hui) 憲友會

Xiao Guobin (Hsiao Kuo-pin) 蕭國斌

Xiao Liangchen (Hsiao Liang-ch'en) 蕭良臣

Xiao Xingyuan (Hsiao Hsing-yüan) 蕭星垣

xie (hsieh) 協

xiexiang (hsieh-hsiang) 協餉

Xiliang (Hsi-liang) 錫良

Xinhai julebu (Hsin-hai chü-le-pu) 辛亥俱樂部

Xinjian lujun (Hsin-chien lu-chün) 新建陸軍

xinjun (hsin-chün) 新軍

Xiong Bingkun (Hsiung Ping-k'un) 熊秉坤

Xiong Chengji (Hsiung Ch'eng-chi) 熊成基

Xiong Shili (Hsiung Shih-li) 熊十力

Xiong Xiling (Hsiung Hsi-ling) 熊希齡

xiucai (hsiu-ts'ai) 秀才

xuebingying (hsüeh-ping-ying) 學兵營

xuejie (hsüeh-chieh) 學界

xuexiguan (hsüeh-hsi-kuan) 學習官

Xunfangdui (Hsün-fang-tui) 巡防隊

xunjingjun (hsün-ching-chün) 巡警軍

Xu Shaozhen (Hsü Shao-chen) 徐紹楨

Xu Shichang (Hsü Shih-ch'ang) 徐世昌

Xu Xilin (Hsü Hsi-lin) 徐錫麟

*Yamatodamashii 大和魂

Yang Du (Yang Tu) 楊度

Yang Jincheng (Yang Chin-ch'eng) 楊藎誠

Yang Shande (Yang Shan-te) 楊善德

Yang Shixiang (Yang Shih-hsiang) 楊士驤

Yang Shu (Yang Shu) 楊樞

Yang Zanxu (Yang Tsan-hsü) 楊瓚緒

Yao Hongfa (Yao Hung-fa) 姚鴻法

yibing (i-bing) 醫兵

Yinchang (Yin-ch'ang) 廕昌

ying (ying) 營

Ying Longxiang (Ying Lung-hsiang) 應龍翔

yingwuchu (ying-wu-ch'u) 營務處

Yin Ziheng (Yin Tzu-heng) 殷子衡

Yizhihui (I-chih-hui) 易知會

yongying (yung-ying) 勇營

youdeng tebie xunzhang (yu-teng t'e-pieh hsün-chang) 優等特別勳章

Yuan Baoyi (Yüan Pao-i) 袁保義

Bibliography

Andreski, Stanislav, *Military Organization and Society,* Berkeley, 2nd ed., 1968.

Anon., 'Junren zhi jiaoju' 軍人之教育 [Education of the soldier], *Youxue yibian* 遊學譯篇 [Translations by overseas students], 7 (August 1903), *junshi* [military affairs], pp. 38-40.

——, 'Lishishang youmin zhi shangwuguo' 歷史上有名之尚武國 [Famous countries in history that exalted militarism], *Guominbao huibian* 國民報彙編 [The Chinese National Magazine] (1904), pp. 196-8.

Baili 百里 [Jiang Fangzhen 蔣方震], 'Junguomin zhi jiaoyu' 軍國民之教育 [Military national education], *Xinmin congbao* 新民叢報 [The New People's Journal], 22 (December 1902), pp. 33-52.

Bays, Daniel H., *China Enters the Twentieth Century: Chang Chih-tung and the Issues of a New Age, 1895-1909,* Ann Arbor, 1978.

Bergere, Marie-Claire, 'The Role of the Bourgeoisie', in Mary Clabaugh Wright (ed.), *China in Revolution: The First Phase, 1900-1913,* New Haven, 1968, pp. 229-95.

Boorman, Howard L. (ed.), *Biographical Dictionary of Republican China,* 4 vols, New York, 1967-71.

Brissaud-Desmaillet, 'Situation de l'armee chinoise au 1ᵉʳ Mars 1910', vol. 75 (May 1910), pp. 412-33; trans. into English in *Journal of the Royal United Service Institution,* 53 (September 1910), pp. 1181-95. Reproduced in United States Navy Department, Office of Naval Intelligence, attached to No. A-4-a, reg. no. 159.

Brunnert, H.S. and V.V. Hagelstrom, *Present Day Political Organization of China,* A. Beltchenko and E. Moran, trans., n.p., 1911, reprinted in Taipei, n.d.

Buck, David D., 'The Provincial Elite in Shantung During the Republican Period: Their Successes and Failures', *Modern China,* I, 4 (October 1975), pp. 417-46.

Cai Jiou 蔡寄鷗 , *Ezhou xueshi* 鄂州血史 [The bloody history of Hubei], Shanghai, 1958.

Cameron, Maribeth E., *The Reform Movement in China, 1898-1912,* Stanford, 1936.

Cao Yabo 曹亞伯 , *Wuchang geming zhenshi* 武昌革命眞史 [The true history of the Wuchang revolution], 2 vols, Shanghai, 1930.

Chang Chung-li, *The Chinese Gentry: Studies in Their Role in Nineteenth Century Chinese Society,* Seattle, 1955.

Chang Hao, *Liang Ch'i-ch'ao and Intellectual Transition in China, 1890-1907,* Cambridge, Mass., 1971.

Chan Lau Kit-Ching, *Anglo-Chinese Diplomacy 1906-1920 in the Careers of Sir John Jordan and Yüan Shih-kai*, Hong Kong, 1978.

——, 'British Policy of Neutrality during the 1911 Revolution in China', *Journal of Oriental Studies*, VII, 2 (1970), pp. 357-79.

Cheng, Shelley H., 'The T'ung-meng-hui: Its Organization, Leadership and Finances, 1905-1912', unpublished Ph.D. disseration, University of Washington, 1962.

Ch'en Jerome, *Yuan Shih-kai*, Stanford, 2nd ed., 1972.

——, 'Defining Chinese Warlords and Their Factions', *Bulletin of the School of Oriental and African Studies*, 31 (1968), pp. 563-600.

——, 'A Footnote on the Chinese Army in 1911-12', *T'oung Pao*, XLVIII, (1960), pp. 425-46.

Chen Kuilong 陳夔龍, *Yonghe shangshu zouyi* 庸盦尚書奏議 [The memorials of Chen Kuilong], n.p., 1913.

Chen Qitian 陳啟天, *Jindai Zhongguo jiaoyushi* 近史中國教育史 [A history of modern Chinese education], Taipei, 1969.

Chen Xizhang 陳錫璋, *Beiyang cangsang shihua* 北洋滄桑史話 [The history of the ups and downs of the Beiyang army] 2 vols., Tainan, 1967.

Chinese Historical Association 中國史學會, *Xinhai geming* 辛亥革命 [The Revolution of 1911], Chai Degeng 柴德賡 et al. (comps), 8 vols, Shanghai, 1957.

Chorley, Katherine C., *Armies and the Art of Revolution*, London, 1943.

Chu, Samuel C., *Reformer in Modern China: Chang Chien, 1853-1926*, New York, 1965.

Cohen, Paul H., 'Ch'ing China: Confrontation with the West, 1850-1900', in James B. Crowley (ed.), *Modern East Asia: Essays in Interpretation*, New York, 1970, pp. 29-61.

Committee on Written Historical Materials of the National Committee of the Chinese People's Political Consultative Conference 中國人民政治協商會議全國委員會文史資料研究委員會 (ed.), *Xinhai geming huiyilu* 辛亥革命回憶錄 [Recollections of the 1911 Revolution], 6 vols, Peking, 1961.

Da Qing Guangxu xinfaling 大清光緒新法令, [New decrees and regulations in the reign of Emperor Guangxu of the Great Qing Dynasty], compiled by *Shangwu yinshuguan* 商務印書館 The Commercial Press, 20 *ce*, Shanghai, 1910.

Deng Muhan 鄧慕韓, 'Guangzhou xinjun yundong junshi zhangcheng shitiao' 廣州新軍運動軍事章程十條 [Ten regulations for the subversion of the New Army in Canton], Guomindang Archives 352/8.

Deng Wenhui 鄧文翬, 'Gongjinhui di yuanqi jiqi rogan zhidu', 共進會的原起及其若干制度

[The Origins of the Society for Common Advancement and some aspects of its system]. *Jindaishi ziliao* 近代史資料 [Materials on modern history], 3 (August 1956), pp. 7-25.

Des Forges, R.V., *Hsi-liang and the Chinese National Revolution*, New Haven, 1973.

Dingle, Edwin J., *China's Revolution: An Historical and Political Record of the Civil War*, Shanghai, 1912.

_____, *Across China on Foot*, New York, 1911.

Ding Zhongjiang 丁中江, *Beiyang junfa shihua* 北洋軍閥史話 [History of the Beiyang warlords], 4 vols, Taipei, 1972.

Dongfang zazhi 東方雜誌 [The Eastern miscellany], Taipei, reprint, 1967.

Dreyer, Edward L. 'Military Continuities: The PLA and Imperial China', in William W. Whitson (ed.), *The Military and Political Power in China in the 1970s*, New York, 1972, pp. 3-24.

Dutt, Vidya Prakash, 'The First Week of the Revolution: The Wuchang Uprising', in Wright (ed.), *China in Revolution*, pp. 383-416.

Editorial Committee on Documentary Collections for the 50th Anniversary of the Founding of the Chinese Republic 中華民國開國五十週年 開國文獻編纂委員會 (comp.), *Zhonghua minguo kaiguo wushinian wenxian* 中華民國開國五十年文獻 [Documents on the 50th anniversary of the founding of the Chinese Republic] 2 *bian* (series), Taipei, 1964.

Eisenstadt, S.N. *The Political Systems of Empires*, London, 1963.

Elvin, Mark, 'The Gentry Democracy in Chinese Shanghai, 1905-14', in Jack Gray (ed.), *Modern China's Search for a Political Form*, London, 1969, pp. 41-65.

Esherick, Joseph W., *Reform and Revolution in China: The 1911 Revolution in Hunan and Hubei*, Berkeley, 1976.

_____, '1911: A review', *Modern China*, 2, 2 (April, 1976), a special issue entitled 'A Symposium on the 1911 Revolution', pp. 141-84.

Fairbank, John K., *The United States and China*, Cambridge, Mass., 1958.

_____, Edwin O. Reischauer and Albert M. Craig. *East Asia: The Modern Transformation*, Boston, 1965.

Fang Dongying 方東瀛 'Liu Ri shiguanxi yu minguo zhengtan (1)' 留日士官系與民初政壇 (一) [The Japanese-educated officers' clique and the politics of the early republic], *Yiwenzhi* 藝文誌 [Art and literature], 54 (1959), pp. 14-18.

Fang Zhaoying 房兆楹, *Qingmo minchu yangxue xuesheng timinglu chuji* 清末民初洋學生題名錄初輯 [A draft list of Chinese overseas students in the late Qing and early republican periods], Taipei, 1962.

Far Eastern Review, 'The Chinese Army', October 1909, pp. 171, 175-88.

——, 'China's Army and Navy', August 1910, pp. 85-6, 90-7.

Fass, Josef, 'The Role of the New Style Army in the 1911 Revolution in China', *Archiv Orientální*, 30 (1962), pp. 183-91.

——, 'Revolutionary Activity in the Province Hu-pei and the Wu-ch'ang Uprising of 1911', *Archiv Orientální*, 28 (1960), pp. 127-49.

Feisheng 飛生 (pseud.), 'Zhen junren', 眞軍人 [The true solider], *Zhejiangchao* 浙江潮 [The tide of Zhejiang], 3 (April 1903), pp. 65-72.

Fen Gesheng 奮翮生 [Cai E 蔡鍔], 'Junguomin bian', 軍國民篇 [On militant citizenry], *Xinmin congbao*, 1 (February 1902), pp. 79-88; 3 (March 1902), pp. 65-72; 11 (July 1902), pp. 45-52.

Feng Yuxiang 馮玉祥, *Wodi shenghuo* 我的生活 [My life], Shanghai, 1947.

Feng Ziyou 馮自由, *Geming yishi* 革命逸史 [Reminiscences of the revolution]. 4 vols, Chongqing and Shanghai, 1939-47.

——, *Zhonghua minguo kaiguoqian gemingshi* 中華民國開國前革命史 [A history of the revolution before the founding of the Chinese republic]. 2 vols, Chongqing, 1944, Taipei reprint, 1954.

Fincher, John. 'Political Provincialism and the National Revolution', in Wright, *China in Revolution*, pp. 185-226.

——, 'Elite Militarism, Populist Tax Protest and China's National Revolution', *Papers on Far Eastern History*, 19 (March 1979), pp. 223-36.

Fung, Edmund S.K., 'Revolution and the Chinese Army, 1911-1913', *Papers on Far Eastern History*, 19 (March 1979), pp. 13-54.

——, 'Post-1949 Chinese Historiography on the 1911 Revolution', *Modern China*, 4, 2 (April 1978), pp. 181-214.

——, 'Military Subversion in the Chinese Revolution of 1911', *Modern Asian Studies*, 9, 1 (1975), pp. 103-23.

——, 'Li Yüan-hung and the Revolution of 1911', *Monumenta Serica*, XXXI (1974-1975), pp. 151-71.

——, 'The T'ung-meng-hui Central China Bureau and the Wuchang Uprising', *Journal of the Institute of Chinese Studies*, 7, 2 (1974), pp. 477-96.

——, 'The Kung-chin-hui: A Late Ch'ing Revolutionary Society', *Journal of Oriental Studies*, 11, 2 (July 1973), pp. 193-206.

——, 'The T'ang Ts'ai-ch'ang Revolt', *Papers on Far Eastern History*, 1 (March 1970), pp. 70-114.

Gascoyne-Cecil, William, Lord, *Changing China*, New York, 1910.

Gillin, Donald G., *Warlord: Yen Hsi-shan in Shansi Province*

1911-1949, Princeton. 1967.

Gittings, John, 'The Chinese Army', in Jack Gray (ed.), *Modern China's Search for a Political Form*, London, 1969, pp. 187-224.

Great Britain, Foreign Office Archives, Public Record Office, London.

FO 17, General Correspondence before 1906 China.

FO 228, Embassy and Consular Archives, China Correspondence Series I.

FO 371, General Correspondence after 1906 Political.

FO 405, Confidential Print, China.

_____, Parliamentary Papers (Blue Books).

China, No. 1 (1912). Correspondence Respecting the Affairs of China (cd. 6148).

China, No. 3 (1912). Further Correspondence Respecting the Affairs of China (cd. 6447).

China, No. 3 (1913). Further Correspondence Respecting the Affairs of China (cd. 7054).

_____, War Office Archives, Public Record Office, London.

WO 33, Reports and Miscellaneous Papers 1853-1948.

WO 106, Directorate of Military Operations and Intelligence 1837-1948.

Guo Tingyi 郭廷以, *Jindai Zhongguo shishi rizhi* 近代中國史事日誌 [A daily chronology of events in modern Chinese history], 2 vols, Taipei, 1963.

Hackett, Roger F., 'Chinese Students in Japan, 1900-1910', *Papers on China*, III (May 1949), pp. 134-69.

Hatano Yoshihiro, 'The New Armies', in Wright, *China in Revolution*, pp. 365-82.

Hedtke, Charles H., 'Reluctant Revolutionaries: Szechwan and the Ch'ing Collapse, 1898-1911', unpublished Ph. D. dissertation, University of California, Berkeley, 1968.

History of the Chinese Republic Chronology Editorial Committee 中華民國史事紀要編輯委員會 (ed.), *Zhonghua minguo shishi jiyao (chugao) 1911*. 中華民國史事紀要 1911 [A chronology of events in the Chinese Republic 1911], Taipei, 1973.

Hobsbawn, E.J., *Primitive Rebels: Studies in the Archaic Forms of Social Movements in the 19th and 20th Centuries*, Manchester, 1959.

Ho Ping-ti, *The Ladder of Success in Imperial China*, New York, 1964.

Hsiao Kung-ch'üan, *Rural China: Imperial Control in the Nineteenth Century*, Seattle, 1960.

Hsieh Pao-chao, *The Government of China (1644-1911)*, Baltimore 1925.

Hsüeh Chün-tu, *Huang Hsing and the Chinese Revolution*, Stanford, 1961.

Huang, Philip C., *Liang Ch'i-ch'ao and Modern Chinese Liberalism*, Seattle, 1972.

Huang Yuanyong 黃遠庸, *Yuan-*

sheng yizhu 遠生遺著 [Posthumous collection of the writings of Huang Yuanyong], 2 vols, no. 19 in the series *Yuan Shikai shiliao huikan* 袁世凱史料彙刊 [Collected historical materials on Yuan Shikai], edited by Shen Yunlong, 沈雲龍 Taipei, 1966.

Hubei xueshengjie 湖北學生界 [The Hubei student circle], Tokyo, 1903.

Hubei Committee of the Chinese People's Political Consultative Conference 中國人民政治協商會議湖北省委員會 (ed.), *Xinhai shouyi huiyilu* 辛亥首義回憶錄 [Recollections of the first [Wuchang] uprising in 1911], 3 vols, Wuhan, 1957.

Hubei wenxian 湖北文獻 [Documents on Hubei], Taipei, 1966.

Hu Egong 胡鄂公 , *Xinhai geming beifang shilu* 辛亥革命北方實錄 [A true account of the revolution in North China], Shanghai, 1948.

Hu Hanmin 胡漢民 , *Hu Hanmin zizhuan* 胡漢民自傳 [The autobiography of Hu Hanmin], reprinted in Taipei, 1969.

Hummel, Arthur W. (ed.), *Eminent Chinese of the Ch'ing Period, 1644-1912*, Washington, 1943-4; Taipei reprint, 1964.

Huntington, Samuel P., *Political Order in Changing Societies*, New York, 1968.

Hu Poyu 胡璞玉 , *Kaiguo zhanshi* 開國戰史 [A military history of the founding of the Re-

public]. Taipei, 1974.

Ichiko Chūzō, 'The Role of the Gentry: An Hypothesis', in Wright, *China in Revolution*, pp. 297-317.

——, 'The Railway Protection Movement in Szechwan in 1911', *Memoirs of the Research Department of the Toyo Bunko*, 14 (1955), pp. 47-69.

Institute of Historical Research, Chinese Academy of Science 中國科學院歷史研究所 (ed.), *Yunnan Guizhou xinhai geming ziliao* 雲南貴州辛亥革命資料 [Materials on the 1911 Revolution in Yunnan and Guizhou], Peking, 1959.

——, *Xiliang yigao zougao* 錫良遺稿奏稿 [A posthumous draft of Xiliang's memorials], Peking, 1959.

Institute of Historical Research, Jilin Branch, Chinese Academy of Science, and the History Department of the Jilin Normal University 中國科學院吉林省分院歷史研究所吉林師範大學歷史系 (eds.), *Jindai dongbei renmin yundongshi* 近代東北人民運動史 [A modern history of the mass movement in the north-east [of China]], Changchun, 1960.

International Encyclopedia of the Social Sciences, New York, 1968.

Janowitz, Morris, *The Military in the Political Development of New Nations*, Chicago, 1964.

Jiang Zuobin 蔣作賓 , *Jiang Zuobin huiyilu* 蔣作賓回憶錄 [The memoris of Jiang Zuobin],

Taipei, 1967.

Jia Shiyi 賈士毅 , *Minguo chunian di jiren caizheng zongzhang* 民國初年的幾任財政總長 [The vairous ministers of finance in the early republic] Taipei, 1967.

Johnson, William R., 'China's 1911 Revolution in the Provinces of Yunnan and Kweichow', unpublished Ph.D. dissertation, University of Washington, 1962.

Joint Hubei Philosophy and Social Science Association 湖北省哲學社會科學會聯合會 (eds), *Xinhai geming wushi zhounian jinian luwenji* 辛亥革命五十週年紀念論文集 [An anthology in celebration of the jubilee of the 1911 Revolution], 2 vols, Hankow, 1962.

Ju Zheng 居正 , *Ju Juesheng xiansheng quanji* 居覺生先生全集 [The collected works of Ju Zheng], Taipei, 1954.

Kapp, Robert A., *Szechwan and the Chinese Republic: Provincial Militarism and Central Power, 1911-1938*, New Haven, 1973.

Kent, Percy H., *The Passing of the Manchus*, London, 1912.

Kuhn, Philip A., *Rebellion and Its Enemies in Late Imperial China: Militarization and Social Structure, 1796-1864*, Cambridge, Mass., 1970.

Kupper, Samuel Yale, 'Revolution in China: Kiangsi Province, 1905-1913', unpublished Ph.D. dissertation, University of Michigan, 1973.

Lan Tianwei 藍大蔚 , 'Junjie' 軍解 [The meaning of soldiers], *Hubei xueshengjie*, 1 (February 1903), pp. 57-62.

____, 'Junguomin sixiang pujilun' 軍國民思想普及論 [The popularisation of the idea of militant citizenry], *Hubei xueshejie*, 3 (April 1903), pp. 41-6.

____, 'Junshi yu guojia zhi guanxi' 軍事與國家之關係[The relationship between the state and military affairs], *Hubei xueshengjie*, 4 (May 1903), pp. 49-62.

Lary, Diana, *Region and Nation: The Kwangsi Clique in Chinese Politics*, Cambridge, 1974.

Leonard, Captain Henry. 'The Chinese Army', in United States General Records, Central Files, 1906-29, Numerical file, 1906-10, vol. 217, encl. to no. 2106/2-5.

Levenson, Joseph R., *Confucian China and Its Modern Fate: A Trilogy*, Berkeley, 1958.

Lewis, Charlton M., *Prologue to the Chinese Revolution: The Transformation of Ideas and Institutions in Hunan Province 1891-1907*, Cambridge, Mass., 1976.

____, 'The Hunanese Elite and the Reform Movement, 1895-1898', *Journal of Asian Studies*, XXIX, 1 (November 1969), pp. 35-42.

Liang Qichao 梁啟超 , *Yinbingshi quanji* 飲冰室全集 [The collected works of the ice-drinking studio], Shanghai, n.d.

Li, Dun J. (ed.), *The Road to Communism: China Since 1912*, New York. 1969.

Liew Kit Siong, *Struggle for Democracy: Sung Chiao-jen and the 1911 Revolution*, Canberra and Berkeley, 1971.

Li Jiannong 李劍農, *Zuijin san-shinian Zhongguo zhengzhi shi* 最近三十年中國政治史 [A political history of China in the last thirty years], Taipei, reprint, 1974.

Li Lianfang 李廉方, *Xinhai Wu-chang shouyiji* 辛亥武昌首義記 [A record of the 1911 Wuchang uprising], n.p. 1947, reprinted in Taipei, n.d.

Li Liejun 李烈鈞, *Li Liejun jiang-jun zizhuan* 李烈鈞將軍自傳 [The autobiography of General Li Liejun], Chongqing, 1944.

Li Liuru 李六如, *Liushinian di bianqian* 六十年的變遷 [Changes in the last sixty years], 2 vols, Peking, 1962.

Li Shiyue 李時岳, *Xinhai ge-ming shiqi lianghu diqu di geming yundong* 辛亥革命時期兩湖地區的革命活動 [The revolutionary movement in the Hunan-Hubei region during the period of the 1911 revolution], Peking, 1957.

Li Shoukong 李守孔, 'Tang Cai-chang yu zhilijun 唐才常與自立軍 [Tang Caichang and the independence army], in Wu Xiangxiang 吳湘相 (ed.), *Zhongguo xiandaishi congkan* 中國現代史叢刊 [Selected writings on modern Chinese history], vol. 6, pp. 41-160.

Liu Fenghan 劉鳳翰, *Xinjiang lujun* 新建陸軍 [The new-founded army], Taipei, 1967.

Liu, F.F., *A Military History of Modern China, 1924-1949*, Princeton, 1956.

Liu Housheng 劉厚生 *Zhang Jian zhuanji* 張謇傳記 [The biography of Zhang Jian], Shanghai, 1958.

Liu Yusheng 劉禺生, *Shizaitang zayi* 世載堂雜憶 [Miscellaneous recollections of Shizaitang], Shanghai ?, n.d.

Li Yuanhong 黎元洪, *Li fuzong-tong zhengshu* 黎副總統政書 [The official correspondence of Vice-President Li], edited by Yi Guogan 易國幹, Taipei, reprint, 1962.

Lu Chun 陸純 (ed.), *Yuan da-zongtong shudu huibian* 袁大總統書牘彙編 [The collected works of President Yuan], no. 11 in the series *Yuan Shikai shiliao huikan*, Taipei, 1966.

Luo Jialun 羅家倫 (comp.), *Ge-ming wenxian* 革命文獻 [Documents on the revolution], vols 1-4, Taipei, 1953.

McKenzie, F.A., *The Unveiled East*, London, 1907.

_____, 'Four Hundred Million Chinamen Awaken' (an interview with Morrison), *London Magazine*, 25, 150 (February 1911), pp. 695-707.

MacKinnon, Stephen R., 'The Peiyang Army, Yuan Shih-k'ai and the Origins of Modern Chinese Warlordism', *Journal of Asian Studies*, XXXII, 3 (May 1973), pp. 405-23.

_____, 'Yüan Shih-kai in Tientsin and Peking: The Sources and Structure of his Power', unpublished Ph.D. dissertation, University of California, Davis, 1971.

Minlibao 民立報 [The Independent People's Daily], Shanghai, 1910-11, reprinted in Taipei, 1970.

Minyoushe 民友社 [Society of the Friends of the People] (ed.), 'Wubei jiaoyu' 武備教育 [Military education], *Youxue yibian*, 1 (November 1902), *junshi* [military affairs], pp. 1-7; 2 (December 1902), *junshi*, pp. 13-16; 4 (February 1903), *junshi*, pp. 17-20.

Morrison, George Ernest, The Papers of George Ernest Morrison, 1850-1932, Mitchell Library, New South Wales Library, Sydney.

Munholland, J. Kim, 'The French Connection That Failed', *Journal of Asian Studies*, XXXII, 1 (November 1972), pp. 77-95.

Nagai Michio 永井道雄, Hara Yoshio 原芳男, and Tanaka Hiroshi 田中宏, *Ajia ryugakusei to Nihon* アジア留学生と日本 [Asian overseas students and Japan], Tokyo, 1973.

Needham, Joseph, 'The Past in China's Present', *The Centennial Review*, 4 (1964), pp. 145-78.

North-China Herald and Supreme Court and Consular Gazette, Shanghai, weekly, 1895-1911.

Peake, Cyrus, *Nationalism and Education in Modern China*, New York, 1932.

Pekin Shina Kenkyūkai 北京支那研究會 (ed.), *Saishin Shina kanshin roku* 最近支那官紳錄 [A most recent record of Chinese officials and gentry], Tokyo, 1918.

Powell, Ralph L., *The Rise of Chinese Military Power, 1895-1912*, Princeton, 1955.

Pye, Lucian W., 'Armies in the Process of Political Modernisation', in John J. Johnson (ed.), *The Role of the Military in Underdeveloped Countries*, Princeton, 1962, pp. 69-90.

Qingchao xuwenxian tongkao 清朝續文獻通考 [Supplementary documents on the Qing dynasty], 300 *juan*, reprinted in Taipei, 1958.

Qingshigao 清史稿 [A draft history of the Qing Dynasty] comps. Zhao Ersun 趙爾巽 et al, 536 *juan*, Peking, 1927.

Qingshi liezhuan 清史列傳 [Biographies of the Qing dynasty], 80 *ce* Shanghai, 1928, reprinted in Taipei, 1964.

Quan Hansheng 全漢昇, 'Tielu guoyu wenti yu xinhai geming' 鐵路國有問題與辛亥革命 [The question of railway nationalisation and the 1911 Revolution], in *Zhongguo xiandaishi congkan*, 1 (1960), pp. 209-71.

Qu Lihe 瞿立鶴, *Qingmo liuxue jiaoyu* 清末留學教育 [Overseas studies in the late Qing period], Taipei, 1973.

Rankin, Mary Backus, *Early Chinese Revolutionaries: Radical Intellectuals in Shanghai* and Chekiang, 1902-1911, Cambridge, Mass., 1971.

Rawlinson, John L., *China's Struggle for Naval Development, 1839-1895*, Cambridge, Mass., 1967.

Reid, J.G., *The Manchu Abdication and the Powers, 1908-1912*, Berkeley, 1935.

Rhoads, Edward J.M., *China's Republican Revolution: The Case of Kwangtung, 1895-1913*, Cambridge, Mass., 1975.

——, 'Merchant Associations in Canton, 1895-1911', in Mark Elvin and G. William Skinner (eds), *The Chinese City Between Two Worlds*, Stanford, 1974, pp. 97-117.

Rosenbaum, Arthur L., 'Gentry Power and the Changsha Rice Riot of 1910', *Journal of Asian Studies*, XXXIV, 3 (May 1975), pp. 689-715.

Ross, Edward A., *The Changing Chinese*, New York, 1911.

Schiffrin, Harold Z., *Sun Yat-sen and the Origins of the Chinese Revolution*, Berkeley, 1968.

Shao Baichang 邵百昌, 'Xinhai Wuchang shouyi zhi qianyin houguo jiqi zuozhan jingguo', 辛亥武昌首義之前因後果及其作戰經過 [The causes of the Wuching uprising of 1911 and its military operations], *Hubei wenxian*, 10 (January 1969), pp. 8-22.

Sharman, Lyon, *Sun Yat-sen: His Life and Its Meaning: A Critical Biography*, Stanford, reprint, 1968.

Sheling Waishi (pseud.) 射陵外

史, 'Baoding junguan xuexiao cangsang shi' 保定軍官學校滄桑史 [A turbulent history of the Baoding military school], *Chunqiu* 春秋 [Spring and autumn], 63 (1960), pp. 63-71.

Shen Jian 沈鑑, 'Xinhai geming qianxi woguo zhi lujun jiqi junfei', 辛亥革命前後我國之陸軍及其軍費 [The army of our country and its finances on the eve of the 1911 Revolution], *Shehui kexue* 社會科學 [The social sciences], II, 2 (January 1937), pp. 343-408.

Shen Yunlong 沈雲龍, *Li Yuanhong pingzhuan* 黎元洪評傳 [A critical biography of Li Yuanhong], Taipei, 1968.

Shen Zuxian 沈祖憲 and Wu Kaisheng 吳闓生, *Rongan diziji* 容庵弟子記 [Records kept by the disciples of Rongan], n.p., 1913.

Sheridan, James E., *Chinese Warlord: The Case of Feng Yu-hsiang*, Stanford, 1966.

——, *China in Disintegration: The Republican Era in Chinese History 1912-1949*, New York, 1975.

Shi Jin 石錦, *Zhongguo xiandaihua yundong yu Qingmo liuRi xuesheng* 中國現代化運動與清末留日學生 [The modernisation of China and Chinese students in Japan in the late Qing period], Taipei, 1967.

Shrecker, John E., *Imperialism and Chinese Nationalism: Germany in Shantung*, Cambridge, Mass., 1971.

Shuntian Shibao 順天時報 [Peking

News], Peking, 1912-13.

Smedley, Agnes, *The Great Road: The Life and Times of Chu Te*, New York, 1956.

Smythe, E. Joan, 'The Tzu-li Hui: Some Chinese and Their Rebellions', *Papers on China*, XII (December 1958), pp. 51-68.

Su An 素庵 and Shi Sheng適生, 'Yunnan lujun jiangwutang di kaikuang' 雲南陸軍講武堂的 概況 [The condition of the Yunnan officers' school], in the Institute of History, Chinese Academy of Science (ed.), *Yunnan Guizhou xinhai geming ziliao*, pp. 14-19.

Subao 蘇報 [The Jiangsu Journal], Shanghai, 1903.

Sutton, Donald Sinclair, 'The Rise and Decline of the Yunnan Army, 1909-1925', unpublished Ph.D. dissertation, Cambridge University, 1970.

Swift, Major Eben, 'The Chinese Army — Its Development and Present Strength', in George H.B. Blakeslee (ed.), *China and the Far East*, New York, 1910, pp. 177-86.

Tao Juyin 陶菊隱, *Beiyang junfa tongzhi shiqi shihua* 北洋軍閥 統治時期史話 [A history of the Beiyang warlords], 6 vols, Peking, 1957.

Teng Ssu-yu and John K. Fairbank (eds), *China's Response to the West, A Documentary Survey*, 1862-1874, Stanford, 1957.

The China Year Book, edited by Montague H.T. Bell and H.G.W. Woodhead, London, 1912-16.

The Times, London.

Thomson, John Stuart, *China Revolutionised*, Indianapolis, 1913

Tsang Chiu-san, *Nationalism in School Education in China*, Hong Kong, 2nd ed., 1967.

United States, Department of State, Decimal File, China, Internal Affairs, 1910-29, National Archives Microfilm Publications, Washington, D.C.

____, Navy Department, Office of Naval Intelligence, National Archives Microfilm Publications, Washington, D.C.

____, War Department, General Staff, National Archives Microfilm Publications, Washington, D.C.

Wan Dixiu 萬迪㑇, 'Wan Dixiu yu Zeng Shengsan lun xinhai shouyi jieyaoshu', 萬迪㑇與曾 省三論辛亥肖義節要書 [A letter from Wan Dixiu to Zeng Shengsan discussing the 1911 uprising], Guomindang Archives 353/3.

Wang Jingyu 汪敬虞, *Zhongguo jindai gongyeshi zhiliao, dierji, 1895-1914 nian* 中國近代工業 史資料第二輯1895-1914 年[Historical materials on modern Chinese industry, vol. 2, 1895-1914], Peking, 1957.

Wang Ranzhi 王冉之, *Jiang Baili jiangjun yu qi junshi sixiang* 蔣百里將軍與其軍事思想 [General Jiang Baili and his military thought], Taipei, 1975.

Welch, Claude E. Jr (ed.), *Poli-*

tical Modernization: A Reader in Comparative Political Change, Belmont, 2nd ed., 1971.

Wen Gongzhi 文公直, *Zuijin san-shinian Zhongguo junshishi* 最近三十年中國軍事史[A military history of China in the last thirty years], 2 vols, Taipei, 1962.

Wong Young-tsu, 'Popular Unrest and the Revolution in Jiangsu', *Modern China*, vol. 3, no. 3 (July 1977), pp. 321-44.

Wright, Mary Clabaugh (ed.), *China in Revolution: The First Phase, 1900-1913*, New Haven, 1968.

____, *The Last Stand of Chinese Conservatism: The T'ung-chih Restoration, 1862-1874*, Stanford, 1957.

Wu Tiecheng 吳鐵城, *Wu Tiecheng huiyilu* 吳鐵城回憶錄 [The memoirs of Wu Tiecheng], Taipei, 2nd ed., 1971.

Wu Xiangxiang 吳湘相, *Minguo zhengzhi renwu* 民國政治人物 [Political figures of the republic], 2 vols, Taipei, 1969.

Xinmin congbao 新民叢報 [The New People's Journal], Yokohama, 1902-7).

Xu Daolin 徐道鄰, *Xu Shuzheng xiansheng wenji nianpu hekan* 徐樹錚先生文集年譜合刊 [Collected writings and chronological biography of Xu Shuzheng, published in one volume], Taipei, 1962.

Xu Tongxin 許同莘, *Zhang Wenxianggong nianpu* 張文襄公年譜 [A chronological study of Zhang Zhidong] 2 vols, Shanghai, 1947.

Yan Xishan 嚴錫山, *Yan Xishan zaonian huiyilu* 嚴錫山早年回憶錄 [The memoirs of Yan Xishan in his early years], Taipei, 1968.

Yang Duo 楊鐸, 'Wuchang geming zhenshi zhi shangque' 武昌革命眞史之商榷 [A reappraisal of the true history of the Wuchang uprising], *Jiangsu bowuguan yuekan* 江蘇博物館月刊 [The Jiangsu Museum Monthly], vol. 2, no. 1, pp. 1-6 (date unknown).

Yang Shiji 楊世驥, *Xinhai geming qianhou Hunan shishi* 辛亥革命前後湖南史事 [A history of Hunan before and after the 1911 Revolution], Changsha, 1958.

Yang Yuru 楊玉如, *Xinhai geming xianzhuji* 辛亥革命先著記 [A first account of the 1911 Revolution], Peking, 1957.

Young, Ernest P., *The Presidency of Yuan Shih-k'ai: Liberalism and Dictatorship in Early Republican China*, Ann Arbor, 1977.

____, 'Nationalism, Reform and Republican Revolution: China in the Early Twentieth Century', in James B. Crowley (ed.), *Modern East Asia: Essays in Interpretation*, New York, 1970, pp. 151-79.

____, 'Yuan Shih-k'ai's Rise to the Presidency', in Wright (ed.), *China in Revolution*, pp. 419-42.

_____, 'The Reformer as a Conspirator', in Albert Feuerwerker *et al.* (eds), *Approaches to Modern Chinese History*, Berkeley, 1967.

Zeng Shengsan 曾省三, 'Wuchang shouyi zhi yuanqi' 武昌首義之原起 [The origins of the Wuchang uprising], Guomindang Archives 355/7.

Zhang Guogan 張國淦, *Xinhai geming shiliao* 辛亥革命史料 [Historical materials on the 1911 Revolution], Shanghai, 1958.

Zhang Nanxian 張難先, *Hubei geming zhizhilu* 湖北革命知之錄 [The known record of the revolution in Hubei], Shanghai, 1945.

Zhang Pengyuan (Chang P'engyüan) 張朋園, *Lixianpai yu xinhai geming* 立憲派與辛亥革命 [The constitutionalists and the 1911 Revolution], Taipei, 1969.

_____, 'The Constitutionalists', in Wright, *China in Revolution*, pp. 143-83.

Zhang Shoubo 張壽波, *Zuijin Hankou gongshangye yiban* 最近漢口工商業一班 [An outline of the commerce and industry in recent Hankow], Hankow, 1911.

Zhang Yukun 章裕昆, *Wenxueshe Wuchang shouyi jishi* 文學社武昌首義紀實 [A factual account of the literary society's uprising in Wuchang], Peking, 1952.

Zhang Zhidong 張之洞, *Zhang Wenxianggong quanji* 張文襄公全集 [The complete works of Zhang Zhidong], comp. Wang Jinqing 王晉卿 *et al.*, reprinted in Taipei, 1963.

Zhejiangchao 浙江潮 [The tide of Zhejiang], Tokyo, 1903.

Zhengfu gongbao 政府公報 [Government Gazette], Peking, 1912-28, reprinted 1912-16, Taipei, n.d.

Zhou Kaiqing 周開慶 (ed.), *Sichuan yu xinhai geming* 四川與辛亥革命 [Sichuan and the 1911 Revolution], Taipei, 1964.

Zhou Shanpei 周善培, *Xinhai Sichuan zhenglu qinliji* 辛亥四川爭路親歷記 [Personal experience of the railway dispute in Sichuan], Chongqing, 1957.

Zhu Wu 竹塢, 'Woguo zhi lujun' 我國之陸軍 [The army of our country], *Guofengbao* 國風報 [The national spirit], 1, 21 (1910), pp. 47-74.

Zhu Yanjia 朱炎佳, 'Wu Luzhen yu Zhongguo geming' 吳祿貞與中國革命 [Wu Luzhen and the Chinese revolution], in *Zhongguo xiandaishi congkan*, no. 6, pp. 161-232.

Zou Lu 鄒魯, *Zhongguo Guomindang shigao* 中國國民黨史稿 [A draft history of the Chinese Nationalist Party], Taipei, reprint, 1965.

Index

Edmund S.K. Fung, born in Canton in 1943, was brought up and educated in Hong Kong where he earned his BA (Hons) and MA in History from the University of Hong Kong. He also holds a PhD from the Australian National University for a thesis on the Hubei revolutionary movement in late Qing China. After publishing several articles out of his thesis, he started work on a broader study of the New Army, for which he had spent some time in the Public Record Office, London.

Dr Fung is a Senior Lecturer in the School of Modern Asian Studies, Griffith University, Brisbane. Before that he had taught modern Chinese history in Monash University and the University of Singapore.

Type set and printed in Hong Kong by Colorcraft Ltd,